Lecture Notes in Computer Science   10134

Commenced Publication in 1973
Founding and Former Series Editors:
Gerhard Goos, Juris Hartmanis, and Jan van Leeuwen

More information about this series at http://www.springer.com/series/7407

Jonathan P. Bowen · Huibiao Zhu (Eds.)

Unifying Theories of Programming

6th International Symposium, UTP 2016
Reykjavik, Iceland, June 4–5, 2016
Revised Selected Papers

 Springer

Editors
Jonathan P. Bowen
London South Bank University
London
UK

Huibiao Zhu
East China Normal University
Shanghai
China

ISSN 0302-9743   ISSN 1611-3349   (electronic)
Lecture Notes in Computer Science
ISBN 978-3-319-52227-2   ISBN 978-3-319-52228-9   (eBook)
DOI 10.1007/978-3-319-52228-9

Library of Congress Control Number: 2016962028

LNCS Sublibrary: SL1 – Theoretical Computer Science and General Issues

Printed on acid-free paper

This Springer imprint is published by Springer Nature
The registered company is Springer International Publishing AG
The registered company address is: Gewerbestrasse 11, 6330 Cham, Switzerland

Preface

Interest in the fundamental problem of the combination of formal notations and theories of programming has grown consistently in recent decades. The theories define, in various different ways, many common notions, such as abstraction, refinement, choice, termination, feasibility, locality, concurrency, and communication. Despite these differences, such theories may be unified in a way that greatly facilitates their study and comparison. Moreover, such a unification offers a means of combining different languages describing various facets and artifacts of software development in a seamless and logically consistent manner.

C.A.R. Hoare and Jifeng He's *Unifying Theories of Programming* (UTP) is widely acknowledged as one of the most significant such unification approaches. Based on their pioneering work, the aims of the UTP Symposium series are to reaffirm the significance of ongoing UTP research efforts and to stimulate advancement of the state of the art in the field. The symposium provides a focus for the sharing of results by those already actively contributing, as well as raising awareness of the benefits of such unifying theoretical frameworks among the wider computer science and software engineering communities.

The UTP 2016 Symposium was held over two days (June 4–5, 2016) in conjunction with the Integrated Formal Methods (iFM) 2016 Conference in the capital city of Reykjavik, Iceland, on the campus of Reykjavik University. The iFM 2016 general chair, Marjan Sirjani, and the workshop chair, Marcel Kyas, both of Reykjavik University, were especially helpful in the organization of the UTP Symposium.

UTP 2016 was co-sponsored by Reykjavik University itself and also East China Normal University. It was the sixth symposium in the UTP series. Previous, UTP symposia have been held successfully every two years in Durham, UK (2006), Dublin, Republic of Ireland (2008), Shanghai, China (2010), Paris, France (2012), and Singapore (2014).

A pleasing feature of the UTP 2016 Symposium was the presence for the first time of both of the founding fathers of UTP, Prof. Sir Tony Hoare (Microsoft Research Laboratory, Cambridge, UK) and Prof. Jifeng He (East China Normal University, Shanghai, China). They previously worked together at the Programming Research Group within the Oxford University Computing Laboratory in the UK, where they developed their ideas that led to their co-authored foundational book on UTP, published in 1998. Both gave keynote talks that added considerably to the UTP 2016 program.

In addition, a panel discussion chaired by Prof. Jonathan Bowen on "UTP Past, Present and Future Directions" was held at the end of the first day, with contributions by panelists Tony Hoare, Andrew Butterfield (Trinity College Dublin, Republic of Ireland), Ana Cavalcanti, and Jim Woodcock (both of University of York, UK). The panelists discussed how they first became involved and interested in UTP, gave an overview of their current work in UTP, and provided their thoughts on where they saw

UTP going in the future. Later, Andrew Butterfield delivered an entertaining and apposite after-dinner speech at the symposium dinner, held in a historic building at a lakeside location in central Reykjavik.

As well as the keynote talks and panel discussion, eight peer-reviewed papers were presented at the UTP 2016 Symposium. Drafts of the papers were given to symposium attendees on USB sticks and revised version of the papers are included in these proceedings.

In summary, we hope that you enjoy this volume, providing a selection of recent research developments and perspectives in the area of Unifying Theories of Programming (UTP). Further information related to the UTP 2016 Symposium can be found online under: http://utp2016.ecnu.edu.cn

November 2016

Jonathan P. Bowen
Huibiao Zhu

Organization

Program Committee

Jonathan Bowen	London South Bank University, UK
Andrew Butterfield	Trinity College Dublin, Ireland
Ana Cavalcanti	University of York, UK
Yifeng Chen	Peking University, China
Jeremy Gibbons	University of Oxford, UK
Lindsay Groves	Victoria University of Wellington, New Zealand
Walter Guttmann	University of Canterbury, New Zealand
Ian J. Hayes	University of Queensland, Australia
Jeremy Jacob	University of York, UK
Zhiming Liu	Birmingham City University, UK
David Naumann	Stevens Institute of Technology, USA
Marcel V. M. Oliveira	Universidade Federal do Rio Grande do Norte, Brazil
Shengchao Qin	Teesside University, UK
Georg Struth	University of Sheffield, UK
Jun Sun	Singapore University of Technology and Design, Singapore
Meng Sun	Peking University, China
Burkhart Wolff	University of Paris-Sud, France
Frank Zeyda	Teesside University, UK
Naijun Zhan	Institute of Software, Chinese Academy of Sciences, China
Yongxin Zhao	East China Normal University, China
Huibiao Zhu	Software Engineering Institute, East China Normal University, China

Additional Reviewers

Chen, Xiaohong
Yan, Gaogao
Zhu, Jiaqi

Contents

A Discrete Geometric Model of Concurrent Program Execution

Bernhard Möller[1]([✉]), Tony Hoare[2], Martin E. Müller[1], and Georg Struth[3]

[1] Institut für Informatik, Universität Augsburg, Augsburg, Germany
bernhard.moeller@informatik.uni-augsburg.de
[2] Microsoft Research, Cambridge, UK
[3] Department of Computer Science, The University of Sheffield, Sheffield, UK

Abstract. A trace of the execution of a concurrent object-oriented program can be displayed in two-dimensions as a diagram of a non-metric finite geometry. The actions of a programs are represented by points, its objects and threads by vertical lines, its transactions by horizontal lines, its communications and resource sharing by sloping arrows, and its partial traces by rectangular figures.

We prove informally that the geometry satisfies the laws of Concurrent Kleene Algebra (CKA); these describe and justify the interleaved implementation of multithreaded programs on computer systems with a lesser number of concurrent processors. More familiar forms of semantics (e.g., verification-oriented and operational) can be derived from CKA.

Programs are represented as sets of all their possible traces of execution, and non-determinism is introduced as union of these sets. The geometry is extended to multiple levels of abstraction and granularity; a method call at a higher level can be modelled by a specification of the method body, which is implemented at a lower level.

The final section describes how the axioms and definitions of the geometry have been encoded in the interactive proof tool Isabelle, and reports on progress towards automatic checking of the proofs in the paper.

Keywords: Concurrent Kleene Algebra · Laws of programming · Trace algebra · Semantic models · Refinement · Unifying theories

1 Introduction

The intent of this paper is to make a modest but seminal contribution towards an ambitious long-term goal. The goal is to provide a secure conceptual foundation for the design, implementation and effective use of future program debugging tools. They will assist in unit testing, component integration, and evolution of concurrent and distributed systems software on an enterprise scale. Such tools will provide differential analysis of changed code, generation of effective test cases, run-time detection of errors, and assistance in their location, diagnosis and correction. The errors will include generic errors defined by the programming language (e.g., overflows), violation of properties explicitly defined as assertions

© Springer International Publishing AG 2017
J.P. Bowen and H. Zhu (Eds.): UTP 2016, LNCS 10134, pp. 1–25, 2017.
DOI: 10.1007/978-3-319-52228-9_1

or assumptions in the program, as well as violations of behavioural design patterns originally laid down by the system architect. The tools will communicate with the programming teams by displaying a navigable trace of events leading up to the suspected anomalies – a technology known as "time-travel debugging".

Our modest contribution is to formalise a discrete geometry governing diagrams of program behaviour. The diagrams will include actions of the program that are relevant to an anomaly, as well as communications and other causal dependencies between the actions.

We provide an example of the application of the geometry to a concurrent object-oriented program. The set of all possible traces of execution of a particular program is a mathematical formalisation (model) of its meaning. Technically, it is known as a denotational semantics. We prove that this semantics satisfies the star-free laws of a Concurrent Kleene Algebra (CKA); this gives an algebraic semantics that justifies program transformation rules applied in optimisation. From the algebraic semantics it is possible to derive other familiar and widely applied forms of semantics (e.g., operational and verification-oriented). We offer this as evidence of the potential applicability of geometry to current and future programming practice.

Further evidence is provided by quoting the many sources of ideas that have been amalgamated into our theories. Our geometric foundation is inspired by graphical research tools developed and applied to the analysis of relaxed memory models, [1,19]. The pattern of horizontal and vertical lines in our diagrams is taken from Message Sequence Charts (MSC) [8] which are widely used to plan and record the architecture of a large-scale computer application. Our concept of a transaction matches the transition of a Petri Net, [23]. Our assertion language for specification of traces is Concurrent Separation Logic [6,22], widely used by seekers of proofs for concurrent programs. Finally, our motivation and methodology are those of past and current research into Unifying Theories of Programming [14].

Summary

In Sect. 2 the primitive concepts of our geometry are enumerated as points, lines and figures, drawn on a two-dimensional surface. The vertical dimension represents time, the horizontal one space. Actions of a program are represented by points, objects by vertical lines, and transactions by horizontal lines. Points occur only at the intersection of a vertical with a horizontal line. Arrows are defined as segments of lines between two neighbouring points on a line. A figure contains a subset of points, and its perimeter is the set of arrows which connect its internal points to points in its external environment.

A figure (called a tracelet) is a trace of execution of some component of a structured program. It may be decomposed into two disjoint but neighbouring subsets p and q in two ways: one of them $(p; q)$ represents sequential composition, and the other $(p|q)$ represents concurrent composition. The arrows between p and q form the common part of the perimeter that separates them. A tracelet containing a single transaction cannot be further decomposed.

Section 3 introduces the concept of a tracelet as a figure representing the execution of some nested component of the program structure. Typical components are $(p; q)$ or $(p|q)$, standing for sequential or concurrent composition of subordinate components p and q. The actions of the original (bracketed) tracelet may then be split disjointly into separate tracelets for p and for q, which therefore share no actions. The arrows between them form a shared part of the perimeter of both of them. A line that passes through all the shared arrows can be drawn horizontally in the case of sequentiality or vertically in the case of concurrency. The splitting process may be continued until every tracelet contains only a single transaction, which cannot be further decomposed. The empty tracelet represents execution of a null command of the program, which of course does nothing.

Section 4 defines a pre-ordering relation $p \leq q$ between tracelets. It means that p is a possibly more interleaved version of q. If the converse relation also holds, the two tracelets are regarded as equal. From the definition of the ordering we prove informally all the laws of CKA whose variables range over single tracelets. They are as follows:

1. The operators ; and | are both associative, and both have the null command as unit.
2. Both operators are monotonic, for example $p \leq q$ implies $p; r \leq q; r$ and $r; p \leq r; q$.
3. Finally, an "interchange" law expresses a characteristic property of interleaving: $(p|q); (p'|q') \leq (p; p')|(q; q')$.

In an example proof we use a combination of all these laws to derive a fully interleaved version of an example tracelet.

Section 5 defines a program as the family of all its possible executions. The family is therefore downward closed, in that it contains all the more interleaved versions of any tracelet that it contains. A non-deterministic choice between programs is simply the set union of their two families. This disjunction has all the usual algebraic properties: associativity, commutativity, and idempotence; in addition, both ; and | distribute through it. The unit of disjunction is the empty family of traces, denoting a program which has no executions. This is the fate of a program containing a syntax error or a type error, or other errors which the language definition requires to be detected at compile time. Section 6 gives a simpler (more abstract) model of CKA. It abstracts from the intricate network of internal actions and arrows of a tracelet, and defines the two composition operators solely in terms of the perimeters of the operands. The common part of their perimeters is removed, and the rest forms the perimeter of the result of the composition. The function which maps a tracelet to its perimeter is a homomorphism w.r.t. ; and |, and therefore preserves all the star-free algebraic properties of the CKA. For some purposes, this perimeter model is an oversimplification, because it fails to model the phenomenon of deadlock resulting from a cyclic chain of causation. Cyclicity is a programming error that halts a group of threads, when each of them is waiting for occurrence of actions of other members of the cycle. This problem is solved by a second model, which retains the internal causal connectivity between the arrows of the perimeter. This model enables absence of deadlock to be proved, or at least detected. Section 7 reports early steps towards a formalisation of the geometric model in Isabelle. So far it provides the concepts and mechanical proofs of most concepts of the previous section. It gives a summary of the remaining steps towards a complete formalisation.

2   Primitive Concepts

We model a concurrent computer program as the set of all its possible executions on any computer system that offers an implementation of its programming language. Each execution is modelled by a discrete geometric diagram called a trace, which is drawn on a two-dimensional surface. The horizontal axis represents spatial distribution of locations in the memory of the computer system. The vertical axis represents the interval of time during which the program is executed.

The primitive components of our discrete geometry include analogues of the points, the lines and the figures familiar from Euclidean geometry. We have no concept of measurement of time or of distance in space. We maintain a distinction between horizontal and vertical coordinates; but whenever convenient, they are not drawn straight. Labels may be attached to a component: they describe its interpretation in the actual program execution.

A point represents a primitive action performed inside or in the immediate vicinity of the computer system during a single execution of the complete program. Every point is the unique member of the intersection of a horizontal and a vertical coordinate; all other such intersections are empty.

A *vertical line* is a non-empty sequence of points along a vertical coordinate that represent the sequential behaviour of an object stored at a particular location of the computer memory. This location number or name serves as a label unique to the line. Typical objects are threads or (possibly structured) variables. The topmost point of the line represents the primitive action of allocation of the object (or forking of a thread), and its bottommost point represents its disposal (or join of a thread). The intermediate points represent the temporal sequence of actions in which the object engages while it exists.

A *horizontal line* is a non-empty sequence of points along a horizontal coordinate whose actions appear to take place simultaneously as a single transaction. It is labelled by a reference to the basic command in the program which called for its execution. Apparent simultaneity will be ensured by disallowing any state of memory which records the performance of only some of the actions of a transaction, while omitting the rest. This follows the familiar definition of atomicity, without placing any constraint on how it is implemented.

A frequent type of transaction contains just two actions, one from the thread issuing the instruction that triggered the action, and the other from an object (usually owned by that thread) which performs the action required by the instruction. A transaction containing just a single action of a single object represents an autonomous behaviour of the object. Other transactions involve more than two objects. For example, a communication on a synchronised channel requires simultaneous actions of six objects: two threads, an output port and an input port for the channel, and finally two variables which supply and receive the communicated value.

A pair of consecutive points on the same line is called an *arrow*. On a vertical line, the higher point is called the source, and the lower one is the target. On a horizontal line, an arrow may point either to the left or to the right. A vertical arrow is labelled by the value stored in its location of memory during the interval between its source action and its target action.

A subset of horizontal and vertical arrows represent *buffered communications* between threads. A horizontal communication arrow is labelled by the value of the message communicated. A vertical communication arrow conveys ownership of the object from one thread to another. It is convenient to draw communication arrows sloping at a slight angle from their nominal orientation.

A *tracelet* contains, surrounded by a rectangle, the subset of the points of a trace which occurred during execution of a single syntactic component of a structured program, i.e., a node in its abstract syntax tree (AST). This means that the complete trace is an execution of the root of the AST; and a typical leaf of the AST is a basic command of the program whose execution is a tracelet containing a single transaction. An *empty tracelet* (which we will call **1**) is an execution of the null command, which of course does nothing.

To summarise the basic concepts of our discrete geometry, we introduce names for infinite mathematical universes, containing all conceivable instances of the primitive concepts of our geometry. Let Pt be the set of all conceivable points; let Vert be the universe of all pairs of points that might feature as the tail or the head of an arrow in a vertical line. Let Hor be the set of all pairs of points that might feature as tail and head of a horizontal arrow. Let Comm be the set of all communication arrows (often drawn diagonally); they are also either in Vert or in Hor. Define Dep = Vert + Hor, where + denotes the union of

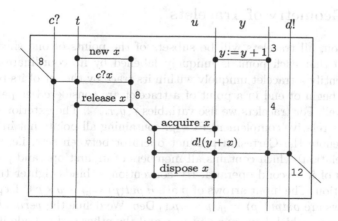

Fig. 1. A sample tracelet

disjoint sets. Its pairs are called arrows or dependences, because it is impossible for the tail action of an arrow to be performed before its head action.

Example 2.1. Figure 1 shows a typical small tracelet. Its points are enclosed in a rectangular perimeter. There are six vertical lines, carrying the labels $c?, t, x, u, y$ and $d!$. Each label stands for the name or location of the object whose behaviour is recorded in the labelled line. All the vertical lines (except x, which is local to this tracelet) extend beyond the rectangle, both above it and below it. The lines t and u stand for threads, x and y are variables, $c?$ is the input port of a channel, and $d!$ is the output port of a different channel.

There are also seven horizontal lines. Two of them extend beyond the perimeter of the tracelet, one on the left and the other on the right. The three lines on the left each contain an action of the thread t, which issues the command for the transaction to occur. Similarly, the four lines on the right are executions of commands from the thread u. The other actions in each transaction are performed by objects (variables) owned by the threads: x is owned by t on the left and by u on the right.

The diagonal arrow in the middle of the diagram is a vertical arrow representing transfer of ownership of the variable x from the thread t to the thread u. The diagonal arrows entering and leaving the perimeter on the left and on the right are inputs and outputs of values on the buffered channels c and d, respectively.

The example shows a trace of the life history of the variable x. It begins with the allocation by its initial owner, the thread t. The next action is the allocation of an initial value to the new object. The value is acquired by input from channel c. The next two actions are a release of ownership by t, and its acquisition by the other thread u. This thread then outputs on channel d the value of the variable y, incremented by the current value of x. Finally, the variable x is disposed by its current owner.   □

3   The Geometry of Tracelets

In this section, all tracelets will be subsets of the points of one single overall trace. Recall that each point is uniquely labelled by its coordinates. We can therefore identify a tracelet uniquely within its trace by the set of its points. All arrows that begin or end in a point of a tracelet are considered as part of that tracelet as well. For tracelets we use variables $p, q, r, \ldots$ The exterior $-p$ of p is defined as its relative complement $\mathsf{Pt} - p$, containing all points not in p.

Let $\times$ denote the Cartesian product operator between sets, i.e. the set of pairs (the relation) which contains all members of its first operand paired with all members of its second operand. By convention $\times$ binds tighter than union and intersection. The input arrows of p are $input(p) =_{df} -p \times p \cap \mathsf{Dep}$, and the output arrows are $output(p) =_{df} p \times -p \cap \mathsf{Dep}$. We define the *perimeter* of p as the set of arrows which have one end in p and the other end outside it; or more formally, $perimeter(p) = input(p) + output(p)$.

As mentioned in Example 2.1, a tracelet p is drawn as a rectangle which encloses all the points in p, and excludes all points in $-p$. That rectangle does not pass through any of these points; it passes just once through each of the perimeter arrows.

Note (for interest) that the bounding rectangle is a closed curve that satisfies an analogue of the Jordan Curve theorem. Define a continuous line as a finite non-repeating sequence of arrows, in which the source or target of each arrow is also the target or source of one of its pair of neighbours within the sequence, or of its only neighbour in the case of endpoint of the chain. Every chain of arrows from one endpoint inside the rectangle to another endpoint outside it must cross at least one rectangle edge. This is proved by a simple induction on the length of the chain.

The perimeter of a rectangle is partitioned into its four edges. A horizontal edge does not contain any horizontal arrows, unless they are (sloping) communication arrows. Similarly, a vertical edge does not contain any vertical arrows unless they are transfers of ownership (also sloping). In drawing a perimeter, the top and bottom edges are horizontal and the left and right edges are vertical.

Each horizontal edge of the perimeter defines the state of part of the memory of the computer system at the relevant time coordinate. It is known in separation logic as a statelet. The top edge defines the initial state that is passed to the tracelet when it starts, and the bottom edge is passed as the final state on completion of execution.

The *content* of the memory at each horizontal edge is defined by the labels on the arrows that pass through the edge. It is defined in the standard way as a partial function which maps the location of each arrow crossing the edge (say $l_1, l_2, \dots$) to the value (say $v_1, v_2, \dots$) which labels that arrow. The function is written in the notation of separation logic. The infix binary operator $*$ stands for the disjoint union of the functions on either side of it. The function $(l \mapsto v)$ is a singleton function, whose whole domain is the singleton $\{l\}$ and which maps l to v. The value of the whole statelet is written in the form

$$(l_1 \mapsto v_1) * (l_2 \mapsto v_2) * \cdots$$

In separation logic, this formula is interpreted as an assertion that the value of l_1 is v_1, and the value of l_2 is v_2, etc.

The content of a vertical edge of a tracelet is defined similarly. But first, we must supply distinct names for all the messages that cross the edge. In the case of a communication channel, we use the channel name subscripted by the index of the message in the sequence of all messages passed on the channel, for example: $(c_4 \mapsto 12)$.

The specification of a tracelet contains the formula for all four edges of its perimeter. The formula for Fig. 1 is written on separate lines for each edge.

$(y \mapsto 3) * (c?, d!, t, u \mapsto \_)$	at the Top
$(d_{27} \mapsto 12)$	on the Right
$(y' \mapsto 4) * (c?, d!, t, u \mapsto \_)$	on the Bottom
$(c_9 \mapsto 8)$	on the Left

The first line states that the initial value of y is 3, and that the other named objects have been allocated. The second line says that (say) the 27th message sent on channel d was 12. The third line gives the final value of y, and states that the other objects are still allocated. The fourth line states that channel c received the value 8 as the 9th message.

3.1   Sequential and Concurrent Composition

Our definition of the ; and | operators will be unconventional. Instead of defining how two tracelets can be composed to give the required result, we describe how the result can be decomposed to give the tracelets of its parts. It seems to be easier to learn first how to take something apart, and how to put it together later.

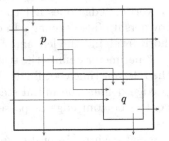

Fig. 2. Sequential composition

Consider a node of the program AST labeled by the operator of sequential composition. Let r be the tracelet for the considered node, and let p and q be the tracelets for its two immediate offspring in the corresponding AST. We describe this situation by the equation $r = p;q$. Now draw a horizontal coordinate internal to the rectangle for r, with all points in p above it, and all points in q below it. The diagram (see Fig. 2) makes it clear that the rectangle for p shares its top edge with r, and its bottom edge with q; similarly, the bottom edge of q is shared with that of r. The left and right edges of r are split into two disjoint parts, and the two top parts are assigned to p and the lower parts to q.

A defining feature of sequential composition is that an implementation can execute it by completing the execution of it first operand before starting execution of the second operand. This would be impossible if any action of the first operand were dependent on any action of the second operand. So the drawing of a horizontal edge is subject to the constraint that no arrow should point from its second operand to its first. That is assured by the fact that a horizontal edge contains only vertical and sloping horizontal arrows, and they all point downwards.

The practical consequence of this constraint is that is impossible to violate the atomicity of a transaction, except at one of its sloping arrows. Memory is represented by a horizontal edge; so any memory that records the result of the action at one end of a non-sloping horizontal arrow must also record the action at the other end. Otherwise the constraint is violated.

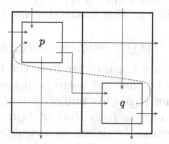

Fig. 3. Concurrent composition

A similar diagram can be drawn for concurrent composition (see Fig. 3), with a new vertical edge instead of a horizontal one. It leads to a similar pattern of sharing of left and right vertical edges, and a similar splitting of the top and bottom horizontal edges. Again, the vertical edge can contain only horizontal and sloping arrows pointing from left to right.

The practical consequence of this constraint is that no object can be owned by more than one thread at any one time. The only way that an object can be shared between two threads is by passing ownership between them by means a sloping vertical arrow. In a conventional view of sharing, ownership is passed between every pair of its actions. Such an object is represented geometrically by a vertical line, all of whose arrows are sloping.

If any of the constraints described above are violated, we simply say that the diagram for $p; q$ or for $p|q$ is undefined; it is just not a tracelet. A composition is also undefined if the values which label any arrow in the edge differ in the two operands. Further reasons for the undefinedness of transactions that executed basic commands are given in the definition of these commands, which should be given in the definition of any particular programming language. Further pursuit of this topic is beyond the scope of this paper.

Summary. To summarise and complement our decompositional definitions of the operators, we give a bottom-up formal presentation of some of the details. We start with a diagrammatic presentation. Figures 2 and 3 show explicitly the pattern of arrows that cross the internal and external edges of a tracelet split horizontally or vertically. Each arrow of the figures represents a (maybe empty) set of arrows in a diagram. Arrow sets that must be empty are simply not shown. We use the convention that horizontal arrows leave their rectangle through the right edge, and enter it through the left edge.

The equations given below are derived by studying the figures. Let $T(p)$ be the set of arrows crossing the top edge of p, and let $B(p), L(p)$, and $R(p)$ be defined similarly as the bottom, left and right edges. Then Fig. 3 shows that

$$T(p \mid q) = T(p) + T(q), \qquad B(p \mid q) = B(p) + B(q).$$

The disjoint union is the separating conjunction that defines the initial and the final states of $p \mid q$: we have $B(p) \cap T(q) = \{\} = T(p) \cap B(q)$. There are no vertical arrows between p and q. This means that no state of memory is passed between them:

$$L(p \mid q) = (L(p) - R(q)) + (L(q) - R(p)).$$

The horizontal inputs of p are taken either from the horizontal inputs of q or from the environment of $p \mid q$ (but not both); and similarly for the horizontal inputs of q. The equation for $R(p \mid q)$ is similar, with L and R interchanged.

Note the dashed curved arrow from $R(q)$ to $L(p)$. Since p is on the left of q, the arrow from p to q cannot be drawn as a straight line in two dimensions while observing the above convention. One could imagine that it was drawn on the back of the paper on which the diagram is drawn. Or one could maintain a uniform left-to-right direction of horizontal arrows by imagining the whole diagram drawn on the curved surface of a cylinder.

Figure 2 shows the graph for sequential composition. It differs from Fig. 3 in two ways. Firstly, the curved arrow is removed, because it would violate our intended meaning of sequential composition. It would actually prevent an implementation of sequential composition from executing the whole of p before starting the execution of q. Secondly, a new internal arrow is introduced to stand for the transmission of the state of memory on termination of p and initiation of q. That is surely another part of our intention when using semicolon.

Derivation of the equations for sequential composition from this diagram is left as an exercise.

3.2   Quadrangulation

We now describe a process for splitting a complete trace or tracelet into all its component tracelets, so that it matches the AST of the program whose execution it represents. The splitting described above for $p;q$ or $p|q$ is repeated on p and on q, and then repeatedly on the smaller tracelets that result from earlier splittings. Once a tracelet has been split it cannot be split again as a whole — only its parts might be split further. Therefore no arrow can be split more than once by a horizontal or a vertical edge. By analogy with the familiar triangulation of figures in Euclidean geometry, we call the process *quadrangulation*. The process is *complete* when all splittable arrows have been split exactly once.

The completely quadrangulated tracelet is a tree which exactly matches the AST of its program. The points of each tracelet in it are the disjoint union of the points of each of its offspring. So any tracelet includes all points of any of its descendants, and is included among the points of all its ancestors. It is helpful to use the text of the program itself as a linear representation for the whole quadrangulated tracelet. Typical examples of such terms are $p \mid (q \mid r)$ and $(p \mid q) ; (p' \mid q')$, where $p, q, \dots$ are variables standing for further descendant tracelets, or (in the case of a leaf) the corresponding basic command of the program.

Example 3.1. Figures 4 and 5 show the result of the first three steps in two different quadrangulations of the tracelet shown in Fig. 1. To avoid distraction, the labels that are irrelevant to our current purposes have been removed. The titles on the figures are the formulae that describe the quadrangulations. They use bracketing to indicate the order in which the splits were made.

$$(p|q); (p'; q')$$

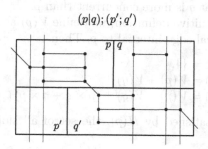

Fig. 4. Tracelet from Fig. 1 split as $(p|q); (p'; q')$

In Fig. 4 the first split is horizontal and the next two are vertical, whereas in Fig. 5 this order is reversed.

$$(p; p')|(q; q')$$

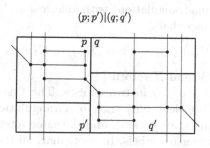

Fig. 5. Tracelet from Fig. 1 split as $(p; p')|(q'; q')$

Otherwise, the figures are very similar. All the points and arrows internal to each of the rectangles p, p', q, q' are identical on both figures, and all the internal arrows and splits within them are the same. The only difference is at the centre of the diagram, where the sloping communication arrow is split horizontally in Fig. 4, whereas it has been split vertically in Fig. 5.   □

4   Algebra of Tracelets

In this section, we will continue to use the single word tracelet for a quadrangulated tracelet. Our algebra is a pre-order algebra, in the sense that it uses a pre-order relation $\leq$ (i.e., a reflexive and transitive relation), in place of the more usual equality symbol $=$ between the left and right hand sides of an equation. In an order algebra, an analogue of equality is re-introduced as an equivalence, again written as $=$, defined as the conjunction of $\leq$ and its converse. In our geometry, the ordering $p \leq q$ between tracelets p, q has an informally expressed meaning that p represents a more sequential execution than the one represented by q or equivalently that q is more concurrent than p.

To formalise this intuitive definition, we define $V(p)$ as the set of all sloping arrows crossing a vertical edge internal to p. Then

$$V(1) = \{\},$$
$$V(p\,;q) = V(p) + V(q)$$
$$V(p \mid q) = V(p) + V(q) + (p \times q + q \times p) \cap \mathsf{Hor}.$$

Similar equations are satisfied by $H(p)$, the set of all sloping arrows crossing horizontal edges in p:

$$H(1) = \{\}$$
$$H(p\,;q) = H(p) + H(q) + p \times q \cap \mathsf{Vert}$$
$$H(p \mid q) = H(p) + H(q)$$

Every internal sloping arrow of p may be in $V(p)$ or $H(p)$, but never in both. If p is completely quadrangulated then the sets $V(p)$ and $H(q)$ are complements of each other relative to the set $\mathsf{Comm} \cap p \times p$ of all sloping arrows within p. Hence, if p and q are complete quadrangulations with identical underlying tracelets then by contraposition it follows that

$$V(p) \subseteq V(q) \iff H(q) \subseteq H(p).$$

For an unsplit tracelet, V and H return $\{\}$.

We define the relation $p \leq q$ in two clauses. The first requires that p and q are entirely equal as tracelets; only their quadrangulations can differ. Hence the two tracelets have the same actions, and the same internal arrows, with the same orientations and the same labels. In particular, all the arrows not split by the quadrangulations match exactly in p and q. The second clause requires that $V(p)$ is contained in $V(q)$ and $H(q)$ is contained in $H(p)$. By the above remark, if $V(p)$ and $H(p)$ as well as $V(q)$ and $H(q)$ are relative complements (which holds, in particular, for complete quadrangulations p, q) then we may use either alternative at convenience. The definition allows a sloping arrow that crosses a horizontal edge in p to cross a vertical edge in q. Because set inclusion is a partial order, so is the relation $\leq$.

Example 4.1. Let r and r' be the quadrangulations in Figs. 4 and 5, respectively, and let a be the only diagonal arrow there. Then we have $V(r) = \{\}$ and $H(r) = \{a\}$, whereas $V(r') = \{a\}$ and $H(r') = \{\}$. Since there is exacly the communication arrow a in both r and r', $V(r)$ and $H(r)$ as well as $V(r')$ and $H(r')$ are relative complements of each other. According to the remarks above and in Example 3.1 therefore $r \leq r'$. Below we will see that this is a special instance of a general law.   □

From the definition we will now derive a set of algebraic laws governing sequential and concurrent composition; they are the basic laws of a Concurrent Kleene Algebra (CKA) [17]. For simplicity, we restrict ourselves here to complete quadrangulations. This allows us in each case to choose the simpler of the equations for V and H. There is a treatment of the general case which will be presented in a follow-up paper.

Theorem 4.2 (example). $p \,;q \leq p \,|\, q$ and $q \,;p \leq p \,|\, q$.

Proof. $V(p\,;q) = V(q\,;p) = V(p) + V(q) \subseteq V(p\,|\,q)$, by the definition of V. □

This theorem justifies the implementation of the concurrent composition by executing the operands in either order. However the justification is void in the case that the left hand side is undefined. The existence of dependences between one operand and the other will make one or both of the interleavings void.

Note that both interleavings of $p\,|\,q$ are below it in the ordering, but that $|$ is not itself commutative. Thus our model does not satisfy the standard definition of sequential consistency, that concurrency is a non-deterministic choice of all its possible interleavings. An asymmetric example of concurrency is the chaining operator $>>$ of CSP which allows communication only from left to right.

Theorem 4.3 (unit). $p\,|\,1 = p = 1\,|\,p$ *(and the same for* $;$*)*.

Proof. $V(p\,|\,1) = V(p) + V(1) + p \times \{\} \cap \mathsf{Hor} \cap \mathsf{Comm} = V(p)$. The second and third terms on the rhs are both empty. In words: there are no points in 1, and therefore no arrow can cross its (invisible) perimeter. □

Theorem 4.4 (association). $p\,|\,(q\,|\,r) = (p\,|\,q)\,|\,r$ *(and the same for* $;$*)*.

Proof. $H(rhs) = H(p\,|\,q) + H(r) = H(p) + H(q) + H(r) =$
$\qquad H(p) + H(q\,|\,r) = H(lhs)$.
The proof for $;$ is similar, using V instead of H. □

Theorem 4.5 (monotonicity). If $p \leq q$ then $p\,;r \leq q\,;r$ *(and the same for* $|$*)*.

Proof. Assume $V(p) \subseteq V(q)$. Then, by monotonicity of $+$ and the hypothesis,

$$V(p\,;r) = V(p) + V(r) \subseteq V(q) + V(r).$$

The proof for $|$ uses H instead of V. □

Theorem 4.6 (interchange). $(p\,|\,q)\,;(p'\,|\,q') \leq (p\,;p')\,|\,(q\,;q')$.

Proof. Let $K = V(p) + V(q) + V(p') + V(q')$. Then

$$V(lhs) = K + (p \times q + p' \times q') \cap \mathsf{Hor} \cap \mathsf{Comm} \subseteq$$
$$K + (p + p') \times (q + q') \cap \mathsf{Hor} \cap \mathsf{Comm} = V(rhs),$$

because $\times$ distributes through $+$. □

Corollary 4.7 (frame). $(p \mid q) ; p' \leq (p ; p') \mid q$ and $p ; (p' \mid q') \leq (p ; p') \mid q'$.

Proof. For the first law substitute 1 for q'. By the unit law, the occurrences of 1 can be cancelled. The second law follows symmetrically.   □

Note that Theorem 4.2 follows by setting $p' = 1$ and substituting q for q' in the second law and by setting $p = 1$ and substituting p for p' in the first law.

The purpose of algebraic laws is to permit an implementation to replace the text of a submitted program by another text derived from it by algebraic reasoning. The hope is that the executed code will be better adapted to the structure and the detail of the capabilities of the executing hardware. Such transformations may be made by a compiler or by an instruction pipeline in the hardware of a computer chip.

For example, suppose the executing computer system has less processors than the number of threads initiated by the running program. In this case, concurrency has to be replaced by interleaving (time-sharing), in which an execution of several threads may be an interleaving of their separate sequential traces. In fact, repeated application of all the laws proved above can generate arbitrary interleaved executions of any pair (or group) of concurrent program.

This is demonstrated by an example of a fully algebraic proof. To avoid clutter, semicolons are omitted except when they are necessary to indicate how the interchange law is to be applied. Also, the use of monotonicity remains tacit.

$$
\begin{aligned}
& abcd \mid xyzw \\
= \quad & \{\!\mid (\text{assoc } ;) \mid\!\} \\
& (a ; bcd) \mid (xy ; zw) \\
\geq \quad & \{\!\mid (\text{interchange}) \mid\!\} \\
& (a \mid xy) ; (bcd \mid zw) \\
\geq \quad & \{\!\mid (\text{assoc } ;) \mid\!\} \\
& a \mid (x ; y) ; (b ; cd \mid zw) \\
\geq \quad & \{\!\mid (\text{frame}) \mid\!\} \\
& (a \mid x) ; y ; (b \mid zw) ; cd \\
\geq \quad & \{\!\mid (\text{Theorem } 4.2) \mid\!\} \\
& axybzwcd.
\end{aligned}
$$

Interleaving is introduced by each step that uses the interchange law or its corollary. The position of the semicolon indicates a scheduling decision that the two semicolons on the rhs of the law will be reached simultaneously by both threads, at exactly the moment when the lhs reaches its single semicolon. Different scheduling decisions would use different associations at each step, and thereby generate all possible different interleavings.

5   From Tracelets to Programs: Lifting

So far we have dealt with single tracelets. A *program* is identified by and with the set of all possible tracelets of its execution, which is what we will explore next. This section explains how all the operators defined on tracelets can be lifted to sets of tracelets in such a way that all the laws proven for operators on tracelets are preserved.

5.1   Elementwise Lifting

We do not consider arbitrary sets of tracelets. Rather, we adopt a downward closure condition which ensures that a relation $\leq$ between programs can be defined as simple set inclusion. A set P of tracelets is *downward closed* w.r.t. the pre-order $\leq$ if $p \in P$ and $p' \leq p$ imply $p' \in P$ as well. Downward closure codifies our intention that any program that can validly be executed concurrently can also be validly executed more sequentially.

If $\circ$ is a binary, possibly partial, operator on tracelets then its *elementwise lifting* to programs P, P' is defined as the downward closure of the set of all defined compositions between P and P', i.e., the set of all tracelets q such there are $p \in P$ and $p' \in P'$ with defined $p \circ p'$ and $q \leq p \circ p'$.

Since we do not only use equational laws but also inequational ones, we have to define a relation $\leq$ between programs if we want to lift laws to programs. While it is clear what equality means for sets, there are several ways to extend a pre-order like $\leq$ to sets. We choose the following definition: $P \leq P'$ holds iff every tracelet in P is below some tracelet in P'. For downward closed sets (and hence programs) $\leq$ coincides with inclusion $\subseteq$. This means that we can use ordinary union to introduce non-deterministic choice into our algebra of programs, and define it as set union. Furthermore, it means that an implementation can make an arbitrary choice from any non-deterministic variants allowed by the program under execution, giving our intended interpretation of non-determinism a demonic flavour.

Let T, T' be terms involving variables and operators on tracelets, and consider the inequational law $T \leq T'$. A sufficient condition for lifting this law from tracelets to programs is *linearity*, viz. that every variable occurs at most once on both sides of the law and that all variables in the left hand side T also occur in the right hand side T'. Examples are the frame and exchange laws. For equations a sufficient condition is *bilinearity*, meaning that both inequations that constitute an equation are linear. Examples are associativity, commutativity and neutrality; a counterexample is distributivity. The main result is as follows.

Theorem 5.1. *If a linear law $T \leq T'$ holds for tracelets then it also holds when all variables in T, T' are interpreted as variables for programs and the operators are interpreted as the elementwise liftings of the corresponding trace operators.*

A detailed proof for general pre-orders can be found in [18]. The technique is classical in mathematics; for related results see among others [10,11] (and also [4] for a survey).

We illustrate the gist of the proof for the case of the law $P \,;\, P' \leq P \mid P'$ lifted from Theorem 4.2. Assume $r \in P \,;\, P'$. By the above definition there are $p \in P, p' \in P'$ such that $r \leq p \,;\, p'$. Since the frame law holds at the trace level, we have $p \, ; p' \le p \, | \, p'$. Moreover, $p \, | \, p'$ is in the set of all $|$-combinations of traces from P with traces from P' and hence also in its downward closure $P \, | \, P'$, so that we are done.

5.2   Errors, Recursion and Iteration

There are further useful consequences of our definition of programs. The set $\mathcal{P}$ of all programs forms a complete lattice w.r.t. the inclusion ordering; it has been called the *Hoare power domain* in the theory of denotational semantics (e.g. [5, 20, 24]).

The least element of $\mathcal{P}$ is the empty program $\emptyset$ which can also serve as an error element, modelling a completely faulty module without any sensible tracelet. A more detailed, elementwise, error handling is already contained in the definition of the elementwise lifting of operators: all erroneous, undefined combinations of tracelets are ruled out from the combination of the containing programs. This was already stated in Sect. 3.1.

The greatest element of $\mathcal{P}$ is the program U consisting of all tracelets. Infimum and supremum in $\mathcal{P}$ coincide with intersection and union, since downward closed sets are also closed under these operations.

Therefore we can define (unbounded) choice between a set $\mathcal{Q} \subseteq \mathcal{P}$ of programs as

$$\lceil\!\rceil \, \mathcal{Q} =_{df} \bigcup \mathcal{Q}$$

with binary choice as the special case

$$P \lceil\!\rceil P' =_{df} P \cup P'.$$

The lifted versions of monotonic tracelet operators are monotonic again (see [18]), but even distribute through arbitrary choices between programs.

Monotonicity of the lifted operators, together with completeness of the lattice of programs and the Tarski-Knaster fixed point theorem, guarantees that recursion equations have least and greatest solutions. More precisely, let $f : \mathcal{P} \to \mathcal{P}$ be a monotonic function. Then f has a least fixed point μf and a greatest fixed point νf, given by the following formulas:

$$\mu f = \bigcap \{P \, | \, f(P) \subseteq P\}, \qquad \nu f = \bigcup \{P \, | \, P \subseteq f(P)\}.$$

With our operator $;$ this can be used to define the Kleene star (see e.g. [7]), i.e., unbounded finite sequential iteration, of a program P as $P^* =_{df} \mu f_P$, where

$$f_P(X) =_{df} \mathsf{skip} \lceil\!\rceil (P \, ; X),$$

where $\mathsf{skip} =_{df} \{1\}$ is the idle program. Since f_P, by the above remark, distributes through arbitrary choices between programs, it is even continuous and Kleene's fixed point theorem tells us that $P^* = \mu f_P$ has the iterative representation

$$P^* = \bigcup \{f_P^i(\emptyset) \, | \, i \in \mathbb{N}\}, \tag{1}$$

which transforms into the well known representation of star, viz.

$$P^* = \bigcup \{P^i \mid i \in \mathbb{N}\}$$

with $P^0 =_{df}$ skip and $P^{i+1} =_{df} P\,;P^i$.

Infinite iteration P^ω can be defined as the greatest fixed point νg_P where

$$g_P(X) =_{df} P\,;X.$$

Along the same lines, unbounded finite and infinite concurrent iteration of a program can be defined. For further forms of iteration we refer to [18].

We conclude this section with a brief description how pre-post-condition semantics can be integrated into our approach. As in [17] one can define, for programs P, P' and Q, the Hoare triple

$$P\,\{Q\}\,P' \iff_{df} P\,;Q \subseteq P'.$$

It expresses that, after any tracelet in "pre-history" P, execution of Q is guaranteed to yield an overall tracelet in P'. From this one can derive the standard properties of Hoare logic and separation logic; for further details we refer to [15, 17].

6 Interfaces and Specifications

We now deal with *specifications* that abstract, to a certain extent, from the interior arrows of tracelets but preserve their interfaces, i.e., their perimeters. For this analysis the distinction between horizontal and vertical arrows is inessential; we only reason about the overall dependence relation Dep.

6.1 Two Types of Specifications

A first, quite radical, abstraction reduces a tracelet just to its perimeter that describes the interaction of the tracelet with its environment. It presents a pure black-box view of the tracelet.

This abstraction can be formalised as follows. The *input points* $in(p)$ of p are the end points of the input arrows to p, while the *output points* $out(p)$ of p are the starting points of the output arrows of p. Now the set of points of $perspec(p)$ is $in(p) \cup out(p)$, while its arrow set is given by $perimeter(p)$. This implies

$$perimeter(perspec(p)) = perimeter(p). \tag{2}$$

A second, more refined, abstraction $connspec(p)$ of p records connections in the form of dependences between input and output points of p. It can be drawn as a tracelet containing only chains with at most three arrows, namely an input, an output and possibly an intermediate arrow. If present, the latter records the existence of a direct or indirect dependence between its source and target within p; however, the whole chain of intermediate internal points is omitted.

This abstraction allows an analysis which of the input arrows are actually useful in that they "contribute" to the outputs. Input arrows that are not connected to any output arrows could, together with the internal arrow chains emanating from them, be safely removed without affecting the observable behaviour of the tracelet. They will, inside p, lead to end points or, in the case of deadlock, to cycles of points that do not have outgoing arrows to points outside the cycles; therefore they cannot contribute to values in labels of output arrows from p.

The set of points of $connspec(p)$ is again $in(p) \cup out(p)$. The arrows of $connspec(p)$ are the input and output arrows of p plus a set Dep'_p of fresh arrows for each pair in $in(p) \times out(p) \cap \mathsf{Dep}^+_p$, where $\mathsf{Dep}_p =_{df} p \times p \cap \mathsf{Dep}$ is the local dependence relation for p. Using transitive rather than reflexive transitive closure ensures that a point e in $in(p) \cap out(p)$ does not receive an extra arrow (e, e) in $connspec(p)$. This takes care of singleton tracelets of the form $+\!\!\!\to \bullet +\!\!\!\to$ (where the brackets indicate the rectangle around the tracelet).

For tracelet p we have the decomposition

$$arrows(p) = perimeter(p) + \mathsf{Dep}'_p,$$

where again $+$ denotes disjoint union.

Both specification functions $s \in \{perspec, connspec\}$ are idempotent, i.e., satisfy $s(s(p)) = s(p)$.

6.2 Specification and (De-)Composition

To make such abstractions useful for the analysis of larger tracelets, they have to behave well w.r.t. composition or decomposition of tracelets. We will now show that this is indeed the case.

For this we use a generic (de)composition operator $\circ$ like in [18]. For tracelets p, p' with disjoint point sets,

$$p \circ p' =_{df} (p + p', arrows(p) \cup arrows(p')).$$

Both operators $|$ and $;$ from Sect. 3.1 can be seen as instances of $\circ$, since they administer the arrows involved in precisely that way.

Theorem 6.1. *For both specification functions $s \in \{perspec, connspec\}$ we have the homomorphic equation*

$$s(p \circ q) = s(s(p) \circ s(q)).$$

The equation is homomorphic in the following sense. One can define a new operator $\circ'$ on specification tracelets r, t by $r \circ' t =_{df} s(r \circ t)$. Then $s(p \circ q) = s(p) \circ' s(q)$.

We present the gist of the proof; full details can be found in the technical report [16]. Automated proofs of some parts are under way, see Sect. 7.

First we establish the behaviour of perimeter and local dependence on composed tracelets:

$$\left. \begin{array}{l} perimeter(p \circ p') = (perimeter(p) \cup perimeter(p')) - intf(p, p'), \\ \mathsf{Dep}_{p \circ p'} = \mathsf{Dep}_p \cup \mathsf{Dep}_{p'} \cup intf(p, p'), \end{array} \right\} \quad (3)$$

where $intf(p, p') =_{df} arrows(p) \cap arrows(p')$ is the interface between p and p'. Using (2) we obtain, moreover,

$$intf(perspec(p), perspec(p')) = intf(p, p'). \quad (4)$$

With the help of these properties easy calculations show that $s = perspec$ satisfies the homomorphic equation of Theorem 6.1.

For the specification operator $connspec$ it suffices to consider the local dependence relations of the tracelets on both sides of the homomorphic equations, since their perimeters coincide by the homomorphic property of $perspec$ anyway. This also implies that the analogue of (4) holds for $connspec$ as well:

$$intf(connspec(p), connspec(p')) = intf(p, p').$$

For the local dependences we proceed in two steps. First, we have the following properties.

Lemma 6.2. *Set* $\hat{p} =_{df} connspec(p)$ *and likewise for* p'.

1. $\mathsf{Dep}_{\hat{p} \circ \hat{p}'} = \mathsf{Dep}_{\hat{p}} \cup \mathsf{Dep}_{\hat{p}'} \cup intf(p, p')$.
2. $\mathsf{Dep}_{connspec(\hat{p} \circ \hat{p}')} \subseteq \mathsf{Dep}_{connspec(p \circ p')}$.

The calculations are not too hard. However, showing the reverse inclusion

$$\mathsf{Dep}_{connspec(p \circ p')} \subseteq \mathsf{Dep}_{connspec(\hat{p} \circ \hat{p}')}$$

is much more laborious. Using the definitions this spells out to

$$(\mathsf{Dep}_p \cup \mathsf{Dep}_{p'} \cup \mathsf{C})^+ \cap in \times out \subseteq (\mathsf{Dep}_{\hat{p}} \cup \mathsf{Dep}_{\hat{p}'} \cup \mathsf{C})^+ \cap in \times out, \quad (5)$$

where $in =_{df} in(p) \cup in(p')$, $out =_{df} out(p) \cup out(p')$ and $\mathsf{C} =_{df} intf(p, p')$.

Let us first give an intuitive idea why (5) holds. Consider event-disjoint tracelets p, p' and events $e \in in(p), e' \in out(p')$ such that $(e, e') \in (\mathsf{Dep}_p \cup \mathsf{Dep}_{p'} \cup \mathsf{C})^+$. Consider an arbitrary path P from e to e' within $p + p'$. According to (3) we can group P into maximal pieces whose arrows are purely within Dep_p, purely within $\mathsf{Dep}_{p'}$ or consist only of "bridging" arrows in C. In Fig. 6, pieces of the first kind are indicated by dotted arrows, while interface and bridging arrows have solid lines.

The reason is that arrows from Dep_p cannot connect directly with those from $\mathsf{Dep}_{p'}$, because their end points lie in disjoint event sets. They can only connect via "bridges" in C. Now each of the maximal pieces within Dep_p or $\mathsf{Dep}_{p'}$ can be contracted to a single Dep_p^+ or $\mathsf{Dep}_{p'}^+$ edge, as is done by $connspec$. By maximality they have to start and end in events in $in(p) \cup out(p)$ or $in(p') \cup out(p')$, resp.,

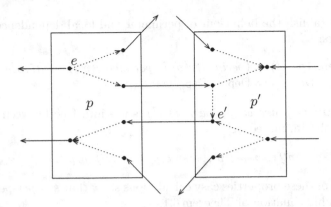

Fig. 6. Connection paths in a composition

which makes their contractions belong to $\mathsf{Dep}_{\hat{p}}$ or $\mathsf{Dep}_{\hat{p}'}$, resp. Therefore it does not matter if we contract a composition tracelet directly or first contract the maximal path pieces in its components and then contract the result further.

The formal proof uses regular algebra to good advantage; we denote relational composition by juxtaposition. We have to deal with the subexpression $(\mathsf{Dep}_p \cup \mathsf{Dep}_{p'} \cup \mathsf{C})^+$ occurring in the left hand side of (5), where we know from the definitions of $\mathsf{Dep}_p, \mathsf{Dep}_{p'}$ and $E \cap E' = \emptyset$ that $\mathsf{Dep}_p\mathsf{Dep}_{p'} = \emptyset = \mathsf{Dep}_{p'}\mathsf{Dep}_p$. We abstract a bit and show the following properties.

Lemma 6.3. *Consider relations* R, S, T.

1. $(R \cup S)^+ = R^+ \cup R^*(SR^*)^+$.
2. *If* $RS = \emptyset = SR$ *then* $(R \cup S)^+ = R^+ \cup S^+$ *and* $(R \cup S)^* = R^* \cup S^*$.
3. *If* $RS = \emptyset = SR$ *then* $(R \cup S \cup T)^+ = R^+ \cup S^+ \cup D(TD)^+$, *where* $D =_{df} R^* \cup S^*$.

For the expression occurring in the left hand side of (5) we obtain from Part 3

$$(\mathsf{Dep}_p \cup \mathsf{Dep}_{p'} \cup \mathsf{C})^+ = \mathsf{Dep}_p^+ \cup \mathsf{Dep}_{p'}^{'+} \cup D(\mathsf{C}D)^+, \tag{6}$$

where $D = \mathsf{Dep}_p^* \cup \mathsf{Dep}_{p'}^{'*}$. This is the formal counterpart of the above-mentioned path decomposition.

From this, further intensive use of regular algebra finally leads to a proof of (5), which establishes Theorem 6.1 for $s = connspec$.

7   Verification Tool Development

For practical uses of the geometric model in verifying concurrent programs, tool support is mandatory. This section outlines exemplarily how this can be achieved by formalising the CKAs exhibited in Sect. 4 together with the model of Sect. 6 in an interactive theorem prover. Isabelle/HOL [21] is used as an example.

We have already built mathematical components for variants of Kleene algebras, regular algebras and relation algebras in Isabelle and integrated some of them into verification components for sequential programs [3,12,13], local reasoning with separation logic [9] and the rely-guarantee calculus [2]. In all of them, an abstract algebraic layer has been linked via formal soundness proofs with concrete computational models, e.g. for the program store. The use of algebra makes the resulting components small and allows us to carry out large parts of the development by automated theorem proving. Here we follow the same approach. The underlying Isabelle theories can be found online[1].

7.1   Formalising CKA

A first step towards a verification component based on the geometric model consists in formalising CKA as an axiomatic type class in Isabelle.

class $cka = kleene\text{-}algebra +$
  fixes $pcomp :: \, 'a \Rightarrow \, 'a \Rightarrow \, 'a$ (**infixl** $\parallel$ 70)
  assumes $pcomp\text{-}assoc$: $x \parallel (y \parallel z) = (x \parallel y) \parallel z$
  and $pcomp\text{-}comm$: $x \parallel y = y \parallel x$
  and $pcomp\text{-}oner$ $[simp]$: $x \parallel 1 = x$
  and $pcomp\text{-}annir$ $[simp]$: $x \parallel 0 = 0$
  and $pcomp\text{-}distribl$: $x \parallel (y + z) = x \parallel y + x \parallel z$
  and $interchange$: $(w \parallel x) \cdot (y \parallel z) \leq (w \cdot y) \parallel (x \cdot z)$

This class extends the operators and axioms of Kleene algebra by the concurrent composition operator and six further axioms. A concurrent iteration operator can be added along these lines. The extension brings all facts proved for Kleene algebras automatically into scope. It is easy, for instance, to derive the small interchange laws or the laws in Lemma 6.3 by automated theorem proving with Isabelle's Sledgehammer tool. Sledgehammer calls external automated theorem provers and SMT solvers and reconstructs their outputs by internally verified tools. This validates them relative to Isabelle's small trustworthy core.

7.2   Formalising Tracelets and Specifications

A second step is the formalisation of the tracelet model. We restrict our attention to the generic model from Sect. 6, which uses the dependency relation from Sect. 3. A refinement to models with several kinds of arrows is straightforward.

type-synonym $'a$ $graph = \, 'a$ rel

abbreviation $vertices$ $g \equiv Field$ g

definition $tracelets$ $g = Pow$ $(vertices$ $g)$

---

[1] http://staffwww.dcs.shef.ac.uk/people/G.Struth/isa/GCKA/GCKA.thy.

definition $str\ \tau\ g \equiv \tau \in tracelets\ g$

definition $A\ \tau\ g = (if\ str\ \tau\ g\ then\ \lceil \tau \rceil\ ;\ g \cup g\ ;\ \lceil \tau \rceil\ else\ undefined)$

A graph is formalised as a binary relation of type α, hence as the set of its arrows. Its set of points or vertices is thus the field of the relation; the union of its domain and range elements. Following Sect. 2, the set of tracelets of a graph is the power set of its vertex set. The subtracelet relation $str\ \tau\ g$ is defined next in the obvious way. It is generally used as a proviso on definitions and theorems (a tracelet type would have to depend on the graph). Finally, the set $A\ \tau\ g$ of arrows of τ in g consists of those arrows of g that have at least one point in τ, provided that τ is a subtracelet of g. It is undefined otherwise. In this definition, the function $\lceil \_ \rceil$ lifts the set V to the subidentity relation $\{(v,v)\ |\ v \in V\}$ to support relation-algebraic reasoning.

Additional notions such as input and output arrows or vertices of tracelets can now be defined as partial functions relative to an underlying graph as well.

definition $iA\ \tau\ g = (if\ str\ \tau\ g\ then\ \lceil -\tau \rceil\ ;\ A\ \tau\ g\ else\ undefined)$

definition $oA\ \tau\ g = (if\ str\ \tau\ g\ then\ A\ \tau\ g\ ;\ \lceil -\tau \rceil\ else\ undefined)$

definition $iV\ \tau\ g = (if\ str\ \tau\ g\ then\ Range\ (iA\ \tau\ g)\ else\ undefined)$

definition $oV\ \tau\ g = (if\ str\ \tau\ g\ then\ Domain\ (oA\ \tau\ g)\ else\ undefined)$

The function $-$ denotes set complementation. Various laws relating these vertices and arrows could then be derived easily be automated theorem proving. These enable automated proofs of some more intricate facts from Sect. 6. In addition, they allow us to define the perimeter, abbreviated as ioA, as $iA\ \tau\ g \cup oA\ \tau\ g$, and the associated specification *perspec*, for which we write S.

definition $S\ \tau\ g = (if\ str\ \tau\ g\ then\ iV\ \tau\ g \cup oV\ \tau\ g\ else\ undefined)$

By contrast to previous sections, $S\ \tau\ g$ is thus a set of vertices, and not a pair. In fact, the specifications from previous sections are neither subtraces of the underlying graph nor graphs themselves. This leads to complications in Isabelle's strongly typed setting. Instead, in the case of *perspec*, specifications are tracelets with respect to the perimeter of the underlying tracelet: $str\ (S\ \tau\ g)\ (ioA\ \tau\ g)$ holds whenever τ is a tracelet in g. Obviously, *connspec* of a tracelet has the same vertex set as *perspec*, but is a tracelet with respect to a different set of arrows. We therefore do not distinguish between the two in the above definition. Analogues of property (2) and idempotency of the specification function can be proved fully automatically for *perspec*, that is, $ioA\ (S\ \tau\ g)\ (ioA\ \tau\ g) = ioA\ \tau\ g$ and $S\ (S\ \tau\ g)\ (ioA\ \tau\ g) = S\ \tau\ g$, whenever τ is a subtracelet of g. For *connspec*, the arrow sets in formulas must be adapted. Additional facts can be found online.

Another essential ingredient of the graph model is the generic (de)composition operation from Sect. 6.2. We have formalised it as a partial function in Isabelle.

partial-function (*tailrec*) *tcomp* :: $'a\ set \Rightarrow\ 'a\ set \Rightarrow\ 'a\ graph \Rightarrow\ 'a\ set$ **where**
  tcomp σ τ g = (*if str* σ g $\wedge$ *str* τ g $\wedge$ $\sigma \cap \tau = \{\}$ *then* $\sigma \cup \tau$ *else undefined*)

The sequential and concurrent compositions from Sect. 3.1 can be defined likewise. It is easy to prove the commutative monoidal properties of composition, subject to definedness. A variant of Theorem 6.1 for *perspec* is more tedious.

lemma *pS-tcomp*:
  assumes *str* σ g and *str* τ g and $\sigma \cap \tau = \{\}$
  shows *pS* (*tcomp* (*pS* σ g) (*pS* τ g) g) (*ioA* σ g $\cup$ *ioA* τ g) = *pS* (*tcomp* σ τ g) g

7.3 Further Formalisation Steps

The following steps are needed for completing the verification component. They follow the design of our previous verification components [3, 13] closely.

Enriching the Model. Various kinds of edges, sequential and concurrent compositions, labels for programming concepts such as actions or transactions, and notions of memory location must be added to the extant tracelet model to obtain the full-fledged geometric model outlined in Sect. 2.

Tracelet and Powerset Algebra. The interchange laws for tracelets (Sect. 4) must be derived. The enriched tracelet model must be lifted to the powerset level and the CKA structure must be established at this level.

Formal Soundness Proof. An interpretation statement is needed to formalise soundness of the enriched tracelet model with respect to CKA within Isabelle's type class framework. All statements proved for CKA are then available within the model. This is important for verification condition generation with the Hoare logic outlined in Sect. 5.2 and for program refinement.

This completes the development of a verification component prototype based on the geometric tracelet model. Program verification is possible by using a shallow embedding of an appropriate programming syntax into the graph model. Alternatively, program syntax could be mapped into the model as usual.

One merit of the approach outlined is that the resulting verification component is correct by construction relative to Isabelle's small trustworthy core. Due to the link with CKA and the genericity of the tracelet formalisation used, the approach should also be robust to minor changes to the model, which has undergone a considerable evolution over time. Beyond a proof of concept and the formal verification of the results in this article, the component could therefore serve as a reference that can be refined and modified easily by other researchers. Because of its simplicity and declarative nature it may also be useful as a template for implementing practical verification tools.

Acknowledgements. We are grateful for valuable input from discussions with Jade Alglave, Peter OHearn, Peter Höfner, Matthew Parkinson, Stephan van Staden, Ian Wehrman, John Wickerson and Huibiao Zhu.

References

1. Alglave, J.: A formal hierarchy of weak memory models. Formal Methods Syst. Des. **41**(2), 178–210 (2012)
2. Armstrong, A., Gomes, V.B.F., Struth, G.: Algebraic principles for rely-guarantee style concurrency verification tools. In: Jones, C., Pihlajasaari, P., Sun, J. (eds.) FM 2014. LNCS, vol. 8442, pp. 78–93. Springer, Cham (2014)
3. Armstrong, A., Gomes, V.B.F., Struth, G.: Building program construction and verification tools from algebraic principles. Formal Aspects Comput. **28**(2), 265–293 (2016)
4. Brink, C.: Power structures. Algebra Univ. **30**(2), 177–216 (1993)
5. Brink, C., Rewitzky, I.: A Paradigm for Program Semantics: Power Structures and Duality. CSLI Publications, Stanford (2001)
6. Brookes, S.: A semantics for concurrent separation logic. Theoret. Comput. Sci. **375**, 227–270 (2007)
7. Conway, J.H.: Regular Algebra and Finite Machines. Chapman and Hall, London (1971)
8. Damm, W., Harel, D.: LSCs - breathing life into message sequence charts. Formal Methods Syst. Des. **19**(1), 45–80 (2001)
9. Dongol, B., Gomes, V.B.F., Struth, G.: A program construction and verification tool for separation logic. In: Hinze, R., Voigtländer, J. (eds.) MPC 2015. LNCS, vol. 9129, pp. 137–158. Springer, Cham (2015)
10. Gautam, N.: The validity of equations of complex algebras. Arch. Math. Logik Grundl. Mat. **443**, 117–124 (1957)
11. Goldblatt, R.: Varieties of complex algebras. Ann. Pure Appl. Logic **44**, 173–242 (1989)
12. Gomes, V.B.F., Struth, G.: Program construction and verification components based on Kleene algebra. Archive of Formal Proofs (2016)
13. Gomes, V.B.F., Struth, G.: Modal Kleene algebra applied to program correctness. In: Fitzgerald, J., Heitmeyer, C., Gnesi, S., Philippou, A. (eds.) FM 2016. LNCS, vol. 9995, pp. 310–325. Springer, Heidelberg (2016)
14. Hoare, C.A.R., He, J.: Unifying Theories of Programming. Prentice Hall, Upper Saddle River (1998)
15. Hoare, C.A.R., Hussain, A., Möller, B., O'Hearn, P.W., Petersen, R.L., Struth, G.: On locality and the exchange law for concurrent processes. In: Katoen, J.-P., König, B. (eds.) CONCUR 2011. LNCS, vol. 6901, pp. 250–264. Springer, Heidelberg (2011)
16. Hoare, T., Möller, B., Müller, M.: Tracelets and Specifications. Dept of Informatics, University of Augsburg (2016). No. 2017-01
17. Hoare, T., Möller, B., Struth, G., Wehrman, I.: Concurrent Kleene algebra and its foundations. J. Log. Algebr. Program. **80**(6), 266–296 (2011)
18. Hoare, T., van Staden, S., Möller, B., Struth, G., Zhu, H.: Developments in concurrent Kleene algebra. J. Log. Algebr. Meth. Program. **85**(4), 617–636 (2016)
19. Horn, A., Alglave, J.: Concurrent Kleene Algebra of partial strings. arXiv.org, July 2014

20. Main, M.: A powerdomain primer – a tutorial for the bulletin of the EATCS 33. Technical report CU-CS-375-87 (1987). Paper 360, Univ. Colorado at Boulder, Dept of Computer Science (1987). http://scholar.colorado.edu/csci_techreports/360
21. Nipkow, T., Wenzel, M., Paulson, L.C. (eds.): Isabelle/HOL – A Proof Assistant for Higher-Order Logic. LNCS, vol. 2283. Springer, Heidelberg (2002)
22. O'Hearn, P.W., Petersen, R.L., Villard, J., Hussain, A.: On the relation between concurrent separation logic and concurrent Kleene algebra. J. Log. Algebr. Meth. Program. 84(3), 285–302 (2015)
23. Petri, C.A.: Communication with automata. Technical report RADC TR 65-377, RADC, Research and Technology Division, New York (1966)
24. Winskel, G.: On power domains and modality. Theoret. Comput. Sci. 36, 127–137 (1985)

A New Roadmap for Linking Theories of Programming

He Jifeng[(⊠)]

Shanghai Key Laboratory of Trustworthy Computing,
International Research Center of Trustworthy Software,
East China Normal University, Shanghai, China
jifeng@sei.ecnu.edu.cn

Abstract. Formal methods advocate the crucial role played by the algebraic approach in specification and implementation of programs. Traditionally, a top-down approach (with denotational model as its origin) links the algebra of programs with the denotational representation by establishment of the *soundness* and *completeness* of the algebra against the given model, while a bottom-up approach (a journey started from operational model) introduces a variety of bisimulations to establish the equivalence relation among programs, and then presents a set of algebraic laws in support of program analysis and verification. This paper proposes a new roadmap for linking theories of programming. Our approach takes an algebra of programs as its foundation, and generates both denotational and operational representations from the algebraic refinement relation.

1 Introduction

Formal methods advocate the crucial role played by the algebra of programs in specification and implementation of programs. Study leads to the conclusion that both the top-down approach (with denotational model as its origin) and the bottom-up approach (a journey started from operational model) can meet in the middle:

- Top-down approach usually begins with construction of a specification-oriented model [1,2,4,10,15], then links the algebra of programs with the denotational framework by establishment of the *soundness* and *completeness* of the algebra [8,13] against the given model.
- Bottom-up approach starts with an operational semantics [12] and introduces a rich variety of bisimulations [5,11] to identify the equivalence relation among programs, and then presents a set of algebraic laws in support of program analysis and verification.

This paper proposes a new roadmap for linking theories of programming. Our framework takes an algebra of programs as its basis, and generates both denotational and operational representations from the algebraic refinement relation. This new strategy consists of the following steps:

© Springer International Publishing AG 2017
J.P. Bowen and H. Zhu (Eds.): UTP 2016, LNCS 10134, pp. 26–43, 2017.
DOI: 10.1007/978-3-319-52228-9_2

Step 1: Within a given program algebra $(\mathcal{P}, \sqsubseteq_A)$, investigate the algebraic properties of the test operator $\mathcal{T}$ which has test case tc and testing program P as its arguments

$$\mathcal{T}(tc, P)$$

In case of the Guarded Command Language [3], tc is represented by a total constant assignment $x, y, .., z := a, b, .., c$ and the test operator $\mathcal{T}$ composes tc and P in sequence:

$$\mathcal{T}(tc, P) =_{df} (tc; P)$$

For CSP [7,14], a test case has the same alphabet as the testing process, and takes the form of a generalised prefix process $s \to \Phi$ where s is a sequence of events in the alphabet of the process P, and Φ a choice construct $x : X \to Stop$ which is added to test the status of P after its engagement in the events of sequence s. The test $\mathcal{T}(tc, P)$ behaves like the system composed of processes tc and P interacting in lock-step synchronisation

$$\mathcal{T}(tc, P) =_{df} (tc \parallel P)$$

Step 2: Explore the dependency between the test outcome with the test case in the following form

$$\mathcal{T}(tc, P) =_A \sqcap Obs$$

where Obs denotes the set of visible observations one can record during the execution of the test and $\sqcap$ means the non-deterministic choices.

For the Guarded Command Language, an observation can be either a total constant assignment or the chaotic program $\perp$ which represents the worst outcome. In case of CSP an observation has a very similar form as test case.

Step 3: Based on the algebra of test, identify a program P as a binary relation $[P]$ which relates the test case with the final observation

$$[P] =_{df} \{(tc, obs) \mid \mathcal{T}(tc, P) \sqsubseteq_A obs\}$$

and select the set inclusion as the refinement relation $\sqsubseteq_{rel}$

$$P \sqsubseteq_{rel} Q =_{df} ([P] \supseteq [Q])$$

Based on the algebra of programs, we can prove

$$\sqsubseteq_{rel} = \sqsubseteq_A$$

Step 4: Propose an algebraic definition of the *consistency* of step relation of the transition system of programs such that any consistent transition system $(O, \sqsubseteq_O)$ satisfies

$$\sqsubseteq_O = \sqsubseteq_A$$

Furthermore, our approach shows how to *generates* the transition rules for CSP combinators directly from the closure properties of the *canonical processes* presented in the consistent criterion of the step relation.

The paper is organised in the following way:
Section 2 adopts this new roadmap to re-establish the semantical models of the Guarded Command Language, where

- Section 2.1 provides an algebraic representation of *machine state* and exmaines its properties.
- Section 2.2 introduces the notion of test cases.
- Section 2.3 presents a test-based model, where each program is identified as a binary relation between test case and visible observation recorded during the execution of the test. It is shown that the refinement relation $\sqsubseteq_{rel}$ in the test model is equivalent to the algebraic refinement $\sqsubseteq_A$.
- Section 2.4 reconstructs the double predicate model with a simplified version of the refinement relation $\sqsubseteq_{dp}$ satisfying $\sqsubseteq_{dp} = \sqsubseteq_A$.
- Section 2.5 revisits the predicate transformer model with the refinement relation $\sqsubseteq_{wp}$, and presents its link with the algebra of programs by showing $\sqsubseteq_{wp} = \sqsubseteq_A$.
- Section 2.6 links Hoare triple proof system with the test-based model of Sect. 2.3.

Section 3 proposes a formal definition for the consistency of step relation of transition system against the algebra of programs. Moreover, it provides a transition system for the Guarded Command Language, and establishes its correctness.

The paper ends with a short summary in Sect. 4. We leave the proof of some theorems in the appendix. We will extends the paper by adopting this new approach on CSP and probabilistic programming languages in the near future.

2   Guarded Command Language

This section investigates how to rediscover a variety of well-established semantical models from the program algebra presented in [9] for the Guarded Command Language:

$$P ::= \bot$$
$$| \ var := exp$$
$$| \ P \lhd bexp \rhd P$$
$$| \ P; P$$
$$| \ P \sqcap P$$
$$| \ \mu X \bullet P(X)$$

where the notation *bexp* stands for a Boolean expression.

Rather than following up an inductive approach to assign meaning to programs, this section develops a new mathematical framework where the behaviours of a program are described by those observations one can make during the testing of a program. To achieve this goal, we first introduce an algebra of tests and then deduce a simplified version of refinement relation in this algebra. Later we are going to derive a family of well-known denotational models [3,4,6,9,10] from the algebra of tests, and revalidate those familiar properties of programming operators.

2.1   Machine State

An operational approach usually defines the relationship between a program and its possible execution by machine. In an abstract way, a computation consists of a sequence of individual steps with the following features

- each step takes the machine from one state to a closely similar state
- each step is drawn from a very limited repertoire.

In a stored program computer, the machine states are represented as pairs

$$(s,\ P)$$

where

(1) s is a text, defining the *data state* as an assignment of constants to all variables of the alphabet

$$x,\ y,\ ...,\ z := a,\ b,\ ...,\ c$$

(2) P is a program text, representing the rest of the program that remains to be executed. When P becomes the empty text ϵ, there is no more program to be executed. The machine state $(t,\ \epsilon)$ is the last state of any execution sequence that contains it, and t presents the final value of the variables in the end of execution.

The following lemma indicates that data states are the best programs.

Lemma 2.1

$$(s \sqsubseteq_A P) \text{ implies } (s =_A P).$$

Algebraic refinement relation on data state sets is the same as set inclusion.

Lemma 2.2

$$\sqcap \{s_i \mid 1 \le i \le n\} \sqsubseteq_A t \text{ iff } t \in \{s_i \mid 1 \le i \le n\}$$

Corollary

$$\sqcap \{s_i \mid 1 \le i \le m\} \sqsubseteq_A \sqcap \{t_j \mid 1 \le j \le n\} \text{ iff } \{s_i \mid 1 \le i \le m\} \supseteq \{t_j \mid 1 \le j \le n\}$$

2.2   Test

The execution of program $(s; P)$ can be seen as a *test* on P with the test case s. The result of such a testing gives rise to a set of possible outcomes *obs*. We are then able to compare the behaviours of two programs based on testing.

Formally, the test operator for the Guarded Command Language is defined by

$$\mathcal{T}(s,\ P) =_{df} (s; P)$$

When $\bot$ is taken as the test case, we obtain

$$\mathcal{T}(\bot,\ P) =_A \bot$$

A test may end with delivery of a set of data states, or fail to produce any meaningful result.

Theorem 2.1

For any test $T(s, P)$, either there exists a finite nonempty set $\{t_i \mid 1 \leq i \leq n\}$ of total constant assignments such that

$$T(s, P) =_A \sqcap \{t_i \mid 1 \leq i \leq n\}$$

or $T(s, P) =_A \bot$

Proof. Any finite program P can be converted into the finite normal form [9]

$$\bot \lhd b \rhd Q$$

where Q is a nondeterministic choice on a finite nonempty set of total assignments

$$Q = \sqcap \{(v := e_i) \mid 1 \leq i \leq m\}$$

In this case, we conclude that

$$(v := c); P =_A \begin{cases} \bot & \text{if } b[c/v] = true \\ \sqcap \{v := e_i[c/v] \mid 1 \leq i \leq m\} & \text{if } b[c/v] = false \end{cases}$$

where $b[c/v]$ stands for result of substituting all free occurrences of variables v in the Boolean expression b by constants c.

The behaviour of an infinite program can be represented as an infinite sequence of expressions [9]

$$S = \{S_n \mid n \in Nat\}$$

where each S_n is a finite normal form, and each S_{n+1} is stronger than its predecessor S_n:

$$(S_{n+1} \sqsupseteq_A S_n) \quad \text{for all } n \in Nat$$

This is called the *descending chain condition*. It allows the later members of the sequence to exclude more and more of impossible behaviours. The exact behaviour of the program is captured by the *least upper bound* of the whole sequence, written

$$\sqcup \{S_n \mid n \in Nat\}$$

In fact, the desending chain $\{(\bot \lhd b_n \rhd Q_n) \mid n \in Nat\}$ satisfies the following stronger order

$$(\bot \lhd b_n \rhd Q_n) =_A (\bot \lhd b_n \rhd Q_{n+k})$$

for all n, k. That is once n is high enough for b_n to be false, all assignments Q_m remain the same as Q_n for all m greater than n. The conclusion of the theorem follows from the continuity of sequential composition:

$$((v := c); \sqcup \{S_n \mid n \in Nat\} =_A \begin{cases} \bot & \text{if } \forall n \in Nat \bullet (b_n[c/v] = true) \\ (v := c); Q_m & \text{if } b_m[c/v] = false \end{cases}$$

The following theorem reveals the compositionality of the testing process by demonstrating how to derive the test outcome of a composite program from those of its components.

Theorem 2.2

(1) $\mathcal{T}(s, (P \sqcap Q)) = \mathcal{T}(s, P) \sqcap \mathcal{T}(s, Q)$
(2) $\mathcal{T}(s, (P \lhd b \rhd Q)) = \mathcal{T}(s, P) \lhd (s; b) \rhd \mathcal{T}(s, Q)$ where $(v := c); b =_{df} b[c/v]$
(3) $\mathcal{T}(s, (P; Q)) =_A \sqcap \{\mathcal{T}(t, Q) \mid \mathcal{T}(s, P) \sqsubseteq_A t\}$
(4) $\mathcal{T}(s, \mu X \bullet P(X)) =_A \sqcup \{\mathcal{T}(s, P^n(\bot)) \mid n \in Nat\}$ where

$$P^0(\bot) =_{df} \bot \quad \text{and} \quad P^{n+1}(\bot) =_{df} P(P^n(\bot))$$

Proof of (3). From Theorem 2.1 we only need to consider two cases:
Case 1: $\mathcal{T}(s, P) =_A \sqcap \{t_i \mid 1 \le i \le n\}$.

$\mathcal{T}(s, (P; Q))$	{assumption}
$=_A \sqcap \{t_i \mid 1 \le i \le n\}; Q$	$\{(U \sqcap V); W =_A (U; W) \sqcap (V; W)\}$
$=_A \sqcap \{\mathcal{T}(t_i, Q) \mid 1 \le i \le n\}$	{Lemma 2.2}
$=_A \sqcap \{\mathcal{T}(t, Q) \mid \mathcal{T}(s, P) \sqsubseteq_A t\}$	

Case 2: $\mathcal{T}(s, P) =_A \bot$. The conclusion follows from the fact

$$\mathcal{T}(\bot, Q) =_A \bot$$

Theorem 2.3. $P =_A Q$ iff for every data state s, $\mathcal{T}(s, P) =_A \mathcal{T}(s, Q)$

2.3   A Test-Based Model

As described in the previous section, the execution of test $\mathcal{T}(s, P)$ may yield a finite nonempty set of outcomes. In the worst case, it may end with a chaotic state. In this sense, each testing program P can be treated as a binary relation on test cases and final observations. This section is going to construct a relation model from the test algebra.

Definition 2.1
A program P can be identified as a binary relation $[P]$ between test case s with the final data state t it may enter in the end of testing.

$$[P] =_{df} \{(s, t) \mid \mathcal{T}(s, P) \sqsubseteq_A t\}$$

As usual we define the refinement relation $\sqsubseteq_{rel}$ on the relational model by the set inclusion

$$P \sqsubseteq_{rel} Q =_{df} ([P] \supseteq [Q])$$

Theorem 2.4

$$\sqsubseteq_{rel} = \sqsubseteq_A$$

Proof. Assume that $P \sqsubseteq_{rel} Q$.
Case 1: $\mathcal{T}(s, Q) =_A \bot$

$\mathcal{T}(s, Q) \sqsubseteq_A \bot$	{Definition 2.1}
$\Rightarrow \ \mathcal{T}(s, P) \sqsubseteq_A \bot$	{assumption}
$\Rightarrow \ \mathcal{T}(s, P) \sqsubseteq_A \mathcal{T}(s, Q)$	

Case 2: $\mathcal{T}(s, Q) =_A \sqcap\{t_i \mid 1 \leq i \leq n\}$.

$$\mathcal{T}(s, Q) =_A \sqcap\{t_i \mid 1 \leq i \leq n\} \qquad \{\text{Lemma 2.2}\}$$

$$\Rightarrow \quad \forall i \in \{1, .., n\} \bullet (\mathcal{T}(s, Q) \sqsubseteq_A t_i) \qquad \{\text{Definition 2.1}\}$$

$$\Rightarrow \quad \forall i \in \{1, .., n\} \bullet (\mathcal{T}(s, P) \sqsubseteq_A t_i) \qquad \{\text{monotonicity of } \sqcap\}$$

$$\Rightarrow \quad \mathcal{T}(s, P) \sqsubseteq_A \sqcap\{t_i \mid 1 \leq i \leq n\} \qquad \{\text{assumption}\}$$

$$\Rightarrow \quad \mathcal{T}(s, P) \sqsubseteq_A \mathcal{T}(s, Q)$$

The conclusion $P \sqsubseteq_A Q$ follows from Theorem 2.3.

The opposite inequation ($\sqsubseteq_A \subseteq \sqsubseteq_{rel}$) follows from Theorem 2.2(1) and the definition of $\sqsubseteq_{rel}$.

Moreover, the mapping $[\,]$ is a homomorphism.

Theorem 2.5

(1) $[P \sqcap Q] = [P] \cup [Q]$
(2) $[P \lhd b \rhd Q] = [P] \lhd (s; b) \rhd [Q]$
(3) $[P; Q] = [P] \circ [Q]$
(4) $[\mu X \bullet P(X)] = \bigcap_n [P^n(\bot)]$

Proof of (3)

$$(s, t) \in [P; Q] \qquad \{\text{Definition 2.1}\}$$

$$\equiv \quad \mathcal{T}(s, (P; Q)) \sqsubseteq_A t \qquad \{\text{Theorem 2.2(3)}\}$$

$$\equiv \quad \sqcap\{\mathcal{T}(u, Q) \mid \mathcal{T}(s, P) \sqsubseteq_A u\} \sqsubseteq_A t \qquad \{\text{Lemma 2.2}\}$$

$$\equiv \quad \exists u \bullet (\mathcal{T}(s, P) \sqsubseteq_A u) \wedge (\mathcal{T}(u, Q) \sqsubseteq_A t) \qquad \{\text{Definition 2.1}\}$$

$$\equiv \quad \exists u \bullet ((s, u) \in [P]) \wedge ((u, t) \in [Q]) \qquad \{\text{Definition of } \circ\}$$

$$\equiv \quad (s, t) \in ([P] \circ [Q])$$

2.4   Double Predicates Model

In [6], a precondition is defined as a predicate describing the initial values of program variables of a program before it is activated, whereas a postcondition is a predicate only mention of the final values of program variables after the execution of a program terminates. Following the VDM approach [10] we permit a postcondition to refer to both initial and final values of program variables in the following discussion.

Definition 2.2 (Double predicates)

$$\mathbf{pre}(P)(v_0) =_{df} \neg(\mathcal{T}(v := v_0, P) \sqsubseteq_A \bot)$$
$$\mathbf{post}(P)(v_0, v') =_{df} \mathcal{T}(v := v_0, P) \sqsubseteq_A (v := v')$$

where v_0 and v' stand for the initial and final values of the program variables v.

In the above definition, the postcondition meets the following constraint, which enables us to simplify the definition of refinement in the double predicate model later.

Theorem 2.6. $\mathbf{post}(P) \equiv (\mathbf{pre}(P) \Rightarrow \mathbf{post}(P))$
The refinement order $\sqsubseteq_{dp}$ on the double predicate model is defined by

$$P \sqsubseteq_{dp} Q =_{df} \forall v_0 \bullet (\mathbf{pre}(P) \Rightarrow \mathbf{pre}(Q)) \wedge \forall v_0, v' \bullet (\mathbf{post}(Q) \Rightarrow \mathbf{post}(P))$$

Theorem 2.7

$$\sqsubseteq_A = \sqsubseteq_{dp}$$

$$
\begin{aligned}
& P \sqsubseteq_A Q && \{\text{Theorem 2.3}\} \\
\equiv\ & \forall v_0 \bullet \mathcal{T}(v := v_0, P) \sqsubseteq_A \mathcal{T}(v := v_0, Q) && \{\text{Theorem 2.1}\} \\
\equiv\ & \forall v_0 \bullet \left(\begin{array}{l} \left(\begin{array}{l} \mathcal{T}(v := v_0, Q) \sqsubseteq_A \perp) \Rightarrow \\ (\mathcal{T}(v := v_0, P) \sqsubseteq_A \perp \end{array} \right) \wedge \\ \forall v' \bullet \left(\begin{array}{l} (\mathcal{T}(v := v_0, Q) \sqsubseteq_A (v := v')) \Rightarrow \\ (\mathcal{T}(v := v_0, P) \sqsubseteq_A (v := v')) \end{array} \right) \end{array} \right) && \{\text{Definition 2.2}\} \\
\equiv\ & \left(\begin{array}{l} \forall v_0 \bullet (\mathbf{pre}(P) \Rightarrow \mathbf{pre}(Q)) \wedge \\ \forall v_0, v' \bullet (\mathbf{post}(Q) \Rightarrow \mathbf{post}(P)) \end{array} \right) && \{\text{Def of } \sqsubseteq_{dp}\} \\
\equiv\ & P \sqsubseteq_{dp} Q
\end{aligned}
$$

Definition 2.2 enables us to transform the original definition of the programming combinators in the double predicates model [9,10] into a set of the compositional laws in our test-generated model:

Theorem 2.8

(1) $\mathbf{pre}(\perp) \equiv \mathbf{false}$

(2) $\mathbf{pre}(P \sqcap Q) \equiv \mathbf{pre}(P) \wedge \mathbf{pre}(Q)$

(3) $\mathbf{pre}(P \lhd b(v) \rhd Q) \equiv \mathbf{pre}(P) \lhd b(v_0) \rhd \mathbf{pre}(Q)$

(4) $\mathbf{pre}(P; Q) \equiv \mathbf{pre}(P) \wedge \neg\exists c \bullet (\mathbf{post}(P)[c/v'] \wedge \neg\mathbf{pre}(Q)[c/v_0])$

(5) $\mathbf{pre}(\mu X \bullet P(X)) = \bigvee_n \mathbf{pre}(P^n(\perp))$

Proof of (4)

$$
\begin{aligned}
& \neg\mathbf{pre}(P; Q)(v_0) && \{\text{Defintion 2.2}\} \\
\equiv\ & \mathcal{T}(v := v_0, (P; Q)) =_A \perp && \{\text{Theorem 2.2(3)}\} \\
\equiv\ & \mathcal{T}(v := v_0, P) =_A \perp \vee \\
& \exists t \bullet \mathcal{T}(v := v_0, P) \sqsubseteq_A t \wedge \mathcal{T}(t, Q) =_A \perp && \{\text{Definition 2.2}\} \\
\equiv\ & \neg\mathbf{pre}(P)(v_0) \vee \exists c \bullet \mathbf{post}(P)(v_0, c) \wedge \neg\mathbf{pre}(Q)(c)
\end{aligned}
$$

Theorem 2.9

(1) $\mathbf{post}(\bot) \equiv \mathbf{true}$

(2) $\mathbf{post}(P \sqcap Q) \equiv \mathbf{post}(P) \vee \mathbf{post}(Q)$

(3) $\mathbf{post}(P \lhd b(v) \rhd Q) \equiv \mathbf{post}(P) \lhd b(v_0) \rhd \mathbf{post}(Q)$

(4) $\mathbf{post}(P; Q) \equiv \exists c \bullet (\mathbf{post}(P)[c/v'] \wedge \mathbf{post}(Q)[c/v_0])$

(5) $\mathbf{post}(\mu X \bullet P(X)) \equiv \bigwedge_n \mathbf{post}(P^n(\bot))$

Proof From Theorem 2.2.

2.5 Predicate Transformer

Given a postcondition r and a proposed design of a final program segment Q, it is possible to deduce the *weakest* precondition under which the execution of Q will end with the states that satisfy the postcondition r. This precondition can often be strengthening, and then taken as the postcondition in the design of the next preceding segment of the program. In this method, a program is identified as a predicate transformer mapping the given postcondition to the corresponding weakest precondition [3]. Based on the algebra of tests, this section redefines the predicate transformer as follows:

Definition 2.3 (Weakest precondition)
Define
$$\mathbf{wp}(Q, r)(v_0) =_{df} \mathcal{T}(v := v_0, Q) \sqsupseteq_A \sqcap\{v := c \mid r(c)\}$$

In our method, the refinement relation $\sqsubseteq_{wp}$ is defined by

$$P \sqsubseteq_{wp} Q =_{df} \forall r, \forall v_0 \bullet (\mathbf{wp}(P, r)(v_0) \Rightarrow \mathbf{wp}(Q, r)(v_0))$$

Theorem 2.10

$$\sqsubseteq_{wp} = \sqsubseteq_A$$

Proof

$$
\begin{array}{lll}
& P \sqsubseteq_A Q & \{\text{Theorem 2.3}\} \\
\equiv & \forall v_0 \bullet (\mathcal{T}(v := v_0, P) \sqsubseteq_A \mathcal{T}(v := v_0, Q)) & \{\text{Transitivity of } \sqsubseteq_A\} \\
\equiv & \forall r, \forall v_0 \bullet & \\
& \left(\begin{array}{l} \mathcal{T}(v := v_0, P) \sqsubseteq_A \sqcap\{v := c \mid r(c)\} \Rightarrow \\ \mathcal{T}(v := v_0, Q) \sqsubseteq_A \sqcap\{v := c \mid r(c)\} \end{array} \right) & \{\text{Definition 2.3}\} \\
\equiv & \forall r, \forall v_0 \bullet (\mathbf{wp}(P, r)(v_0) \Rightarrow \mathbf{wp}(Q, r)(v_0)) & \{\text{Definition of } \sqsubseteq_{wp}\} \\
\equiv & P \sqsubseteq_{wp} Q &
\end{array}
$$

Like in Sects. 2.3 and 2.4, the new definition of the predicate transformer enables us to verify the following family of so called *healthiness* conditions presented in [3].

Theorem 2.11

(1) $\mathbf{wp}(Q, \mathit{false}) = \mathit{false}$

(2) $\mathbf{wp}(Q, r_1 \wedge r_2) = \mathbf{wp}(Q, r_1) \wedge \mathbf{wp}(Q, r_2)$

Proof of (2)

$$
\begin{array}{lll}
& \mathbf{wp}(Q, r_1) \wedge \mathbf{wp}(Q, r_2) & \{\text{Definition 2.3}\} \\
\equiv & \left(\begin{array}{l} T(v := v_0, Q) \sqsupseteq_A \sqcap\{v := c \mid r_1(c)\} \wedge \\ T(v := v_0, Q) \sqsupseteq_A \sqcap\{v := c \mid r_2(c)\} \end{array} \right) & \{\text{Corollary of Lemma 2.2}\} \\
\equiv & T(v := v_0, Q) \sqsupseteq_A \sqcap\{v := c \mid (r_1 \wedge r_2)(c)\} & \{\text{Definition 2.3}\} \\
\equiv & \mathbf{wp}(Q, r_1 \wedge r_2) &
\end{array}
$$

The next theorem links the double predicates model with the predicate transformer model.

Theorem 2.12
$$\mathbf{wp}(Q, r(v)) \equiv \mathbf{pre}(Q) \wedge \neg \exists c \bullet (\mathbf{post}(Q)[c/v'] \wedge \neg r(c))$$

$$
\begin{array}{lll}
& \mathbf{wp}(Q, r(v)) & \{\text{Definition 2.3}\} \\
\equiv & T(v := v_0, Q) \sqsupseteq_A \sqcap\{v := c \mid r(c)\} & \{\text{Theorem 2.1}\} \\
\textbf{Proof} \quad \equiv & \left(\begin{array}{l} (T(v := v_0, Q) \neq_A \bot) \wedge \\ \forall t \bullet (T(v := v_0, Q) \sqsubseteq_A t) \Rightarrow (t \in \{v := c \mid r(c)\}) \end{array} \right) & \{\text{Definition 2.2}\} \\
\equiv & \mathbf{pre}(Q) \wedge \forall c \bullet (\mathbf{post}(Q)[c/v'] \Rightarrow r(c)) & \{\text{calculation}\} \\
\equiv & \mathbf{pre}(Q) \wedge \neg \exists c \bullet (\mathbf{post}(Q)[c/v'] \wedge \neg r(c)) &
\end{array}
$$

Corollary

(1) $\mathbf{pre}(P) \equiv \mathbf{wp}(P, \mathbf{true})$

(2) $\mathbf{post}(P) \equiv \neg\mathbf{wp}(P, v \neq v')$

The following theorem validates the original definition of the predicate transformer given in [3].

Theorem 2.13

(1) $\mathbf{wp}(\bot, r) \equiv \mathbf{false}$
(2) $\mathbf{wp}(P \sqcap Q, r) \equiv \mathbf{wp}(P, r) \wedge \mathbf{wp}(Q, r)$
(3) $\mathbf{wp}(P \lhd b(v) \rhd Q, r) \equiv \mathbf{wp}(P, r) \lhd b(v_0) \rhd \mathbf{wp}(Q, r)$
(4) $\mathbf{wp}(P; Q, r) \equiv \mathbf{wp}(P, \mathbf{wp}(Q, r)))$
(5) $\mathbf{wp}(\mu X \bullet P(X)) \equiv \bigvee_n \mathbf{wp}(P^n(\bot), r)$

Proof of (4)

$$\mathbf{wp}(P, \mathbf{wp}(Q, r)) \qquad\qquad \text{\{Theorem 2.12\}}$$

$$\equiv \quad \mathbf{pre}(P) \wedge \neg\exists c \bullet \begin{pmatrix} \mathbf{post}(P)[c/v'] \wedge \\ \neg\mathbf{wp}(Q, r)[c/v_0] \end{pmatrix} \qquad\qquad \text{\{Theorem 2.12\}}$$

$$\equiv \quad \begin{pmatrix} \mathbf{pre}(P) \wedge \\ \neg\exists c \bullet \left(\begin{pmatrix} \mathbf{post}(P)[c/v'] \wedge \\ \begin{pmatrix} \neg\mathbf{pre}(Q)[c/v_0] \vee \\ \exists d \bullet \begin{pmatrix} \mathbf{post}(Q)[c, d/v_0, v'] \wedge \\ \neg r(d) \end{pmatrix} \end{pmatrix} \end{pmatrix} \right) \end{pmatrix} \qquad \text{\{calculation\}}$$

$$\equiv \quad \begin{pmatrix} \mathbf{pre}(P) \ \wedge \neg\exists c \bullet \begin{pmatrix} \mathbf{post}(P) \wedge \\ \neg\mathbf{pre}(Q)[c/v_0] \end{pmatrix} \ \wedge \\ \neg\exists d \bullet \begin{pmatrix} \exists c \bullet \begin{pmatrix} \mathbf{post}(P)[c/v_0] \wedge \\ \mathbf{post}(Q)[c, d/v_0, v'] \end{pmatrix} \ \wedge \\ \neg r(d) \end{pmatrix} \end{pmatrix} \qquad \text{\{Theorem 2.8 and 2.9\}}$$

$$\equiv \quad \mathbf{pre}(P; Q) \wedge \neg\exists d \bullet (\mathbf{post}(P; Q)[d/v'] \wedge \neg r(d)) \qquad \text{\{Theorem 2.12\}}$$

$$\equiv \quad \mathbf{wp}(P; Q, r)$$

2.6   Hoare Triple

In [6], the correctness of a program was interpreted as the triple

$$precondition \ \{program\} \ postcondition$$

known as a Hoare triple, where the postcondition only refers to the final values of program variables.

Definition 2.4 (Hoare triple)
Define

$$p\{Q\}r \ =_{df} \ \forall v_0 \bullet (p(v_0) \Rightarrow (\mathcal{T}(v := v_0, Q) \sqsupseteq_A \sqcap\{v := c \mid r(c)\}$$

Theorem 2.14

$$p\{Q\}r \ \equiv \ \forall v_0 \bullet (p(v_0) \Rightarrow \mathbf{wp}(Q, r(v)))$$

Proof. From Definitions 2.3 and 2.4.

Based on the new definition of Hoare triple we are able to reestablish the soundness of Hoare logic used for verification of programs.

Theorem 2.15 (Hoare triple proof rules)

(1) If $p\{Q\}r_1$ and $p\{Q\}r_2$ then $p\{Q\}(r_1 \wedge r_2)$
(2) If $p\{Q\}r$ and $q\{Q\}r$ then $(p \vee q)\{Q\}r$
(3) If $p\{Q\}r$ then $p\{Q\}(q \vee r)$
(4) $r(e)\{v := e\}r(v)$
(5) If $(p \wedge b)\{Q_1\}r$ and $(p \wedge \neg b)\{Q_2\}r$ then $p\{Q_1 \lhd b \rhd Q_2\}r$
(6) If $p\{Q_1\}q$ and $q\{Q_2\}r$ then $p\{Q_1; Q_2\}r$

(7) If $p\{Q_1\}r$ and $p\{Q_2\}r$ then $p\{Q_1 \sqcap Q_2\}r$
(8) $false\{Q\}r$

Proof of (6)

$$
\begin{array}{lll}
 & p\{Q_1; Q_2\}r & \{\text{Theorem 2.14}\} \\
\equiv & \forall v_0 \bullet (p(v_0) \Rightarrow \mathbf{wp}(Q_1; Q_2, r)) & \{\text{Theorem 2.13(4)}\} \\
\equiv & \forall v_0 \bullet (p(v_0) \Rightarrow \mathbf{wp}(Q_1, \mathbf{wp}(Q_2, r))) & \{\text{Theorem 2.11(2) and } q\{Q_2\}r\} \\
\Leftarrow & \forall v_0 \bullet (p(v_0) \Rightarrow \mathbf{wp}(Q_1, q)) & \{p\{Q_1\}q\} \\
\equiv & true &
\end{array}
$$

3 Operational Approach

Let $\rightarrow$ be a step relation on machine states. Its *reflexive transitive closure* is defined by

$$\rightarrow^* \ =_{df} \ \nu X \bullet (id \vee (\rightarrow; X))$$

where $\nu X.G(X)$ stands for the *greatest fixed point* of function G.
We define the concept of *divergence*, being a machine state that can lead to an infinite execution

$$(s, P) \uparrow \ =_{df} \ \forall n, \exists t, Q \bullet ((s, P) \rightarrow^n (t, Q))$$

where $\rightarrow^1 =_{df} \rightarrow$
and $\rightarrow^{n+1} =_{df} (\rightarrow^1; \rightarrow^n)$

Definition 3.1
A step relation is *consistent* with the algebraic semantics if for any machine state (s, P)

(1) $\mathcal{T}(s, P) =_A \ \sqcap \{\mathcal{T}(t, Q) \mid (s, P) \rightarrow (t, Q)\}$, and
(2) $(s, P) \uparrow$ implies $\mathcal{T}(s, P) =_A \perp$

In the following discussion we will extend the definition of the test operator to cope with the empty program text

$$\mathcal{T}(s, \epsilon) =_{df} s$$

Theorem 3.1
If $\rightarrow$ is consistent then

$$\mathcal{T}(s, P) =_A \ \perp \lhd (s, P) \uparrow \rhd \sqcap \{t \mid (s, P) \rightarrow^* (t, \epsilon)\}$$

Proof. First we show that $\mathcal{T}(s, P) =_A \perp \ \Rightarrow \ (s, P) \uparrow$
From Theorem 2.2 and the condition (1) of Definition 3.1 it follows that there exists machine state (t, Q) such that

$$(s, P) \rightarrow (t, Q) \quad \text{and} \quad \mathcal{T}(t, Q) =_A \perp$$

With induction we conclude that for all $n \geq 0$ there exists a machine state (t_n, Q_n) satisfying

$$\mathcal{T}(t_n, Q_n) =_A \perp \text{ and } (s, P) \to^n (t_n, Q_n)$$

which leads to the conclusion $(s, P) \uparrow$

If (s, P) is not divergent, then from the condition (1) of Definition 3.1 we can show by induction

$$\mathcal{T}(s, P) =_A \sqcap \{t \mid (s, P) \to^* (t, \epsilon)\}$$

Definition 3.1 explores the following correspondence between the step relation of the operational semantics with the refinement relation of algebraic semantics

(1) Whenever a machine state (s, P) is divergent, then the execution of test $\mathcal{T}(s, P)$ will end with a chaotic state.

(2) If (s, P) is not divergent, then the final states that it can reach via step transitions are exactly those delivered by the execution of the test $\mathcal{T}(s, P)$.

Definition 3.2 (Operational Refinement)
Let $\to$ be a consistent step relation. Define

$$P \sqsubseteq_O Q =_{df} \left(\begin{array}{l} \forall s \bullet ((s, Q) \uparrow \Rightarrow (s, P) \uparrow) \wedge \\[2ex] \forall t \bullet ((s, Q) \to^* (t, \epsilon)) \Rightarrow \left(\begin{array}{l} (s, P) \uparrow \vee \\ ((s, P) \to^* (t, \epsilon)) \end{array} \right) \end{array} \right)$$

Theorem 3.2

$$\sqsubseteq_O = \sqsubseteq_A$$

Proof

$$\begin{array}{ll} P \sqsubseteq_A Q & \{\text{Theorem 2.3}\} \\[1ex] \equiv \forall s \bullet (\mathcal{T}(s, P) \sqsubseteq_A \mathcal{T}(s, Q)) & \{\text{Theorem 2.1}\} \\[1ex] \equiv \forall s \bullet \left(\begin{array}{l} (\mathcal{T}(s, Q) =_A \perp) \Rightarrow (\mathcal{T}(s, P) =_A \perp) \\ \wedge \\ \forall t \bullet (\mathcal{T}(s, Q) \sqsubseteq_A t) \Rightarrow (\mathcal{T}(s, P) \sqsubseteq_A t) \end{array} \right) & \{\text{Lemma 2.2 and Theorem 3.1}\} \\[3ex] \equiv \forall s \bullet \left(\begin{array}{l} ((s, Q) \uparrow \Rightarrow (s, P) \uparrow) \wedge \\ \forall t \bullet ((s, Q) \to^* (t, \epsilon)) \Rightarrow \\ \left(\begin{array}{l} (s; P) \uparrow \vee \\ ((s, P) \to^* (t, \epsilon)) \end{array} \right) \end{array} \right) & \{\text{Definition 3.2}\} \\[3ex] \equiv P \sqsubseteq_O Q \end{array}$$

If (s, P) is not divergent, then from the condition (1) of Definition 3.1 we can show by induction

$$\mathcal{T}(s, P) =_A \sqcap \{t \mid (s, P) \to^* (t, \epsilon)\}$$

Definition 3.1 explores the following correspondance between the step relation of the operational semantics with the refinement relation of algebraic semantics

(1) Whenever a machine state (s, P) is divergent, then the execution of test $T(s, P)$ will end with a chaotic state.
(2) If (s, P) is not divergent, then the final states that it can reach via step transitions are exactly those delivered by the execution of the test $T(s, P)$.

Definition 3.3
In [9], the following transition system was given to the Guarded Command Language:

(1) Assignment
   $(s, v := e) \rightarrow (s; (v := e), \epsilon)$, where $(v := c); (v := e) = (v := e[c/v])$

(2) Choice
   (a) $((s, P \sqcap Q) \rightarrow (s, P)$
   (b) $((s, P \sqcap Q) \rightarrow (s, Q)$

(3) Conditional
   (a) $(s, P \lhd b \rhd Q) \rightarrow (s, P)$ if $(s; b) = true$
   (b) $(s, P \lhd b \rhd Q) \rightarrow (s, Q)$ if $(s; b) = false$

(4) Composition
   (a) $(s, P; Q) \rightarrow (t, R; Q)$ if $(s, P) \rightarrow (t, R)$
   (b) $(s, P; Q) \rightarrow (t, Q)$ if $(s, P) \rightarrow (t, \epsilon)$

(5) Recursion
   $(s, \mu X \bullet P(X)) \rightarrow (s, P(\mu X \bullet P(X)))$

(6) Chaos
   $(s, \bot) \rightarrow (s, \bot)$

In the following we are going to establish the consistency of the step relation of Definition 3.3 with respect to the algebra of programs.

First, we show that the step relation of Definition 3.3 meets the condition (1) of Definition 3.1.

Theorem 3.3
$T(s, P) =_A \sqcap \{T(t, Q) \mid (s, P) \rightarrow (t, Q)\}$

Proof: Direct from Theorem 2.2 and the rule (1)–(7) of Definition 3.3.

Theorem 3.4
If P is a finite program, then

$$(s, P) \uparrow \Rightarrow T(s, P) =_A \bot$$

Proof: We give an induction proof based on the structure of program text P:

Base case: Clearly the conclusion holds for the case $P = v := e$ and $P = \bot$

Inductive step:

$$(s, P_1 \sqcap P_2) \uparrow \qquad\qquad \{\text{Rule (2) in Definition 3.3}\}$$
$$\Rightarrow (s, P_1) \uparrow \sqcap (s, P_2) \uparrow \qquad\qquad \{\text{Induction hypothesis}\}$$
$$\Rightarrow (T(s, P_1) =_A \bot) \vee (T(s, P_2) =_A \bot) \qquad \{\text{Theorem 2.2(1)}\}$$
$$\Rightarrow T(s, P_1 \sqcap P_2) =_A \bot$$

$$(s, P_1 \lhd b \rhd P_2) \uparrow \qquad\qquad \{\text{Rule (3) in Definition 3.3}\}$$
$$\Rightarrow (s, P_1) \uparrow \lhd s; b \rhd (s, P_2) \uparrow \qquad\qquad \{\text{Induction hypothesis}\}$$
$$\Rightarrow (T(s, P_1) =_A \bot) \lhd s; b \rhd (T(s, P_2) =_A \bot) \qquad \{\text{Theorem 2.2(2)}\}$$
$$\Rightarrow T(s, P_1 \lhd b \rhd P_2) =_A \bot$$

$$(s, P_1; P_2) \uparrow \qquad\qquad \{\text{Rule (4) in Definition 3.3}\}$$
$$\Rightarrow (s, P_1) \uparrow \vee \exists t \bullet \begin{pmatrix} (s, P_1) \to (t, \epsilon) \wedge \\ (t, P_2) \uparrow \end{pmatrix} \qquad \{\text{Induction hypothesis}\}$$
$$\Rightarrow T(s, P_1) =_A \bot \vee$$
$$\exists t \bullet (T(s, P_1) \sqsubseteq_A t \wedge T(t, P_2) =_A \bot) \qquad \{\text{Theorem 2.2(3)}\}$$
$$\Rightarrow T(s, P_1; P_2) =_A \bot$$

Finally we are going to tackle infinite programs.

Lemma 3.1

If $(s, G(Q)) \to^* (t, \epsilon)$, then either $(s, G(\bot)) \uparrow$ or $(s, G(\bot)) \to^* (t, \epsilon)$.

Proof: See Appendix.

Lemma 3.2

(1) $(s, F(P)) \uparrow \Rightarrow (s, \mathcal{F}(\bot)) \uparrow$ for any program P.
(2) $(s, F(\mu X \bullet P(X))) \uparrow \Rightarrow (s, F(P(\mu X \bullet P(X)))) \uparrow$

Proof: See Appendix.

Theorem 3.5

$(s, F(\mu X \bullet P(X)) \uparrow \Rightarrow T(s, F(\mu X \bullet P(X))) =_A \bot$

Proof:

$$(s, F(\mu X \bullet P(X))) \uparrow \qquad\qquad \{\text{Lemma 3.2(2)}\}$$
$$\Rightarrow \forall n \bullet (s, F(P^n(\mu X \bullet P(X)))) \uparrow \qquad\qquad \{\text{Lemma 3.2(1)}\}$$
$$\Rightarrow \forall n \bullet (s, F(P^n(\bot))) \uparrow \qquad\qquad \{\text{Theorem 3.4}\}$$
$$\Rightarrow \forall n \bullet T(s, F(P^n(\bot))) =_A \bot \qquad\qquad \{\text{Continuity of } F\}$$
$$\Rightarrow T(s, F(\mu X \bullet P(X))) =_A \bot$$

Combining Theorems 3.3, 3.4 and 3.5 we conclude

Theorem 3.6
The step relation defined in Definition 3.3 is consistent.

4   Conclusion

This paper proposes a new roadmap for linking theories of programming. From the investigation of the Guarded Command Language it becomes clear that algebraic refinement relation plays a key role in building varies denotational models and their links. Our work also shows that the formalisation of consistency of operational semantics can be simplified by separation progress requirement (condition (1) in Definition 3.2) from livelock-free constraint (condition (2)):

- The first requirement excludes the error of omission of a transition. Validation of the consistent condition (1) is quite straightforward, because it only needs to examine one step transition.
- the second requirement avoids the inclusion of too many transitions. To handle this type of livelock free properties, this paper adopts quite tedious structural induction because it has to deal with recursion and multiple step transition.

We will extend this paper by applying this algebraic approach to build the mathematical framework for CSP and probabilistic programming languages in the near future.

Acknowledgements. This work is supported by National Natural Science Foundation of China (Grant No. 61321064), Shanghai Knowledge Service Platform Project (No. ZF1213) and the NSFC-Zhejiang Joint Fund for the Integration of Industrialization and Informatization (No. U1509219).

Appendix

Lemma 3.1
If $(s, G(Q)) \rightarrow^* (t, \epsilon)$, then either $(s, G(\perp)) \uparrow$ or $(s, G(\perp)) \rightarrow^* (t, \epsilon)$.

Proof: Induction on the structure of G.

Base case: $G(Q) = Q$. The conclusion follows from From Rule (6)

$$(s, \perp) \rightarrow (s, \perp)$$

in Definition 3.2.

Inductive step:
(1) $G(Q) = G_1(Q) \sqcap G_2(Q)$.

$$(s, G(Q)) \rightarrow^* (t, \epsilon) \qquad \qquad \{\text{Role (2) in Def 3.2}\}$$

$$\Rightarrow \begin{pmatrix} (s, G_1(Q)) \rightarrow^* (t, \epsilon) \vee \\ (s, G_2(Q)) \rightarrow^* (t, \epsilon) \end{pmatrix} \qquad \{\text{Induction hypothesis}\}$$

$$\Rightarrow \begin{pmatrix} (s, G_1(\perp)) \uparrow \ \vee \ (s, G_1(\perp)) \rightarrow^* (t, \epsilon) \vee \\ (s, G_2(\perp)) \uparrow \ \vee \ (s, G_2(\perp)) \rightarrow^* (t, \epsilon) \end{pmatrix} \qquad \{\text{Role (2) in Def 3.2}\}$$

$$\Rightarrow \ (s. G(\perp)) \uparrow \vee (s, G(\perp)) \rightarrow^{ast} (t, \epsilon)$$

(2) $G(Q) = G_1(Q) \lhd b \rhd G_2(X)$

$$(s, G(Q)) \to^* (t, \epsilon) \qquad \{\text{Role (3) in Def 3.2}\}$$

$$\Rightarrow \begin{pmatrix} (s, G_1(Q)) \to^* (t, \epsilon) \\ \qquad\qquad \lhd(s;b)\rhd \\ (s, G_2(Q)) \to^* (t, \epsilon) \end{pmatrix} \qquad \{\text{Induction hypothesis}\}$$

$$\Rightarrow \begin{pmatrix} (s, G_1(\bot)) \uparrow \ \lor \ (s, G_1(\bot)) \to^* (t, \epsilon) \\ \qquad\qquad \lhd(s;b)\rhd \\ (s, G_2(\bot)) \uparrow \ \lor \ (s, G_2(\bot)) \to^* (t, \epsilon) \end{pmatrix} \qquad \{\text{Role (3) in Def 3.2}\}$$

$$\Rightarrow \quad (s. G(\bot)) \uparrow \lor (s, G(\bot)) \to^{ast} (t, \epsilon)$$

(3) $G(Q) = G_1(Q); G_2(Q)$

$$(s, G(Q)) \to^* (t, \epsilon) \qquad \{\text{Role (4) in Def 3.2}\}$$

$$\Rightarrow \quad \exists u \bullet \begin{pmatrix} (s, G_1(Q)) \to^* (u, \epsilon) \ \lor \\ (u, G_2(Q)) \to^* (t, \epsilon) \end{pmatrix} \qquad \{\text{Induction hypothesis}\}$$

$$\Rightarrow \quad \exists u \bullet \begin{pmatrix} (s, G_1(\bot)) \uparrow \ \lor \ (s, G_1(\bot)) \to^* (u, \epsilon) \ \lor \\ (u, G_2(\bot)) \uparrow \ \lor \ (u, G_2(\bot)) \to^* (t, \epsilon) \end{pmatrix} \qquad \{\text{Role (4) in Def 3.2}\}$$

$$\Rightarrow \quad (s. G(\bot)) \uparrow \lor (s, G(\bot)) \to^{ast} (t, \epsilon)$$

(4) $G(Q) = \mu X \bullet P(Q, X)$

$$(s, \mu X \bullet P(G, X)) \to (t, \epsilon) \qquad \{\text{Role (5) in Def 3.2}\}$$

$$\Rightarrow \quad (s, P(G, \mu X \bullet P(G, X))) \to (t, \epsilon) \qquad \{\text{Induction hypothesis}\}$$

$$\Rightarrow \begin{pmatrix} (s, P(\bot, \mu X \bullet P(\bot, X))) \uparrow \ \lor \\ (s, P(\bot, \mu X \bullet P(\bot, X))) \to (t, \epsilon) \end{pmatrix} \qquad \{\text{Role (5) in Def 3.2}\}$$

$$\Rightarrow \begin{pmatrix} (s, \mu X \bullet P(\bot, X)) \uparrow \ \lor \\ (s, \mu X \bullet P(\bot, X)) \to (t, \epsilon) \end{pmatrix}$$

Lemma 3.2

(1) $(s, F(P)) \uparrow \Rightarrow (s, \mathcal{F}(\bot)) \uparrow$

(2) $(s, F(\mu X \bullet P(X))) \uparrow \Rightarrow (s, F(P(\mu X \bullet P(X)))) \uparrow$

Proof (1). Based on induction on the structure of F.

Base case: $F(X) = X$. The conclusion follows from the rule (6).
Inductive Step:

$$(s, F_1(Q) \sqcap F_2(Q)) \uparrow \qquad \{\text{rule (2)}\}$$

$$\Rightarrow \quad (s, F_1(Q)) \uparrow \lor (s, F_2(Q)) \uparrow \qquad \{\text{induction hypothesis}\}$$

$$\Rightarrow \quad (s, F_1(\bot)) \uparrow \lor (s, F_2(\bot)) \uparrow \qquad \{\text{rule (2)}\}$$

$$\Rightarrow \quad (s, (F_1(\bot) \sqcap F_2(\bot))) \uparrow$$

$$(s, F_1(Q) \lhd b \rhd F_2(Q)) \uparrow \qquad \{\text{rule (3)}\}$$

$$\Rightarrow \quad (s, F_1(Q)) \uparrow \ \lhd(s;b) \rhd \ (s, F_2(Q)) \uparrow \qquad \{\text{induction hypothesis}\}$$

$$\Rightarrow \quad (s, F_1(\bot)) \uparrow \ \lhd(s;b) \rhd \ (s, F_2(\bot)) \uparrow \qquad \{\text{rule (3)}\}$$

$$\Rightarrow \quad (s, (F_1(\bot) \lhd b \rhd F_2(\bot))) \uparrow$$

$(s, F_1(Q); F_2(Q)) \uparrow$ {rule (4)}

$\Rightarrow$ $(s, F_1(Q)) \uparrow \lor$

$\exists t \bullet (s, F_1(Q)) \rightarrow^* (t, \epsilon) \land (t, F_2(Q)) \uparrow$ {Lemma 3.1}

$\Rightarrow$ $(s, F_1(\bot)) \uparrow \lor (s, F_1(\bot)) \rightarrow^* (t, \epsilon) \land (t, F_2(\bot)) \uparrow$ {rule (4)}

$\Rightarrow$ $(s, F_1(\bot); F_2(\bot)) \uparrow$

Proof of (2): Similar to (1).

References

1. Abrial, J.-R.: The B-Book: Assigning Programs to Meanings. Cambridge Press, Cambridge (1996)
2. Abrial, J.-R.: Modelling in Event-B: System and Software Engineering. Cambridge Press, Cambridge (2010)
3. Dijkstra, E.W.: A Discipline of Programming. Prentice-Hall, Englewood Cliffs (1976)
4. Henner, E.C.R.: Predicative programming, Part 1, 2. Commun. ACM **27**(2), 134–151
5. Hennessy, M.C.: Algebraic Theory of Process. The MIT Press, Cambridge (1988)
6. Hoare, C.A.R.: An axiomatic basis for computer programming. Commun. ACM **12**, 576–583 (1969)
7. Hoare, C.A.R.: Communicating Sequential Processes. Prentice Hall, Upper Saddle River (1985)
8. Hoare, C.A.R., et al.: Laws of programming. Commun. ACM **30**(8), 672–686 (1987)
9. Hoare, C.A.R., He, J.: Unifying Theories of Programming. Prentice Hall, Englewood Cliffs (1998)
10. Jones, C.B.: Systematic Software Development Using VDM. Prentice Hall, Englewood Cliffs (1986)
11. Milner, R.: Communicating and Mobile Systems: The π-Calculus. Cambridge Univ. Press, Cambridge (1999)
12. G.D. Plotkin. A structural approach to operational semantics. Technical report, DAIMI-FN-19, Aarhus University, Denmark, (1981)
13. Roscoe, A.W.: Laws of occam programming. Theoret. Comput. Sci. **60**, 177–229 (1988)
14. Roscoe, A.W.: The Theory and Practice of Concurrency. Prentice Hall (1998)
15. Spivey, J.M., Notation, T.Z.: A Reference Manual. Prentice Hall, Englewood Cliffs (1992)

Towards a UTP Semantics for Modelica

Simon Foster[1]([⊠]), Bernhard Thiele[2], Ana Cavalcanti[1], and Jim Woodcock[1]

[1] Department of Computer Science, University of York, York, UK
{simon.foster,ana.cavalcanti,jim.woodcock}@york.ac.uk
[2] PELAB, Linköping University, Linköping, Sweden
bernhard.thiele@liu.se

Abstract. We describe our work on a UTP semantics for the dynamic systems modelling language Modelica. This is a language for modelling a system's continuous behaviour using a combination of differential-algebraic equations and an event-handling system. We develop a novel UTP theory of hybrid relations, inspired by Hybrid CSP and Duration Calculus, that is purely relational and provides uniform handling of continuous and discrete variables. This theory is mechanised in our Isabelle implementation of the UTP, Isabelle/UTP, with which we verify some algebraic properties. Finally, we show how a subset of Modelica models can be given semantics using our theory. When combined with the wealth of existing UTP theories for discrete system modelling, our work enables a sound approach to heterogeneous semantics for Cyber-Physical systems by leveraging the theory linking facilities of the UTP.

1 Introduction

Cyber-Physical Systems (CPS) are a class of computerised system that integrate discrete computation with continuous physical processes. CPS are typically developed using a combination of discrete and continuous models, often in differing heterogeneous languages. This makes verification of trustworthiness challenging. There is a need for unifying semantic models to allow the integration of heterogeneous system components, whilst ensuring that a given set of safety properties is supported. Hoare and He's Unifying Theories of Programming (UTP) has been designed as a framework in which the integration of languages, through the common semantic domain of the alphabetised relation calculus, can be achieved. Semantic models for discrete modelling languages in UTP are already numerous [13,26,30,36], and, therefore, in this paper we focus on semantics of continuous models in the Modelica language.

Modelica [22] is a widely used language for description and modelling of hybrid dynamical systems that compose a continuously evolving physical plant with a discrete controller. Such systems are described using a mixture of differential-algebraic equations (DAEs), and event guards that trigger discontinuous jumps in system behaviour by execution of discrete equations and algorithms – so called "hybrid DAEs". Modelica has a number of commercial

© Springer International Publishing AG 2017
J.P. Bowen and H. Zhu (Eds.): UTP 2016, LNCS 10134, pp. 44–64, 2017.
DOI: 10.1007/978-3-319-52228-9_3

implementations including Dymola[1], Wolfram SystemModeler[2], MapleSim[3] and the open-source implementation, OpenModelica[4]. However, the Modelica language has an incomplete formal semantics; though the semantics of DAEs is well known, the event iteration system currently does not have a formal semantics. Here we give a denotational semantics to a fragment of Modelica using a UTP theory of hybrid relations. Additionally to clarifying the semantics of Modelica, this allows us to consider the combination of continuous and discrete models through common theoretical factors and theory linking.

Our approach to giving a semantics to Modelica is three-fold. Firstly, we create a UTP theory of hybrid relations, building on the work of He [14,15], Zhou [32,33], Zhan [21], and others. This theory extends the alphabet of UTP predicates with continuous variables $\underline{c} \in con\alpha$ and is defined by novel healthiness conditions that characterise these variables as piecewise continuous functions.

Secondly, we define the operators of our hybrid relational calculus, which is similar to the imperative subset of $\mathcal{HCSP}$ [34], but extended with an interval operator [33] that provides a continuous specification statement. In particular we provide support for semi-explicit DAEs and continous variable preemption. As with Hybrid CSP, we base the denotational semantics around the Duration Calculus [33], though the semantics is purely relational. Moreover, we provide a uniform account of both discrete and continuous variables by linking the latter to discrete "copy" variables that give the valuation at the beginning and end of a continuous evolution. Thus, both discrete and continuous variables can be manipulated with the same operators; in the latter case this provides initial value constraints. Our model of hybrid relations has also mechanised in our UTP proof assistant, *Isabelle/UTP* [10], that provides theorem proving facilities.

Thirdly, we define a preliminary denotational semantics for Modelica through a mapping into the hybrid relational calculus. This mapping primarily considers the event-handling mechanism of Modelica, whereby specific conditions on continuous variables can lead to both discontinuous jumps in variables, and also changes to the equations active in the DAE system.

The remainder of our paper is structured as follows. In Sect. 2, we provide background on hybrid systems by briefly surveying the literature, with particular emphasis on works related to the UTP. In Sect. 3 we briefly describe the UTP, and in Sect. 4 we introduce the Modelica language. In Sect. 5, we describe our UTP theory of hybrid relations. In Sect. 6, we use our UTP theory to build a hybrid relational calculus, including operators for specifying continuous invariants, differential equations, and preemption. In Sect. 7, we outline our mechanisation of the hybrid relational calculus in Isabelle [10,23]. In Sect. 8, we use our hybrid relational calculus to give a high-level denotational semantics to the Modelica language, focusing principally on the interaction between evolution of DAEs and the event handling system. Finally in Sect. 9, we draw conclusions.

---

[1] http://www.3ds.com/products-services/catia/products/dymola.
[2] http://www.wolfram.com/system-modeler/.
[3] http://www.maplesoft.com/products/maplesim/.
[4] https://www.openmodelica.org/.

2   Related Work: Hybrid Systems

The majority of the work on hybrid systems takes inspiration from Hybrid Automata [16], an extension of finite state automata that allows the specification of continuous behaviour. A hybrid automaton consists of a finite set of states labelled by ODEs, a state invariant, and initial conditions. The states (or "modes") are connected by transitions that are labelled with jump conditions and (optionally) events. Whilst in a state the continuous variables evolve according to the system of ODEs and the given invariant; this is known as a *flow* as the variable values continuously flow from one value to another. When one of the jump conditions of an outgoing edge is satisfied, the event, if present, can instantaneously execute, potentially resulting in a discontinuity, and the targeted hybrid state is activated. Thus a hybrid automata is characterised by behaviour that includes both continuous flows also discrete jumps. Hybrid automata are given a denotational semantics in terms of piecewise continuous functions [16] $\mathbb{R} \to \mathbb{R}^n$, also called trajectories, that are continuous except for in a finite number of places.

Verification of hybrid systems was made possible through the seminal work of Platzer [27]. This work develops a logic called Differential Dynamic Logic ($d\mathcal{L}$) that allows us to specify invariants over both discrete and continuous variables. Hybrid systems are modelled using a language of hybrid programs, that combines the usual operators of an imperative language with continuous behaviour specified by differential equations. Hybrid programs are equipped with a relational semantics, and a proof calculus for $d\mathcal{L}$ allows reasoning about hybrid programs. An implementation of $d\mathcal{L}$ called *KeYmaera* [27] allows the automated verification of systems modelled as hybrid programs. Our notion of hybrid relation is inspired by Platzer's hybrid programs, though we focus on a UTP denotational semantics as opposed to an operational semantics. Our own setting of the Duration Calculus [33] provides us with the necessary machinery to similarly justify a dynamic logic. Moreover, we observe that, with a UTP model, we are in a strong position to extend the work to deal with concurrent hybrid programs, a notion that $d\mathcal{L}$ does not consider.

Concurrency is considered in Hybrid CSP [14,34] ($\mathcal{HCSP}$), an extension of Hoare's process calculus CSP [17] that adds support for continuous variables as described by differential equations and modelled by standard trajectories, in a similar manner to hybrid automata. $\mathcal{HCSP}$ [14] extends CSP with continuous variables whose behaviour is described by differential equations of the form $\mathcal{F}(\dot{s}, s) = 0$. Interaction between discrete and continuous behaviour takes the form of preemption conditions on continuous variables, timeouts, and interruption of a continuous evolution through CSP events. $\mathcal{HCSP}$ has a denotational semantics that is presented in a predicative style similar to the UTP [18].

Further work on $\mathcal{HCSP}$ [34] enriches the language to allow explicit interaction between discrete and continuous variables. This is achieved through a novel denotational semantics in terms of the Extended Duration Calculus [35], which treats variables as piecewise continuous functions. This allows a more precise semantics for operators like preemption that are defined in terms of suitable variable limits. A Hoare logic for this calculus is presented in [21], through the adoption of Platzer's differential invariants, along with an operational semantics. Our work is heavily influenced by $\mathcal{HCSP}$, though we focus on formalising the sequential aspects of hybrid systems, and so formalise a subset of the operators with refined definitions. Our operators formalise continuous after variables by explicitly considering left-limits which is important for Modelica event iteration.

A theorem prover for $\mathcal{HCSP}$ called, HHL Prover [37], has also been developed and applied to verification of Simulink diagrams through a mapping into $\mathcal{HCSP}$ [31]. More recently the fundamentals of hybrid system modelling have been studied in a purely UTP relational setting [15]. This work has produced a language called the Hybrid Relational Modelling Language [15] (HRML), which draws on $\mathcal{HCSP}$, but uses signals rather than CSP's events as the main communication abstraction. Our notation is agnostic in this respect, and could be extended either to support the event or signal paradigm.

Duration Calculus [33] ($\mathcal{DC}$) provides specification of invariants over the continuous time domain, in order to facilitate verification real-time systems. For example, we can write $\lceil x^2 > 7 \rceil$, which specifies all possible intervals of over which $x^2 > 7$ is invariant. The chop operator $P \circ Q$ specifies that an interval may be broken into two subsequent intervals, over which P and then Q hold, respectively. $\mathcal{DC}$ has been extended to provide a semantics for hybrid real-time systems modelling [35], which is then used to give semantics to $\mathcal{HCSP}$ [34]. $\mathcal{DC}$ can also be used to give an account to typical operators of modal and temporal logics. Thus, grounding our semantics in $\mathcal{DC}$ enables us to form continuous specifications about hybrid systems. Different to $\mathcal{DC}$ we provide a purely relational UTP semantics, and also explictly distinguish continuous and discrete variables, instead of modelling the latter as step functions. This distinction allows us to retain standard relational definitions of the majority of discrete UTP operators.

3   Unifying Theories of Programming

Unifying Theories of Programming [4,18] (UTP) is a framework for the specification of formal semantics. It is based on the idea that any temporal model can be expressed as an alphabetised predicate that describes how variables change over time. This idea of "programs-as-predicates" means that the duality of programs and specifications all but disappea‚rs, as programs are just a subclass of specifications. This powerful idea provides a strong basis for unification of heterogeneous languages and semantic models, since many different shapes of models can be given a uniform view. The UTP further allows that different semantic presentations, such as denotational, algebraic, axiomatic, and operational, can be formally linked through mutual embeddings. This ensures that consistency is maintained between semantic models and that tools that implement them can be combined for multi-pronged analysis and verification of models [10].

Concretely, an alphabetised relation is a pair $(\alpha P, P)$ where αP is the alphabet and P is a predicate all of whose free variables belong to αP. The alphabet can in turn be subdivided $\alpha(P) = in\alpha(P) \cup out\alpha(P)$, with input variables

$x, y \in \text{in}\alpha(P)$ and output variables $x', y' \in \text{out}\alpha(P)$. The calculus provides the operators typical of first order logic. UTP predicates are ordered by a refinement partial order $P \sqsubseteq Q$ that also defines a complete lattice. Imperative programs can be described using relational operators, such as sequential composition $P \,;\, Q$, if-then-else conditional $P \lhd b \rhd Q$, assignment $x :=_A v$ (for expression v and alphabet A), and skip II_A, all of which are given predicative interpretations.

More sophisticated language constructs can be expressed by enriching the theory of alphabetised relations to create UTP theories. A UTP theory consists of (i) a set of observational variables, (ii) a signature, and (iii) a set of healthiness conditions. The observational variables record behavioural semantic information about a particular program. For example, we may have an observational variable for recording the current time called $clock : \mathbb{R}$. The signature uses these operational variables to encode the main operators of the target **ht** language.

The domain of a UTP theory can be constrained through healthiness conditions, which act as invariants over the observational variables. For example, it is intuitively the case that time only moves forward, and so a relational observation like $C \triangleq clock = 3 \wedge clock' = 1$ ought not to be possible. We can eliminate this kind of behaviour description with an invariant $clock \leq clock'$. In the UTP such conditions are expressed as idempotent functions, for example **HT**$(P) = P \wedge clock \leq clock'$, so that healthiness of a predicate P can be expressed as a fixed point equation: $P = \textbf{HT}(P)$. If we apply **HT** to C, the result is miraculous predicate **false** and thus C is excluded from the theory signature.

UTP theories can be used to describe a domain useful for modelling particular problems – for instance, we can add further conditions to **HT** to provide a theory of real-time programs. UTP theories can also be composed to produce modelling domains that combine different language aspects. Put more simply, UTP theories provide the building blocks for a heterogeneous language's denotational semantics [9]. Such a denotational semantics provides the "gold standard" for the meaning of language constructs and can then be used to derive other presentations, such as operational and, very often, algebraic.

4   Modelica

Modelica is an equation-based object-oriented language for describing the dynamic behaviour of CPS, standardised by the Modelica Language Specification (MLS) [22]. The MLS is described using English; therefore, its semantics is to some extent subject to interpretation. Quoting from [22, Sect. 1.2]: "The semantics of the Modelica language is specified by means of a set of rules for translating any class described in the Modelica language to a flat Modelica structure. A class must have additional properties in order that its flat Modelica structure can be further transformed into a set of differential, algebraic and discrete equations (= flat hybrid DAE). Such classes are called simulation models."

Figure 1 illustrates the basic idea. The squiggle arrow denotes a degree of fuzziness — a simulation result is an *approximation* to the, in general, inaccessible exact solution of the equation system and the specification does not prescribe a particular solution approach. A classical model for a hybrid systems is the bouncing ball. A possible Modelica implementation for a ball with mass 1 kg and an impact coefficient of 0.8 that falls from an initial height of $h = 1$ m is given in Fig. 2. When the ball hits the ground, it changes its velocity v discontinuously and bounces back. der(h) and der(v) denote the time derivatives $\dot{h}$ and $\dot{v}$ of variables h and v, respectively. The acceleration to the ground is determined by earth's gravitational acceleration $g = 9.81$ m/s^2. The discontinuous change of variable v is modelled using a conditionally activated reinitialization equation. The ball hits the ground when condition $h < 0$ becomes true. The reinit() operator is used for reinitializing v with the negative value of v (times the impact coefficient) just before condition $h < 0$ becomes true (pre(v) returns the left limit of variable v at the event instant).

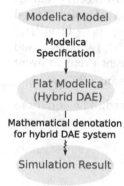

Modelica Model

Modelica Specification

Flat Modelica (Hybrid DAE)

Mathematical denotation for hybrid DAE system

Simulation Result

```
model BouncingBall
   Real h; Real v;
   initial equation
      h = 1.0;
   equation
      v = der(h);
      der(v) = -9.81;
      when h<0 then
         reinit(v, -0.8*pre(v));
      end when;
end BouncingBall;
```

Fig. 1. From model to simulation result.

Fig. 2. Bouncing ball in Modelica.

Several formal specification approaches have been used to give semantics to subsets of the Modelica language. Most of the approaches describe the instantiation and flattening of Modelica models (*i.e.*, the *static semantics*, corresponding to the first stage in Fig. 1) [1,20,28] while others are restricted to discrete-time language subsets [29].

Flat Modelica can be conceptually mapped to a set of differential, algebraic and discrete equations of the following form [22, Appendix C]:

1. *Continuous-time behaviour.* The system behaviour *between* events is described by a system of differential and algebraic equations (DAEs):

$$f\big(x(t), \dot{x}(t), y(t), t, m(t_e), m_{\mathrm{pre}}(t_e), p, c(t_e)\big) = 0 \qquad (1\mathrm{a})$$
$$g\big(x(t), y(t), t, m(t_e), m_{\mathrm{pre}}(t_e), p, c(t_e)\big) = 0, \qquad (1\mathrm{b})$$

where t denotes time; p is a vector of parameters and constants; $x(t)$ is a vector of dynamic variables of type Real and $\dot{x}(t)$ is the vector of its derivatives; $y(t)$ is a vector of algebraic variables of type Real; $m(t_e)$ is a vector of discrete-time variables of type discrete Real, Boolean, Integer, or String which changes only at event instants t_e; $m_{\text{pre}}(t_e)$ are the values of m immediately before the current event at event instant t_e; and $c(t_e)$ is a vector containing all Boolean condition expressions, e.g., if-expressions.

2. *Discrete-time behaviour.* The behaviour at an event at time t_e is described by following discrete equations:

$$m(t_e) := f_m\big(x(t_e), \dot{x}(t_e), y(t_e), m_{\text{pre}}(t_e), p, c(t_e)\big) \qquad (2)$$

$$c(t_e) := f_e\big(m^{\mathbf{B}}(t_e), m^{\mathbf{B}}_{\text{pre}}(t_e), p^{\mathbf{B}}, rel(v(t_e))\big). \qquad (3)$$

An event fires if any of the conditions $c(t_e)$ change from **false** to **true**. The vector-valued function f_m specifies new values for the discrete variables $m(t_e)$. The vector $c(t_e)$ is defined by the vector-valued function f_e, which contains all Boolean condition expressions evaluated at the most recent event t_e; $rel(v(t_e)) = rel([x(t); \dot{x}(t); y(t); t; m(t_e); m_{\text{pre}}(t_e); p])$ is a Boolean-typed vector-valued function containing variables v_i, e.g., $v_1 > v_2$, $v_3 \geq 0$; $m^{\mathbf{B}}(t_e)$ is a vector of discrete-time variables of type Boolean, $m^{\mathbf{B}}(t_e) \subseteq m(t_e)$, and $m^{\mathbf{B}}_{\text{pre}}(t_e)$ are the values of $m^{\mathbf{B}}$ immediately before the current event at event instant t_e; $p^{\mathbf{B}}$ are parameters and constants of type Boolean, $p^{\mathbf{B}} \subseteq p$.

Simulation means that an initial value problem (IVP) is solved. The equations define a DAE which may have discontinuities and a variable structure and may be controlled by a discrete-event system.

5   Theory of Hybrid Relations

We now proceed to describe our theory of hybrid relations to enable the definition of a relational calculus for modelling sequential hybrid processes. Our model unifies the treatment of discrete and continuous variables so that the same operators may be used for manipulating both. In Modelica, DAEs are used to describe continuously evolving dynamic behaviour of a system. Thus, in the UTP, we first introduce a theory of continuous time processes that embeds trajectories into alphabetised predicates and shows how continuous variables evolve over a given interval. These intervals are used to divide up the evolution of a system into piecewise continuous segments.

Our theory is based on vanilla UTP alphabetised relations, and so is insensitive to termination and stability of continuous processes. Following the UTP philosophy, we consider hybrid behaviour in isolation, and then later augment it with additional structure to allow the finer expression of such properties. Our theory can, for instance, be embedded into timed reactive designs [13,30].

Alphabet. Our model of continuous time introduces observational variables $ti, ti' : \mathbb{R}_{\geq 0}$ that define the start and end time of the current computation interval, as in $\mathcal{DC}$ [35]. We also introduce the expression ℓ to denote the duration of the current interval, where $\ell \triangleq ti' - ti$.

As already said, the alphabetised relational calculus divides the alphabet into input $in\alpha(P)$ and output variables $out\alpha(P)$. Inspired by [15], we add a further subdivision $\underline{x}, \underline{y}, \underline{z} \in \mathrm{con}\alpha(P)$, the set of continuous variables, that is orthogonal to the discrete program variables, that is $\mathrm{con}\alpha(P) \cap (\mathrm{in}\alpha(P) \cup \mathrm{out}\alpha(P)) = \emptyset$. The elements of $\mathrm{con}\alpha(P)$ are the variables to be used in differential equations and other continuous constructs.

We assume that all variables consist of a name, type, and optional decoration. For example, the name in the variables x, x', and $\underline{x}$ is the same – x – but the decorations differ. We introduce the distinguished continuous variable $\underline{t}$ that denotes the current instant in an algebraic or differential equation. An alphabetised predicate P whose alphabet can be so partitioned, i.e. $\alpha(P) = \mathrm{in}\alpha(P) \cup \mathrm{out}\alpha(P) \cup \mathrm{con}\alpha(P)$, is called a *hybrid relation*.

Continuous variables come in two varieties that allows us to talk about a particular instant or about the whole time continuum:

- instant variables – these are continuous variables of type $\mathbb{R}$ that refer to the value at a particular instant;
- trajectory variables – these are time-dependent variables of type $\mathbb{R}_{\geq 0} \to \mathbb{R}$ and give the values over a whole trajectory.

Trajectory variables are total rather than partial functions. This has the advantage that composition operators need not consider explicit combination of trajectories through overriding. Instead, composition further constrains the trajectory functions, potentially over disjoint time domains (as is the case for;). Valuations of the trajectory exist outside $[ti, ti')$, but they have no relevance.

We require that each trajectory variable $\underline{x} : \mathbb{R}_{\geq 0} \to \mathbb{R}$ is accompanied by discrete before and after "copy" variables with the same name – $x, x' : \mathbb{R}$ – that record the values at the start and limit of the current interval. This, crucially, allows us to use the standard operators of relational calculus for manipulating continuous variables via discrete copies. This allows us to consider the set of purely discrete variables that are not discrete copies of a continuous variable:

$$\mathrm{dis}\alpha(P) = \{x \in \mathrm{in}\alpha(P) \mid \underline{x} \notin \mathrm{con}\alpha(P)\} \cup \{x' \in \mathrm{out}\alpha(P) \mid \underline{x} \notin \mathrm{con}\alpha(P)\}$$

We introduce the following @ operator borrowed from [6] that lifts a predicate in instant variables to one in trajectory variables.

Definition 1. *Continuous variable lifting*

$$P @ \tau \triangleq \{\underline{x} \mapsto \underline{x}(\tau) \mid \underline{x} \in \mathrm{con}\alpha(P) \setminus \{\underline{t}\}\} \dagger P$$

The dagger (†) operator is a nominal substitution operator. It applies the given partial function, which maps variables to expressions, as a substitution to the given predicate, so that $P[v/x] = \{x \mapsto v\} \dagger P$. We construct a substitution that maps every flat continuous variable (other than the distinguished time variable $\underline{t} \in [ti..ti')$) to a corresponding variable lifted over the time domain. The effect of this is to state that the predicate holds for values of continuous variables at a particular instant τ, a variable that is potentially free in P. Each flat continuous variable $\underline{x} : T$ is thus transformed to have a time-dependent function $\underline{x} : \mathbb{R} \to T$ type. This operator is used to lift time predicates over intervals.

Table 1. Signature of hybrid relational calculus

$$P, Q ::= P \; ; Q \mid P \vartriangleleft b \vartriangleright Q \mid x := e \mid P^* \mid P^\omega \mid [\![P]\!] \mid \langle F_n \mid b \rangle \mid P [b] Q$$

Healthiness conditions. We introduce two healthiness conditions:

$$HCT1(P) \triangleq P \wedge ti \leq ti'$$

$$HCT2(P) \triangleq P \wedge \left(ti < ti' \Rightarrow \bigwedge_{\underline{v} \in \text{con}\alpha(P)} \left(\begin{array}{l} \exists I : \mathbb{R}_{\text{oseq}} \bullet \text{ran}(I) \subseteq \{ti \ldots ti'\} \\ \wedge \{ti, ti'\} \subseteq \text{ran}(I) \wedge \\ \wedge (\forall n < \#I - 1 \bullet \\ \quad \underline{v} \text{ cont-on } [I_n, I_{n+1})) \end{array} \right) \right)$$

where
$$\mathbb{R}_{\text{oseq}} \triangleq \{x : \text{seq} \, \mathbb{R} \mid \forall n < \#x - 1 \bullet x_n < x_{n+1}\}$$
$$f \text{ cont-on } [m, n) \triangleq \forall t \in [m, n) \bullet \lim_{x \to t} f(x) = f(t)$$
HCT1 states that
time may only ever go forward, as should be the case, and thus the time interval is well-defined. **HCT2** states that every continuous variable $\underline{v}$ should be piecewise continuous, that is, that for non-empty intervals there exists a finite number of points (range of I) between ti and ti' where discontinuities occur. We define the set of totally ordered sequences $\mathbb{R}_{\text{oseq}}$ that captures this set of discontinuities, and the continuity of f is defined in the usual way by requiring that at each point in $[ti, ti')$, the limit correctly predicts where the function goes.

HCT1 and **HCT2** are idempotent, monotone, and commutative as they are both conjunctive. We then have that **HCT = HCT2 ∘ HCT1** also satisfies all these properties. Furthermore it defines a complete lattice.

Theorem 1. HCT *predicates form a complete lattice under* $\sqcap$ *and* $\sqcup$, *with* $\top_H = $ **HCT(true)** *and* $\perp_H = $ **false**.

Proof. By conjunctivity of **HCT**. Properties of conjunctive healthiness conditions are proved in [12]. □

6   Hybrid Relational Calculus

The signature of our theory is given in Table 1. It consists of the standard operators of the alphabetised relational calculus together with operators to specify intervals $[\![P]\!]$, differential algebraic equations $\langle F_n \mid b \rangle$, and preemption $P [b] Q$. Using this calculus, we can describe the bouncing ball example from Fig. 2:

Example 1. Bouncing ball in hybrid relational calculus

$$h, v := 1, 0 \; ; \left(\left\langle \underline{\dot{h}} = \underline{v}; \; \underline{\dot{v}} = -9.81 \right\rangle [\underline{h} < 0] \, v := -v \cdot 0.8) \right)^\omega$$

This hybrid program has two continuous variables for height $\underline{h}$ and velocity $\underline{v}$. Initially we set these two variables to 1 and 0, and then initiate the system of ODEs. The system evolves until $\underline{h} < 0$, at which point a discrete command is executed that assigns $-v \cdot 0.8$ to v, that is, the velocity is reversed with a dampening factor. The system infinitely iterates, allowing the system dynamics to continue evolving, but with new initial values. Such a system only requires an ODE with no algebraic equations; to illustrate DAEs we give another example.

Example 2. Cartesian pendulum in hybrid relational calculus

$$\left\langle \; \underline{\dot{x}} = \underline{u}; \; \underline{\dot{u}} = \lambda \cdot \underline{x}; \; \underline{\dot{y}} = \underline{v}; \; \underline{\dot{v}} = \lambda \cdot \underline{y} - 9.81 \; \middle| \; \underline{x}^2 + \underline{y}^2 = l^2 \; \right\rangle$$

This system consists of four differential and one algebraic equation in terms of the position (x, y), horizontal and vertical velocities u and v, and the length l of the pendulum cable. The differential equations describe the horizontal and vertical components of the pendulum's movement vector, governed by the laws of conservation of energy and gravity using a constant λ previously defined. The algebraic equation ties x and y together through the Pythagorean theorem, ensuring that the length of the cable must be respected by the movement. □

We note that many of the standard operators of the alphabetised relational calculus retain their standard denotational semantics [18] in this setting, but over the expanded alphabet. Indeed, an alphabetised relation is simply a hybrid relation with the degenerate alphabet $con\alpha(P) = \emptyset$. For continuous variables, sequential composition behaves like conjunction. In particular, if we have $P \; ; \; Q$, with P and Q representing evolutions over disjoint intervals, then their sequential composition combines the corresponding trajectories when they agree on variable valuations. Put another way, the final condition of P also defines the initial condition for Q as in the Z schema composition operator.

Similarly, other operators like the Kleene star and Omega iteration operators P^* and P^ω, being defined solely in terms of sequential composition, disjunction (internal choice), $\mathbb{I}$, and fixed point operators, also remain valid in this context. Thus we already have the core operators of an imperative programming language at our disposal. We prove that these core operators satisfy our two healthiness conditions in Isabelle (cf. Sect. 7), but for now we state the following theorem.

Theorem 2. *The following operators of relational calculus $P \; ; \; Q$, $P \lhd b \rhd Q$, P^*, $\mathbb{I}$, $x := v$, and **false** are **HCT** closed.*

The maximally nondeterministic relation **true** is of course not **HCT** healthy, and so we supplement our theory with $\textbf{true}_H \triangleq \textbf{HCT}(\textbf{true})$. We define the interval operator from $\mathcal{DC}$ [33] and our own variant.

Definition 2. *Interval operators*

$$\lceil P \rceil \triangleq \textbf{HCT2}(\ell > 0 \wedge (\forall \underline{t} \in [ti, ti') \bullet P @ \underline{t}))$$

$$\lceil\!\lceil P \rceil\!\rceil \triangleq \lceil P \rceil \wedge \bigwedge_{\underline{v} \in con\alpha(P)} (v = \underline{v}(ti) \wedge v' = \lim_{t \to ti'} (\underline{v}(t))) \wedge \mathbb{I}_{dis\alpha(P)}$$

$\lceil P \rceil$ is a continuous specification statement that P holds at every instant over all non-empty right-open intervals from ti to ti'; it corresponds to the standard $\mathcal{DC}$ operator. We apply **HCT2** to ensure that all variables are also piecewise continuous. In this setting we can use sequential composition $P \, ; \, Q$ to express the $\mathcal{DC}$ chop operator $(P \circ Q)$ to decompose an interval. Our additional interval operator $\llbracket P \rrbracket$ pairs continuous variables with discrete variables at the start and limit of the interval, whilst holding other discrete variables constant. The initial condition of each continuous variable $\underline{x}$ in the interval is constrained by the valuation of the corresponding discrete copy x. Likewise, the condition at the limit of the interval is recorded in the corresponding discrete after variable x'.

Crucially, this provides a uniform view of discrete and continuous variables when handled over an interval, and allows the use of standard relational operators for their manipulation. Moreover, by taking the limit rather than the final value of a continuous variable we do not constrain the trajectory valuation at ti' meaning it can be defined by a suitable discontinuous discrete assignment at this instant. Following [14] we ground our definition of differential equation systems in this interval operator. This will, for example, allow us to formally refine a DAE, under given initial conditions, to a suitable solution expressed using the interval operator. Intervals satisfy a number of standard laws of $\mathcal{DC}$ illustrated in Table 2, which we prove in Sect. 7.

Table 2. Algebraic laws of durations

$$\lceil true \rceil = \ell > 0 \qquad\qquad \lceil false \rceil = \textbf{false}$$
$$\lceil P \wedge Q \rceil = \lceil P \rceil \wedge \lceil Q \rceil \qquad \lceil P \vee Q \rceil \sqsubseteq \lceil P \rceil \vee \lceil Q \rceil$$
$$\llbracket P \rrbracket \sqsubseteq \llbracket P \rrbracket \, ; \, \llbracket P \rrbracket$$

We next introduce an operator, adapted from $\mathcal{HCSP}$ [21,34], to describe the evolution of a system of differential-algebraic equations.

Definition 3. *DAE system in semi-explicit form*

$$\langle \, \underline{\dot{v}}_1 = f_1; \, \cdots \, ; \, \underline{\dot{v}}_n = f_n \, | \, 0 = b_1; \, \cdots \, ; \, 0 = b_m \, \rangle$$
$$\triangleq \llbracket (\forall \, i \in 1..n, \forall \, j \in 1..m \bullet \underline{\dot{v}}_i(\underline{t}) = f_i(\underline{t}, \underline{v}_1(\underline{t}), \cdots, \underline{v}_n(\underline{t}), \underline{w}_1(\underline{t}), \cdots, \underline{w}_m(\underline{t})))$$
$$\wedge \, 0 = b_j(\underline{t}, \underline{v}_1(\underline{t}), \cdots, \underline{v}_n(\underline{t}), \underline{w}_1(\underline{t}), \cdots, \underline{w}_m(\underline{t})) \rrbracket$$

A DAE $\langle \, F_n \, | \, B_m \, \rangle$ consists of a set of n functions $f_i : \mathbb{R} \times \mathbb{R}^n \times \mathbb{R}^m \to \mathbb{R}$ each of which defines the derivative of variable $\underline{v}_i$ in terms of the independent time variable $\underline{t}$ and $n + m$ dependent variables. It also contains algebraic constraints $b_j : \mathbb{R} \times \mathbb{R}^n \times \mathbb{R}^m \to \mathbb{R}$ that must be invariant for any solution and do not refer to derivatives. For $m = 0$ the DAE corresponds to an ODE, which we write as $\langle \, F_n \, \rangle$. The DAE operator is defined using the interval operator to be all non-empty intervals over which a solution satisfying both the ODEs and algebraic constraint exists. Non-emptiness is important as it means that a DAE must make progress: it cannot simply take zero time since $\ell > 0$, and so a DAE cannot directly cause "chattering Zeno" effects when placed in the context of a loop, though normal Zeno effects remain a possibility.

As previously explained, at the initial time (ti) each continuous variable $\underline{v}_i$ of the system is equated to the value of the corresponding discrete input variable v_i. To obtain a well defined problem description, we require the following conditions to hold [2]: (i) the system of equations is consistent and neither underdetermined nor overdetermined; (ii) the discrete input variables v_i provide consistent initial conditions (ICs[5]); (iii) the equations are specific enough to define a unique solution during the interval ℓ. The system is then allowed to evolve from this point in the interval between ti and ti' according to the DAEs. At the end of the interval, the corresponding output discrete variables are assigned. During the evolution all discrete variables and unconstrained continuous variables are held constant.

Finally, we define the preemption operator, adapted from $\mathcal{HCSP}$.

Definition 4. *Preemption operator*

$$P\,[\,B\,]\,Q \triangleq (Q \lhd B\,@\,ti \rhd (P \wedge \lceil \neg B \rceil)) \vee ((\lceil \neg B \rceil \wedge B\,@\,ti' \wedge P)\,;\,Q)$$

Intuitively, P is a continuous process that evolves until the predicate B is satisfied, at which point Q is activated. This operator is used to capture events in Modelica. The semantics is defined as a disjunction of two predicates. The first predicate states that, if B holds in the initial state of ti, then Q is activated immediately. Otherwise, P is activated and can evolve while B remains false (potentially indefinitely). The second predicate states that $\neg B$ holds on the interval $[ti, ti')$ until instant ti', when B switches to a true valuation; during that inverval P is executing. Following this, P is terminated and Q is activated.

7   Mechanisation in Isabelle/UTP

Our Isabelle [23] mechanisation serves two purposes: firstly it validates the model by enabling us to prove algebraic laws, and secondly it enables theorem proving for hybrid programs. It is based in a shallow embedding of the UTP[6], which provides direct proof automation through a combination of *Isabelle/Circus* [5] and our own deep model [10]. UTP relations are represented by predicates over bindings, and bindings over a given alphabet are represented using record types, where each field corresponds to a variable. The model is based on a UTP expression type $('a,\, '\alpha)\ uexpr$ ranging over alphabet type $'\alpha$ and with return type $'a$.

---

[5] Notice that in the general case ICs for DAE systems may actually involve derivatives $\underline{\dot{v}}_i$ of $\underline{v}_i$ [25]. Modelica supports the general case and sophisticated algorithms for finding consistent ICs from "guess" values exist [2,24]. However, numerical/symbolic methods for solving IVPs is not within the scope of our current work. Hence, we only consider less general ICs and presume that consistent ICs are provided.

[6] See https://github.com/isabelle-utp/utp-main/tree/shallow.

Alphabetised predicates $'\alpha$ *upred* are expressions with a boolean return type, and relations are predicates over a product type $('\alpha \times '\beta)$ *upred*.

We mimic the syntax of UTP predicates as given in most standard publications (e.g. [4,18]). Where this is not possible, we supplement the same syntax with an added subscript u. For example, equality in Isabelle "=" denotes HOL equality, so we use $=_u$ for UTP equality. Input variable and output variable expressions are written $\$x$ and $\$x\,'$ respectively. We also make use of Isabelle's implementation of Cauchy real numbers and analysis [7,11]. Our proofs make heavy use of Isabelle's automated proof facilities like auto and sledgehammer [3]. This has allowed us to use Isabelle to validate the healthiness conditions and definitions given in the previous sections. We prove that they respect appropriate laws, which increases confidence in the correctness of our UTP theory. This section has been compiled using Isabelle's document preparation system: all definitions and theorems have been mechanically verified[7].

> **record** $('d, 'c)$ *hyst* =
> $state_u$ :: $'d \times 'c$
> $time_u$ :: *real*
> $traj_u$ :: *real* $\Rightarrow 'c$

> **type-synonym** $('d, 'c)$ *hyrel* = $('d, 'c)$ *hyst hrelation*

A hybrid state $('d, 'c)$ *hyst* represents the alphabet, or equivalently the state of the hybrid relation, at a particular instant. We represent this using a record with three fields: $state_u$ denoting the state variables, $time_u$ denoting the time, and $traj_u$ denoting the trajectory of continuous variables. The record type is parametrised by the discrete portion of the alphabet, denoted by type $'d$ and the continuous portion denoted by type $'c$. The state field's type is a product of the discrete and continuous state, whilst the trajectory refers only to the continuous state. Intuitively, this encodes the distinction between discrete and continuous variables. A hybrid relation is then a homogeneous relation (*hrelation*) over the hybrid state. We next give the healthiness conditions of our theory.

> **definition** $HCT1(P) = (P \wedge \$time \geq_u 0 \wedge \$time \leq_u \$time')$

$HCT1$ is broadly the same as in Sect. 6, though we additionally require that the initial time be no less than zero; this is due to our use of the standard type *real* that also encompasses negative numbers.

> **definition** $HCT2(P) =$
> $(P \wedge (\$time' >_u \$time \Rightarrow$
> $(\exists\, I \cdot \{\$time, \$time'\}_u \subseteq_u ran_u(I) \wedge ran_u(I) \subseteq_u \{\$time \mathrel{..} \$time'\}_u$
> $\wedge (\forall\, n \cdot n <_u \#_u(I) - 1 \Rightarrow \$traj\ cont{-}on_u\ \{I(\!|n|\!)_u \mathrel{..}< I(\!|n+1|\!)_u\}_u)$
> $\wedge sorted_u(I) \wedge distinct_u(I))))$

$HCT2$ also explicitly requires that the trajectory sequence I is both sorted and distinct, which equates to it being linearly sorted as required.

> **definition** $HTRAJ(P) = (P \wedge \$traj =_u \$traj')$

---

[7] Our Isabelle/UTP theory development, including all omitted proofs, is available at http://www.cs.york.ac.uk/~simonf/utp2016.

We also have to add an auxiliary healthiness condition *HTRAJ*. This allows us to use standard HOL binary relations, where there is only inputs and outputs, to represent hybrid relations. Specifically, we have two copies of the trajectory, a before version and an after version and so this healthiness condition ensures the trajectory remains constant throughout. Monotonicity and idempotence of the healthiness conditions is proved by our automated relational calculus tactic.

With our healthiness conditions defined, we can proceed to define the operators. The basic operators, such as II and @ are elided here, and we instead focus on the continuous operators. We first define the two interval operators.

definition
$$hInt\ P = HCT(\$time' >_u \$time \wedge (\forall\ t \in \{\$time\ ..< \$time'\}_u \cdot P \bullet_u t))$$

Definition *hInt* corresponds to the interval operator $\lceil P \rceil$, and has an almost identical definition. In our mechanisation, an interval can be written as $\lceil P \rceil_H$ where P is a predicate with the time variable τ free.

definition
$$hDisInt\ P = (hInt\ P \wedge \pi_1(\$state') =_u \pi_1(\$state) \wedge \pi_2(\$state) =_u \$traj(\!|\$time|\!)_u$$
$$\wedge\ \pi_2(\$state') =_u lim_u(x \to \$time'^-)(\$traj(\!|x|\!)_u))$$

Our modified interval operator $\lceil\!| P |\!\rceil$, represented here by *hDisInt* conjoins the standard interval operator with predicates that ensure that discrete variables remain const and that continuous variable copies match the initial value in the trajectory, and the left limit of the trajectory at the end. Here π_n is a function that returns the *n*th element of a product, $f(\!|x|\!)_u$ represents function application, and $lim_u(x \to t^-)$ denotes the left-limit. This interval operator is written $\lceil\!| P |\!\rceil_H$, again with τ free.

Next we define the operators for ODEs and DAEs. The first step is to formally mechanise the notion of time derivatives ($\dot{x}$). Thus we define a predicate *hasDerivAt* that relates ODEs to solution functions using the lifting package [19].

type-synonym $'c\ ODE = real \times\ 'c \Rightarrow\ 'c$

lift-definition *hasDerivAt* ::
  $(real \Rightarrow\ 'c :: real\text{-}normed\text{-}vector) \Rightarrow\ 'c\ ODE \Rightarrow real \Rightarrow ('a,\ 'b)\ relation$
  (- *has*−*deriv* - *at* - [90, 0, 91] 90)
  is $\lambda\ \mathcal{F}\ \mathcal{F}'\ \tau\ A.\ (\mathcal{F}\ has\text{-}vector\text{-}derivative\ (\mathcal{F}'\ (\tau,\ \mathcal{F}\ \tau)))\ (at\ \tau\ within\ \{0..\})$.

An explicit system of ODEs ($'c\ ODE$) is encoded as a function $real \times\ 'c \Rightarrow\ 'c$, where the real is the time parameter, and $'c$ is a vector of real variables. We require that $'c$ be within the type class *real-normed-vector* of real vector spaces. Isabelle's Multivariate Analysis library contains a function *has-vector-derivative* that relates a solution function $\mathcal{F} : \mathbb{R} \to \mathbb{R}^n$ with its derivatives $\dot{\mathcal{F}} : \mathbb{R}^n$ at instant τ within a particular range. It represents the Fréchet derivative of differential equations in a vector space. We use this to define a construct $\mathcal{F}\ has−deriv\ \mathcal{F}'\ at\ \tau$ where $\mathcal{F}$ is a solution function, $\mathcal{F}'$ is the system of ODEs. This predicate is accompanied by a large number of rules that can be used to certify derivatives of polynomial functions. We now use these to encode operators for ODEs, DAEs, and ODEs under an initial condition.

definition $\langle \mathcal{F}' \rangle_H = (\exists\ \mathcal{F} \cdot \lceil\ \mathcal{F}\ has{-}deriv\ \mathcal{F}'\ at\ \tau \wedge \&con\alpha =_u \mathcal{F}(\!(\tau)\!)_u\ \rceil_H)$

definition $\langle \mathcal{F}'|B \rangle_H = (\langle \mathcal{F}' \rangle_H \wedge \lceil |B| \rceil_H)$

definition $\mathcal{I} \models \langle \mathcal{F}' \rangle_H = (\langle \mathcal{F}' \rangle_H \wedge \$traj(\!(\$time)\!)_u =_u \mathcal{I})$

We choose to implement ODEs and DAEs as separate constructs, as the definitions are simpler, though equivalent to those in the previous section. An ODE $\langle \mathcal{F}' \rangle_H$ specifies that a solution function $\mathcal{F}$ to the given ODE must exist and that at each point of the interval the values of all continuous variables ($con\alpha$) track this solution function. A DAE $\langle \mathcal{F}'|B \rangle_H$ is then simply an ODE constrained with the algebraic predicate throughout the interval. We also provide a representation of ODEs as explicit initial value problems by $\mathcal{I} \models \langle \mathcal{F}' \rangle_H$ where $\mathcal{I}$ gives initial values to all continuous variables.

Finally, we prove some key laws about our hybrid relational calculus. Firstly we show that sequential composition is *HCT* closed, which partly validates our healthiness conditions with respect to the standard relational calculus. This is proved by an apply-style Isabelle proof which is omitted.

> **theorem** *seq-r-HCT-closed*:
> **assumes** P *is HCT* **and** Q *is HCT*
> **shows** $(P\ ;;\ Q)$ *is HCT*
> **by** (*metis HCT-seq-r Healthy-def' assms(1) assms(2)*)

In order to demonstrate the use of ODEs in this framework, we take the ODE from the bouncing ball example, and show how its solution can be expressed as a refinement statement.

> **theorem** *gravity-ode-refine*:
> $((v_0, h_0)_u \models \langle \lambda\ (t, v, h).\ (-\ g,\ v) \rangle_H \wedge \$time =_u 0) \sqsubseteq$
> $(\lceil\ \&con\alpha =_u (v_0 - g{\cdot}\tau,\ v_0{\cdot}\tau - g{\cdot}(\tau{\cdot}\tau)\ /\ 2 + h_0)_u\ \rceil_H \wedge \$time =_u 0)$
> **by** (*rel-tac ; rule exI ; auto ; vderiv-tac*)

As in Example 1, we specify the ODE with two variables, v and h that will give the velocity and height about the ground of the ball. We refine this in the window $time = 0$ as it makes the solution simpler via an appropriate conjunction. Given initial conditions of v_0 and h_0 for the respective variables, solutions to the ODE equations are $v_0 - g{\cdot}\tau$ and $(v_0{\cdot}\tau - g{\cdot}\tau^2)/2 + h_0$, respectively. The solutions are proved correct in Isabelle automatically by application of our relational calculus tactic *rel-tac*, followed by existential introduction (*exI*) to introduce the ODE solution, application of the *auto* tactic, and then finally application of our own tactic vderiv-tac. This tactic recursively applies the set of introduction for differentiation in an effort to show that a given ODE is the derivative of a given solution. This example serves to demonstrate how a theorem prover can reason about differential equations in terms of their solution intervals making use of refinement and the Duration Calculus.

8 Modelica Semantics

In this section we give a semantics for flat Modelica whose models are given by a set of conditional differential, algebraic, and discrete equations. More specifically, we assume that a Modelica model consists of a set of dynamic variables x, algebraic variables y, and discrete variables q, and

- a set of $k \in \mathbb{N}_{>0}$ conditional DAEs, consisting of:
  - differential equations $\dot{x} = \mathcal{F}_i(x, y, q)$ for $i \in 1..k$;
  - algebraic equations $y = \mathcal{B}_i(x, y, q)$ for $i \in 1..k$;
  - boolean DAE guards $\mathcal{G}_i(x, y, q)$ for $i \in 1..k - 1$, that give the conditions under which the corresponding set of differential and algebraic equations is active in terms of the values of discrete and continuous variables at initialisation or the previous event. We assume that at least one set of equations is active at any time;
- a set of $l \in \mathbb{N}$ boolean event conditions $\mathcal{C}_i(x, y, q)$ for $i \in 1..l$, that trigger an event when changing value. These must be specified in terms of the core Modelica relational operators, namely $\leq$, $<$, $=$, and $\neq$;
- a set of $m \in \mathbb{N}$ conditional discrete equation blocks, consisting of:
  - n boolean discrete-event guards $\mathcal{H}_{i,j}(x, y, q, q_{pre})$ for $i \in 1..m, j \in 1..n$;
  - n discrete equations/algorithms $\mathcal{P}_{i,j}(x, y, q, q_{pre})$ for $i \in 1..m, j \in 1..n$.
  We assume the discrete equations are sorted into a suitable sequence.

Each conditional DAE describes a possible continuous behaviour using a collection of differential and algebraic equations. The particular behaviour to be executed is chosen based on the evaluation of the guards, which take as input the valuations of the discrete and continuous variables at the (re)start of the continuous evolution. The possible events that can occur are described by a collection of boolean event conditions, which act as guards that can stop the continuous evolution. Once one or more of these guards changes value an event is fired, and possible discrete behaviour is executed. Usually such guards are implemented in terms of a zero crossing function, though our semantics specifies them abstractly. The appropriate discrete behaviours are then chosen through a collection of discrete event guards, and the resulting behaviour by an appropriate discrete equation that may be specified by a suitable algorithm.

We give the semantics for such a Modelica model $\mathcal{M}$, which is shown in Fig. 3, in terms of four main definitions.

Init denotes the initialisation phase of a Modelica model, where initial values are assigned to the discrete and continuous variables. For now, we assume that initial values u, v, and w can be unambiguously assigned to each. Following initialisation, an infinite loop is entered representing the main body of behaviour.

DAE denotes the conditional system of differential and algebraic equations active during the continuous evolution of the model. It is represented by a conditional predicate that selects an appropriate set of differential and algebraic equations based on initial values of discrete and continuous variables.

Events denotes the event preemption condition, and is a disjunction of all possible event conditions ("relations" in Modelica terminology) in the Modelica model. In this way, the DAE remains active until one of the event conditions changes from its initial value, at which point it is preempted.

Finally, Discr describes possible discrete behaviour to be executed during event iteration; a finite event loop adapted from the pseudo code given on page

$$\mathcal{M} \;=\; \mathsf{Init} \;;\; (\mathsf{DAE}\,[\,\mathsf{Events}\,]\,\mathsf{Discr})^{\omega}$$

$$\mathsf{Init} \;=\; \underline{x}, \underline{y}, q := u, v, w$$

$$\mathsf{DAE} \;=\; \big\langle\, \underline{x} = \mathcal{F}_1(\underline{\dot{x}}, \underline{y}, q) \,\big|\, \mathcal{B}_1(\underline{x}, \underline{y}, q) \,\big\rangle \lhd \mathcal{G}_1 \rhd \cdots$$
$$\lhd \mathcal{G}_{n-1} \rhd \big\langle\, \underline{\dot{x}} = \mathcal{F}_n(\underline{x}, \underline{y}, q) \,\big|\, \mathcal{B}_n(\underline{x}, \underline{y}, q) \,\big\rangle$$

$$\mathsf{Events} \;=\; \bigvee_{i \in \{1..k\}} \mathcal{C}_i(\underline{x}, \underline{y}, q) \neq \mathcal{C}_i(x, y, q)$$

$$\mathsf{Discr} \;=\; \textbf{\textit{var}}\ q_{pre} \;\bullet$$
$$\quad\textbf{\textit{until}}\ q_{pre} = q\ \textbf{\textit{do}}$$
$$\qquad q_{pre} := q\ ;$$
$$\qquad \mathcal{P}_{1,1}(\underline{x}, \underline{y}, q, q_{pre}) \lhd \mathcal{H}_{1,1}(\underline{x}, \underline{y}, q, q_{pre}) \rhd \mathcal{P}_{1,2}(\underline{x}, \underline{y}, q, q_{pre}) \lhd \cdots\;;\;\cdots\;;$$
$$\qquad \mathcal{P}_{m,1}(\underline{x}, \underline{y}, q, q_{pre}) \lhd \mathcal{H}_{m,1}(\underline{x}, \underline{y}, q, q_{pre}) \rhd \mathcal{P}_{m,2}(\underline{x}, \underline{y}, q, q_{pre}) \lhd \cdots\;;$$
$$\quad\textbf{\textit{od}}$$

Fig. 3. Overall semantics of a Modelica model $\mathcal{M}$

263 of [22]. The initial value of all discrete variables is first copied by creation of a local variable q_{pre} that holds the initial value of q. Each conditional discrete equation is then evaluated, which may lead to updates to q, and then the procedure iterates. The event iteration terminates when no more updates to q are made: a fixed point is reached. In Modelica the existence of a fixed point is not guaranteed and event iteration can potentially lead to an infinite loop.

To illustrate, we use the bouncing ball Modelica example from Fig. 2. It has continuous variables representing the height of the ball above the ground h and the velocity of the ball v. For giving a semantics to this we convert the when expression to an if expression, so we need only consider semantics of the latter, using the conceptual mapping in Sect. 8.3.5.1 of [22], which will yield:

```
c = h<0;
if (c and not(pre(c))) then
   reinit(v, -0.8*pre(v));
end if;
```

An additional variable c of type Boolean is added, and assigned the condition of the when statement. The when equation itself is replaced by an if equation whose condition is that c is true now, and was not true previously – i.e. it has become true at the current instant. We can now give the semantics of this model.

Example 3. Bouncing ball semantics in hybrid relational calculus

$$h, v, c := 1, 0, false \; ;$$
$$(\langle\, \dot{\underline{v}} = -9.81; \; \dot{\underline{h}} = \underline{v}\, \rangle$$
$$[(\underline{h} < 0) \neq (h < 0)]$$
$$\textbf{\textit{var}}\; c_{pre} \bullet$$
$$\textbf{\textit{until}}\; (c_{pre} = c)\; \textbf{\textit{do}}$$
$$c_{pre} := c \; ; \; c := h < 0 \; ;$$
$$v := -0.8 \cdot v \; \lhd \; c \wedge \neg c_{pre} \; \rhd \; \mathbb{I}$$
$$\textbf{\textit{od}})^{\omega}$$

We assign initial values for the three variables, and assume that the condition c is false initially. The DAE is then activated and evolves until the valuation of the if guard $h < 0$ at time t is different from the initial value, that is $(\underline{h} < 0) \neq (h < 0)$. We note that $\underline{h}$ and h are two different variables: $\underline{h}$ denotes h at time t, whilst h denotes its value at the beginning of the present DAE evolution, so the inequality corresponds to the value of this boolean guard changing. At this point, the event iteration begins. We create a variable to denote the previous value of c, and then enter into the event loop. We then assign c to c_{pre}, and evaluate the discrete equations. First of all, we evaluate the new value of c, which is the event condition. Secondly, if c is true and different from its previous value, we also update v, otherwise we skip. The loop terminates once the value of c has stablised (which it has in the second iteration). Following this, we iterate the whole loop and restart the DAE with the new initial values.

This example serves to illustrate the behaviour of a Modelica model in the hybrid relational calculus. Our preliminary semantics considers a fragment of the event handling mechanism, excluding practical problems of initialization and numerical integration of DAEs. Present limitations include the separation of continuous and discrete equations during the event handling mechanism. More complete Modelica semantics require to solve a *mixed* system of the discrete and continuous equations during events. We will consider these in future iterations of this semantics, define a more complete translation, and apply it to more substantive examples.

9 Conclusions

We have presented a denotational semantics for the dynamical systems modelling language Modelica, in terms of a hybrid relational calculus that has been mechanised in Isabelle. The semantics elaborates the event iteration system, showing how continuous evolution transitions to discrete behaviour and vice-versa. Nevertheless, our translation is currently relatively informal and thus in future work we will define a comprehensive mapping from Modelica to hybrid relations, including its expression language and collection of imperative language constructs. We will also combine our theory of hybrid relations with timed reactive designs [13] to provide a rich semantic model providing termination, stability, and concurrency in the form of CSP.

This work supports the goals of a large EU project called INTO-CPS[8], which aims at building an integrated tool-chain for model based development of Cyber-Physical Systems. This tool-chain will support the integration of heterogeneous discrete and continuous system models through the Functional Mockup Interface [8] (FMI), a language that allows the composition of continuous time and discrete event models, and their concurrent simulation to support empirical evaluation. We will use our UTP theory of hybrid relations combined with timed reactive designs to develop a common semantic domain into which all these language can be mapped and verified.

We also plan to further experiment with theorem proving in Isabelle, for example through a mechanisation of Hybrid Hoare Logic [37]. As stated in Sect. 8, Modelica does not guarantee that event iteration terminates and so we could use such a prover, in the context of reactive designs, to verify termination.

References

1. Åkesson, J., Ekman, T., Hedin, G.: Implementation of a Modelica compiler using JastAdd attribute grammars. Sci. Comput. Program. **75**(1–2), 21–38 (2010). Special Issue on ETAPS 2006 and 2007 Workshops on Language Descriptions, Tools, and Applications (LDTA 2006 and 2007)
2. Bachmann, B., Aronsson, P., Fritzson, P.: Robust initialization of differential algebraic equation. In: 5th International Modelica Conference, Austria, September 2006
3. Blanchette, J.C., Bulwahn, L., Nipkow, T.: Automatic proof and disproof in Isabelle/HOL. In: Tinelli, C., Sofronie-Stokkermans, V. (eds.) FroCoS 2011. LNCS (LNAI), vol. 6989, pp. 12–27. Springer, Berlin (2011). doi:10.1007/978-3-642-24364-6_2
4. Cavalcanti, A., Woodcock, J.: A tutorial introduction to CSP in *unifying theories of programming*. In: Cavalcanti, A., Sampaio, A., Woodcock, J. (eds.) PSSE 2004. LNCS, vol. 3167, pp. 220–268. Springer, Berlin (2006). doi:10.1007/11889229_6
5. Feliachi, A., Gaudel, M.-C., Wolff, B.: Isabelle/*Circus*: a process specification and verification environment. In: Joshi, R., Müller, P., Podelski, A. (eds.) VSTTE 2012. LNCS, vol. 7152, pp. 243–260. Springer, Berlin (2012). doi:10.1007/978-3-642-27705-4_20
6. Fidge, C.J.: Modelling discrete behaviour in a continuous-time formalism. In: Araki, K., Galloway, A., Taguchi, K. (eds.) Proceedings of the 1st International Conference on Integrated on Integrated Formal Methods, pp. 170–188. Springer, Heidelberg (1999)
7. Fleuriot, J.D.: On the mechanization of real analysis in Isabelle/HOL. In: Aagaard, M., Harrison, J. (eds.) TPHOLs 2000. LNCS, vol. 1869, pp. 145–161. Springer, Berlin (2000). doi:10.1007/3-540-44659-1_10
8. FMI development group. Functional mock-up interface for model exchange and co-simulation, 2.0 (2014). https://www.fmi-standard.org
9. Foster, S., Miyazawa, A., Woodcock, J., Cavalcanti, A., Fitzgerald, J., Larsen, P.: An approach for managing semantic heterogeneity in systems of systems engineering. In: Proceedings of the 9th International Conference on Systems of Systems Engineering. IEEE (2014)

---

[8] *An Integrated Tool-chain for Model-based Design of Cyber-Physical Systems.* EU H2020 grant agreement 644047. http://into-cps.au.dk/.

10. Foster, S., Zeyda, F., Woodcock, J.: Isabelle/UTP: a mechanised theory engineering framework. In: Naumann, D. (ed.) UTP 2014. LNCS, vol. 8963, pp. 21–41. Springer, Cham (2015). doi:10.1007/978-3-319-14806-9_2

11. Harrison, J.: A HOL theory of euclidean space. In: Hurd, J., Melham, T. (eds.) TPHOLs 2005. LNCS, vol. 3603, pp. 114–129. Springer, Berlin (2005). doi:10.1007/11541868_8

12. Harwood, W., Cavalcanti, A., Woodcock, J.: A theory of pointers for the UTP. In: Fitzgerald, J.S., Haxthausen, A.E., Yenigun, H. (eds.) ICTAC 2008. LNCS, vol. 5160, pp. 141–155. Springer, Berlin (2008). doi:10.1007/978-3-540-85762-4_10

13. Hayes, I.J., Dunne, S.E., Meinicke, L.: Unifying theories of programming that distinguish nontermination and abort. In: Bolduc, C., Desharnais, J., Ktari, B. (eds.) MPC 2010. LNCS, vol. 6120, pp. 178–194. Springer, Berlin (2010). doi:10.1007/978-3-642-13321-3_12

14. He, J.: From CSP to hybrid systems. In: Roscoe, A.W. (ed.) A Classical Mind: Essays in Honour of C.A.R. Hoare, pp. 171–189. Prentice Hall (1994)

15. He, J.: HRML: a hybrid relational modelling language. In: IEEE International Conference on Software Quality, Reliability and Security, QRS 2015, August 2015

16. Henzinger, T.A.: The theory of hybrid automata, pp. 278–292. IEEE (1996)

17. Hoare, T.: Communicating Sequential Processes. Prentice-Hall, Englewood Cliffs (1985)

18. Hoare, T., He, J.: Unifying Theories of Programming. Prentice-Hall, Englewood Cliffs (1998)

19. Huffman, B., Kunčar, O.: Lifting and transfer: a modular design for quotients in Isabelle/HOL. In: Gonthier, G., Norrish, M. (eds.) CPP 2013. LNCS, vol. 8307, pp. 131–146. Springer, Cham (2013). doi:10.1007/978-3-319-03545-1_9

20. Kågedal, D., Fritzson, P.: Generating a Modelica compiler from natural semantics specifications. In: Proceedings of 1998 Summer Computer Simulation Conference, SCSC 1998 (1998)

21. Liu, J., Lv, J., Quan, Z., Zhan, N., Zhao, H., Zhou, C., Zou, L.: A calculus for hybrid CSP. In: Ueda, K. (ed.) APLAS 2010. LNCS, vol. 6461, pp. 1–15. Springer, Berlin (2010). doi:10.1007/978-3-642-17164-2_1

22. Modelica Association. Modelica - A Unified Object-Oriented Language for Systems Modeling - Version 3.3 Revision 1. Standard Specification, July 2014

23. Nipkow, T., Wenzel, M., Paulson, L.C. (eds.): Isabelle/HOL: A Proof Assistant for Higher-Order Logic. LNCS, vol. 2283. Springer, Berlin (2002)

24. Ochel, L.A., Bachmann, B.: Initialization of equation-based hybrid models within OpenModelica. In: 5th International Workshop on Equation-Based Object-Oriented Modeling Languages and Tools, Nottingham, UK, pp. 97–103, April 2013

25. Pantelides, C.: The consistent initialization of differential-algebraic systems. SIAM J. Sci. Stat. Comput. 9(2), 213–231 (1988)

26. Perna, J.I., Woodcock, J.: UTP semantics for handel-C. In: Butterfield, A. (ed.) UTP 2008. LNCS, vol. 5713, pp. 142–160. Springer, Berlin (2010). doi:10.1007/978-3-642-14521-6_9

27. Platzer, A.: Logical Analysis of Hybrid Systems. Springer, Heidelberg (2010)

28. Satabin, L., Colao, J., Andrieu, O., Pagano, B.: Towards a formalized Modelica subset. In: 11th International Modelica Conference, September 2015

29. Thiele, B., Knoll, A., Fritzson, P.: Towards qualifiable code generation from a clocked synchronous subset of modelica. Model. Identif. Control 36(1), 23–52 (2015)

30. Wei, K., Woodcock, J., Cavalcanti, A.: *Circus Time* with reactive designs. In: Wolff, B., Gaudel, M.-C., Feliachi, A. (eds.) UTP 2012. LNCS, vol. 7681, pp. 68–87. Springer, Berlin (2013). doi:10.1007/978-3-642-35705-3_3

31. Zhao, H., Yang, M., Zhan, N., Gu, B., Zou, L., Chen, Y.: Formal verification of a descent guidance control program of a lunar lander. In: Jones, C., Pihlajasaari, P., Sun, J. (eds.) FM 2014. LNCS, vol. 8442, pp. 733–748. Springer, Cham (2014). doi:10.1007/978-3-319-06410-9_49

32. Zhou, C., Hansen, M.R.: Chopping a point. In: Proceedings of 7th BCS-FACS Refinement Workshop. Springer, Heidelberg (1996)

33. Zhou, C., Hoare, C.A.R., Ravn, A.P.: A calculus of durations. Inf. Process. Lett. **40**(5), 269–276 (1991)

34. Chaochen, Z., Ji, W., Ravn, A.P.: A formal description of hybrid systems. In: Alur, R., Henzinger, T.A., Sontag, E.D. (eds.) HS 1995. LNCS, vol. 1066, pp. 511–530. Springer, Berlin (1996). doi:10.1007/BFb0020972

35. Chaochen, Z., Ravn, A.P., Hansen, M.R.: An extended duration calculus for hybrid real-time systems. In: Grossman, R.L., Nerode, A., Ravn, A.P., Rischel, H. (eds.) HS 1991–1992. LNCS, vol. 736, pp. 36–59. Springer, Berlin (1993). doi:10.1007/3-540-57318-6_23

36. Zhu, H., Yang, F., He, J.: Generating denotational semantics from algebraic semantics for event-driven system-level language. In: Qin, S. (ed.) UTP 2010. LNCS, vol. 6445, pp. 286–308. Springer, Berlin (2010). doi:10.1007/978-3-642-16690-7_15

37. Zou, L., Zhan, N., Wang, S., Fränzle, M.: Formal verification of simulink/stateflow diagrams. In: Finkbeiner, B., Pu, G., Zhang, L. (eds.) ATVA 2015. LNCS, vol. 9364, pp. 464–481. Springer, Cham (2015). doi:10.1007/978-3-319-24953-7_33

A Two-Way Path Between Formal and Informal Design of Embedded Systems

Mingshuai Chen[1], Anders P. Ravn[2], Shuling Wang[1], Mengfei Yang[3],
and Naijun Zhan[1(✉)]

[1] State Key Laboratory of Computer Science, Institute of Software,
Chinese Academy of Sciences, Beijing, China
{chenms,wangsl,znj}@ios.ac.cn
[2] Department of Computer Science, Aalborg University, Aalborg, Denmark
[3] Chinese Academy of Space Technology, Beijing, China

Abstract. It is well known that informal simulation-based design of embedded systems has a low initial cost and delivers early results; yet it cannot guarantee the correctness and reliability of the system to be developed. In contrast, the correctness and reliability of the system can be thoroughly investigated with formal design, but it requires a larger effort, which increases the development cost. Therefore, it is desirable for a designer to move between formal and informal design. This paper describes how to translate Hybrid CSP (HCSP) formal models into Simulink graphical models, so that the models can be simulated and tested using a MATLAB platform, thus avoiding expensive formal verification if the development is at a stage where it is considered unnecessary. Together with our previous work on encoding Simulink/Stateflow diagrams into HCSP, it provides a two-way path in the design of embedded systems, so that the designer can flexibly shift between formal and informal models. The translation from HCSP into Simulink diagrams is implemented as a fully automatic tool, and the correctness of the translation is justified using Unifying Theories of Programming (UTP).

Keywords: Simulink · HCSP · UTP · Verification · Hybrid systems

1 Introduction

Correct and efficient design of complex embedded systems is a grand challenge for computer science and control theory. Model-based design (MBD) is thought to be an effective solution. This approach begins with an abstract model of the system to be developed. Extensive analysis and verification of the abstract model are then performed so that errors can be identified and corrected at a very early stage. Then the higher-level abstract model is refined to step by step to more detailed models till a level where the system can be built with existing components or a few newly developed ones.

Many MBD approaches targeting embedded systems have been proposed and used in industry and academia. These approaches can be simulation-based informal ones such as Simulink/Stateflow [1,2], Modelica [3], SysML [4],

© Springer International Publishing AG 2017
J.P. Bowen and H. Zhu (Eds.): UTP 2016, LNCS 10134, pp. 65–92, 2017.
DOI: 10.1007/978-3-319-52228-9_4

MARTE [5], or they can be verification based like Metropolis [6], Ptolemy [7], hybrid automata [8], CHARON [9], HCSP [10,11], Differential Dynamic Logic [12], Hybrid Hoare Logic [13]. It is evident that informal design of embedded systems has a low initial cost and is intuitively appealing, because simulations give results early on, but it cannot fully guarantee the correctness and reliability of the system to be developed; in contrast, the correctness and reliability of the system can be thoroughly investigated with formal design, but the cost is higher and it requires specialized skills. Therefore, it is desirable to provide a two-way path between formal and informal approaches for a designer.

The first contribution of this paper is to provide one lane of this path. It takes a formal model and translates it automatically to a Simulink model. The other lane has been developed in previous work [14,15]. The translation from the formal to informal model presented here, is implemented as a fully automatic tool. Another contribution of this paper is to provide a justification of the correctness of the translation. To this end, we define a UTP semantics for Simulink and a UTP semantics for HCSP, and then establish a correspondence between the two. Due to lack of space, the implementation and a case study on a lunar lander have been omitted and can be found in [16].

1.1 Related Work

There has been a range of works on translating Simulink/Stateflow into modelling formalisms supported by analysis and verification tools. Mathworks itself released a tool named *Simulink Design Verifier* [17] (SDV) for formal analysis of Simulink/Stateflow models. However, currently, SDV can only be used to detect low-level errors such as integer overflow, dead logic, array access violation, division by zero, and so on, in blocks of a model, but not system-level properties of the complete model with the physical and environmental aspects taken into account.

Simulation-based verification [18] can be used to verify system-level properties in a bounded time, but cannot be applied for unbounded verification. Thus there is work on translating Simulink into other modelling formalisms, for which analysis and verification tools are developed. Tripakis *et al.* [19] presented an algorithm of translating discrete-time Simulink models to Lustre, a synchronous language developed with formal semantics and a number of tools for validation and analysis, and later extended the work by incorporating a subset of Stateflow [20]. Cavalcanti *et al.* [21] presented a semantics for discrete-time Simulink diagrams using Circus [22], a combination of Z and CSP. Meenakshi *et al.* [23] gave an algorithm that translates a subset of Simulink intothe input language of model checker NuSMV. Sifakis *et al.* proposed a translation into BIP in [24]. BIP [25] stands for Behaviour, Interaction and Priority, which is a component-based formal model for real-time concurrent systems. These works do not consider continuous time models of Simulink. This is considered in the follpwing works. Yang and Vyatkin [26] translate Simulink into Function Blocks. Zhou and Kumar investigated how to translate Simulink into *Input/Output Hybrid*

Automata [27], while the translation of both discrete and continuous time fragments of Simulink into *SpacEx Hybrid Automata* was considered in [28]. In [29], Chen *et al.* translates Simulink models to a real-time specification language Timed Interval Calculus (TIC). In this, continuous Simulink diagrams can be analyzed by a theorem prover. However, the translation is limited as it handles only continuous blocks whose outputs can be represented explicitly by a mathematical relation on inputs. In contrast, in [14] is a translation from Simulink into HCSP which handles all continuous blocks using the notion of differential equations and invariants.

Contract-based frameworks for Simulink are described in [30,31]. In [30], Simulink diagrams are represented by SDF graphs, and discrete-time blocks are specified by contracts with pre/post-conditions. Then sequential code is generated from the SDF graph, and the code is verified using traditional refinement-based techniques. In [31], Simulink blocks are annotated with rich types, then the SimCheck tool extracts verification conditions from the Simulink model and the annotations, and submits them to an SMT solver for verification. While in our approach, all Simulink/Stateflow models can be specified and verified using Hybrid Hoare Logic and its deductive verification techniques.

In [32], a compositional formal semantics built on predicate transformers was proposed for Simulink, based on which, a tool for verification of Simulink blocks was reported in [33], consisting of two components: a translator from Simulink hierarchical block diagrams into predicate transformers and an implementation of the theory of predicate transformers in Isabelle. The UTP semantics of Simulink/Stateflow defined here is quite similar to the one given in [32].

There have been several formal semantics defined for HCSP. In He's original work on HCSP [10], an algebraic semantics of HCSP was given. Subsequently, a Duration Calculus (DC) based semantics for HCSP was presented in [11]. These two original formal semantics of HCSP are very restrictive and incomplete, for example, it is unclear whether the set of algebraic rules defined in [10] is complete, and *super-dense computations* and recursion are not well handled in [11]. In [13,34–36], operational, axiomatic and DC-based denotational semantics for HCSP are proposed, and the relations among them are discussed. In this paper, we re-investigate the semantics of HCSP by defining its simulation semantics using Simulink and its UTP-based denotational semantics, and study the correspondence between the two semantics.

The rest of this paper introduces HCSP and Simulink in Sect. 2, Sect. 3 presents the translation from HCSP into Simulink. Section 4 presents a justification of the translation by proving consistency of the UTP semantics. A conclusion is in Sect. 5.

2   Preliminaries

HCSP [10,11,34] is a language for describing hybrid systems. It extends the well-known language of Communicating Sequential Processes (CSP) with timing constructs, interrupts, and differential equations for modelling continuous evolution. Data exchange among processes is confined to instantaneous synchronous communication, avoiding shared variables between parallel processes.

Simulink [1] is an interactive platform for modelling, simulating and analyzing multidomain dynamic and embedded systems. It provides a graphical block diagramming tool and a customizable set of block libraries for building executable models.

2.1 Hybrid CSP (HCSP)

The syntax of HCSP processes is given below:

$$P ::= \text{skip} \mid x := e \mid ch?x \mid ch!e \mid P;Q \mid B \to P \mid P \sqcup Q \mid P^*$$
$$\mid \langle F(\dot{s}, s) = 0 \& B \rangle \mid \langle F(\dot{s}, s) = 0 \& B \rangle \trianglerighteq \|_{i \in I}(io_i \to Q_i)$$
$$S ::= P \mid S \| S$$

Here x and s stand for variables, B and e are conventional Boolean and arithmetic expressions. P, Q, Q_i are sequential processes; and io_i stands for a communication event, which is either $ch?x$ or $ch!e$, and ch for a channel name. A system S is either a sequential process, or a parallel composition of several sequential processes.

The processes taken from CSP, skip, $x := e$ (assignment), $ch?x$ (input), $ch!e$ (output), $P;Q$ (sequential composition), $B \to P$ (conditional statement), P^* (repetition), $P \sqcup Q$ (internal choice), and $S\|S$ (parallel composition) have their standard meaning.

The evolution statement is $\langle F(\dot{s}, s) = 0 \& B \rangle$, where s represents a vector of real variables and $\dot{s}$ the first-order time derivative of s. It forces s to evolve according to the differential equations defined by the functional F as long as B holds, and it terminates immediately when B becomes false.

The process $\langle F(\dot{s}, s) = 0 \& B \rangle \trianglerighteq \|_{i \in I}(io_i \to Q_i)$ behaves like $\langle F(\dot{s}, s) = 0 \& B \rangle$, except that the evolution is preempted as soon as one of the communications io_i occurs. That is followed by the respective Q_i. However, if the evolution statement terminates before a communication occurs, then the process terminates immediately.

2.2 Simulink

A Simulink model contains a set of blocks, subsystems, and wires, where blocks and subsystems cooperate by setting values on the wires between them. An elementary block gets input signals and computes the output signals. However, to make Simulink more useful, almost every block in Simulink contains some user-defined parameters to alter its functionality. One typical parameter is *sample time* which defines how frequently the computation is. done. Two special values, 0 and -1, may be set for sample time, where the sample time 0 indicates that the block is used for simulating the physical environment and hence computes continuously, and -1 signifies that the sample time of the block is not set, it will be determined by the sample times of the in-going wires to the block. Thus,

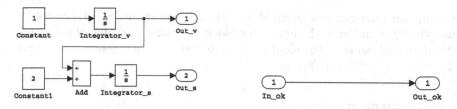

Fig. 1. $\dot{v} = 1, \dot{s} = v + 2$ **Fig. 2.** skip statement

blocks are classified into two categories, i.e. *continuous* and *discrete*, according to their sample times.

Blocks and subsystems in a Simulink model receive inputs and compute outputs in parallel, and wires specify the data flow between blocks and subsystems. Computation in a block takes no time and the output is delivered immediately to its receiver.

As a convention, in the sequel, when describing Simulink diagrams, we use x to stand for the input signal on in-port In_x, x' for the output signal on out-port Out_x, possibly with a subscript to indicate which subsystem the signal belongs to. For instance, x'_P indicates an output signal on Out_x inside a subsystem P.

3 From HCSP to Simulink

The translation from HCSP processes into graphical Simulink models starts from the most basic ingredients, i.e. expressions, to primitive statements and then is followed by compositional components.

3.1 Expressions

Arithmetic expressions in HCSP are translated to a normal subsystem in Simulink. A variable x is encoded into an input block of the subsystem, a constant c into a constant block with corresponding value, and parentheses determine priority of the computation. As for the operations over reals, a sequence of $+$ and $-$ (or $*$ and $/$) is shrunk into a sum (or product) block with multiple input signals in Simulink. In the example for assignment in Fig. 3 is included the Simulink subsystem for the expression $x + y * z$. *Boolean expressions* are translated similarly.

3.2 Differential Equations

The syntax of differential equations in HCSP is $F \triangleq \dot{s} = e \mid F, F$, where s stands for a continuous variable, $\dot{s}$ is the time derivative of s, and F, F indicates a group of differential equations that evolve simultaneously over time.

Each single differential equation is encoded into a continuous integrator block with an input signal of the value of e and an output signal of s; equations in the same group are a normal subsystem in Simulink. For example, $\dot{v} = 1, \dot{s} = v + 2$, becomes the block in Fig. 1, the integrator block of s takes the value of $v + 2$ and an internal initial value s_0 to calculate the integral and then generate a signal of s, i.e. $s(t) = \int_{t_0}^{t} (v(t) + 2)dt + s_0$.

3.3 skip Statement

In HCSP, skip terminates immediately with no effect on the process, and thus there is intuitively no need to draw anything in Simulink diagrams. However, blocks and subsystems in a Simulink model are running inherently in parallel, but processes in HCSP can be executed sequentially, thus we need a mechanism to specify sequential execution in a Simulink diagram. Inspired by UTP [37], we introduce Boolean signals ok and ok' into each subsystem to represent initiation and termination. Whenever ok' is false, the process has not terminated and the final values of the process variables are unobservable. Similarly, when ok is false, the process has not started and even the initial values are unobservable. These conventions permit translation of sequential composition. Both ok and ok' are local to each HCSP process, and they never occur in expressions.

In a Simulink subsystem ok and ok' are given by an in-port In_ok and an out-port Out_ok respectively. Since skip does nothing and terminates instantly, the subsystem for skip in Simulink in Fig. 2 has $ok' = ok$, indicating that whenever skip starts, it terminates immediately without any effect.

3.4 Assignment

Figure 3 illustrates the subsystem in Simulink with an example of assignment $x := x + y * z$, where for ease of understanding, we unpack the subsystem of arithmetic expression e. The output signals are computed by the following equations:

$$ok' = ok \qquad x' = \begin{cases} x'_{new}, & ok \wedge \neg d(ok) \\ x, & \neg ok \wedge \neg d(ok) \\ d(x'), & d(ok) \end{cases} \qquad \mathbf{u'} = \mathbf{u}$$

Here, $\mathbf{u}$ stands for the set of signals that are not processed by the current subsystem, i.e. y and z in this example. x'_{new} represents the newly computed signal, here produced by block Add1. Moreover, we use $d(x)$ to denote the value of x in the previous period. It is kept through a unit delay block that holds its input for one period of the sample time.

3.5 Continuous Evolution

The Simulink diagram translated from an evolution in HCSP is shown in Fig. 4, where the group of differential equations $\mathcal{F}$ and the Boolean condition B are encapsulated into a single subsystem respectively. The enabled subsystem F

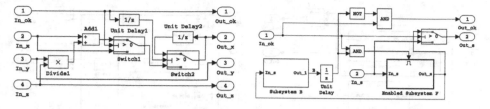

Fig. 3. $x := x + y * z$ **Fig. 4.** Continuous evolution

contains a set of integrator blocks corresponding to the vector s of continuous variables, and executes continuously whenever the value of the input signal, abbreviated as en, on the enable-port is positive. Intuitively, subsystem B guards the evolution of subsystem F by taking the output signals of F as its inputs, i.e. $s_B = s'_F$, and partially controlling the enable signal of F via its output Boolean signal, denoted by B. As a consequence, an algebraic loop occurs between subsystem B and F which is not allowed in Simulink, the simple solution is to introduce a unit delay block with an initial value 1 inserted after subsystem B. Thus the boundary condition is evaluated after completion of an integrator step. Formally, given inputs, the output signals are computed by the following equations:

$$en = ok \wedge d(B) \qquad ok' = ok \wedge \neg d(B) \qquad s' = \begin{cases} s'_F, & ok \\ s, & \neg ok \end{cases}$$

3.6 Conditional Statement

Figure 5 illustrates the translation from a conditional statement of HCSP into a Simulink diagram. In most cases, subsystem B and P share the same group of input signals x, and for those distinct input signals, we add corresponding inports for B or P, which is not presented in Fig. 5. Accordingly, the output signals are computed according to

$$ok_P = ok \wedge B \qquad ok' = \begin{cases} ok'_P, & B \\ ok, & \neg B \end{cases} \qquad x' = x'_P.$$

3.7 Internal Choice

Given an internal choice $P \sqcup Q$, we use $outSigs(\mathrm{P})$ and $outSigs(\mathrm{Q})$ to represent the set of output signals (including ok') of subsystem P and Q respectively, and encode the random choice according to the following two situations.

– For each $x' \in outSigs(\mathrm{P}) \cap outSigs(\mathrm{Q})$, we introduce a switch block in Simulink diagrams for signal routing, which switches x' between x'_P from P and x'_Q from Q based on the value of the second input.
– For each $y' \in outSigs(\mathrm{P}) - outSigs(\mathrm{Q})$, we directly output the signal y'_P from P as the final value of y', because in case that P is not chosen by the system, y' stays unchanged. For each $z' \in outSigs(\mathrm{Q}) - outSigs(\mathrm{P})$, analogously.

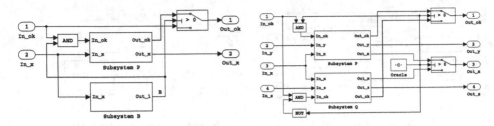

Fig. 5. Conditional statement   **Fig. 6.** Internal choice

Figure 6 illustrates a pattern to implement the above two cases. In order to guarantee that only one process in the internal choice is switched on, every switch block here needs to share exactly the same *switching condition*. As shown in Fig. 6, the two switch blocks share a common criteria (> 0) for passing first input as well as an identical second input signal, abbreviated as *Ran*, generated by an *oracle* that provides a non-deterministic signal[1]. The computation of signal *ok* and *ok'* can be formalized as

$$\begin{cases} ok_P = ok \wedge Ran \\ ok_Q = ok \wedge \neg Ran \end{cases} \qquad ok' = \begin{cases} ok'_P, Ran \\ ok'_Q, \neg Ran \end{cases}$$

3.8   Sequential Composition

An essential work in translating sequential composition into Simulink models, is to construct the initiation and termination of a process, which has already been done by introducing *ok* and *ok'* signals in connection with the *skip* process.

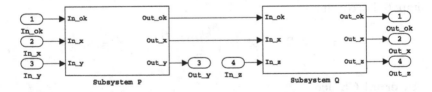

Fig. 7. Sequential composition

Figure 7 illustrates a straightforward encoding of sequential composition into Simulink diagrams. For exclusive signals y and z, we draw corresponding ports independently for subsystem P and Q. The set of common signals x processed by

---

[1] An oracle that interprets non-determinism is none of the blocks in Simulink library, inasmuch as the random block provided by Simulink generates pseudo random numbers, which is in itself deterministic.

both P and Q is linked sequentially from P to Q, and the same happens for ok and ok'.

$$okP = ok \quad okQ = ok'_P \quad ok' = ok'_Q \qquad x_P = x \quad x_Q = x'_P \quad x' = x'_Q$$

3.9 Repetition

The basic idea in encoding repetition is to link the outputs of subsystem P back into its in-ports, and we need to specify a finite random number N to control the number of times that P executes.

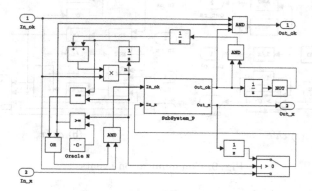

Fig. 8. Repetition

The integrated pattern to encode repetition p^* into Simulink diagrams is elaborated in Fig. 8. Here, a unit delay block with an initial value of 0 is introduced to break the algebraic loop that occurs when we link the outputs of P back. Besides, we introduce an oracle carrying a non-negative random number N to specify the number of repetitions of subsystem P. The update of variables is formulated as the following equations:

$$n = ok \times (d(n) + d(ok'_P \wedge \neg d(ok'_P))) \qquad ok' = ok \wedge ok'_P \wedge (n \geq N)$$

$$okP = ok \wedge (n == d(n) \vee n \geq N) \qquad x_P = \begin{cases} d(x'_P), n > 0 \\ x, \quad n == 0 \end{cases}$$

3.10 Communication Events

For each communication event, either a *sender* ($ch!e$) or a *receiver* ($ch?x$), we construct a subsystem in Simulink to deliver the message along ch for the matching pair of events. In order to synchronise the interaction, we introduce another pair of Boolean signals re and re' (re is short for ready) into each subsystem that corresponds to a communication event. re indicates whether the matching event is ready for the communication, while re' indicates whether the event itself is ready for the communication.

A communication along channel ch takes place as soon as both re_{ch} and re'_{ch} are true, then both the sending and the receiving parties are ready, otherwise one or both sides must wait. Additionally, re and re' are local signals, which never occur in the process statements. Furthermore, re and re' in a Simulink subsystem are constructed as an in-port signal named In_re and an out-port signal named Out_re respectively. Figure 9 illustrates the Simulink diagrams that interpret communication events, which can be elaborated in the following two parts.

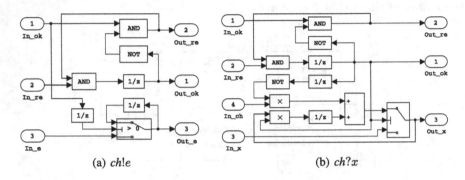

(a) $ch!e$ (b) $ch?x$

Fig. 9. Communication events

– For a sender $ch!e$, the output signals are computed according to

$$re' = ok \wedge \neg ok' \quad ok' = f(d(re \wedge re')) \quad e' = \begin{cases} e, & \neg d(ok) \\ d(e'), & d(ok) \end{cases},$$

where the *keep* pattern $f(s(t)) = ok(t) \wedge (s(t) \vee f(s(t-1)))$ for $t > cnow$, with $f(s(t)) = 0$ for $t \in [cnow, cnow+1)$, here $cnow$ is the current time. This is to keep ok' true since the communication is finished, i.e., since both re and re' turn true.

– For a receiver $ch?x$, the output signals are computed according to

$$re' = ok \wedge \neg ok' \quad ok' = f(d(re \wedge re'))$$
$$x' = \begin{cases} x, & \text{if } \neg ok' \\ \neg d(ok') \times ch + d(ok') \times d(x'), & \text{otherwise} \end{cases}$$

3.11 Parallel

For $P \| Q$, we consider the following two cases:

Without communications. This is a trivial case that we draw a subsystem encapsulating the two subsystems in terms of P and Q, but without any wires (except those carrying ok, ok') between the two subsystems, as shared variables are not allowed in HCSP. Specifically, we set $ok_P = ok_Q = ok$, and $ok' = ok'_P \wedge ok'_Q$.

With communications. As for a parallel process $P\|Q$ with inter-communications along a set of common channels $comChan(P,Q)$, we draw a subsystem containing the subsystems corresponding to P and Q, as well as some additional wires to bind all channels in $comChan(P,Q)$ and deliver messages along them.

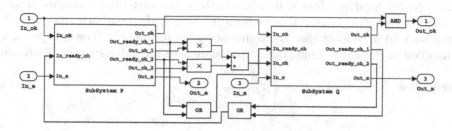

Fig. 10. Parallel $e := 0; ch!e; < \dot{e} = 1 \& e < 2 >; ch!e \| x := 3; ch?x; ch?x$

We elaborate the above idea by showing a Simulink diagram corresponding to a parallel process in Fig. 10, where the signals relevant to communications are attached with subscripts to specify the name of the common channel and the distinctive events corresponding to the same channel. Suppose that there are m and n events relevant to ch in subsystem P and Q respectively, then the computation in Fig. 10 is done by

$$ok_P = ok_Q = ok \quad ok' = ok'_P \wedge ok'_Q \quad re_{ch\_P} = \bigvee_{i=1}^{n} re'_{ch\_i\_Q} \quad re_{ch\_Q} = \bigvee_{j=1}^{m} re'_{ch\_j\_P}$$

indicating that the two subsystems in parallel are activated simultaneously when the system starts, and the parallel process terminates when both P and Q terminate. Furthermore, the channel ch on one side claims ready to the other side if either of its involved events is ready, which means that the communication events on different parties of a common channel are matched dynamically during the execution. Moreover, the value that Q receives along channel ch is computed as $ch_Q = \sum_{j=1}^{m} re'_{ch\_j\_P} \times ch'_{j\_P}$.

3.12 External Choice by Communications

As a subcomponent of interruption in HCSP, the external choice $[]_{i \in I}(io_i \rightarrow Q_i)$ waits until one of the communications io_i takes place, and then it is followed by the respective Q_i, where I is a non-empty finite set of indices, and $\{io_i\}_{i \in I}$ are communication events, i.e. either $ch!e$ or $ch?x$. In addition, if more than one among $\{io_i\}_{i \in I}$ are ready simultaneously, only one of them executes, this is determined randomly by the system. Thus, if the matching side of every io_i involved is ready for communication, then the external choice degenerates to internal choice. Besides, the syntax $(io_i \rightarrow Q_i)$ actually indicates a sequential composition $(io_i \rightarrow \text{skip} ; Q_i)$, to which the translation approach already has been introduced above.

Taking $P \parallel R$ as an example, where $P \hat{=} io_1; Q_1$ and $R \hat{=} io_2; Q_2$, then the ok signal of P can be computed by $ok_P = f(ok \wedge re_P \wedge (\neg re_R \vee (Ran < 0)))$. This means that when the external choice starts $(ok = 1)$ and the matching event of io_1 is ready $(re_P = 1)$, P is chosen to execute if either the matching event of io_2 is not ready $(re_R = 0)$, or the random number Ran, where $Ran \in [-1, 1)$, occurs to be negative $(Ran < 0)$ when both of the matching event are ready. A *keep* pattern $f(s)$ is used here to keep the signal ok_P true, otherwise it may jump back to false after that the communication terminates. The subsystem R is handled analogously. Thus, the output signals of the subsystem of $P \parallel R$ are given by $ok' = ok'_P \vee ok'_R$, $x' = \begin{cases} x'_P, \, ok'_P \\ x'_R, \, ok'_R \\ x, \quad \neg ok'_P \wedge \neg ok'_R \end{cases}$.

3.13   Interruption

Obviously, $\langle F(\dot{s}, s) = 0 \& B \rangle \trianglerighteq [\![_{i \in I}(io_i \to Q_i)$ is equivalent to $\langle F(\dot{s}, s) = 0 \& (B \wedge \neg re'_R) \rangle; re'_R \to [\![_{i \in I}(io_i \to Q_i)$, where $re'_R = f\left(\bigvee_{i \in I} re'_{oi_i}\right)$, and the translation rules can be composed in a semantic-preserving way (see Sect. 4). Hence, translating an interruption into a Simulink diagram becomes a composition of translating various components that have been illustrated in previous subsections.

4   Correctness of the Translation

In this section, we define UTP semantics both for HCSP constructs and the corresponding Simulink diagrams; proving the consistency of the two semantics is then a justification of the correctness of the translation from HCSP processes to Simulink diagrams.

UTP is a relational calculus based on first-order logic, which is intended for unifying different programming paradigms. In UTP, a *sequential program* (possibly nondeterministic) is represented by a *design* $D = (\alpha, P)$, where α denotes the set of state variables (called observables). Each state variable comes in an unprimed and a primed version, denoting respectively the pre- and the post-state value of the execution of the program. In addition to the program variables and their primed versions such as x and x', the set of observables includes two designated Boolean variables, ok and ok', denoting termination and stability of the program, respectively. P stands for the construct, $p(x) \vdash R(x, x')$, which is defined as

$$(ok \wedge p(x)) \Rightarrow (ok' \wedge R(x, x')).$$

It means that if the program is activated in a stable state, ok, where the *precondition* $p(x)$ holds, the execution will terminate, ok', in a state where the *postcondition* R holds; thus the post-state x' and the initial state x are related by relation R. We use *pre.D* and *post.D* to denote the pre- and post-conditions of D, respectively. If $p(x)$ is *true*, then P is shortened as $\vdash R(x, x')$.

Refinement

Let $D_1 = (\alpha, P_1)$ and $D_2 = (\alpha, P_2)$ be two designs with the same alphabet. D_2 is a *refinement* of D_1, denoted by $D_1 \sqsubseteq D_2$, if $\forall x, x', ok, ok'. (P_2 \Rightarrow P_1)$. Aslo, let $D_1 = (\alpha_1, P_1)$ and $D_2 = (\alpha_2, P_2)$ be two designs with possible different alphabets $\alpha_1 = \{x, x'\}$ and $\alpha_2 = \{y, y'\}$. D_2 is a *data refinement* of D_1 over $\alpha_1 \times \alpha_2$, denoted by $D_1 \sqsubseteq_d D_2$, if there is a relation $\rho(y, x')$ s.t. $\rho(y, x'); D_1 \sqsubseteq D_2; \rho(y, x')$.

In UTP the domain of designs forms a complete lattice with the refinement partial order, and *true* corresponding to **abort** (*false* corresponding to **miracle**) is the smallest (largest) element of the lattice. Furthermore, this lattice is closed under the classical programming constructs. These fundamental mathematical properties ensure that the domain of designs is a proper semantic domain for sequential programming languages.

Concurrent and Reactive Designs

Semantics of *concurrent and reactive programs* is defined by the notion of *reactive designs* with an additional Boolean observable *wait* that denotes suspension of a program. A design P is a *reactive design* if it is a fixed point of $\mathcal{H}'$, i.e. $\mathcal{H}'(P) = P$, where

$$\mathcal{H}'(p \vdash R) \widehat{=} (\vdash \wedge_{x \in \alpha(P)} x' = x \wedge wait' = wait) \lhd wait \rhd (p \vdash R). \tag{1}$$

$P_1 \lhd b \rhd P_2$ is a conditional statement, which means if b holds then P_1 else P_2, where b is a Boolean expression and P_1 and P_2 are designs. Informally, Eq. (1) says that if a reactive system (a reactive design) waits for a response from the environment (i.e., *wait* holds), it will keep waiting and do nothing (i.e., keep program variables unchanged), otherwise its function $(p \vdash R)$ will be executed.

Adaptation to Dynamical Systems

Obviously, hybrid systems are concurrent and reactive systems, so the UTP semantics of a hybrid system should satisfy the UTP *healthiness condition*. On the other hand, hybrid systems show some additional features, like real-time and the mixture of discrete and continuous dynamics. For specifying these additional features, we have to extend the notion of *reactive design* in UTP to admit function variables, and quantifications over functions, as in a real-time setting, program variables and channels are interpreted as functions over time. For specifying locality, higher-order quantifications are inevitable. So, UTP will become higher-order, rather than first-order. In addition, the derivative of a variable is allowed in a predicate. Therefore, strictly speaking, we extend the relational calculus of UTP to the combined theory of ordinary differential equations and timed traces with higher-order quantification.

In order to deal with real-time, a system variable *now* is introduced, which stands for the starting time. Correspondingly, *now'* stands for the ending time of a process.

Another point is that synchronization can only block discrete dynamics and keep discrete variable unchanged, it cannot block the evolution of continuous dynamics; time does not stop. So, given a hybrid system S, say $p \vdash P$, with continuous variables $\mathbf{s}$ and discrete variables $\mathbf{x}$, whose continuous dynamics is modeled as $\langle F(\dot{\mathbf{s}}, \mathbf{s}) = 0 \& B \rangle$, written $S_C{}^2$, then the healthiness condition of reactive designs should be changed to

$$\mathcal{H}(S) = S, \text{ where} \tag{2}$$

$$\mathcal{H}(S) \,\widehat{=}\, (\vdash \mathbf{x}' = \mathbf{x} \wedge wait' = wait \wedge S_C) \lhd wait \rhd S. \tag{3}$$

A design that meets the healthiness condition (2) is called a *hybrid design*. For simplicity, we will denote the left side of $wait$ in Eq. (3) by Π_H in the sequel.

For convenience, for each channel ch, we introduce two Boolean functions over time $ch!$ and $ch?$. $ch!(t)$ means that ch is ready for sending at time t, similarly, $ch?(t)$ means that ch is ready for receiving at time t. In addition, $Periodic(ch^*, st)$ denotes $\forall n \in \mathbb{N}. \; t = n * st \Rightarrow ch^*(t)$, which means that the communication event ch^* is ready periodically with period st. Also, *maximal synchronization* semantics is adopted, i.e.,

$$\forall t \geq 0. \; (ch?(t) \wedge ch!(t)) \Rightarrow (\neg ch?'(t) \wedge \neg ch!'(t)), \tag{4}$$

which means that when a synchronization is ready, it takes place immediately.

4.1   UTP Semantics for Simulink

For each Simulink construct C, the observables of C include the inputs in, outputs out, the user defined parameters, and some auxiliary variables that are introduced for defining the semantics. Some output(s) may be also input(s), i.e. $out_i = in'_j$, but we will uniformly use out_i instead of in'_j as output in the semantics. Also, we use $cnow$ to denote the current time. Now the semantics is a predicate denoted by $[\![C]\!]$.

Blocks. As pointed out in [38], it is natural to interpret each block of a Simulink diagram as a predicate relating its inputs to the outputs. The behavior of a block can be divided into a set of sub-behaviors, each guarded by a condition. Moreover, these guards are exclusive and complete, i.e., the conjunction of any two of them is unsatisfiable and the disjunction of all of them is valid. So, each sub-behavior can be further specified as a predicate over input and output signals. Additionally, for each discrete block (diagram), it is assumed that its input signals from outside are available at each sampling point. So, it can be represented by a UTP formula of the form:

$$[\![B(ps, in, out)]\!]$$

$$\widehat{=} \mathcal{H}(Ass \vdash out(0) = ps.init \wedge \bigwedge_{k=1}^{m} (B_k(ps, in) \Rightarrow P_k(ps, in, out))), \tag{5}$$

---

^{2} We always assume time evolution is modeled in S_C, i.e., it contains $\dot{now} = 1$.

which means that in case the environment satisfies Ass (the *precondition*), the behaviour of a block is specified by the formula at the right side of $\vdash$ (the *postcondition*). We use ps to denote a family of user-set parameters that may change the functionality of the block. As explained previously, $\bigvee_{k=1}^{m} B_k(ps, in)$, and $\neg(B_i(ps, in) \wedge B_j(ps, in))$ for any $i \neq j$, always hold.

Thus the UTP semantics of a continuous block has the following form:

$$\llbracket CB(ps, in, out) \rrbracket \,\,\hat{=}\,\, \mathcal{H}(in! \vdash out(0) = ps.init \,\wedge$$
$$\left(\left(\begin{matrix} B_1(in, ps) \Rightarrow F_1(\dot{out}, out, in, ps) = 0 \wedge \cdots \wedge \\ B_m(in, ps) \Rightarrow F_m(\dot{out}, out, in, ps) = 0 \end{matrix} \right) \wedge out!)),$$

where $F_i(\dot{out}, out, in, ps) = 0$ models the continuous evolution if B_i holds. In this case, $wait \hat{=} \neg out?$, which means that the continuous evolution will be interrupted by outputting to the environment. Thus, Eq. (2) holds with the maximal synchronization assumption in Eq. (4).

Correspondingly, the UTP semantics of a discrete block is

$$\llbracket DB(ps, in, out) \rrbracket \,\,\hat{=}\,\, \mathcal{H}(\text{Periodic}(in!, ps.st) \wedge \text{Periodic}(out?, ps.st) \vdash out(0) = ps.init \,\wedge$$
$$\text{Periodic}(out!, ps.st) \wedge (\exists n \in \mathbb{N}. \,\, cnow = n * st) \Rightarrow$$
$$\left(\begin{matrix} B_1(in, ps) \Rightarrow \llbracket P_{comp_1}(in, out, ps) \rrbracket \wedge \cdots \wedge \\ B_m(in, ps) \Rightarrow \llbracket P_{comp_m}(in, out, ps) \rrbracket \end{matrix} \right)),$$

where $\llbracket P_{comp_i}(in, out, ps) \rrbracket$ stands for the UTP semantics of the i-th discrete computation, which can be obtained in a standard way (see [37]). The precondition says that the environment should periodically input to and output from the block. In this case, $wait$ is set as $\neg \exists n \in \mathbb{N}. \,\, cnow = n * st$ and its continuous is $\dot{cnow} = 1$, meaning that the block keeps waiting (idle) except for the periodic points at which discrete jumps happen.

Example 1. As an illustration, we show how to concretize the UTP semantics for some basic Simulink blocks including Constant, Divide, Not, Or, Relational, Switch, Delay and Integrator. We treat Constant and Delay as continuous blocks, although they can also be treated as discrete blocks in a similar way.

A Constant block generates a scalar constant value:

$$\llbracket \text{Constant}(ps.c, out) \rrbracket \hat{=} \mathcal{H}(\vdash out(0) = c \wedge \dot{out} = 0 \wedge out!).$$

The design inside $\mathcal{H}$ is equivalent to $\vdash out = c \wedge out!$, which is $\vdash out(cnow) = c \wedge out!(cnow)$. Analogous remarks apply for the following.

Similarly, the UTP semantics for the Divide block is as follows:

$$\llbracket \text{Divide}(ps.I, ps.\{sn_i\}_{i \in I}, \{in_i\}_{i \in I}, out) \rrbracket$$
$$\hat{=} \mathcal{H}(\wedge_{i \in I}\text{Periodic}(in_i!, ps.st) \wedge \text{Periodic}(out?, ps.st) \vdash \text{Periodic}(out!, ps.st) \,\wedge$$
$$((\exists n \in \mathbb{N}. \,\, cnow = n * ps.st) \Rightarrow out = \prod_{i \in I} sin_i) \,\wedge$$
$$(sn_i =' *' \Rightarrow sin_i = in_i) \wedge (sn_i =' /' \Rightarrow sin_i = 1/in_i)).$$

The logical operator blocks $\mathtt{Not}$ and $\mathtt{Or}$ respectively perform the specified logical operations on their inputs, whose UTP semantics are given by

$$[\![\mathtt{Not}(in, out)]\!] \cong \mathcal{H}(\mathrm{Periodic}(in!, ps.st) \wedge \mathrm{Periodic}(out?, ps.st) \vdash \mathrm{Periodic}(out!, ps.st) \wedge$$
$$\exists n \in \mathbb{N}. \ cnow = n * ps.st \Rightarrow out = \neg in),$$

$$[\![\mathtt{Or}(ps, \{in_i\}_{i \in I}, out)]\!]$$
$$\cong \mathcal{H}(\wedge_{i \in I}\mathrm{Periodic}(in_i!, ps.st) \wedge \mathrm{Periodic}(out?, ps.st) \vdash \mathrm{Periodic}(out!, ps.st) \wedge$$
$$\exists n \in \mathbb{N}. \ cnow = n * ps.st \Rightarrow out = \bigvee_{i \in I} in_i),$$

The $\mathtt{Relational}$ operator block compares two inputs using the relational operator parameter $ps.op$, and outputs either 1 (*true*) or 0 (*false*); its UTP semantics is given by

$$[\![\mathtt{Relational}(ps.op, in_1, in_2, out)]\!]$$
$$\cong \mathcal{H}(\mathrm{Periodic}(in_1!, ps.st) \wedge \mathrm{Periodic}(in_2!, ps.st) \wedge \mathrm{Periodic}(out?, ps.st) \vdash$$
$$\mathrm{Periodic}(out!, ps.st) \wedge \exists n \in \mathbb{N}. \ cnow = n * ps.st \Rightarrow out = ps.op(in_1, in_2)).$$

The $\mathtt{Switch}$ block passes through the first input or the third input based on the value of the second input, thus its UTP semantics is:

$$[\![\mathtt{Switch}(ps, in_1, in_2, in_3, out)]\!]$$
$$\cong \mathcal{H}(\wedge_{i=1}^{3}\mathrm{Periodic}(in_i!, ps.st) \wedge \mathrm{Periodic}(out?, ps.st) \vdash \mathrm{Periodic}(out!, ps.st) \wedge$$
$$(\exists n \in \mathbb{N}. \ cnow = n * ps.st) \Rightarrow \left(\begin{array}{l} ps.op(in_2, ps.c) \Rightarrow out = in_1 \wedge \\ \neg ps.op(in_2, ps.c) \Rightarrow out = in_3 \end{array} \right)).$$

A $\mathtt{Delay}$ block holds and delays its input by one sample period, therefore its UTP semantics is:

$$[\![\mathtt{Delay}(ps, in, out)]\!] \cong \mathcal{H}(in! \vdash \left(\begin{array}{l} cnow < ps.st \Rightarrow out(cnow) = ps.init \wedge \\ cnow \geq ps.st \Rightarrow out(cnow) = in(cnow - ps.st) \end{array} \right) \wedge out!).$$

An $\mathtt{Integrator}$ block outputs the value of the integral of its input signal with respect to time, so its UTP semantics is given by

$$[\![\mathtt{Integrator}(ps, in, out)]\!] \cong \mathcal{H}(in! \vdash out(0) = ps.init \wedge (\dot{out} = in \wedge out!)).$$

Diagrams. A diagram is a set of blocks with connecting wires. W.l.o.g., consider a diagram D consisting of m continuous blocks and n discrete blocks, which are connected via a set of wires. The UTP semantics for blocks were defined above. Let therefore the semantics for the continuous blocks be $[\![CB_i(ps_i, \{in_i\}_{i \in I_i}, out_i)]\!]$ for $i = 1, \ldots, m$, and for the discrete blocks be $[\![DB_j(ps'_j, \{in'_i\}_{j \in J_j}, out'_j)]\!]$ for $j = 1, \ldots, n$.

Then the UTP semantics of D can be represented by

$$[\![D(ps^*, \{in_i^*\}_{i\in I}, \{out_i^*\}_{i\in J})]\!]$$
$$\hat{=}\ \exists \cup_{i=1}^m \{in_i\}_{i\in I_i} - \{in_i^*\}_{i\in I_C}, \exists \cup_{j=1}^n \{in_j'\}_{j\in J_j} - \{in_i^*\}_{i\in I_D},$$
$$\exists \{out_1, \ldots out_m\} - \{out_i^*\}_{i\in J_C}, \exists \{out_1', \ldots, out_n'\} - \{out_i^*\}_{i\in J_D}.$$
$$\mathcal{H}(\wedge_{k\in I_D}\text{Periodic}(in_k^*!, ps^*.st) \wedge \wedge_{k\in I_C} in_k^*! \wedge \wedge_{k\in J_D}\text{Periodic}(out_k^*?, ps_k^*.st)$$
$$\vdash\ \wedge \wedge_{k\in J}\, out_k^*(0) = ps_k^*.init \wedge \wedge_{k\in J_C} out_k^*!$$

$$\wedge \wedge_{i=1}^m [\![CB_i(ps_i, \{in_i\}_{i\in I_i}, out_i)]\!] \wedge \wedge_{j=1}^n (out_j'(0) = ps_j'.init)[\sigma, \rho] \wedge$$
$$(\exists n \in \mathbb{N}.\ cnow = n * \text{GCD}(ps_1'.st, \cdots, ps_n'.st)) \Rightarrow (\wedge_{j=1}^n ps_j'.st \mid cnow \Rightarrow$$
$$\left(\begin{array}{l} B_{j1}(\{in_i'\}_{j\in J_j}, ps_j')[\sigma, \rho] \Rightarrow [\![P_{comp_{j1}}(ps_j', \{in_i'\}_{j\in J_j}, out_j')]\!][\sigma, \rho] \wedge \cdots \wedge \\ B_{jm}(\{in_i'\}_{j\in J_j}, ps_j')[\sigma, \rho] \Rightarrow [\![P_{comp_{jm}}(ps_j', \{in_i'\}_{j\in J_j}, out_j')]\!][\sigma, \rho] \end{array} \right)))),$$

where GCD computes the *greatest common divisor*, and

$$\{in_i^*\}_{i\in I_C} = \cup_{i=1}^m \{in_i\}_{i\in I_i} - (\{out_1, \ldots out_m\} \cup \{out_1', \ldots, out_n'\}),$$
$$\{in_i^*\}_{i\in I_D} = \cup_{j=1}^n \{in_j'\}_{j\in J_j} - (\{out_1, \ldots out_m\} \cup \{out_1', \ldots, out_n'\}),$$
$$\{out_i^*\}_{i\in J_C} = \{out_1, \ldots out_m\} - (\cup_{i=1}^m \{in_i\}_{i\in I_i} \cup \cup_{j=1}^n \{in_j'\}_{j\in J_j}),$$
$$\{out_i^*\}_{i\in J_D} = \{out_1', \ldots, out_n'\} - (\cup_{i=1}^m \{in_i\}_{i\in I_i} \cup \cup_{j=1}^n \{in_j'\}_{j\in J_j});$$

I_C and I_D stand for the dangling inputs for continuous and discrete blocks after the composition, thus $I = I_C \cup I_D$ is the set of inputs of D; J_C and J_D stand for the dangling outputs for continuous and discrete blocks after the composition, thus $J = J_C \cup J_D$ is the set of outputs of D; and σ and ρ stand for the substitutions that replace the local input signals and input channels by the corresponding output signals and channels with the common names among these blocks (continuous and discrete) in each block, respectively. Furthermore, we set in this case

$$wait \hat{=} \wedge_{i=1}^m \neg out_i? \wedge \neg\exists n \in \mathbb{N}.\ cnow = n * \text{GCD}(ps_1'.st, \cdots, ps_n'.st).$$

Example 2. Consider the diagram Diag performing $out = in + c$. According to the above discussion, its UTP semantics can be given as

$$[\![\text{Diag}(ps, in, out)]\!]$$
$$\hat{=} \exists out'.\mathcal{H}(\text{Periodic}(in!, ps.st) \wedge \text{Periodic}(out?, ps.st) \vdash ([\![\text{Constant}(ps, out')]\!] \wedge$$
$$[\![\text{Add}(ps, \{+1, +1\}, \{in_1, in_2\}, out)]\!][in/in_1, out'/in_2]).$$

Subsystems

Normal Subsystems. A normal subsystem has a set of blocks and wires that specify the signal connections. Actually, a normal subsystem can be seen as a diagram by flattening, i.e., connecting the external inputs of the inside blocks with the inputs of the subsystem and the external outputs of the inside blocks with the outputs of the subsystem. Suppose a normal subsystem NSub with a set of inputs $\{in_i\}_{i \in I}$ and a set of outputs $\{out_j\}_{j \in J}$, and its inside blocks form a diagram Diag with a set of external inputs $\{in'_i\}_{i \in I'}$ and $\{out'_j\}_{j \in J'}$. Let σ be the mapping to relate $\{in_i\}_{i \in I}$ with $\{in'_i\}_{i \in I'}$, and $\{out'_j\}_{j \in J'}$ with $\{out_j\}_{j \in J}$, then the UTP semantics of it can be easily defined as

$$[\![\text{NSub}(ps, \{in_i\}_{i \in I}, \{out_j\}_{j \in J})]\!] \mathrel{\widehat{=}} [\![\text{Diag}(ps, \{in'_i\}_{i \in I'}, \{out'_j\}_{j \in J'})]\!][\sigma].$$

Enabled Subsystems. A normal subsystem is enabled by adding an enabled block. It executes each simulation step when the enabling signal has a positive value, otherwise holds the states so they keep their most recent values. So, its UTP semantics can be defined as follows:

$$[\![\text{ESub}(ps, \{in_i\}_{i \in I}, en, \{out_j\}_{j \in J})]\!]$$
$$\mathrel{\widehat{=}} \quad en(now) > 0 \Rightarrow [\![\text{NSub}(ps, \{in_i\}_{i \in I}, en, \{out_j\}_{j \in J})]\!] \wedge$$
$$en(now) \leq 0 \Rightarrow out(now) = out(now - ps.st).$$

Theorem 1. *Given a Simulink diagram C, its UTP semantics $[\![C]\!]$ satisfies the healthiness condition in Eq. (2), that is*

$$\mathcal{H}([\![C]\!]) = [\![C]\!].$$

Proof. It is straightforward by the definition of $[\![C]\!]$.   □

4.2   UTP Semantics for HCSP

As advocated by Hoare and He [37], a reactive system can be identified by the set of all possible observations of that system. As usual, an alphabet is attached to a system P (and its with the following constituents: $\mathcal{V}(P)$: the set of both continuous and discrete variable names, which is arranged as a vector $\mathbf{v}$, $i\Sigma(P)$: the set of input channel names, and $o\Sigma(P)$: the set of output channel names. Together the latter two form $\Sigma(P) \mathrel{\widehat{=}} i\Sigma(P) \cup o\Sigma(P)$, which is arranged as a vector ch_P.

Given a hybrid system, its timed observation is the tuple $\langle now, \mathbf{v}, \mathbf{f_v}, re_{ch*}, msg_{ch} \rangle$. Here now is the start point and now' the end point of a time interval of an observation i. The initial values of variables are $\mathbf{v}$, and $\mathbf{v}'$ are the final values at termination. The vector $\mathbf{f_v}$ contains of real-valued functions over the time interval $[now, now']$ that record the values of $\mathbf{v}$, evidently with $\mathbf{f_v}(now) = \mathbf{v}, \mathbf{f_v}(now') = \mathbf{v}'$. The vector re_{ch*} of $\{0, 1\}$-valued Boolean functions over $[now, now']$, indicates whether communication events $ch*$ are ready for communication. The vector msg_{ch}, of real-valued functions over $[now, now']$ records the values passed along channels ch. We further define

$$const(\mathbf{f}, \mathbf{b}, t_1, t_2) \mathrel{\widehat{=}} \forall t \in [t_1, t_2].\ \mathbf{f}(t) = \mathbf{b},$$
$$const^l(\mathbf{f}, \mathbf{b}, t_1, t_2) \mathrel{\widehat{=}} \forall t \in [t_1, t_2).\ \mathbf{f}(t) = \mathbf{b},$$
$$const^r(\mathbf{f}, \mathbf{b}, t_1, t_2) \mathrel{\widehat{=}} \forall t \in (t_1, t_2].\ \mathbf{f}(t) = \mathbf{b}.$$

Using the UTP timed observations, the HCSP constructs can be defined as follows.

The skip statement, which does not alter the program state, is the relational identity:

$$[\![skip]\!] \widehat{=} \mathcal{H}(\vdash now' = now \land \mathbf{v}' = \mathbf{v} \land const(\mathbf{f_v}, \mathbf{v}, now, now') \land$$
$$const(re_{ch*}, \mathbf{0}, now, now') \land const(msg_{ch}, msg_{ch}(now), now, now')).$$

As skip terminates immediately, *wait* is equivalent to *false* in this case. Hereafter, let

$$RE \widehat{=} const(re_{ch*}, \mathbf{0}, now, now') \land const(msg_{ch}, msg_{ch}(now), now, now').$$

The assignment of e to a variable x is modelled as setting x to e and keeping all other variables (denoted by $\mathbf{u}$) constant:

$$[\![x := e]\!] \widehat{=} \mathcal{H}(\vdash now' = now \land x' = e \land \mathbf{u}' = \mathbf{u} \land const(\mathbf{f}_x, e, now, now') \land$$
$$const(\mathbf{f_u}, \mathbf{u}, now, now') \land RE).$$

As an assignment process terminates immediately, *wait* is equivalent to *false* here.

An evolution process says that the system waits, while it is evolving until the domain constraint becomes false. So, the UTP semantics is the following hybrid design

$$[\![\langle F(\dot{s}, s) = 0 \& B \rangle]\!] \widehat{=} (\vdash F(\dot{s}, s = 0) \land t = 1) \lhd B \rhd [\![skip]\!].$$

Obviously, in this case *wait* is equivalent to B.

The conditional statement behaves according to whether the condition holds or not: $[\![B \rightarrow P]\!] \widehat{=} [\![P]\!] \lhd B \rhd [\![skip]\!]$, and internal choice is interpreted as a non-deterministic selection between two operands: $[\![P \sqcup Q]\!] \widehat{=} ([\![P]\!] \lor [\![Q]\!])$.

In order to define sequential and parallel composition, we introduce two semantic operators.

Let H_1 and H_2 be two hybrid designs with

$$H_1 \widehat{=} (\vdash \wedge_{x \in \mathcal{V}(H_1)} x' = x \land wait'_{H_1} = wait_{H_1} \land S_{H_1}) \lhd wait_{H_1} \rhd (p_{H_1} \vdash R_{H_1}),$$
$$H_2 \widehat{=} (\vdash \wedge_{x \in \mathcal{V}(H_2)} x' = x \land wait'_{H_2} = wait_{H_2} \land S_{H_2}) \lhd wait_{H_2} \rhd (p_{H_2} \vdash R_{H_2}),$$

which satisfy the healthiness condition in Eq. (2). The sequential composition of H_1 and H_2, denoted by $H_1 \,\raisebox{0.2ex}{;}\, H_2$ is defined by

$$H_1 \,\raisebox{0.2ex}{;}\, H_2 \widehat{=} \exists wait_{H_1}, wait_{H_2}. \, \exists \mathbf{v}_{H_1}, now_{H_1}, ok_{H_1}.$$
$$\exists \mathbf{f}_{\mathbf{v}_{H_1}}, re_{ch_{H_1}*}, msg_{ch_{H_1}}, f_{\mathbf{v}_{H_2}}, re_{ch_{H_2}*}, msg_{ch_{H_2}}.$$
$$(\vdash (wait_{H_1} \Rightarrow \Pi_{H_1}) \land (wait_{H_2} \Rightarrow \Pi_{H_2}) \land wait' = wait) \lhd wait \rhd$$

$$(\neg wait_{H_1} \wedge wait_{H_2} \wedge r_{H_1} \vdash R_{H_1})\sigma_{H_1} \wedge$$
$$(\neg wait_{H_1} \wedge \neg wait_{H_2} \wedge r_{H_2} \vdash R_{H_2})\sigma_{H_2} \wedge$$
$$\forall t \in [now, now_{H_1}). \ wait(t) = wait_{H_1}(t) \wedge$$
$$\mathbf{f}_{\mathbf{v}}(t) = \mathbf{f}_{\mathbf{v}_{H_1}}(t) \wedge re_{ch*}(t) = re_{ch_{H_1}*}(t) \wedge msg_{ch}(t) = msg_{ch_{H_1}}(t) \wedge$$
$$\forall t \in [now_{H_1}, now']. \ wait(t) = wait_{H_2}(t) \wedge$$
$$\mathbf{f}_{\mathbf{v}}(t) = \mathbf{f}_{\mathbf{v}_{H_2}}(t) \wedge re_{ch*}(t) = re_{ch_{H_2}*}(t) \wedge msg_{ch}(t) = msg_{ch_{H_2}}(t).$$

where

$$\sigma_{H_1} = [\mathbf{v}_{H_1}/\mathbf{v}', now_{H_1}/now', ok_{H_1}/ok'][\mathbf{f}_{\mathbf{v}_{H_1}}/\mathbf{f}_{\mathbf{v}}, re_{ch_{H_1}*}/re_{ch*}, msg_{ch_{H_1}}/msg_{ch}],$$
$$\sigma_{H_2} = [\mathbf{v}_{H_1}/\mathbf{v}, now_{H_1}/now, ok_{H_1}/ok][\mathbf{f}_{\mathbf{v}_{H_2}}/\mathbf{f}_{\mathbf{v}}, re_{ch_{H_2}*}/re_{ch*}, msg_{ch_{H_2}}/msg_{ch}].$$

In the above,

$$\exists \mathbf{v}_{H_1}, now_{H_1}, ok_{H_1}. \ \exists \mathbf{f}_{\mathbf{v}}^{H_1}, re_{ch_{H_1}*}, msg_{ch_{H_1}}, f_{\mathbf{v}}^{H_2}, re_{ch_{H_2}*}, msg_{ch_{H_2}}.$$
$$(\neg wait_{H_1} \wedge wait_{H_2} \wedge r_{H_1} \vdash R_{H_1})\sigma_{H_1} \wedge (\neg wait_{H_1} \wedge \neg wait_{H_2} \wedge r_{H_2} \vdash R_{H_2})\sigma_{H_2}$$

is essentially equivalent to the sequential composition of the two designs $(\neg wait_{H_1} \wedge wait_{H_2} \wedge r_{H_1} \vdash R_{H_1})$ and $(\neg wait_{H_1} \wedge \neg wait_{H_2} \wedge r_{H_2} \vdash R_{H_2})$ by the theory of UTP [37].

It is easy to see that if H_1 and H_2 satisfy the healthiness condition of hybrid designs, so does $H_1 \,\fatsemi\, H_2$. Hence, $H_1 \,\fatsemi\, H_2$ is still a hybrid design, which implies that hybrid designs are closed under sequential composition.

The parallel composition of H_1 and H_2, denoted by $H_1 \parallel H_2$ is defined

$$H_1 \parallel H_2 \,\hat{=}\, \exists now_{H_1}, now_{H_2}, ok_{H_1}, ok_{H_2}. \ H_1[ok/ok_{H_1}] \wedge H_2[ok/ok_{H_2}] \wedge$$
$$now' = max\{now'_{H_1}, now'_{H_2}\} \wedge (ok' = ok'_{H_1} \wedge ok'_{H_2}) \wedge$$
$$(\forall t \in (now'_{H_1}, now']. \ \mathbf{f}_{\mathbf{v}_{H_1}}(t) = \mathbf{f}_{\mathbf{v}_{H_1}}(now'_{H_1}) \wedge$$
$$re_{ch_{H_1}*}(t) = re_{ch_{H_1}*}(now'_{H_1}) \wedge msg_{ch_{H_2}}(t) = msg_{ch_{H_2}}(now'_{H_2})) \wedge$$
$$(\forall t \in (now'_{H_2}, now']. \ \mathbf{f}_{\mathbf{v}_{H_2}}(t) = \mathbf{f}_{\mathbf{v}_{H_2}}(now'_{H_2}) \wedge$$
$$re_{ch_{H_2}*}(t) = re_{ch_{H_2}*}(now'_{H_2}) \wedge msg_{ch_{H_2}*}(t) = msg_{ch_{H_2}*}(now'_{H_2})).$$

It can be further be proved that

$$H_1 \parallel H_2 \ \Leftrightarrow \ \exists now_{H_1}, now_{H_2}, ok_{H_1}, ok_{H_2}.$$
$$\vdash \begin{pmatrix} wait_{H_1} \Rightarrow \Pi_{H_1} \wedge \\ wait_{H_2} \Rightarrow \Pi_{H_2} \end{pmatrix} \lhd wait_{H_1} \wedge wait_{H_2} \rhd \begin{pmatrix} (p_{H_1} \vdash R_{H_1})[ok/ok_{H_1}] \wedge \\ (p_{H_2} \vdash R_{H_2})[ok/ok_{H_2}] \end{pmatrix} \wedge$$
$$now' = max\{now'_{H_1}, now'_{H_2}\} \wedge (ok' = ok'_{H_1} \wedge ok'_{H_2}) \wedge$$
$$(\forall t \in (now'_{H_1}, now']. \ \mathbf{f}_{\mathbf{v}_{H_1}}(t) = \mathbf{f}_{\mathbf{v}_{H_1}}(now'_{H_1}) \wedge$$
$$re_{ch_{H_1}*}(t) = re_{ch_{H_1}*}(now'_{H_1}) \wedge msg_{ch_{H_2}}(t) = msg_{ch_{H_2}}(now'_{H_2})) \wedge$$
$$(\forall t \in (now'_{H_2}, now']. \ \mathbf{f}_{\mathbf{v}_{H_2}}(t) = \mathbf{f}_{\mathbf{v}_{H_2}}(now'_{H_2}) \wedge$$
$$re_{ch_{H_2}*}(t) = re_{ch_{H_2}*}(now'_{H_2}) \wedge msg_{ch_{H_2}*}(t) = msg_{ch_{H_2}*}(now'_{H_2})).$$

Therefore,also $H_1 \parallel H_2$ satisfies the healthiness condition of hybrid designs. Hence, $H_1 \parallel H_2$ is a hybrid design, which implies that hybrid designs are closed under parallel composition.

Now, given two HCSP processes P and Q, their sequential composition is defined $[\![P; Q]\!] \cong [\![P]\!] \,_9^o\, [\![Q]\!]$, and their parallel composition by $[\![P \parallel Q]\!] \cong [\![P]\!] \parallel [\![Q]\!]$.

A process variable X is interpreted as a predicate variable. Without confusion in the context, we use X to represent the predicate variable corresponding to process variable X, i.e. $[\![X]\!] \cong X$.

The semantics for recursion is defined as the least fixed point of the corresponding recursive predicate by $[\![\mathrm{rec}\, X.P]\!] \cong \mu X.[\![P]\!]$. An HCSP process P^* is thus defined as $P^* \Leftrightarrow \mathrm{rec}\, X.(\mathrm{skip} \sqcup (P; X))$. As discussed above, its semantics is given by $[\![P^*]\!] \Leftrightarrow \exists N.[\![P^N]\!]$, where $P^0 \cong \mathrm{skip}$.

A receiving event can be modelled by $[\![ch?x]\!] \cong \vdash LHS \lhd re_{ch?} \wedge \neg re_{ch!} \rhd RHS$, where $LHS \cong n\dot{o}w = 1 \wedge x' = x \wedge \mathbf{u}' = \mathbf{u}$, and

$$RHS \cong now' = now + d \wedge re'_{ch?} = 0 \wedge re'_{ch!} = 0 \wedge \mathbf{u}' = \mathbf{u} \wedge x' = msg_{ch}(now') \wedge$$
$$const^I(re_{ch?}, 1, now, now') \wedge const^I(re_{ch!}, 0, now, now').$$

Here, $wait \cong re_{ch?} \wedge \neg re_{ch!}$, i.e., the process waits until its dual event becomes ready. The sending event $[\![ch!e]\!]$ can be defined similarly.

The communication interruption can be defined as

$$[\![\langle F(\dot{s}, s) = 0 \& B \rangle \unrhd \,[\!]_{i \in I}(io_i \to Q_i)]\!] \cong [\![\langle F(\dot{s}, s) = 0 \& (B \wedge \neg \Gamma) \rangle;$$
$$\Gamma \to \,[\!]_{i \in I}(io_i \to Q_i)]\!]$$

where $\Gamma \cong \bigvee_{i \in I} re'_{\overline{io_i}}$, and $\overline{io_i}$ stands for the dual communication event with respect to io_i, for instance $\overline{ch?} = ch!$.

To prove whether the UTP semantics of other HCSP constructs satisfies the healthiness condition is mathematically straightforward and thus omitted here. It can be further deduced that the domain of hybrid designs forms a complete lattice with a refinement partial order, on which the classical programming operations are closed.

4.3   Justification of Correctness

Having defined a UTP semantics respectively for the HCSP components and the Simulink diagrams, we justify the translation by checking the semantic equivalence of a Simulink diagram with its corresponding HCSP construct (Theorem 2). Here are several remarks to be noted during the proofs:

1. We set the sample times of all discrete blocks to -1 in the translation, that is, all the generated discrete blocks share a globally identical sample time gst, which will be configured by the user before triggering the simulation.

2. It is assumed that the *In_ok* signal in a subsystem firstly turns true at the first sample point, i.e. $min\{t|In\_ok(t) = 1\} = gst$. Similarly, we use τ to denote the earliest time at which the *Out_ok* signal becomes true, i.e. $\tau \hateq min\{t|Out\_ok(t) = 1\}$.

3. Hereafter we use [[Wires]] to indicate implicitly the entire group of variable substitutions within a subsystem, and blocks are referred to as their abbreviated names with potential identifiers, for instance, Swt1 in the assignment structure stands for the block Switch1 in Fig. 3.

4. Unless otherwise stated, the parameters of a block will be elided in the semantic function for simplicity. Besides, to distinguish the input/output signals of blocks, the leading characters of input/output signals of a subsystem are capitalized.

Theorem 2. *Given an HCSP process P, denote the translated Simulink diagram by* H2S(P). *Suppose there is a correspondence (denoted by EA) between* [[P]] *and* [[H2S(P)]], *i.e.,* $now = gst$, $now' = \tau$, $ok = In\_ok(gst) = \top$, $ok' = Out\_ok(\tau)$, $\mathbf{v} = In\_\mathbf{v}(gst)$, $\mathbf{v}' = Out\_\mathbf{v}(\tau)$, $f_\mathbf{v} = Out\_\mathbf{v}|_{[gst,\tau]}$, $re_{ch*} = Out\_re_{ch*}|_{[gst,\tau]}$, *and* $msg_{ch} = Out\_re_{ch}|_{[gst,\tau]}$, *then*

$$Periodic(in!, ps.gst) \wedge Periodic(out?, ps.gst) \Rightarrow ([[P]] \Leftrightarrow [[H2S(P)]]|_{[gst,\tau]}) \quad (6)$$

as $gst \to 0$.

Proof. By induction on the structure of HCSP components. For simplicity, we use **ch**∗ to denote the local communication events inside of H2S(P) in what follows.

skip: It is easy to see that under the assumptions,

$$Periodic(in!, ps.gst) \wedge Periodic(out?, ps.gst) \Rightarrow ([[\text{skip}]] \Leftrightarrow [[H2S(\text{skip})]]|_{[gst,\tau]}) .$$

Assignment: Without loss of generality, we use [[Diag_e]] to denote the semantics of the diagram which computes the right-hand side of the assignment.

$\quad$ [[H2S(x := e)]]
$\hateq \exists \mathbf{ch}*.[[\text{Wires}]] \wedge [[\text{Diag}_e]] \wedge [[\text{Del1}]] \wedge [[\text{Del2}]] \wedge [[\text{Swt1}]] \wedge [[\text{Swt2}]]$
$\Leftrightarrow Periodic(in!, ps.gst) \wedge Periodic(out?, ps.gst) \vdash Periodic(out!, ps.gst) \wedge$
$\quad \forall t \geq 0. \ (t < gst \Rightarrow out\_Del1(t) = 0) \wedge (t \geq gst \Rightarrow out\_Del1(t) = In\_ok(t - gst)) \wedge$
$\quad\quad (t < gst \Rightarrow out\_Del2(t) = 0) \wedge (t \geq gst \Rightarrow out\_Del2(t) = Out\_x(t - gst)) \wedge$
$\quad (\exists n \in \mathbb{N}. \ cnow = n * ps.gst \Rightarrow$
$\quad\quad (In\_ok(cnow) > 0 \Rightarrow out\_Swt1(cnow) = out\_Diag_e(cnow)) \wedge$
$\quad\quad (In\_ok(cnow) \leq 0 \Rightarrow out\_Swt1(cnow) = In\_x(cnow)) \wedge$
$\quad\quad (out\_Del1(cnow) > 0 \Rightarrow out\_Swt2(cnow) = out\_Del2(cnow)) \wedge$
$\quad\quad (out\_Del1(cnow) \leq 0 \Rightarrow out\_Swt2(cnow) = out\_Swt1(cnow)) \wedge$
$\quad\quad Out\_x(cnow) = out\_Swt2(cnow) \wedge Out\_ok(cnow) = In\_ok(cnow)$

Using the left-hand side of (6) and restricting the time interval, we get the desired result.

$$Periodic(in!, ps.gst) \land Periodic(out?, ps.gst) \land [\![H2S(x := e)]\!]|_{[gst,\tau]}$$

$$\Leftrightarrow (\exists n \in \mathbb{N}.\ cnow = n * ps.gst \land cnow \in [gst, \tau]) \Rightarrow (Out\_ok(cnow) = In\_ok(cnow) \land$$

$$Out\_x(cnow) = out\_Diag_e(cnow))$$

$$\Leftrightarrow ok' \land \tau = now \land x' = e \land const(f_x, e, now, \tau) \land$$

$$\mathbf{u}' = \mathbf{u} \land const(f_{\mathbf{u}}, \mathbf{u}, now, \tau) \land RE \qquad\qquad (gst \to 0,\ EA)$$

Evolution statement: By the defined UTP semantics, it follows

$$[\![H2S(\langle F(\dot{s}, s) = 0\&B)\rangle)]\!] \cong \exists ch*. [\![Wires]\!] \land [\![NSubB]\!] \land [\![ESubF]\!] \land [\![Del]\!] \land$$
$$[\![Not]\!] \land [\![And1]\!] \land [\![And2]\!] \land [\![Swt]\!]$$

$$\Leftrightarrow Periodic(in!, ps.gst) \land Periodic(out?, ps.gst) \vdash Periodic(out!, ps.gst) \land$$
$$\forall t \geq 0.\ (out\_And1(t) > 0 \Rightarrow out\_ESubF(t) = S(t)) \land$$
$$(out\_And1(t) \leq 0 \Rightarrow out\_ESubF(t) = out\_ESubF(t - gst)) \land$$
$$(t < gst \Rightarrow out\_Del(t) = 1) \land (t \geq gst \Rightarrow out\_Del(t) = out\_NSubB(t - gst)) \land$$
$$(\exists n \in \mathbb{N}.\ cnow = n * ps.gst) \Rightarrow$$
$$out\_NSubB(cnow) = B(cnow) \land out\_Not(cnow) = \neg out\_Del(cnow) \land$$
$$out\_And1(t) = (In\_ok(cnow) \land out\_Del(t)) \land out\_And2(t) = (In\_ok(cnow) \land$$
$$out\_Not(cnow)) \land (In\_ok(cnow) > 0 \Rightarrow out\_Swt(cnow) = out\_ESubF(cnow)) \land$$
$$(In\_ok(cnow) \leq 0 \Rightarrow out\_Swt(cnow) = In\_s(cnow)) \land$$
$$Out\_s(cnow) = out\_Swt(cnow) \land Out\_ok(cnow) = out\_And2(cnow)$$

Using the left-hand side of (6) and restricting the time interval, we have

$$Periodic(in!, ps.gst) \land Periodic(out?, ps.gst) \land ok \land [\![H2S(\langle F(\dot{s}, s) = 0\&B)\rangle)]\!]|_{[gst,\tau - gst]}$$

$$\Leftrightarrow Out\_ok(\tau) = \top \land \tau - gst = gst + (\tau - 2 * gst) \land Out\_s(\tau - gst) = S(\tau - 2 * gst) \land$$
$$(\exists n \in \mathbb{N}.\ cnow = n * ps.gst \land cnow \in [gst, \tau)) \Rightarrow out\_NSubB(cnow - gst) \land$$
$$f_s(cnow) = S(cnow - gst)) \land \neg out\_NSubB(\tau - gst) \land$$
$$out\_ESubF(cnow) = out\_ESubF(cnow - gst)$$

$$\Leftrightarrow ok' \land \mathbf{u}' = \mathbf{u} \land const(f_{\mathbf{u}}, \mathbf{u}, now, \tau) \land RE \land$$
$$(B \land \tau = now + d \land s' = S(d) \land \forall t \in [now, \tau].\ f_s(t) = S(t - now) \lor$$
$$\neg B \land s' = s) \qquad\qquad (gst \to 0,\ EA)$$

$$\Leftrightarrow ([\![F(\dot{s}, s) = 0]\!] \lhd B \rhd [\![skip]\!])$$

Thereby the semantics can be proved consistent on the interval $[gst, \tau - gst]$, moreover, when the user-defined sample time $gst \to 0$, we have the desired result.

Conditional: By the definition of H2S and the UTP semantics of Simulink:

$$[\![\text{H2S}(B \to P)]\!] \triangleq \exists ch*.[\![\text{Wires}]\!] \wedge [\![\text{NSubB}]\!] \wedge [\![\text{NSubP}]\!] \wedge [\![\text{And}]\!] \wedge [\![\text{Swt}]\!]$$

$$\Leftrightarrow \text{Periodic}(in!, ps.gst) \wedge \text{Periodic}(out?, ps.gst) \vdash \text{Periodic}(out!, ps.gst) \wedge$$

$$(\exists n \in \mathbb{N}. \; cnow = n * ps.gst) \Rightarrow$$

$$out\_NSubB(cnow) = B(cnow) \wedge [\![\text{NSubP}(in_{ok} = out\_And(cnow))]\!] \wedge$$

$$out\_And(cnow) = (In\_ok(cnow) \wedge out\_NSubB(cnow)) \wedge$$

$$(out\_NSubB(cnow) > 0 \Rightarrow out\_Swt(cnow) = out\_NSubP\_ok(cnow)) \wedge$$

$$(out\_NSubB(cnow) \leq 0 \Rightarrow out\_Swt(cnow) = In\_ok(cnow)) \wedge$$

$$Out\_x(cnow) = out\_NSubP\_x(cnow) \wedge Out\_ok(cnow) = out\_Swt(cnow)$$

It follows

$$\text{Periodic}(in!, ps.gst) \wedge \text{Periodic}(out?, ps.gst) \wedge [\![\text{H2S}(B \to P)]\!]|_{[gst,\tau]}$$

$$\Leftrightarrow (B \wedge [\![P]\!]) \vee (\neg B \wedge ok' \wedge \tau = now \wedge v' = v \wedge const(f_v, v, now, \tau) \wedge RE) \wedge$$

$$\mathbf{u}' = \mathbf{u} \wedge const(f_\mathbf{u}, \mathbf{u}, now, \tau) \wedge RE \qquad\qquad (gst \to 0, \; EA)$$

$$\Leftrightarrow [\![P]\!] \lhd B \rhd [\![\text{skip}]\!]$$

Thus we have the desired result.

Internal choice: This is proved as for the conditional process.

Sequential composition: As shown in Fig. 7, **x** are the set of common signals processed by both P and Q, while **y** and **z** are the respective exclusive signals.

$$[\![\text{H2S}(P; Q)]\!]|_{[gst,\tau]} \triangleq \exists ch*.[\![\text{Wires}]\!]|_{[gst,\tau]} \wedge [\![\text{NSubP}]\!]|_{[gst,\tau]} \wedge [\![\text{NSubQ}]\!]|_{[gst,\tau]}$$

$$\Leftrightarrow [\![\text{NSubP}(in_{ok} = In\_ok(cnow), in_x = In\_x(cnow), in_y = In\_y(cnow))]\!]|_{[gst,\tau]} \wedge$$

$$[\![\text{NSubQ}(in_{ok} = out\_NSubP\_ok(t), in_x = out\_NSubP\_x(t), in_z = In\_z(t))]\!]|_{[gst,\tau]} \wedge$$

$$(\exists n \in \mathbb{N}. \; cnow = n * ps.gst \wedge cnow \in [gst, \tau]) \Rightarrow$$

$$Out\_ok(cnow) = out\_NSubQ\_ok(cnow) \wedge Out\_x(cnow) = out\_NSubQ\_x(cnow) \wedge$$

$$Out\_y(cnow) = out\_NSubP\_y(cnow) \wedge Out\_z(cnow) = out\_NSubQ\_z(cnow)$$

$$\Leftrightarrow (\exists x_m, now_m, ok_m. \; (out\_NSubP\_ok(now_m) \Leftrightarrow ok) \wedge$$

$$[\![\text{NSubP}]\!][x_m/x', ok_m/ok'] \wedge [\![\text{NSubQ}]\!][x_m/x, ok_m/ok] \wedge$$

$$\forall t \geq 0.y(t) = out\_NSubP\_y(t) \wedge x(t) = out\_NSubQ\_x(t) \wedge$$

$$z(t) = out\_NSubQ\_z(t)) \qquad (gst \to 0, \; EA \text{ and Induction Hypothesis})$$

This gives the desired result.

Recursion: We only consider tail recursion, i.e., repetition. General recursion can be proved similarly. As shown in Fig. 8, a random number N, generated by an oracle, is used in the Simulink diagram as the number of iterations of subsystem P. Since $[\![P^*]\!]$ is defined by the least fixed point, it is clear that the inverse direction holds: $\text{Periodic}(in!, ps.gst) \wedge \text{Periodic}(out?, ps.gst) \Rightarrow$ $([\![P^*]\!] \Leftarrow [\![\text{H2S}(P^*)]\!]|_{[gst,\tau]})$. For the other direction, suppose $[\![P^*]\!]$ holds, then according to the semantics, there must exist N such that $[\![P^N]\!]$ holds. We then apply the oracle, to generate the same number N, to control the execution of the Simulink diagram $\text{H2S}(P^*)$, to execute for N times. The fact is thus proved, i.e.

$$\text{Periodic}(in!, ps.gst) \wedge \text{Periodic}(out?, ps.gst) \Rightarrow \left(\llbracket P^* \rrbracket \Rightarrow \llbracket \text{H2S}(P^*) \rrbracket|_{[gst, \tau]}\right).$$

Communication events: By the definition of H2S and the UTP semantics of Simulink given in Sect. 4.1, it follows

$$\text{Periodic}(in!, ps.gst) \wedge \text{Periodic}(out?, ps.gst) \wedge \llbracket \text{H2S}(ch?x) \rrbracket|_{[gst, \tau]}$$

$\Leftrightarrow (\exists n \in \mathbb{N}.\ cnow = n * ps.gst \wedge cnow \in [gst, \tau]) \Rightarrow$

$\quad Out\_re(cnow) = (In\_ok(cnow) \wedge \neg Out\_ok(cnow)) \wedge$

$\quad Out\_ok(cnow) = f(In\_re(cnow - gst) \wedge Out\_re(cnow - gst)) \wedge$

$\quad (\neg Out\_ok(cnow) \Rightarrow Out\_x(cnow) = In\_x(cnow)) \wedge$

$\quad (Out\_ok(cnow) \Rightarrow Out\_x(cnow) = (\neg Out\_ok(cnow - gst)) * In\_ch(cnow))$

$\Leftrightarrow Out\_ok(\tau) = \top \wedge$

$\quad (\exists n \in \mathbb{N}.\ cnow = n * ps.gst) \Rightarrow$

$\quad\quad cnow \in [gst, \tau - gst] \Rightarrow Out\_re(cnow) = 1 \wedge In\_re(t) = 0 \wedge In\_re(\tau - gst) = 1 \wedge$

$\quad\quad cnow \in (\tau - gst, \tau] \Rightarrow Out\_re(cnow) = 0 \wedge In\_re(cnow) = 0 \wedge$

$\quad\quad cnow \in [gst, \tau) \Rightarrow Out\_x(cnow) = In\_x(cnow) \wedge Out\_x(\tau) = In\_ch(\tau)$

$\Leftrightarrow ok' \wedge now' = now + d \wedge const(re_{ch?}, 1, now, now') \wedge$

$\quad const^t(re_{ch!}, 0, now, now') \wedge re_{ch!}(now') = 1 \wedge re'_{ch?}(now') = 0 \wedge re'_{ch!}(now') = 0 \wedge$

$\quad const^t(f_x, x, now, now') \wedge f_x(now') = msg_{ch}(now') \wedge$

$\quad const(\mathbf{f_u}, \mathbf{u}, now, now') \wedge \mathbf{u}' = \mathbf{u} \wedge x' = msg_{ch}(now') \qquad\qquad (gst \to 0,\ EA)$

$\Leftrightarrow (LHS \lhd re_{ch?} \wedge \neg re_{ch!} \rhd RHS)$

Therefore, we get

$$\text{Periodic}(in!, ps.gst) \wedge \text{Periodic}(out?, ps.gst) \Rightarrow \left(\llbracket ch?x \rrbracket \Leftrightarrow \llbracket \text{H2S}(ch?x) \rrbracket|_{[gst, \tau]}\right).$$

The equivalence for sending events can be proved similarly.

Interruption: It is trivial to prove that Theorem 2 holds for communication interruption, inasmuch as it can be interpreted by the sequential composition and conditional statement, for which we have already proved validation of Theorem 2.

Parallel: As shared variables are not allowed in HCSP, we use $\mathbf{y}$ and $\mathbf{z}$ to denote the set of exclusive signals (including re and msg) respectively for P and Q.

Let $\tau_P \widehat{=} min\{t \mid out\_NSubP\_ok(t) = 1\}$, and $\tau_Q \widehat{=} min\{t \mid out\_NSubQ\_ok(t) = 1\}$. Then, according to the definitions, we have

$$[\![H2S(P\|Q)]\!]|_{[gst,\tau]} \widehat{=} \exists ch*.[\![Wires]\!]|_{[gst,\tau]} \wedge [\![NSubP]\!]|_{[gst,\tau]} \wedge [\![NSubQ]\!]|_{[gst,\tau]}$$

$$\Leftrightarrow [\![NSubP(in_{ok} = In\_ok(cnow), in_y = In\_y(cnow))]\!]|_{[gst,\tau]} \wedge$$

$$[\![NSubQ(in_{ok} = In\_ok(cnow), in_z = In\_z(cnow))]\!]|_{[gst,\tau]} \wedge$$

$$(\exists n \in \mathbb{N}.\ cnow = n * ps.gst \wedge cnow \in [gst, \tau]) \Rightarrow$$

$$(\tau_P = \tau \vee \tau_Q = \tau) \wedge (Out\_ok(cnow) = out\_NSubP\_ok(cnow) \vee out\_NSubQ\_ok(cnow)) \wedge$$

$$(\exists n \in \mathbb{N}.\ cnow = n * ps.gst \wedge cnow \in [\tau_P, \tau]) \Rightarrow Out\_y(cnow) = out\_NSubP\_y(\tau_P) \wedge$$

$$(\exists n \in \mathbb{N}.\ cnow = n * ps.gst \wedge cnow \in [\tau_Q, \tau]) \Rightarrow Out\_z(cnow) = out\_NSubQ\_z(\tau_Q) \wedge$$

$$\Leftrightarrow [\![P\|Q]\!] \qquad\qquad (gst \to 0,\ EA \text{ and Induction Hypothesis})$$

It thus follows immediately that Theorem 2 holds for the parallel composition. □

5   Conclusion

In this paper, we presented a translation from HCSP formal models into Simulink graphical models, so that the models can be simulated and tested using a MATLAB platform, thus avoiding expensive formal verification if the development is at a stage where it is considered unnecessary. Together with our previous work on encoding Simulink/Stateflow diagrams into HCSP, it provides a two-way path in the design of embedded systems. In addition, we proposed a justification of the translation, which uses UTP as a main vehicle for arguing formally for the correspondence between the two semantics.

Acknowledgements. The work is supported partly by "973 Program" under grant No. 2014CB340701, by NSFC under grants 91418204 and 91118007, by CDZ project CAP (GZ 1023), and by the CAS/SAFEA International Partnership Program for Creative Research Teams.

References

1. Simulink User's Guide. http://www.mathworks.com/help/pdf_doc/simulink/sl_using.pdf
2. Stateflow User's Guide. http://www.mathworks.com/help/pdf_doc/stateflow/sf_using.pdf
3. Tiller, M.: Introduction to Physical Modeling with Modelica. Springer, New York (2001)
4. SysML V 1.4 Beta Specification (2013). http://www.omg.org/spec/SysML
5. Selic, B., Gerard, S.: Modeling and Analysis or Real-Time and Embedded Systems with UML and MARTE: Developing Cyber-Physical Systems. The Springer International Series in Engineering and Computer Science. The MK/OMG Press, Burlington (2013)

6. Balarin, F., Watanabe, Y., Hsieh, H., Lavagno, H., Passerone, C., Sangiovanni-Vincentelli, A.L.: Metropolis: an integrated electronic system design environment. IEEE Comput. **36**(4), 45–52 (2003)
7. Eker, J., Janneck, J., Lee, E.A., Liu, J., Liu, X., Ludvig, J., Neuendorffer, S., Sachs, S., Xiong, Y.: Taming heterogeneity - the ptolemy approach. Proc. IEEE **91**(1), 127–144 (2003)
8. Henzinger, T.: The theory of hybrid automata. In: LICS 1996, pp. 278–292, July 1996
9. Alur, R., Henzinger, T.A.: Modularity for timed and hybrid systems. In: Mazurkiewicz, A., Winkowski, J. (eds.) CONCUR 1997. LNCS, vol. 1243, pp. 74–88. Springer, Berlin (1997). doi:10.1007/3-540-63141-0_6
10. He, J.: From CSP to hybrid systems. In: A Classical Mind, Essays in Honour of C.A.R. Hoare, pp. 171–189. Prentice Hall International (UK) Ltd. (1994)
11. Chaochen, Z., Ji, W., Ravn, A.P.: A formal description of hybrid systems. In: Alur, R., Henzinger, T.A., Sontag, E.D. (eds.) HS 1995. LNCS, vol. 1066, pp. 511–530. Springer, Berlin (1996). doi:10.1007/BFb0020972
12. Platzer, A.: Differential-algebraic dynamic logic for differential-algebraic programs. J. Log. Comput. **20**(1), 309–352 (2010)
13. Liu, J., Lv, J., Quan, Z., Zhan, N., Zhao, H., Zhou, C., Zou, L.: A calculus for hybrid CSP. In: Ueda, K. (ed.) APLAS 2010. LNCS, vol. 6461, pp. 1–15. Springer, Berlin (2010). doi:10.1007/978-3-642-17164-2_1
14. Zou, L., Zhan, N., Wang, V., Fränzle, M., Qin, S.: Verifying simulink diagrams via a hybrid hoare logic prover. In: EMSOFT 2013, pp. 1–10 (2013)
15. Zou, L., Zhan, N., Wang, S., Fränzle, M.: Formal verification of simulink/stateflow diagrams. In: Finkbeiner, B., Pu, G., Zhang, L. (eds.) ATVA 2015. LNCS, vol. 9364, pp. 464–481. Springer, Cham (2015). doi:10.1007/978-3-319-24953-7_33
16. Chen, M., Ravn, A.P., Wang, S., Yang, M., Zhan, N.: A two-way path between formal and informal design of embedded systems (extended version). http://lcs.ios.ac.cn/~chenms/papers/UTP2016_FULL.pdf
17. Simulink Design Verifier User's Guide (2010). http://www.manualslib.com/manual/392930/Matlab-Simulink-Design-Verifier-1.html#manual
18. Han, Z., Mosterman, P.J.: Towards sensitivity analysis of hybrid systems using simulink. HSCC **2013**, 95–100 (2013)
19. Tripakis, S., Sofronis, C., Caspi, P., Curic, A.: Translating discrete-time simulink to lustre. ACM Trans. Embedded Comput. Syst. **4**(4), 779–818 (2005)
20. Scaife, N., Sofronis, C., Caspi, P., Tripakis, S., Maraninchi, F.: Defining and translating a "safe" subset of simulink/stateflow into lustre. In: EMSOFT 2004, pp. 259–268. ACM (2004)
21. Cavalcanti, A., Clayton, P., O'Halloran, C.: Control law diagrams in *Circus*. In: Fitzgerald, J., Hayes, I.J., Tarlecki, A. (eds.) FM 2005. LNCS, vol. 3582, pp. 253–268. Springer, Berlin (2005). doi:10.1007/11526841_18
22. Woodcock, J., Cavalcanti, A.: The semantics of *Circus*. In: Bert, D., Bowen, J.P., Henson, M.C., Robinson, K. (eds.) ZB 2002. LNCS, vol. 2272, pp. 184–203. Springer, Berlin (2002). doi:10.1007/3-540-45648-1_10
23. Meenakshi, B., Bhatnagar, A., Roy, S.: Tool for translating simulink models into input language of a model checker. In: Liu, Z., He, J. (eds.) ICFEM 2006. LNCS, vol. 4260, pp. 606–620. Springer, Berlin (2006). doi:10.1007/11901433_33
24. Sfyrla, V., Tsiligiannis, G., Safaka, I., Bozga, M., Sifakis, J.: Compositional translation of simulink models into synchronous BIP. In: IEEE Fifth International Symposium on Industrial Embedded Systems, SIES 2010, pp. 217–220. IEEE (2010)

25. Bliudze, S., Sifakis, J.: The algebra of connectors - structuring interaction in BIP. IEEE Trans. Comput. **57**(10), 1315–1330 (2008)

26. Yang, C., Vyatkin, V.: Transformation of simulink models to IEC 61499 Function Blocks for verification of distributed control systems. Control Eng. Pract. **20**(12), 1259–1269 (2012)

27. Zhou, C., Kumar, R.: Semantic translation of simulink diagrams to input/output extended finite automata. Discrete Event Dyn. Syst. **22**(2), 223–247 (2012)

28. Minpoli, S., Frehse, G.: SL2SX translator: from simulink to SpaceEx verification tool. In: HSCC 2016 (2016)

29. Chen, R., Dong, J.S., Sun, J.: A formal framework for modeling and validating simulink diagrams. Formal Asp. Comput. **21**(5), 451–483 (2009)

30. Boström, P.: Contract-based verification of simulink models. In: Qin, S., Qiu, Z. (eds.) ICFEM 2011. LNCS, vol. 6991, pp. 291–306. Springer, Berlin (2011). doi:10.1007/978-3-642-24559-6_21

31. Roy, P., Shankar, N.: Simcheck: a contract type system for simulink. ISSE **7**(2), 73–83 (2011)

32. Preoteasa, V., Tripakis, S.: Refinement calculus of reactive systems. In: EMSOFT 2014, pp. 2:1–2:10 (2014)

33. Dragomir, I., Preoteasa, V., Tripakis, S.: Compositional semantics and analysis of hierarchical block diagrams. In: Bošnački, D., Wijs, A. (eds.) SPIN 2016. LNCS, vol. 9641, pp. 38–56. Springer, Cham (2016). doi:10.1007/978-3-319-32582-8_3

34. Zhan, N., Wang, S., Zhao, H.: Formal modelling, analysis and verification of hybrid systems. In: Liu, Z., Woodcock, J., Zhu, H. (eds.) Unifying Theories of Programming and Formal Engineering Methods. LNCS, vol. 8050, pp. 207–281. Springer, Berlin (2013). doi:10.1007/978-3-642-39721-9_5

35. Wang, S., Zhan, N., Guelev, D.: An assume/guarantee based compositional calculus for hybrid CSP. In: Agrawal, M., Cooper, S.B., Li, A. (eds.) TAMC 2012. LNCS, vol. 7287, pp. 72–83. Springer, Berlin (2012). doi:10.1007/978-3-642-29952-0_13

36. Guelev, D., Wang, S., Zhan, N.: Hoare reasoning about HCSP in the duration calculus (2013, submitted)

37. Hoare, C., He, J.: Unifying Theories of Programming, vol. 14. Prentice Hall, Englewood Cliffs (1998)

38. Zou, L., Lv, J., Wang, S., Zhan, N., Tang, T., Yuan, L., Liu, Y.: Verifying chinese train control system under a combined scenario by theorem proving. In: Cohen, E., Rybalchenko, A. (eds.) VSTTE 2013. LNCS, vol. 8164, pp. 262–280. Springer, Berlin (2014). doi:10.1007/978-3-642-54108-7_14

A Denotational Semantics for Parameterised Networks of Synchronised Automata

Siqi Li[1(✉)] and Eric Madeleine[2]

[1] Shanghai Key Laboratory of Trustworthy Computing, ECNU, Shanghai, China
cathy.lsq09@gmail.com
[2] Université Côte d'Azur, INRIA, I3S, Sophia Antipolis, France

Abstract. Parameterised Networks of Synchronised Automata (pNets) is a machine-oriented semantic formalism used for specifying and verifying the behaviour of distributed components or systems. In addition, it can be used to define the semantics of languages in the parallel and distributed computation area. Unlike other traditional process calculi, pNets only own one pNet node as an operator which composes all subnets running in parallel. Using this single synchronisation artifact, it is capable of expressing many operators or synchronisation mechanisms. In this paper, we explore a denotational semantics for parameterised networks. The denotational semantics of parameterised networks we investigate is based on the behaviours of their subnets. The behaviour of a subnet is determined by both its state and the actions it executes. Based on the traces of a set of subnets, the behaviour of a pNet consisting of those subnets can be deduced. A set of algebraic laws is also explored based on the denotational semantics.

1 Introduction

With the rapid development of network technology, a number of software environments or middlewares emerge for facilitating the development of applications distributed over networks. These tools can be used in a variety of contexts, ranging from multiprocessors or clusters of machines, to local or wide area networks, to pervasive and mobile computing. In order to describe the behaviour of distributed systems and to verify properties of such systems, several formal languages and process calculi have been proposed in [3,9,11].

Parameterised Networks of Synchronised Automata, abbreviated as pNets, is an element of a pragmatic approach based on graphical specifications for communicating and synchronised distributed objects, in which both events (messages) and agents (distributed objects) can be parameterised. In this framework, pNets is a low level semantic model used for expressing the operational semantics of dedicated programming languages or high-level formalisms for distributed systems. The pNet model is based on the general notion of labelled transition systems, and on hierarchical networks of communicating systems (synchronisation networks), with explicit handling of data parameters in communication events and in the topology of processes. The agents in pNets can also be parameterised

J.P. Bowen and H. Zhu (Eds.): UTP 2016, LNCS 10134, pp. 93–113, 2017.
DOI: 10.1007/978-3-319-52228-9_5

to encode sets of equivalent agents running in parallel. In order to realize communications and synchronisation among the agents in the networks, we use a notion of synchronisation vectors inherited from Arnold [1], but augmented with explicit data values. It provides a general and flexible way to compose any number of components, which matches the expressiveness of many different usual process algebras [2]. Recently we have extended the model towards *open pNets*, that contain *Holes* playing the role of process variables. Open pNets are able to express operators of process algebras or distributed systems, and provides us with a methodology to prove properties of program skeletons, or generic algorithms where we don't care about the details of some parts of the system. They are endowed with an operational semantics and a bisimulation based symbolic equivalence [5].

The concept of pNets was targeted towards the behavioural specification of distributed systems. In the last decade, (closed) pNets have been used to model the behaviours of a number of distributed systems featuring queues, futures, component systems, one-to-many communications, or fault-tolerance protocols Also, the pNets model offers good properties as a formalism for defining the semantics of distributed and heterogeneous systems: it provides a compact hierarchical format, easy to produce from source code. It can also be transformed using abstract interpretation of data domains, and the authors use this approach to construct finite pNets that can be analysed by model-checking [2].

Some research has been done on the formal semantics for distributed computing in order to provide a strong theoretical foundation for those languages or frameworks used in this area. Koymans proposed a denotational semantics for a real-time distributed language called Mini CSP-R in [7]. A formal semantics was developed for a distributed programming language named LIPS using Dijkstra's weakest preconditions [10]. Both of the works focus on the parallel execution of the processes but put little emphasis on the hierarchy. As for the pNets model, the study on formalism has just started. An operational semantics and a bisimulation theory for closed pNets are proposed in [4]. Their work also employs some examples to illustrate the expressiveness of pNets. Based on these discussions on formal semantics for pNets, the model checking technology that has been applied to verify the correctness of distributed applications or systems can be improved. Also, it becomes more persuasive and reasonable to be used on safety-critical systems.

This paper proposes a denotational semantics for pNets using UTP theory [6], which can provide another understanding of the formalism complementing the operational approach, and help deduce interesting algebraic properties of parameterised networks. A process (a subnet) in pNets is formalized by a predicate with structured traces and process states. Similar to traditional programming languages, the execution state of a pNet has *completed* state, *waiting* state and *divergent* state to represent the current status and control of the behaviour. A trace is introduced to record the interactions among subnets in the pNets system. The behaviour of a pNets system can be deduced by merging the behaviours of all subnets together. Besides, we investigate the behaviours of pNets composition with sub-pNets filling some holes by merging the traces of the sub-pNet into the upper-level pNet. Based on the formalized denotational semantics, a set of algebraic laws is obtained.

The rest of this paper is organized as follows. Section 2 recalls the formal definition of pNets with the explanation on the notations and term algebra. Section 3 presents the semantic model of parameterised networks. Section 4 explores a denotational semantics defined structurally on the different elements of the pNet model. Section 5 investigates a set of algebraic laws, including a set of laws concerning parallel composition and pNets composition. Also, we show how we prove properties of various constructs from other languages that we encode using pNets.

2 Parameterised Networks (pNets)

In this section, we recall the formal definition of pNets and the notations that are used in the definition. pNets are tree-like structures. Nodes of the tree (pNet nodes) are synchronising artifacts, using a set of *synchronisation vectors* that express the possible synchronisation between the parameterised actions of a subset of the sub-trees. The leaves of the tree are either pLTSs or Holes. pLTSs (*parameterised labelled transition systems*), are transition graphs with explicit data values and assignments. Holes are placeholders for unknown processes, only specified by their set of possible actions, named the *sort*. A pNet tree with at least one hole is called an *open pNet*.

Notations. In the following definitions, indexed structures are extensively used over some countable sets, which are equivalent to mapping over the countable set. We use $a_i^{i \in I}$ to denote a family of elements a_i indexed over the set I. $a_i^{i \in I}$ defines both I the set over which the family is indexed (called range), and a_i the elements of the family. An empty family is denoted $\emptyset$. $\uplus$ is the disjoint union on indexed sets (meaning both indices and elements should be distinct).

Term Algebra. The pNets model relies on the notion of parameterised actions, that are symbolic expressions using data types and variables. We leave unspecified the constructors of the algebra that will allow building actions and expressions. Moreover, we use a generic *action interaction* mechanism, based on (some sort of) unification between two or more action expressions, to express various kinds of communication or synchronisation mechanisms. We denote $\mathcal{P}$ the set of variables and $\mathcal{T}_{\mathcal{P}}$ the term algebra over the set of variables $\mathcal{P}$. Within $\mathcal{T}_{\mathcal{P}}$, we distinguish a set of *action terms* (*parameterised actions*) $\mathcal{A}_{\mathcal{P}}$ and a set of *expression terms* $\mathcal{E}_{\mathcal{P}}$ including a set of *Boolean expressions* (guards) denoted as $\mathcal{B}_{\mathcal{P}}$ (with: $\mathcal{E}_{\mathcal{P}} \cap \mathcal{A}_{\mathcal{P}} = \emptyset \wedge \mathcal{B}_{\mathcal{P}} \subseteq \mathcal{E}_{\mathcal{P}} \wedge \mathcal{A}_{\mathcal{P}} \cup \mathcal{E}_{\mathcal{P}} = \mathcal{T}_{\mathcal{P}}$). Naturally action terms will use data expressions as subterms. To be able to reason about the data flow between pLTSs, we distinguish *input variables* of the form $?x$ within terms. The function $vars(t)$ identifies the set of variables in a term $t \in \mathcal{T}$, and $iv(t)$ returns its input variables.

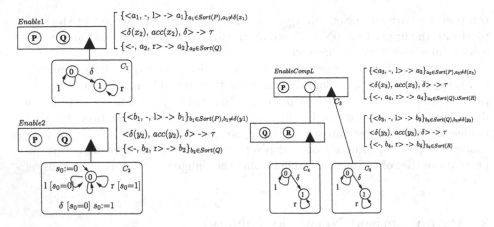

Fig. 1. Two pNets encodings for Enable   **Fig. 2.** Composed pNet for ''P>>(Q>>R)''

pNets can encode naturally the notion of input actions in value-passing CCS [8] or of usual point-to-point message passing calculi, but it also allows for more general mechanisms, like gate negotiation in Lotos, or broadcast communications. Using our notations, value-passing actions *à la* CCS would be encoded as $a(?x_1, ..., ?x_n)$ for inputs, $a(v_1, .., v_n)$ for outputs (in which v_i are action terms containing no input variables). Our action algebras also include a notion of *local actions*, that cannot be further synchronised; to simplify the notations in this paper we shall simply denote them as τ as in CCS.

Example 1. As a running example, we use pNets representing the *Enable* operator of the Lotos specification language. In the Lotos expression "P≫Q", an exit(x) statement within process P terminates P, carrying a value x that is captured by the accept(x) statement of Q. In Fig. 1 we show two possible pNet encodings for the Lotos operator in a graphical format. Figure 2 show a hierarchical pNet representing the expression "P≫(Q≫R)". A pNet is graphically represented by a box, containing circles with a process name, empty circles connected to a subnet and triangles with a line pointing to a box containing a pLTS.

We use a simple action algebra, containing two constructors $\delta(x)$ and $acc(x)$, for any possible value of the variable x, corresponding to the statements exit(x) and accept(x). Both $\delta(x)$ and $acc(x)$ actions are implicitly included in the sorts of all processes. The rest of the graphical elements will be explained below.

To begin with, we present the definition of pLTS: a pLTS is a labelled transition system with variables; variables can be manipulated, defined, or accessed inside states, actions, guards, and assignments. Without loss of generality and to simplify the formalisation, we suppose here that variables are local to each state: each state has its set of variables disjoint from the others, denoted $vars(s)$. Transmitting variable values from one state to the other is done by explicit assignment.

Note that we make no assumption on finiteness of the set of states nor on finite branching of the transition relation.

We first define the set of actions a pLTS can use, let a range over action labels, op are operators, and x_i range over variable names. Action terms are:

$$\alpha \in \mathcal{A} ::= a(p_1, \ldots, p_n) \qquad \text{action terms}$$
$$p_i ::= ?x \mid Exp \qquad \text{parameters (input variable or expression)}$$
$$Exp ::= Value \mid x \mid op(Exp^*) \qquad \text{Expressions}$$

We suppose that each input variable does not appear somewhere else in the same action term: $p_i = ?x \Rightarrow \forall j \neq i . x \notin vars(p_j)$. Input variables are only used as binders local to a pLTS, capturing data values coming from synchronisation with other pNets. They will not appear in the action alphabets of pLTSs and pNets, nor in the synchronisation mechanism.

Definition 1 (pLTS). *A pLTS is a tuple $pLTS \triangleq \langle\!\langle S, s_0, \rightarrow \rangle\!\rangle$ where:*

- *S is a set of states.*
- *$s_0 \in S$ is the initial state.*
- *$\rightarrow \subseteq S \times L \times S$ is the transition relation and L is the set of labels of the form $\langle \alpha, e_b, (x_j := e_j)^{j \in J} \rangle$, where $\alpha \in \mathcal{A}$ is a parameterised action, $e_b \in \mathcal{B}$ is a guard, and the variables $x_j \in P$ are assigned the expressions $e_j \in \mathcal{E}$.*
  If $s \xrightarrow{\langle \alpha, e_b, (x_j := e_j)^{j \in J} \rangle} s' \in \rightarrow$ then $iv(\alpha) \subseteq vars(s')$, $vars(\alpha)\backslash iv(\alpha) \subseteq vars(s)$, $vars(e_b) \subseteq vars(s)$, and $\forall j \in J. vars(e_j) \subseteq vars(s) \wedge x_j \in vars(s')$.

Example 2. Both pNets in Fig. 1 have a pLTS acting as a controller, in a state-oriented style at the top, and a data-oriented style at the bottom. In a pLTS, states have names, and transitions have labels, written as "action [guard] assignment*". The initial state can also have an initial assignment, marked with an arrow. Variables assigned are those of the target state, while variables used in guards or expressions are those of the source state, and input variables of the action. For example the pLTS C_2 has a single state, with a state variable s_0, its transitions include guards (e.g. $[s_0 = 0]$) and assignments (e.g. $s_0 := 1$).

Remark that the conditions on variable sets imply that the local variables of a state s include all input variables received in incoming transitions of s, as well as all local variables explicitly assigned in incoming transitions of s. We denote **Trans**(s) the set of outgoing transitions of s and $tgt(t)$ the target state of t.

Hierarchy and Synchronisation: Now we define the hierarchical operator, called *pNet node* that is the only constructor required for building complex pNets. A pNet node has a set of sub-pNets that can be either pNets or pLTSs, and a set of Holes, playing the role of process parameters. The synchronisation between action of sub-nets is given by a set of *synchronisation vectors*: a synchronisation vector synchronises one or several internal actions, and exposes a single resulting global action. Communication of data between the partners of a synchronisation is done by unification. This synchronisation method is very flexible and generic.

It allows to model classical synchronous communication The selection of specific vectors in the set (depending on the actions offered by subnets) models nondeterminism and interleaving. Channels or queues are not handled directly, they have to be modelled using a pLTS, that will be synchronised with the subnets involved. This is a very versatile and expressive schema, as shown in [4].

Action terms for pNets are simpler than for pLTSs, and defined as follows:

$$\alpha \in \mathcal{A}_S ::= a(Expr_1, \ldots, Expr_n)$$

Definition 2 (pNets). *A pNet is a hierarchical structure where leaves are pLTSs and holes:*
$pNet \triangleq pLTS \mid \langle\langle pNet_i^{i \in I}, S_j^{j \in J}, SV_k^{k \in K} \rangle\rangle$ *where*

- $I \in \mathcal{I}$ *is the set over which sub-pNets are indexed.*
- $pNet_i^{i \in I}$ *is the family of sub-pNets.*
- $J \in \mathcal{I}_\mathcal{P}$ *is the set over which holes are indexed. I and J are* disjoint: $I \cap J = \emptyset$, $I \cup J \neq \emptyset$
- $S_j \subseteq \mathcal{A}_S$ *is a set of action terms, denoting the* Sort *of hole j.*
- $SV_k^{k \in K}$ *is a set of synchronisation vectors* $(K \in \mathcal{I}_\mathcal{P})$. $\forall k \in K, SV_k = \alpha_l^{l \in I_k \uplus J_k} \rightarrow \alpha'_k$ *where* $\alpha'_k \in \mathcal{A}_\mathcal{P}$, $I_k \subseteq I$, $J_k \subseteq J$, $\forall i \in I_k . \alpha_i \in \mathrm{Sort}(pNet_i)$, *and* $\forall j \in J_k . \alpha_j \in S_j$. *The global action of a vector* SV_k *is* $\mathrm{Label}(SV_k) = \alpha'_k$.

Definition 3 (Sorts and Holes of pNets).

- *The sort of a pNet is its signature: the set of actions it can perform. For a pLTS we do not need to distinguish input variables. More formally*[1]:

$$\mathrm{Sort}(\langle\langle S, s_0, \rightarrow \rangle\rangle) = \{\alpha \{\!\!\{x \leftarrow ?x | x \in iv(\alpha)\}\!\!\} \mid s \xrightarrow{\langle \alpha, \, e_b, \, (x_j := e_j)^{j \in J} \rangle} s' \in \rightarrow\}$$
$$\mathrm{Sort}(\langle\langle \overline{pNet}, \overline{S}, \overline{SV} \rangle\rangle) = \{\alpha'_k \mid \alpha_j^{j \in J_k} \rightarrow \alpha'_k \in \overline{SV}\}$$

- *The set of holes of a pNet is defined inductively; the sets of holes in a pNet node and its subnets are all disjoint:*

$$\mathrm{Holes}(\langle\langle S, s_0, \rightarrow \rangle\rangle) = \emptyset$$
$$\mathrm{Holes}(\langle\langle pNet_i^{i \in I}, S_j^{j \in J}, \overline{SV} \rangle\rangle) = J \cup \bigcup_{i \in I} \mathrm{Holes}(pNet_i)$$
$$\forall i \in I. \ \mathrm{Holes}(pNet_i) \cap J = \emptyset$$
$$\forall i_1, i_2 \in I. i_1 \neq i_2 \Rightarrow \mathrm{Holes}(pNet_{i_1}) \cap \mathrm{Holes}(pNet_{i_2}) = \emptyset$$

A pNet Q is *closed* if it has no hole: $\mathrm{Holes}(Q) = \emptyset$; else it is said to be *open*.

Graphical Syntax: When describing examples, we usually deal with pNets with finitely many sub-pNets and holes, and it is convenient to have a more concrete syntax for synchronisation vectors. When $I \cup J = [0..n]$ we denote synchronisation vectors as $< \alpha_1, .., \alpha_n > \rightarrow \alpha$, and elements not taking part in the synchronisation are denoted $-$ as in: $< -, -, \alpha, -, - > \rightarrow \alpha$.

---

[1] $\{\!\!\{x_k \leftarrow e_k\}\!\!\}^{k \in K}$ is the parallel substitution operation.

Example 3. Back to Fig. 1, the first synchronisation vector of pNet `Enable1` means: for every action a_1 in the sort of P with $a_1 \neq \delta(x_1)$ for some x_1, this a_1 action can synchronise with the l action of the controller, and this synchronisation is seen as a global action a_1 of `Enable1`. Vectors are defined in a parameterised manner, using variables universally quantified, and local to each vector.

More examples can be found in [4].

Composition Operator: Open pNets can be composed by replacing one hole (at some arbitrary position in the tree) by a pNet with a compatible sort:

Definition 4 (pNet Composition). *Let $N1 = \ll pNet_i^{i \in I}, S_j^{j \in J}, \overline{SV} \gg$ and $N2$ be two pNets, ho a hole of $N1$ such that $Sort(N2) \subseteq S_{h0}$, their composition denoted $N1[N2]_{ho}$ is:*

if $ho \in J$ then $N1[N2]_{ho} = \ll (pNet_i)^{i \in I} \uplus N2, S_j^{j \in J \setminus \{ho\}}, \overline{SV} \gg$
else $\exists i0 \in I.ho \in Holes(pNet_{i0})$
and $N1[N2]_{ho} = \ll (pNet_i)^{i \in I} [pNet_{i0} \leftarrow pNet_{i0}[N2]_{ho}], S_j^{j \in J}, \overline{SV} \gg$

Remark that the composition operation does not change synchronisation vectors at any level in the pNet structure: only the hole involved is replaced by a subnet, and the sort inclusion condition ensures the actions of the subnets are properly taken into account by the synchronisation vectors. This is essential for keeping the compositional features of the model.

Example 4. Fig. 2 shows that the hole Q in the pNet `Enable1` in Fig. 1 is instantiated by another instance of `Enable1` where $Sort(Enable1) \subseteq Sort(Q)$. The composed pNet represents the Lotos process expression "P $\gg$ (Q $\gg$ R)", denoted as $Enable(P,P')[Enable(Q,R)]_{P'}$. Both C_3 and C_4 contain instances of the controller pLTS. Here a_3, a_4, b_3 and b_4 in the synchronisation vectors are variables that can take any value in the sort of their corresponding holes.

3 The Semantic Model

Now we define the denotational semantic model for pNets based on the UTP theory [6] in this section. UTP uses relational calculus as a unifying basis to define denotational semantics for programs across different programming paradigms. In the semantic models, different programming paradigms are equipped with different *alphabets* and a selection of laws called *healthiness conditions*. An alphabet is a set of observational variables recording external observations of the program behaviour. The healthiness conditions are kind of invariants, imposing constraints on the values and evolution of variables. The observational variables are defined in a structural manner, using relational predicates relating the possible values of the variables of a given program construct with those of its parts.

In our semantic model, we use the notion of *process*, which is widely used in a number of process algebra and calculus, to denote the various forms of processes in the pNet formalism, namely pLTS, sub-pNets, holes and even a whole pNet system. We say that a process *fires* a transition, that means a transition of a pLTS, an action of a hole, or a "global action" generated by the execution of a synchronisation vector in the case of a pNet node.

The predecessor of a pNet process is a process executed just before the current execution step. This process may either have terminated successfully so that the current process can start, or it may have not terminated and its final values are unobservable.

With the understanding of the specific meaning of these notions, we introduce the following variables defined for the alphabet to observe the behaviours of pNets processes.

- **Status** st, st': express the execution state of a process before and after a transition is fired, with values in $\{comp, wait, div\}$.
  - *completed* state: A process may complete all its execution and terminate successfully. "$st = comp$" means that the predecessor of the process has terminated successfully and the control passes into the process for activation. "$st' = comp$" means that the process itself terminates successfully.
  - *waiting* state: A process may wait for receiving messages from its environment. "$st = wait$" indicates that the predecessor of the process is at waiting state. Hence the considered process itself cannot be scheduled. "$st' = wait$" indicates that the current process is at waiting state.
  - *divergent* state: A process may perform an infinite computation and enter into a divergent state. "$st = div$" indicates that the predecessor of the process has entered into a divergent state, whereas "$st' = div$" indicates that the process itself has entered into a divergent state.
- **Current state** cs, cs': denote the state (corresponding to the set of states in pLTS) where the current execution begins and terminates. This is used to help relate all the transitions and figure out which transition should be fired.
- **Data store** $ds(s)^{s \in S}$, $ds(s)'^{s \in S}$: record the values of the local variables of the state s in the set S before and after an observation. We will use the notations $\overline{ds}$ and $\overline{ds}'$ to denote the full set of Stores for simplicity.
- **Trace** tr, tr': record a sequence of observations on the interaction among the subnets. The elements in the trace variable are in the form of $\alpha(v_1, \ldots, v_n)$ where $n \geq 1$ or just a value v. Here, $v_1, \ldots, v_n$ can be values either recorded directly from the message transmission or computed from the expressions.

Notations for Traces. In the following, $t[i]$ is the ith element in the trace t; $t_1 \preceq t_2$ denotes that sequence t_1 is a prefix of sequence t_2; $\langle l^k \rangle$ is the trace where the element l is repeated k times; $\langle l^* \rangle$ the trace where l is repeated in any finite number of times; $t^\frown t'$ the concatenation of traces t and t'; and $s \upharpoonright A$ means trace s is restricted to the elements in set A.

Before we present the denotational semantics of each process in pNets, we will define some healthiness conditions that a pNet process should satisfy. The first point is that the trace variable introduced to our semantics cannot be shortened: an execution step can only add an event to the trace. This is encoded as the

$\mathcal{H}1$ law below: a predicate P defining the semantics of any pNet process must satisfy:

$$(\mathcal{H}1)\quad P = P \wedge Inv(tr) where Inv(tr) =_{df} tr \preceq tr'.$$

The next point deals with divergent processes: "$st = div$" means that the predecessor process has entered the divergent state and the current process will never start. Therefore, a pNets process P has to meet the healthiness condition below:

$$(\mathcal{H}2)\quad P = P \vee (st = div \wedge Inv(tr))$$

A process may wait for receiving message from other subnets or the environment. If the subsequent process is asked to start in a waiting state of its predecessor, it leaves all the states unchanged, including the trace and all its other observational variables. It should satisfy the following healthiness condition:

$$(\mathcal{H}3)\quad P = \mathrm{II} \triangleleft (st = wait) \triangleright P$$

where we denote the logical choice: $P \triangleleft b \triangleright Q =_{df} b \wedge P \vee \neg b \wedge Q$,

the II relation: $\mathrm{II} =_{df} Inv(tr) \triangleleft st = div \triangleright Id$.

and the identity relation: $Id =_{df} (st' = st) \wedge (tr' = tr) \wedge (cs' = cs) \wedge (\overline{ds}' = \overline{ds})$.
Now we give the definition for $\mathcal{H}$-function:

$$\mathcal{H}(X) =_{df} (X \wedge Inv(tr)) \triangleleft st = comp \triangleright (Inv(tr) \triangleleft st = div \triangleright \mathrm{II})$$

From the definition of $\mathcal{H}$-function, we know that $\mathcal{H}(X)$ satisfies all the healthiness conditions. This function can be used in defining the denotational semantics for pNets model.

The definitions here are similar to the one in [6], with the following correspondance with the variables ok and $wait$ from the original UTP theory: $st = comp$ corresponding to the situation that $ok \wedge \neg wait$, $st = wait$ corresponding to $ok \wedge wait$ and $st = div$ corresponding $\neg ok$.

4   Denotational Semantics

In this section, we present the denotational semantics for the four constructs of pNets: pLTSs, Holes, pNet nodes and pNet composition. We use $\mathbf{beh}(P)$ to describe the behaviour of a pNet process after it is activated. Here P can be any type of pNet or a transition of a pLTS.

4.1   Parameterised Labelled Transition System

The order of execution in a pLTS relies on the relations between states and transitions, encoded in its transition relation. The variable cs is used to keep tracking the execution of the pNets processes so that we know at which step the execution will continue. The denotational semantics of a pLTS is given below.

$$\textbf{beh}(\langle\!\langle S, s_0, \rightarrow \rangle\!\rangle) =_{df} \textbf{beh}(\textbf{Init}((x_j := e_j)^{j\in J}), s_0) \,\overset{\circ}{,}\, \textbf{beh}(\langle\!\langle S, s_0, \rightarrow \rangle\!\rangle_{s_0})$$

$$\textbf{beh}(\langle\!\langle S, s_0, \rightarrow \rangle\!\rangle_{cs}) =_{df} \bigvee\nolimits_{t\in\textbf{Trans}(cs)} \left(\textbf{beh}(t) \,\overset{\circ}{,}\, \textbf{beh}(\langle\!\langle S, s_0, \rightarrow \rangle\!\rangle_{\textbf{tgt}(t)})\right)$$

where $P\,\overset{\circ}{,}\,Q$ denotes the sequential composition in the form of relational calculus, meaning that $P\,\overset{\circ}{,}\,Q = \exists obs_0.\,P[obs_0/obs']\wedge Q[obs_0/obs]$. The term obs (resp. obs_0, obs') represents the set of variables st, cs, ds and tr.

The behaviour of a pLTS is the set of traces computed from its initial state. The set of traces computed from an arbitrary state cs is the union of all traces obtained using its set of outgoing transitions $\textbf{Trans}(cs)$, followed by the traces of their target states.

$$\textbf{beh}(\textbf{Init}((x_j := e_j)^{j\in J}), s_0) =_{df}$$

$$\mathcal{H}\left(st' = comp \wedge ds(s_0)' = \{x_j := e_j\}^{j\in J}) \wedge tr' = \langle\,\rangle \wedge cs' = s_0 \right)$$

The above semantics deals with the initialisation on the local variables of the initial state as well as other observational variables.

Now we look into the details of the execution of a transition. For the actions, as we defined in the action terms, we will mainly use action algebras in this form: $\alpha(?x_1, \ldots, ?x_{n_1}, e_1, \ldots, e_{n_2})$. For simplicity, we will use the notation $\alpha(?x, e)$ instead when giving our semantics. Note that the forms of the actions are not limited to this, but are out of the scope of this paper. The execution of one single transition is atomic without interruption by the other processes. If the guard evaluates to `false`, then the trace remains unchanged and the variables stay in the initial state. Otherwise there will be two stages. One stage is the waiting state, at which the process is waiting for input values and all other observational variables stay unchanged. The other stage is the terminating state. If there are input variables in the action, they will be assigned input values. Then, the values of the local variables in the assignments will be updated accordingly.

$$\textbf{beh}(t)=\textbf{beh}(s \xrightarrow{\langle\alpha(?x,e),e_b,(x_j:=e_j)^{j\in J}\rangle} s') =_{df}$$

$$\mathcal{H}\left(\begin{pmatrix} \begin{pmatrix} st' = wait \wedge tr' = tr \wedge cs' = cs \wedge ds(s')' = ds(s') \\ \vee \\ st' = comp \wedge \exists m \in \textbf{Value}. \\ \quad \begin{pmatrix} tr' = tr^\frown\langle\alpha(m,e)\rangle \wedge cs' = s' \wedge \\ ds(s')' = ds(s')[m/x, (e_j/x_j)^{j\in J}] \end{pmatrix} \end{pmatrix} \\ \triangleleft e_b \triangleright \\ st' = comp \wedge tr' = tr \wedge cs' = cs \wedge ds(s')' = ds(s') \end{pmatrix}\right)$$

Here, **Value** stands for all possible values which can be transmitted by subnets in the whole pNet. In the action $\alpha(?x, e)$, there is an input variable x, an expression e whose value will be sent. It is obvious that a value (denoted m here) is assigned to x, thus we have $\alpha(m, e)$ recorded in the trace and the value of x changed in the local variables of the target state s'. Each transition produces a single action, and a single step in the relational semantics. After the execution of the transition, the pLTS moves to the target state at which the next execution will start.

Example 5. Recall the pLTS C_1 from Fig. 1. There are three transitions in the pLTS and we would like to show how its semantics is obtained.

We start unfolding the definitions for Initialization,
$$\mathbf{beh}(C_1) = \mathcal{H}\,(st' = comp \wedge \emptyset \wedge tr' = \langle\,\rangle \wedge cs' = 0)\,\mathbf{;}\,\mathbf{beh}((C_1)_0)$$
Then the definition for states:
$$\mathbf{beh}((C_1)_0) = \mathbf{beh}(0 \xrightarrow{l} 0)\,\mathbf{;}\,\mathbf{beh}((C_1)_0) \vee \mathbf{beh}(0 \xrightarrow{\delta} 1)\,\mathbf{;}\,\mathbf{beh}((C_1)_1)$$
$$\mathbf{beh}((C_1)_1) = \mathbf{beh}(1 \xrightarrow{r} 1)\,\mathbf{;}\,\mathbf{beh}((C_1)_1)$$
and for each transition, e.g.:
$$\mathbf{beh}(0 \xrightarrow{l} 0) = \mathcal{H}(st' = comp \wedge tr' = tr^\frown\langle l \rangle \wedge cs' = 0)$$
Now we apply the semantics of the sequence ($\mathbf{;}$) operator, producing recursive equations on the value of the observational variables:
$$\mathbf{beh}((C_1)_0) = \mathcal{H}(B) \text{ such that}$$
$B = \exists st_1, tr_1, cs_1.\ (st_1 = comp \wedge tr_1 = tr^\frown\langle l \rangle \wedge cs_1 = 0) \wedge B[st_1/st, tr_1/tr, cs_1/cs]$

Unfolding this equation k times, eliminating intermediate variables, and adding the initialisation step finally gives us:
$B = \exists st_0, st_1, ..., st_k, tr_k, cs_k.\ \vee\ (st_k = comp \wedge tr_k = tr^\frown\langle l^k \rangle \wedge cs_k = 0) \wedge B[st_k/st, tr_k/tr, cs_k/cs]$.

Building now the semantics of the full C_1 pLTS yields to a set of mutually recursive equations on predicate variables, with one such variable for each state of the pLTS. Here the solution is $\{tr, cs\}$, where:

$tr = \langle l^* \rangle, cs = s_0 \quad \vee \quad tr = \langle l^* \rangle^\frown\langle\delta\rangle, cs = s_1 \quad \vee \quad tr = \langle l^* \rangle^\frown\langle\delta\rangle^\frown\langle r^* \rangle, cs = s_1.$

Example 6. Consider now the pLTS C_2 in Fig. 1, who has a state variable s_0. The initialization gives:
$$\mathbf{beh}(C_2) = \mathcal{H}\,(st' = comp \wedge ds' = \{s_0 := 0\} \wedge tr' = \langle\,\rangle \wedge cs' = 0)\,\mathbf{;}\,\mathbf{beh}((C_2)_0)$$
Its semantics is $\{tr, ds, cs\}$, where:
$$tr = \langle l^* \rangle,\ ds = \{s_0 := 0\},\ cs = 0.$$
$$\vee \quad tr = \langle l^* \rangle^\frown\langle\delta\rangle,\ ds = \{s_0 := 1\},\ cs = 0$$
$$\vee \quad tr = \langle l^* \rangle^\frown\langle\delta\rangle^\frown\langle r^* \rangle,\ ds = \{s_0 := 1\},\ cs = 0.$$

Example 7. Finally we give an example of a pLTS with value-passing, that is using an input variable.

The set of solutions is $\{tr, ds, cs\}$, where traces a formed by a sequence of i/o actions a finite number of times, eventually followed by a single i action (when moving to state 1). Naturally in each cycle the value carried can be different:

Buffer

A pLTS with a data store

$$tr = Cycles(l),\ ds = \emptyset,\ cs = 0$$

$$\lor\quad tr = Cycles(l)^\smallfrown\langle i(v_{l+1})\rangle,\ ds = \{x := v_{l+1}\},\ cs = 1,\ \forall v_{l+1} \in \textbf{Value}.$$

in which $Cycles(l) = \langle (i(v_k), o(v_k))^* \rangle$ with $\forall k \in [1..l].v_k \in \textbf{Value}$

4.2 Holes

Now we investigate the semantics for the holes, where we benefit from the semantics of transitions in pLTSs. For a hole H with sort $Sort(H)$, we define the maximum behaviour of H by building a single state pLTS, being able to perform any sequence of actions of the sort.

$$MaxLTS(H) = \langle\!\langle \{s_0\}, s_0, \rightarrow \rangle\!\rangle, with \qquad \forall a \in Sort(H).s_0 \xrightarrow{\langle a \rangle} s_0$$

$$\textbf{beh}(H) =_{df} \textbf{beh}(MaxLTS(H))$$

4.3 Parallel Composition

This section investigates the behaviour of a pNets system composed of a set of subnets running in parallel. Let $pNet = \ll pNet_i^{i \in I}, S_j^{j \in J}, \overline{SV} \gg$. Its behaviour is the composition of the behaviours of all the subnets by merging the traces together.

We do not put any constraint on the finiteness of the pNets model - a pNets system is able to compose an unbounded number of subnets. But for readability we assume here $I \cup J = [1, n]$, thus n pairs of (st, tr) are used to observe each subnet, working concurrently to contribute to the composition result. Also remark that the internal states and stores (cs, ds) of subnets are not observed. The composition is described by the following definition:

$$\textbf{beh}(\ll pNet_i^{i \in I}, S_j^{j \in J}, \overline{SV} \gg) =_{df}$$

$$\left(\begin{array}{l} \exists\ st_1, st_1', \ldots, st_n, st_n', tr_1, tr_1', \ldots, tr_n, tr_n', \overline{ds_1}, \overline{ds_1}', \ldots, \overline{ds_n}, \overline{ds_n}' \, . \\ tr_1 = \ldots = tr_n = tr \land st_1 = \ldots = st_n = st \land \\ \forall i \in I.\textbf{beh}(pNet_i)[st_i, st_i', \overline{ds_i}, \overline{ds_i}', tr_i, tr_i'/st, st', \overline{ds}, \overline{ds}', tr, tr'] \land \\ \forall j \in J.\textbf{beh}(S_j)[st_j, st_j', \overline{ds_j}, \overline{ds_j}', tr_j, tr_j'/st, st', \overline{ds}, \overline{ds}', tr, tr'] \land \\ Merge \end{array} \right)$$

in which the $Merge$ predicate captures the behaviours of a parallel composition:
$$Merge =_{df}$$

$$\begin{pmatrix} (\forall i \in [1,n].\, st_i' = comp) \Rightarrow st' = comp \wedge \\ (\exists i \in [1,n].\, st_i' = div) \Rightarrow st' = div \wedge \\ \left(\exists i \in [1,n] \cdot \begin{pmatrix} st_i' = wait \wedge \\ \forall j \in [1,n] \cdot st_j' \neq div \end{pmatrix} \right) \Rightarrow st' = wait \wedge \\ \overline{ds}' = \bigcup_{i \in [1,n]} \overline{ds_i}' \wedge \\ \exists u \in (tr_1' - tr_1 \| \ldots \| tr_n' - tr_n).\, tr' = tr^\frown u \end{pmatrix}$$

The status of the composed behaviour is determined by the n parallel components together. The composition terminates if all the processes terminate and diverges as long as one of the processes diverges. Then the composition stays at waiting state if one of the processes waits and none of the others diverges. Finally, the composition of these n traces is produced by the *trace synchronisation* operator $\|$:

Trace Synchronisation. This operator takes n arguments $tr_i' - tr_i$, each being a subsequence of arbitrary length of actions of the corresponding subnet. It computes a set of subtraces that $Merge$ will append to the traces of the composed pNet.

case-1. If all the input traces are empty, the result is a set of an empty sequence:

$$\langle\rangle \| \ldots \| \langle\rangle = \{\langle\rangle\}$$

case-2. If there is a synchronised action (τ in this paper) in the head of one of the input traces, it is automatically visible at the upper level of the pNet, so we directly record this action in the merged traces.

$$= \exists k \in [1..n].\, e_k = \tau \implies$$

$$\langle e_1\rangle^\frown t_1 \| \ldots \| \langle e_n\rangle^\frown t_n = \{\langle e_k\rangle^\frown l \mid l \in \langle e_1\rangle^\frown t_1 \| \ldots \| t_k \| \langle e_{k+1}\rangle^\frown t_{k+1} \| \ldots \| \langle e_n\rangle^\frown t_n\}$$

case-3. In all other situations, we need to select one synchronisation vector matching an event group within the set of the first observations of all the n input traces (Definition 5) and then figure out a synchronised event. Remember that a synchronisation vector concerns any (non-empty) subset of the subnets of the current pNet node. Let us denote as **Value** the set of all possible values which can be transmitted by subnets in the whole pNet and $vars(SV)$ the variables of a synchronisation vector SV.

Definition 5 (Events Match). *Given a set of events* $\{e_o, e_p, ..., e_q\} \subseteq \{e_1, e_2, ..., e_n\}$, *we say that they match if there exists a synchronisation vector* $SV = \alpha_l^{l \in L} \rightarrow \alpha' \in \overline{SV}$ *and a valuation function* $\phi = \{x \rightarrow \textbf{Value} \mid x \in var(SV)\}$ *that lets both* $(\alpha_l)^{l \in L} \phi = \{e_o, e_p, \ldots e_q\}$ *and* $L = \{o, p, \ldots, q\}$ *satisfied. We write* $\mathsf{EMatch}(SV, \alpha', \phi, e_o, e_p, \ldots, e_q)$.

With this definition, we can complete the definition of trace synchronisation:

$$\mathsf{EMatch}(SV, \alpha', \phi, e_o, e_p, \ldots, e_q) \implies$$

$$\langle e_1\rangle^\frown t_1 \| \ldots \| \langle e_n\rangle^\frown t_n = \{\langle \alpha'\phi\rangle^\frown l \mid l \in \langle e_1\rangle^\frown t_1 \| \ldots \| t_o \| \langle e_{o+1}\rangle^\frown t_{o+1} \|$$

$$\ldots \| t_p \| \langle e_{p+1}\rangle^\frown t_{p+1} \| \ldots \| t_q \| \langle e_{q+1}\rangle^\frown t_{q+1} \| \ldots \| \langle e_n\rangle^\frown t_n\}$$

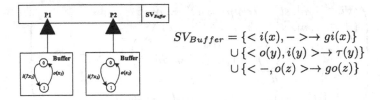

$$SV_{Buffer} = \{< i(x), - > \rightarrow gi(x)\}$$
$$\cup \{< o(y), i(y) > \rightarrow \tau(y)\}$$
$$\cup \{< -, o(z) > \rightarrow go(z)\}$$

Fig. 3. A pNet showing data flow

Example 8. Now we use the pNets example in Fig. 3 with explicit data transmission to present how its denotational semantics is computed by using our definition. In this 2-places buffer, you can see two pLTSs with identical transitions. It is easy to obtain one possible trace for P1, with an arbitrary number of i/o cycles:

$t_{P1} = \langle i(e_1), o(e_1), i(e_2), o(e_2), i(e_3) \rangle$.

And below is a corresponding trace of P2.

$t_{P2} = \langle i(e_1'), o(e_1'), i(e_2') \rangle$.

From the set of synchronisation vectors defined, we can figure out that on the first execution step, P1 receives some value e_1 assigned to its input variable x_1. This uses the first synchronisation vector of the Buffer pNet, and generates the global action $gi(e_1)$. In the next step, P1 emits e_1 of x_1, synchronised with action $i(x_2)$ of P2, thus the x_2 in P2 is assigned the value e_1, using the second vector, and generating action $\tau(e_1)$.

Then we can obtain one trace for the whole pNets by using the trace synchronisation operator. We have omitted the values of variables st and ds, that the reader will easily guess.

$t_{P1} \parallel t_{P2} = \langle gi(e_1) \rangle^\frown l_1$.

where $l_1 \in \langle o(e_1), i(e_2), o(e_2), i(e_3) \rangle \parallel \langle i(e_1'), o(e_1'), i(e_2') \rangle$.
There is only one choice in l_1, matching the 2nd vector of the Buffer pNet:

$t_{P1} \parallel t_{P2} = \langle gi(e_1), \tau(e_1) \rangle^\frown l_2$.

where $l_2 \in \langle i(e_2), o(e_2), i(e_3) \rangle \parallel \langle o(e_1'), i(e_2') \rangle$. Now there are two possible choices, either use the first vector with event $i(e_2)$ (yielding $gi(e_2)$), or the third one with $o(e_1')$ (yielding $go(e_1)$).

Finally the full composition is given by the following regular expression:

$$t_{P1} \parallel t_{P2} = \langle gi(e_1), \tau(e_1), gi(e_2), go(e_1), \tau(e_2), gi(e_3) \rangle$$
$$\vee \langle gi(e_1), \tau(e_1), go(e_1), gi(e_2), \tau(e_2), gi(e_3) \rangle,$$

after which both traces t_{P1} and t_{P2} are exhausted.

4.4   Composition Operator

This section explores the behaviour of the composition of two pNets. In order to simplify the notation, we only consider here a composition operator that replaces a hole at the first (top) level of a pNet tree, that is less general than the composition operator in Definition 4.

Let $N_1 = \ll pNet_i^{i \in I_1}, S_j^{j \in J_1}, \overline{SV_1} \gg$, $N_2 = \ll pNet_i^{i \in I_2}, S_j^{j \in J_2}, \overline{SV_2} \gg$. The pNet composition $N_1[N_2]_{ho}$ indicates that a pNet N_2 fills a hole indexed ho in N_1.

Now we describe the behaviour of $N_1[N_2]_{ho}$:

$\mathbf{beh}(N_1[N_2]_{ho}) =_{df}$

$$
\left(
\begin{array}{l}
\exists st_1, st_1', st_2, st_2', tr_1, tr_1', tr_2, tr_2', \overline{ds_1}, \overline{ds_1'}, \overline{ds_2}, \overline{ds_2'}. \\
st_1 = st_2 = st \wedge tr_1 = tr_2 = tr \wedge \\
\mathbf{beh}(N_1)[st_1, st_1', tr_1, tr_1', \overline{ds_1}, \overline{ds_1'}/st, st', tr, tr', \overline{ds}, \overline{ds'}] \wedge \\
\mathbf{beh}(N_2)[st_2, st_2', tr_2, tr_2', \overline{ds_2}, \overline{ds_2'}/st, st', tr, tr', \overline{ds}, \overline{ds'}] \wedge \\
NM(ho)
\end{array}
\right)
$$

The first four predicates describe the two independent behaviours of pNets N_1 and N_2 being composed (running in parallel in essence). The last predicate $NM(ho)$ mainly does the merging of the contributed traces of the two behaviour branches for recording the communication, which is defined below.

$NM(ho) =_{df}$

$$
\left(
\begin{array}{l}
st_1' = comp \wedge st_2' = comp \Rightarrow st' = comp \wedge \\
st_1' = div \vee st_2' = div \Rightarrow st' = div \wedge \\
st_1' = wait \wedge st_2' \neq div \Rightarrow st' = wait \wedge \\
st_2' = wait \wedge st_1' \neq div \Rightarrow st' = wait \wedge \\
\overline{ds'} = \overline{ds_1'} \cup \overline{ds_2'} \wedge \\
\exists u \in (tr_1' - tr_1)[tr_2' - tr_2]_{ho}. tr' = tr^\frown u
\end{array}
\right)
$$

The control state of the composed behaviour of the pNet is determined by the combination of the status of the two pNets, which is similar to parallel composition. The trace of the composition is a member of the set of traces produced by *trace composition* operator $[\ ]_{ho}$.

Trace Composition. Operator $[\ ]_{ho}$ models how to merge two individual traces (under some constraints) of pNets $N1$ and $N2$ into a set of traces of $N_1[N_2]_{ho}$.

case-1. If both input traces are empty, the result is a set of an empty sequence:

$$\langle \rangle [\langle \rangle]_{ho} = \{\langle \rangle\}$$

case-2. If the trace of the subnet is empty, the result is determined by the first observation of the non-empty trace:

$$\langle e \rangle^\frown t [\langle \rangle]_{ho} = \{\langle e \rangle^\frown l \mid l \in \{\langle \rangle\}\} = \{\langle e \rangle\}$$

case-3. In the situation where the inner input trace is not empty, we need to check first whether these two traces match (see Definition 7). Only two matching traces can be merged. Then we find out the first pair of matching events (see Definition 6) from the matched traces respectively and compute the corresponding action for the merged trace.

Let t_1 and t_2 be two traces of N_1 and N_2 respectively.

Definition 6 (Events Match for pNets Composition). *Given a pair of events e_1 and e_2, we say that they are matched for pNets composition if there exists a synchronisation vector $SV = \alpha_l^{l \in L} \to \alpha' \in \overline{SV_1}$, with $ho \in L$, and a valuation function that lets $\alpha_{ho}\phi_{ho} = e_2$. We have $\alpha'\phi = e_1$ and we define an updated valuation function $\phi' = \phi + \phi_{ho}$ which replaces some of the values defined in ϕ by the ones in ϕ_{ho}. We write $< \alpha', \phi' > = \mathsf{CEMatch}(e_1, e_2, ho)$.*

Definition 7 (Traces Match). *We say that the two traces t_1 and t_2 are matched (denoted as $\mathsf{TMatch}(t_1, t_2, ho)$) if they satisfy such conditions:*

(1) For each element e_2 except synchronised action τ in t_2, there exists an element e_1 in t_1 (where e_1 can be τ) that satisfies $\mathsf{CEMatch}(e_1, e_2, ho)$;

(2) Matching pairs of events are ordered consistently: given two such pairs $(t_1[i] = e_1, t_2[i'] = e_2)$ and $(t_1[j] = e_3, t_2[j'] = e_4)$ such that $\mathsf{CEMatch}(e_1, e_2, ho)$ and $\mathsf{CEMatch}(e_3, e_4, ho)$ are satisfied, then $i < j \implies i' < j'$.

Now we present how the $[\,]_{ho}$ operator works under the third case.

Let $t_1 = s_1^{\frown}\langle e_1 \rangle ^{\frown} r_1$ and $t_2 = s_2^{\frown}\langle e_2 \rangle ^{\frown} r_2$, where we have $\mathsf{TMatch}(t_1, t_2)$, $\neg \mathsf{TMatch}(s_1, s_2)$ and $< \alpha', \phi' > = \mathsf{CEMatch}(e_1, e_2)$ all satisfied. Then:

$$s_1^{\frown}\langle e_1 \rangle^{\frown} r_1 [s_2^{\frown}\langle e_2 \rangle^{\frown} r_2]_{ho} = \{l_1^{\frown}\langle \alpha'\phi' \rangle^{\frown} l_2 \mid l_1 \in s_1 \mid\mid\mid s_2 \wedge l_2 \in r_1[r_2]_{ho}\}$$

where the shuffle operator $\mid\mid\mid$ is defined as:

$$\langle \rangle \mid\mid\mid \langle \rangle = \{\langle \rangle\}; \qquad \langle \rangle \mid\mid\mid \langle e_2 \rangle^{\frown} t_2 = \{\langle e_2 \rangle^{\frown} l \mid l \in \langle \rangle \mid\mid\mid t_2\}$$

$$\langle e_1 \rangle^{\frown} t_1 \mid\mid\mid \langle e_2 \rangle^{\frown} t_2 = \{\langle e_1 \rangle^{\frown} l \mid l \in t_1 \mid\mid\mid \langle e_2 \rangle^{\frown} t_2\} \cup \{\langle e_2 \rangle^{\frown} l \mid l \in \langle e_1 \rangle^{\frown} t_1 \mid\mid\mid t_2\}$$

Example 9. Now we consider the semantics for $\mathrm{Enable}(\mathrm{P},\mathrm{P}')[\mathrm{Enable}(\mathrm{Q},\mathrm{R})]_{P'}$ expressing $P \gg (Q \gg R)$ that we mentioned in Example 4. The behaviours of the composed pNet is computed from the behaviours of two pNets, which may contain a large number of observations. In order to make the illustration more readable, we select single traces from the sets to show the merging of the traces.

Let t_1 and t_2 be two traces of $\mathrm{Enable}(\mathrm{P},\mathrm{P}')$ and $\mathrm{Enable}(\mathrm{Q},\mathrm{R})$ respectively where $t_1 = \langle \alpha_1, \tau, \alpha_2, \alpha_3 \rangle$, $t_2 = \langle \alpha_2, \tau, \alpha_3 \rangle$. We have here $\alpha_1 \in Sort(P)$, $\alpha_2 \in Sort(Q)$ and $\alpha_3 \in Sort(R)$.

According to Definition 6, $< \alpha_2, \{a_4 \mapsto \alpha_2\} > = \mathsf{CEMatch}(\alpha_2, \alpha_2, P')$ and $< \alpha_3, \{a_4 \mapsto \alpha_3\} > = \mathsf{CEMatch}(\alpha_3, \alpha_3, P')$ are satisfied, both firing the synchronisation vector $\{< -, a_4, r > \to a_4\}$ in Fig. 2. Also, a_2 and a_3 are well ordered in t_1 and t_2 conforming with Definition 7. Then we can obtain one trace of the newly constructed pNet by merging the two traces above:

$$t_1[t_2]_{P'} = \langle \alpha_1, \tau, \alpha_2, \alpha_3 \rangle [\langle \alpha_2, \tau, \alpha_3 \rangle]_{P'}$$
$$= \langle \alpha_1, \tau \rangle^{\frown} \langle \alpha_2 \rangle^{\frown} \langle \alpha_3 \rangle [\langle \rangle^{\frown} \langle \alpha_2 \rangle^{\frown} \langle \tau, \alpha_3 \rangle]_{P'} = \langle l_1, \alpha_2, l_2 \rangle$$

where $l_1 \in \langle \alpha_1, \tau \rangle ||| \langle \rangle$ and $l_2 \in \langle \alpha_3 \rangle [\langle \tau, \alpha_3 \rangle]_{P'} = \langle \tau, \alpha_3 \rangle$.

So we get one trace for Enable(P,P')[Enable(Q,R)]$_{P'}$: $\quad \langle \alpha_1, \tau, \alpha_2, \tau, \alpha_3 \rangle$.

5   Algebraic Properties

The main purpose of the formalisation of a programming language is to prove its interesting properties. Most of them are elegantly expressed in the form of algebraic laws and equations. In this section, we explore a set of basic algebraic laws for pNets, based on standard trace semantics: 2 pNets are equivalent if they have same (potentially infinite) set of (finite) traces. pNets being a low level model used to express the semantics of high level languages, we have two categories of properties: general properties about pNets themselves, and specific properties about operators encoded using pNets. We start with a property of the Enable operator of Lotos encoded in Fig. 1.

Associativity of Enable. Consider the two pNets expressing $(P \gg Q) \gg R$ (in Fig. 4(a)), built as Enable(P',R)[Enable(P,Q)]$_{P'}$, and $P \gg (Q \gg R)$ (in Fig. 4(b)), built as Enable(P,P')[Enable(Q,R)]$_{P'}$ respectively. We would like to prove the associativity law: $(P \gg Q) \gg R = P \gg (Q \gg R)$.

Sketch of the Proof: On the left we have traces of Enable(P,Q) and Enable(P',R) whose traces are given below, denoted as t_1 and t_2 respectively.

$$t_1 = \langle a_1^{n_1} \rangle \vee t_1 = \langle a_1^{n_1} \rangle ^\frown \langle \tau \rangle ^\frown \langle a_2^{n_2} \rangle, \forall n_1, n_2 \in \mathbb{N}$$
$$t_2 = \langle a_2^{n_2} \rangle \vee t_2 = \langle a_2^{n_2} \rangle ^\frown \langle \tau \rangle ^\frown \langle a_3^{n_3} \rangle, \forall n_2, n_3 \in \mathbb{N}.$$

Here, we can see that the traces from each set to be merged complying with the form $s_1 ^\frown \langle a_2 \rangle ^\frown t_1 [\langle a_2 \rangle ^\frown t_2]$, where $< \alpha_2, \{a_4 \mapsto \alpha_2\} >=$ CEMatch(α_2, α_2, P') is satisfied. Also, TMatch(t_1, t_2, P') is satisfied if $n_2 = n_3$. Then we deduce the traces for Enable(P',R)[Enable(P,Q)]$_{P'}$:

$$t_{PQ-R} = \langle a_1^{n_1} \rangle \vee t_{PQ-R} = \langle a_1^{n_1} \rangle ^\frown \langle \tau \rangle ^\frown \langle a_2^{n_2} \rangle \vee t_{PQ-R} = \langle a_1^{n_1} \rangle ^\frown \langle \tau \rangle ^\frown \langle a_2^{n_2} \rangle ^\frown \langle \tau \rangle ^\frown \langle a_3^{n_3} \rangle$$

and symmetrically for Enable(P,P')[Enable(Q,R)]$_{P'}$:

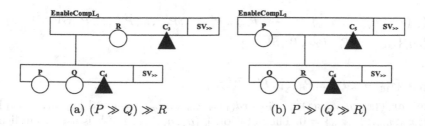

(a) $(P \gg Q) \gg R$ (b) $P \gg (Q \gg R)$

Fig. 4. Two pNets expressing Enable operators

$$t_{P-QR} = \langle a_1^{n_1} \rangle \vee t_{P-QR} = \langle a_1^{n_1} \rangle ^\frown \langle \tau \rangle ^\frown \langle a_2^{n_2} \rangle \vee t_{P-QR} = \langle a_1^{n_1} \rangle ^\frown \langle \tau \rangle ^\frown \langle a_2^{n_2} \rangle ^\frown \langle \tau \rangle ^\frown \langle a_3^{n_3} \rangle$$

Thus, we can say that the behaviours of $(P \gg Q) \gg R)$ and $(P \gg (Q \gg R))$ are equivalent based on traces, and conclude that $(P \gg Q) \gg R = P \gg (Q \gg R)$ is satisfied.   □

Now we list a small number of typical laws that can be proved in a similar manner. For most of them, the proofs are straightforward, but long and tedious. Writing them formally requires a lot of notations that we have not introduced in the paper, and we will not do it here.

Symmetry/Permutation of pNet Nodes. The pNet node as a general parallel operator is symmetric.

For a pNet $\ll pNet_i^{i \in I}, S_j^{j \in J}, SV_k^{k \in K} \gg$, we assume that $I \cup J = [1, n]$ and we abstract each subnet as a process P. Then we alter the pNet node as: $\ll P_1, \ldots, P_n, SV_k^{k \in K} \gg$. It is easy to get

$$\ll P_1, \ldots, P_n, SV_k^{k \in K} \gg = \ll P_{\pi(1)}, \ldots, P_{\pi(n)}, SV_k'^{k \in K} \gg$$

where the structure for each SV_k is $< P_1, \ldots, P_n >$, the structure for each SV_k' is $< P_{\pi(1)}, \ldots, P_{\pi(n)} >$, and π is a permutation on $[1, n]$.

Guarded Choice. We introduce a concept of guarded choice, which enriches the language to support the algebraic laws. The guarded choice is expressed in the form:

$$\{h_1 \to P_1\} [\![\ldots [\![\{h_n \to P_n\}.$$

Each element $h \to P$ of the guarded choice is a guarded component, where h can be a guard in the form of either $\alpha(?x, e)$ or τ. After one of the h_i is performed or fired, the subsequent process is P_i.

(**par-2**)   Let $P_g = \{a_g \to P_g'\} [\![\vert_{i \in I_g} \{\tau \to P_{ig}'\}$,

where $g \in [1, n]$ and a_g is the action that will be synchronised with others according to the synchronisation vectors while τ_{ig} cannot be further synchronised. We here put an index to τ to make it easy to be extended to be in a more flexible form. Then we have:

$$\ll P_1, \ldots, P_g, P_{g+1}, \ldots, P_n, \overline{SV} \gg$$
$$= \{\updownarrow (a_{x_1}, a_{y_1}, \ldots, a_{z_1})^{SV_1} \to \ll P_1, \ldots, P_{x_1}', \ldots, P_{y_1}', \ldots, P_{z_1}', \ldots, P_n, \overline{SV} \gg\}$$

$$\ldots$$

$$[\![\{\updownarrow (a_{x_m}, a_{y_m}, \ldots, a_{z_m})^{SV_m} \to \ll P_1, \ldots, P_{x_m}', \ldots, P_{y_m}', \ldots, P_{z_m}', \ldots, P_n, \overline{SV} \gg\}$$
$$[\![\vert_{i \in I_1} \{\tau_{i1} \to \ll P_{i1}', P_2 \ldots, P_n, \overline{SV} \gg\}$$

$$\ldots$$

$$[\![\vert_{i \in I_n} \{\tau_{in} \to \ll P_1, \ldots, P_{i(n-1)}, P_{in}', \overline{SV} \gg\}$$

where $Card(\{x_1, y_1, \ldots, z_1\})^2 + \ldots + Card(\{x_m, y_m, \ldots, z_m\}) = n$ and $\{x_1, y_1, \ldots, z_1\} \cap \ldots \cap \{x_m, y_m, \ldots, z_m\} = \emptyset$. The notation $\updownarrow (a_x, a_y, \ldots, a_z)^{SV}$ is used to indicate

---

[2] $Card(A)$ returns the number of elements in the set A.

that the parallel execution of all the actions $a_x, a_y, \ldots, a_z$ can trigger a synchronisation presented by SV, of which the result can be either an action to be synchronised or one that cannot be further synchronised.

Identity Operator. A pNet with only one hole indexed 0 of sort S is the identity of pNet composition:

(**ncomp-1**) $I_s[N]_0 = N$ where $I_s := \ll \emptyset, (0 \mapsto S), \{(0 \mapsto a) \to a | a \in S\} \gg$

Composition Operator. If N_2 and N_3 instantiate two holes in N_1 respectively meaning that $Sort(N_2) \subseteq Sort(S_{ho_1})$ and $Sort(N_3) \subseteq Sort(S_{ho_2})$ are satisfied, then we have:

(**ncomp-2**) $(N_1[N_2]_{ho_1})[N_3]_{ho_2} = (N_1[N_3]_{ho_2})[N_2]_{ho_1}$

Proof. Sketch: expanding the definition of $\mathbf{beh}((N_1[N_2]_{h0})$, and removing parts that are trivialy equal, the equation boils down to (here, obs stands for the set of observational variables we defined for our semantics: $\{st, tr, \overline{ds}\}$):

$$LHS = \begin{pmatrix} \exists obs_1, obs_1', obs_2, obs_2'. \, obs_1 = obs_2 = obs \wedge \\ \begin{pmatrix} \exists obs_1, obs_1', obs_2, obs_2'. \\ \mathbf{beh}(N_1)[obs_1, obs_1'/obs, obs'] \wedge \\ \mathbf{beh}(N_2)[obs_2, obs_2'/obs, obs'] \wedge \\ \exists u \in (tr_1' - tr_1)[tr_2' - tr_2]_{ho_1}. \, tr' = tr^\frown u \end{pmatrix} [obs_1, obs_1'/obs, obs'] \wedge \\ \mathbf{beh}(N_3)[obs_2, obs_2'/obs, obs'] \wedge \\ \exists u \in (tr_1' - tr_1)[tr_2' - tr_2]_{ho_2}. \, tr' = tr^\frown u \end{pmatrix}$$

We suppose that any two traces we select to merge are matched according to Definition 7, thus we can always find pairs of events that are matched. If the two pairs of matched events (e, e_2) and (e', e_3) (e_2 and e_3 are events in the trace of N_2 and N_3 respectively, and e and e' are events in the trace they are to be merged.) does not fire the same synchronisation vector, it does not matter which trace merge with the trace of N_1 first. Otherwise, the event $\alpha'\phi'$ recorded in the composed the trace is determined by both e_2 and e_3. Then we have the variables commuted:

$$= \begin{pmatrix} \exists obs_1, obs_1', obs_2, obs_2'. \, obs_1 = obs_2 = obs \wedge \\ \begin{pmatrix} \exists obs_1, obs_1', obs_2, obs_2'. \\ \mathbf{beh}(N_1)[obs_1, obs_1'/obs, obs'] \wedge \\ \mathbf{beh}(N_3)[obs_2, obs_2'/obs, obs'] \wedge \\ \exists u \in (tr_1' - tr_1)[tr_2' - tr_2]_{ho_2}. \, tr' = tr^\frown u \end{pmatrix} [obs_1, obs_1'/obs, obs'] \wedge \\ \mathbf{beh}(N_2)[obs_2, obs_2'/obs, obs'] \wedge \\ \exists u \in (tr_1' - tr_1)[tr_2' - tr_2]_{ho_1}. \, tr' = tr^\frown u \end{pmatrix}$$
$$= RHS$$

In a similar way, if N_2 instantiates one hole in N_1 and one of the holes in N_2 is instantiated by N_3 indicating that $Sort(N_3) \subseteq Sort(S_{ho_2}) \subseteq Sort(S_{ho_1})$ is satisfied, then:

(**ncomp-3**) $N_1[N_2[N_3]_{ho_2}]_{ho_1} = (N_1[N_2]_{ho_1})[N_3]_{ho_2}$

6   Conclusions

In this paper we have formalized a denotational semantics for Parameterised Networks of Processes. A pNet node is considered as an operator composing a number of subnets running in parallel, which ensures the model's flexibility in expressing various operators, and we do not introduce any specific parallel operator to weaken this feature in pNets model. In our semantics, the subnets in the pNets are viewed as processes and the behaviours of each process are investigated by the execution of a subnet. A trace has been introduced to record the interactions among all the subnets in a pNets system. We have investigated the behaviours of subnets including holes. Then the behaviour of a pNet system can be achieved by merging the behaviours of a set of subnets. A set of algebraic laws on both parallel composition and pNet composition has been achieved based on the denotational semantics.

For the future, we plan to continue our formalisation of pNet systems. One aspect of our future work is to explore the algebraic semantics of the pNets model and study the relations among the three semantics: denotational semantics, operational semantics and algebraic semantics. Moreover, the pNets model can be extended by adding other features such as time issues or probabilities. And it is challenging to explore the semantics with these features.

Acknowledgment. This work was partially funded by the Associated Team FM4CPS between INRIA and ECNU, Shanghai. It was also supported by the Danish National Research Foundation and the National Natural Science Foundation of China (No. 61361136002) for the Danish-Chinese Center for Cyber Physical Systems, National Natural Science Foundation of China (Grant No. 61321064), Shanghai Collaborative Innovation Center of Trustworthy Software for Internet of Things (No. ZF1213) and Doctoral Fund of Ministry of Education of China (No. 20120076130003).

References

1. Arnold, A.: Finite Transition Systems - Semantics of Communicating Systems. Prentice Hall International Series in Computer Science. Prentice Hall, Upper Saddle River (1994)
2. Barros, T., Ameur-Boulifa, R., Cansado, A., Henrio, L., Madelaine, E.: Behavioural models for distributed fractal components. Ann. des Télécommun. **64**(1–2), 25–43 (2009)
3. Baude, F., Caromel, D., Dalmasso, C., Danelutto, M., Getov, V., Henrio, L., Pérez, C.: GCM: a grid extension to fractal for autonomous distributed components. Ann. des Télécommun. **64**(1–2), 5–24 (2009)
4. Henrio, L., Madelaine, E., Zhang, M.: pNets: an expressive model for parameterised networks of processes. In: 23rd Euromicro International Conference on Parallel, Distributed, and Network-Based Processing, PDP 2015, Turku, Finland, March 4–6, 2015, pp. 492–496 (2015)
5. Henrio, L., Madelaine, E., Zhang, M.: A theory for the composition of concurrent processes. In: Albert, E., Lanese, I. (eds.) FORTE 2016. LNCS, vol. 9688, pp. 175–194. Springer, Heidelberg (2016). doi:10.1007/978-3-319-39570-8_12

6. Hoare, C.A.R., He, J.: Unifying Theories of Programming. Prentice Hall International Series in Computer Science. Prentice Hall, Upper Saddle River (1998)
7. Koymans, R., Shyamasundar, R., de Roever, W., Gerth, R., Arun-Kumar, S.: Compositional semantics for real-time distributed computing. Inf. Comput. **79**(3), 210–256 (1988)
8. Milner, R.: Communication and Concurrency. Prentice-Hall Inc., Upper Saddle River (1989)
9. Nierstrasz, O.: Piccola - a small composition language. In: Object-Oriented Technology, ECOOP 1999, Workshop Reader, ECOOP 1999 Workshops, Panels, and Posters, Lisbon, Portugal, June 14–18, 1999, Proceedings, p. 317 (1999)
10. Rajan, A., Bavan, S., Abeysinghe, G.: Semantics for a distributed programming language using SACS and weakest pre-conditions. In: International Conference on Advanced Computing and Communications, ADCOM 2006, pp. 434–439, December 2006
11. Schmitt, A., Stefani, J.-B.: The Kell calculus: a family of higher-order distributed process calculi. In: Priami, C., Quaglia, P. (eds.) GC 2004. LNCS, vol. 3267, pp. 146–178. Springer, Heidelberg (2005). doi:10.1007/978-3-540-31794-4_9

UTP Semantics of Reactive Processes with Continuations

Gerard Ekembe Ngondi$^{(\boxtimes)}$ and Jim Woodcock

Department of Computer Science, University of York, York YO10 5GH, UK
gen501@york.ac.uk

Abstract. Based on the Unifying Theories of Programming (UTP) semantic framework, Hoare and He have defined (a means for constructing) a high-level language with labels and jumps, using the concept of continuations. The language permits placing labels at given points within a program and making jumps to these labels when desired. In their work, Hoare and He have limited themselves to the definition of continuations for sequential programs. This paper is concerned with the extension of that work to reactive programs. We first extend their results to include parallelism and Higher Order programs. This is achieved by designing a new control variable $\mathcal{L}$ whose value follows the parallel structure of programs. We then proceed to define reactive (CSP) processes that contain the new control variable $\mathcal{L}$, resulting in the theory of Reactive (Process) Blocks. The encapsulation operator defined by Hoare and He and which may also be used for hiding the control variable $\mathcal{L}$ does readily provide a (functional) link between both UTP theories of Reactive Processes and of Reactive Blocks. The semantics are denotational.

Keywords: Continuations · Denotational semantics · UTP · CSP · Reactive processes

1 Introduction

Implementing a program consists of adding details related to the program's execution on a given platform: the result is called an *implementation*. A detail of particular importance relates to *control flow*, or the order of the execution of the instructions in the program. A device called the *program counter* normally computes and stores the value of the address of the next instruction to be executed. When executing a program, the processor always refers to the program counter.

The method of continuations [10,11] has been devised for giving semantics to programming languages with labels and jumps. As it also allows giving semantics to other programming constructs than jumps, it has resulted in a programming paradigm called continuation-passing style or CPS.

Continuations naturally permit to localise the instructions of a program amongst other instructions. Locations are unique and are ordered according to the order of execution within a given program. Since locations are explicit, a program

© Springer International Publishing AG 2017
J.P. Bowen and H. Zhu (Eds.): UTP 2016, LNCS 10134, pp. 114–133, 2017.
DOI: 10.1007/978-3-319-52228-9_6

must always provide the location of the next program, which is properly called the continuations of its predecessor. High-level programs do not rely on continuations for defining control flow, which is rather associated with the order of evaluation of the instructions of the program.

Process mobility [7] refers to any model or theory that describes the movement of a process from its initial computational environment (or source) to another computational environment (or target). It has two variants: *weak mobility*, in which only the code of the process moves; and *strong mobility*, in which a program is first interrupted, then its code and interrupt state are migrated to a remote target where its execution is to be resumed. Denotational semantics for weak mobility have been defined on the basis of UTP-CSP by Tang and Woodcock [5,6]. We plan to extend their results with semantics for strong mobility.

The resume operation on the remote machine requires the capacity to tell what instruction to execute next, and also to jump to that instruction. However, UTP-CSP [1,4]may rightly be called a high-level language and hence does not provide any jump instruction. The concept of continuations naturally comes to mind for reasoning about control flow in process algebra, and we are not aware of any other model for achieving that. Although some may argue that jumps are a harmful feature at an implementation level, such is not the case as far as semantics are concerned, given that simple elegant models are to be preferred. In sum, we need to extend UTP-CSP with *jump* features in order to define strong mobility, and we propose using continuations as a solution.

Much work is dedicated to continuation-passing style, e.g. [12–16]. However their approach is not directly relevant to our work. In [9], Jahnig et al. provide a denotational semantics for a CSP-like language. Hence, they do not deal directly with CSP either. In the context of UTP, two pieces of work deal with continuations. [1, Chap. 6] provides semantics for sequential programs in general. This work may be used for giving semantics to UTP-CSP processes that have no parallel operator, only. In [8], the authors also use continuations, although they are interested in verifying shared-memory programs. It is not clear from their work why they use continuations. Notwithstanding, their semantics deal with parallel programs in general, hence their work may be used for giving semantics to all UTP-CSP processes. Unfortunately this latter extension is not straightforward and leads us to design a new control variable.

In Sect. 2 we present the UTP semantics for continuations defined in [1, Chap. 6]. They will notably serve as a basis for the formalisation of continuations for parallel programs in general (including the design of the new control variable), discussed in Sect. 3. The corresponding denotational semantics are then presented in Sect. 4. The continuations semantics for UTP-CSP processes are then obtained by applying CSP healthiness conditions to parallel programs (with continuations), thus yielding reactive process blocks, presented in Sect. 5. We then conclude.

2 UTP Background - Continuations for Sequential Programs

2.1 An Overview of UTP

UTP [1] is a formal semantics framework for reasoning about programs, programming theories and the links between theories. The semantics of a program are given by a relation between the initial (undecorated) and final (decorated) observations that can be made of the variables that characterise the program behaviour. Relations are themselves represented as *alphabetised predicates*, i.e. predicates of the form $(\alpha P, P)$. αP is called the *alphabet* of the predicate P, and determines what variables P may mention. αP may be partitioned into two subsets: $in\alpha P$, which represents the initial observations, and $out\alpha P$, which represents the final observations.

Programming languages and paradigms are formalised as UTP theories. A UTP theory is just a collection of predicates, and consists of three elements: an alphabet, containing only those variables that the predicates of the theory may mention; a *signature*, which contains the operators of the theory, and *healthiness conditions* which are laws constricting the set of legal predicates to those that obey the properties expressed by the conditions.

Healthiness conditions generally have the form: $\textbf{NAME} \quad P = f(P)$, for some idempotent function f (i.e. $f \circ f(x) = f(x)$). $\textbf{NAME}$ stands for the name of the healthiness condition and is also used as an alias for f i.e. we write $P = \textbf{NAME}(P)$ and we say that P is $\textbf{NAME}$-healthy.

Specifications are also expressible in UTP, and a theory of refinement permits us to ensure the correctness of a program with regard to a given specification.

The most basic of all UTP theories is the theory of Relations, on top of which every other UTP is built. We define below some program constructs.

Assignment. $x :=_A e$ denotes the assignment of an expression e to a variable x. The meaning of assignment is thus equality: that between x and e after the assignment.

$$x :=_A e \mathrel{\hat=} (x' = e \wedge y' = y \wedge .. \wedge z' = z)$$
$$\alpha(x := e) \mathrel{\hat=} \mathsf{A} \cup \mathsf{A}'$$

Skip. II_A denotes the command that does nothing; it is equivalent to the assignment $x := x$.

$$II_\mathsf{A} \mathrel{\hat=} (x' = x) \qquad where\ \mathsf{A} = \{x, x'\}$$
$$\alpha II_\mathsf{A} \mathrel{\hat=} \mathsf{A}$$

Conditional. $P \lhd b \rhd Q$ stands for 'if b then P else Q', where b is some testable condition. Formally, a *condition* is defined as a predicate not containing dashed variables.

$$P \lhd b \rhd Q \mathrel{\hat=} (b \wedge P) \vee (\neg b \wedge Q) \qquad if\ \alpha b \subseteq \alpha P = \alpha Q$$
$$\alpha(P \lhd b \rhd Q) \mathrel{\hat=} \alpha P$$

Variable Declaration, Undeclaration. $\mathbf{var}\,x$ denotes the declaration of a new program variable x and $\mathbf{end}\,x$ its undeclaration. Let A be an alphabet which includes x and x'. Then:

$$\mathbf{var}\,x \mathrel{\widehat{=}} \exists\,x \bullet II_{\mathsf{A}} \qquad\qquad \alpha(\mathbf{var}\,x) \mathrel{\widehat{=}} \mathsf{A} \setminus \{x\}$$
$$\mathbf{end}\,x \mathrel{\widehat{=}} \exists\,x' \bullet II_{\mathsf{A}'} \qquad\qquad \alpha(\mathbf{end}\,x) \mathrel{\widehat{=}} \mathsf{A} \setminus \{x'\}$$

Alphabet Extension. The scope of x lies between $\mathbf{var}\,x$ and $\mathbf{end}\,x$; beyond, the variable is undefined and cannot be observed. Let $x, x' \in \alpha R$, then:

$$R_{+x} \mathrel{\widehat{=}} R \wedge x' = x$$
$$\alpha R_{+x} = \alpha R \cup \{x, x'\}$$

Floyd Assertion and Assumption. An *assertion* is the statement that a condition, c say, is expected to be true at the point at which it is written; otherwise, the program behaves in a totally unpredictable, chaotic way, i.e. like $\bot$. We also say that the failure is caused by the programmer. An assertion captures the intent of the programmer, that something is meant to be true.

$$c_{\bot} \mathrel{\widehat{=}} II \mathrel{\lhd} c \mathrel{\rhd} \bot$$

On the other hand, an *assumption* is the statement that a condition is true at the point at which it is written; otherwise the program behaves in an impossible, miraculous way, i.e. like $\top$. We also say that the failure is caused by the program. An assumption captures the confidence of the programmer, that something is true.

$$c^{\top} \mathrel{\widehat{=}} II \mathrel{\lhd} c \mathrel{\rhd} \top$$

Reactive Processes

The theory of Relations is too general and may be restricted accordingly by means of healthiness conditions. Here, we give a brief overview of the theory of reactive processes, which permits reasoning about communicating programs.

The alphabet of a reactive process consists of the following:

- $\mathcal{A}$, the set of authorised events; $tr, tr' : \mathcal{A}^*$, the trace; $ref, ref' : \mathbb{P}\mathcal{A}$, the refusal set
- $ok, ok' : \mathbb{B}$, stability and termination; $wait, wait' : \mathbb{B}$, waiting states
- v, v', other variables

The above alphabet alone is not enough to characterise reactive processes. Predicates with such an alphabet must also satisfy the following healthiness conditions.

$$\mathbf{R1} \quad P = P \wedge tr \le tr'$$
$$\mathbf{R2} \quad P = \sqcap\{P[s, s ^\frown (tr' - tr)/tr, tr'] \mid s \in \mathcal{A}^*\}$$
$$\mathbf{R3} \quad P = II_{\mathbf{R}} \mathrel{\lhd} wait \mathrel{\rhd} P$$

where $\Pi_R \mathrel{\widehat{=}} (ok' = ok \wedge wait' = wait \wedge tr' = tr \wedge ref' = ref \wedge v' = v) \lhd ok \rhd$ $(tr \leq tr')$.

R1 states that the occurrence of an event cannot be undone viz. the trace can only get longer. **R2** states that the initial value of tr may not affect the current observation. **R3** states that a process behaves like Π_R when its predecessor has not yet terminated.

Alternatively, we may use the single healthiness condition $R = R1 \circ R2 \circ R3$.

A particular model of reactive processes is provided by the CSP process algebra ([2,3]) whose semantics in UTP are presented subsequently. CSP processes are reactive processes that obey the following additional healthiness conditions:

CSP1 $P = P \lhd ok \rhd tr \leq tr'$

CSP2 $P = P \mathbin{\fatsemi} J$

where $J \mathrel{\widehat{=}} (ok \Rightarrow ok' \wedge wait' = wait \wedge tr' = tr \wedge ref' = ref \wedge v' = v)$

CSP1 states that if a process has not started ($ok = false$) then nothing except for trace expansion can be said about its behaviour. Otherwise the behaviour of the process is determined by its definition. **CSP2** states that a process may always terminate. It characterises the fact that divergence may never be enforced.

Alternatively, we may use the single healthiness condition $CSP = R \circ CSP1 \circ CSP2$.

We present the semantics of some CSP processes subsequently. Some definitions are similar to the ones presented earlier, with some changes. For example, the definitions mention new alphabet elements, and certain healthiness conditions are applied directly, as in assignment below.

Assignment (2). Denoted by $x := e$, is the process that sets the value of the variable x to e on termination, but does not modify the other variables. It does not interact with the environment, always terminates, and never diverges.

$$(x := e) \mathrel{\widehat{=}} R3 \circ CSP1(ok' \wedge \neg wait' \wedge tr' = tr \wedge x' = e \wedge v' = v)$$

A particular kind of assignment is one that leaves everything unchanged, and has already been seen above viz. Π_R.

Skip (2). Denoted by $SKIP$, is the process that refuses to engage in any event, terminates immediately and does not diverge. It is a special instance of Π_R.

$$SKIP \mathrel{\widehat{=}} \exists\, ref \bullet \Pi_R$$

Parallel Composition. Denoted by $P \parallel Q$, is the process that behaves like both P and Q and terminates when both have terminated. P and Q may not share any variable other than the observational variables ($ok, wait, ...$). P and

Q modify separate copies of the shared observational variables which are then merged at the end using the merge predicate M, as defined below.

$$\mathcal{A}(P \parallel Q) \mathrel{\hat{=}} \mathcal{A}P \cup \mathcal{A}Q$$

$$P \parallel Q \mathrel{\hat{=}} P(\mathbf{o}, 1.\mathbf{o}') \wedge Q(\mathbf{o}, 2.\mathbf{o}') \mathbin{;} M(1.\mathbf{o}, 2.\mathbf{o}, \mathbf{o}')$$

$$M \mathrel{\hat{=}} \begin{pmatrix} ok' = (1.ok \wedge 2.ok) \wedge \\ wait' = (1.wait \vee 2.wait) \wedge \\ ref' = (1.ref \cup 2.ref) \wedge \\ (tr' - tr) = ((1.tr - tr) \parallel (2.tr - tr)) \end{pmatrix} \mathbin{;} SKIP$$

2.2 Continuations in UTP

In UTP [1, Chap. 6], the program counter is represented by a variable, denoted l, and referred to as the *control variable*. The set of possible values which l can take is called *continuations set* or simply continuations, and is denoted by αl (αlP, the continuations of a predicate P). The *instructions* of the program are represented by *steps*, which are themselves predicates. An implementation may consist of a 'single' step or of an assembly of such steps.

First, we define programs that may be represented as the sequential repetition of a single step. The value of l is tested before each repetition of the step and determines if the execution of the step starts, continues or ends. Hence, l does also specify *termination*.

Definition 1 (Continuations and execution).

$$P^* \mathrel{\hat{=}} (l \in \alpha lP) * P$$

αlP denotes the set of continuations of P; $l \in \alpha lP$ denotes the control variable for its execution; and P^* denotes the execution of P, defined as a loop, which iterates the step as long as l remains in the continuations set.

For a step P, the value of l determines the start and termination of its execution. When l is outside the continuations of P, P may not be started. Although the behaviour of P in such case may be anything, it is safe to assume that it does nothing, i.e. that its behaviour is II. This is a sound assumption when we consider the execution of P in conjunction with that of other steps.

Definition 2 (Step). *A predicate P is a step if $l \in \alpha lP$ and*

$$P = P \triangleleft l \in \alpha lP \triangleright II$$

As a consequence,

$$((l \notin \alpha lP)_\perp \mathbin{;} P) = (l \notin \alpha lP)_\perp$$

The following theorem gives the closure property of some operators.

Theorem 1 (Step closure). *If P and Q are steps, then*

1. $P \,\fatsemi\, Q$ *is a step.*
2. $P \sqcap Q$ *and* $P \lhd b \rhd Q$ *are also steps whenever* $\alpha l P = \alpha l Q$.
3. *The set of steps is a complete lattice.*

Programs may occupy disjoint storage areas, in which case they are said to be disjoint. This means that two steps which have disjoint continuations are disjoint. It is possible to assemble them into a single program, by using the assembly operator defined below.

Definition 3 (Assembly). *Let P and Q be disjoint steps, i.e.* $\alpha l P \cap \alpha l Q = \{\}$.

$$P \boxplus Q \,\hat{=}\, (P \lhd l \in \alpha l P \rhd Q) \lhd (l \in \alpha l P \cup \alpha l Q) \rhd II$$
$$\alpha l (P \boxplus Q) \,\hat{=}\, \alpha l P \cup \alpha l Q$$

There are two known ways of implementing a program: compilation and interpretation. In what follows we present the former only.

Compilation. Compilation is the transformation of the program into a target program expressed in the machine code of the processor that is to execute it. Compilation conserves the meaning of the source program. The semantics of the target language (or machine code) may equally be given in UTP. Each instruction in the language may be given a meaning as a step.

A single instruction is a step with a single continuation given by the singleton set $\{m\}$.

Definition 4 (Single instruction). *If INST is a machine code instruction then*

$$m : INST \,\hat{=}\, INST \lhd l = m \rhd II$$

is a single instruction.

Single instructions may be assembled together using the assembly operator ($\boxplus$).

Definition 5 (Machine code block). *A* machine code block *is a program expressed as an assembly of single instructions.*

$$S_0 \boxplus S_1 \boxplus \ldots \boxplus S_n$$

Using the preceding definition, it is possible to enter a machine code block at any of its constituent continuation points. In practice, it is common to define a *normal starting point*, denoted by s, and a *normal finishing point*, denoted by f. They relate respectively to the first and last single instructions of the program. s is the value of l when control enters sequentially into the program; any other point should be entered by a jump. f is the value of l when control leaves sequentially through the last instruction. Respectively in each case, we will also talk about *normal start or entry* and *normal termination or exit*. The assumption of normal entry is expressed by the predicate $(l = s)_\top$. The obligation to terminate normally is expressed by the predicate $(l = f)_\bot$. Machine code blocks that have these pre- and post-condition are called *structured*.

Definition 6 (Structured block). *A* structured block *is a program of the form*

$$(l = s)_\top \, \S \, P^* \, \S \, (l = f)_\bot$$

where P is a machine code block. The value of s is called its starting point *and the value of f its* finishing point.

Let $\hat{P}$ denote the target program into which a source program P has been compiled by a compiler. $\hat{P}$ should have the same effect (or behaviour) as P. $l \in \alpha\hat{P}$ but $l \notin \alpha P$ (since P is not a step).

$$P \sqsubseteq (\mathbf{var}\ l \, \S \, \hat{P} \, \S \, \mathbf{end}\ l)$$

Definition 7 (Target code). *A program is in* target code *if it is expressed in the form*

$$\langle s, P, f \rangle \mathrel{\hat{=}} \mathbf{var}\ l \, \S \, (l = s)_\top \, \S \, P^* \, \S \, (l = f)_\bot \, \S \, \mathbf{end}\ l$$

where P is a machine code block. An equivalent formulation is:

$$\langle s, P, f \rangle \mathrel{\hat{=}} \mathbf{var}\ l := s \, \S \, P^* \, \S \, (l = f)_\bot \, \S \, \mathbf{end}\ l$$

According to the fundamental theorem of compilation [1, Chap. 6, Theorem 6.2.10], every program can be expressed in target code.

Theorem 2 (Fundamental theorem of compilation). *Every program can be expressed in target code.*

It is possible to combine low-level language features, such as jumps and labels, with high-level language features. Such a facility was provided by many early programming languages.

High-Level Language with Jumps and Labels. For the combination of a high-level language with jumps and labels to be possible, it is necessary to consider, in addition to s and f, other continuation points viz. those corresponding to entry and exit by a jump. A special value, denoted by $\mathbf{n}$, will be used for both s and f. $\alpha l_0 P$ will denote the set of all entry points; $\alpha l' P$ will denote the set of all exit points; and neither may contain $\mathbf{n}$. If l takes its value in either of these sets, it will signify that the program has been entered or exited by a jump respectively, in contrast to normal entry and exit through $\mathbf{n}$.

Definition 8 (Blocks and proper blocks). *Let S and F be sets of labels (continuation points), and $\mathbf{n} \notin S$, and $\mathbf{n} \notin F$.*

$$(P : S \Rightarrow F) \stackrel{\wedge}{=} P = (P \, \S \, (l \in F \cup \{\mathbf{n}\})_\perp) \lhd l \in S \cup \{\mathbf{n}\} \rhd II)$$

A program is a block *if it satisfies* $P : \alpha l_0 P \Rightarrow \alpha l' P$; *a block is called a* proper block *if* $\alpha l_0 P \cap \alpha l' P = \{\}$.

The construction **label** s permits placing a label within the program at the point intended to be the destination of a jump. **label** s may be entered normally or by a jump, but it always exits normally. The construction **jump** f permits jump-ing to the location indicated by the label f. **jump** f may be entered normally or by a jump, but it always exits by a jump.

Definition 9 (Labels and jumps).

$$\mathbf{label}\, s \stackrel{\wedge}{=} (l := \mathbf{n}) \lhd l \in \{s, \mathbf{n}\} \rhd II \qquad \alpha l_0 \mathbf{label}\, s \stackrel{\wedge}{=} \{s\} \quad \alpha l' \mathbf{label}\, s \stackrel{\wedge}{=} \{\}$$
$$\mathbf{jump}\, f \stackrel{\wedge}{=} (l := f) \lhd l = \mathbf{n} \rhd II \qquad\quad \alpha l_0 \mathbf{jump}\, f \stackrel{\wedge}{=} \{\} \quad \alpha l' \mathbf{jump}\, f \stackrel{\wedge}{=} \{f\}$$

The following theorem gives the permitted operators for blocks having the same alphabets of entry and exit points.

Theorem 3 (Block closure) *The set of blocks $\{P \mid P : S \Rightarrow F\}$ is a complete lattice, and closed with respect to non-deterministic choice and conditional. The same applies to proper blocks.*

Before giving the closure for sequential composition, we first give its continuations. A sequential composition $P \, \S \, Q$ may be entered normally through $\mathbf{n}$, or by a jump. In the second case, the entry point may belong to either P or Q. Similarly, it may be exited normally through $\mathbf{n}$, or by a jump from either P or Q.

Definition 10 (Continuations for sequential composition).

$$\alpha l_0 (P \, \S \, Q) \stackrel{\wedge}{=} \alpha l_0 P \cup \alpha l_0 Q$$
$$\alpha l' (P \, \S \, Q) \stackrel{\wedge}{=} (\alpha l' P \setminus \alpha l_0 Q) \cup \alpha l' Q$$

Theorem 4 (Sequential composition closure) *If $P : S \Rightarrow F$ and $Q : T \Rightarrow G$, then*

$$(P \, \S \, Q) : S \cup T \Rightarrow ((F \setminus T) \cup G)$$

3   Concepts and Formalisation

Note. For ease, we will refer to the work presented in the previous section as HH98 steps or simply HH98. Similarly, we will refer to the work in [8] as WH02 steps or simply WH02.

The CPS transformation (or compiler) is inherently sequential [10,11]. UTP-CSP processes also permit the representation of sequential programs, which form a subset of the class of reactive programs. This suggests that HH98 may be applied at least to sequential UTP-CSP. All that is needed is to extend the alphabet of UTP-CSP sequential processes, and point-wise extend the definition of sequential composition to the control variable l, as suggested in HH98. However, l is not expressive enough for reasoning about control flow in the presence of parallelism.

The problem actually lies with the design of the control variable as *single-valued*. We need a mathematical model that follows more tightly the computation model. For example, using l in the presence of interrupt, it would be as if a single program was interrupted at a time whereas we should be able to say that many programs may be interrupted at a time. The solution is to design a value of the control variable that follows more tightly the structure of processes. This is what is done in [8].

In [8] (hereafter also WH02), Woodcock and Hughes use a *set-valued* control variable, denoted ls instead, and that contains the continuations of all the steps that may be executed in parallel next. Using WH02, we may point-wise extend the UTP-CSP parallel composition operator. However, a number of changes must first be considered. Unlike HH98 steps, a WH02 step may now exit at many points at any one time, implying that a step may be entered simultaneously at multiple entry points. This is a little counter-intuitive but poses no great difficulties. Yet, ls is not sufficient for our purpose. To see this, consider the following illustration.

Let $P = \langle s, P_1, h \rangle \, \raisebox{-0.3ex}{\scriptsize 9} \, \langle h, P_2, f \rangle$, and let $ls = \{s, h\}$. The value of ls is valid, but does not reflect the structure of P. If the programmer was expecting parallel composition, sequential composition will be performed instead, which is an error and will not be detected. Let $Q = \langle s, Q_1, f \rangle \parallel \langle t, Q_2, g \rangle$, and let $ls = \{s\}$. Then Q will behave like Q_1, since Q_2 behaves like *SKIP* (by definition). Again, if parallel composition was expected then only one step will be executed instead of two in parallel, which is an error and will not be detected.

In sum, we have to design a new value for the control variable seeing that neither HH98 variable l nor WH02 variable ls are adequate. $\mathcal{L}$ will denote the new control variable, and we discuss its formalisation subsequently.

Design of the Control Variable $\mathcal{L}$

Parallel composition may be seen as a single block such that when entered sequentially, the steps that compose the block are executed in parallel, and when they have all exited, then the block is also exited. That is, entry into (resp. exit from) a block of parallel steps is identical to entry into (resp. exit from) a sequential block. Sequential and parallel blocks would hence differ in their respective execution order: for the first, only one step may be executed at a single (observation) time, whilst multiple steps may be executed at a single time for the second. In other words, parallel composition acts as an envelop w.r.t. its components. It has its own continuations, that differ from those of its constituents. Let $P = P_1 \parallel P_2$, then the block denoted by P differs from its component blocks P_1 and P_2. P has its own entry and exit points that differ from those of P_1 and P_2.

A *control flow graph* (CFG) is a standard representation of programs with no parallel constructs, using a graph. A CFG and related concepts are appropriate for discussing the structure of UTP-CSP processes. Note that we are not interested in a graphical formalism, but only to use graphs as an adequate means for discussion. In what follows, we sketch what such a graph might look like.

A CFG for Reactive Processes. Figure 1(a) shows an example of such a graph read in a left-right, then top-down, iterative manner, thus indicating the flow of control. P_i nodes may denote either single instructions, sequential blocks, or nested (parallel) blocks. Both the root node (P) and initial nodes (e.g. P_{31}, P_{32}, P_{33}) are indicated by empty circles. A nesting node (e.g. P_3) is indicated by a vertical line starting from the node downwards, as shown in (b). An empty square indicates termination for a horizontal line, whereas it simply serves as a visual aid to indicate the end of a vertical line. A flattened graph (c) shows how control goes through P_3, and then again through P_{312}. More information could have been added for loops, and jumps, and bigger graphs may be conceived, but such are not our main interest. Rather, we may also annotate nodes with their continuations. The annotation procedure would then show how to evaluate the control variable.

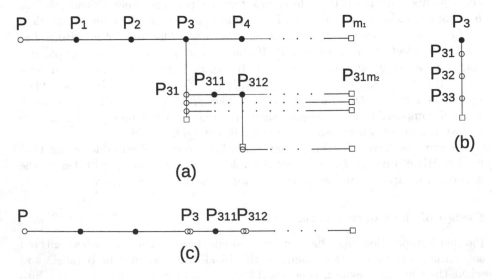

Fig. 1. Example of a CFG for reactive processes

Value of $\mathcal{L}$

Let $\mathcal{L}$ denote the control variable whose value we will be discussing. Then $\alpha\mathcal{L}P$ denotes the continuations of a step P.

To formalise the nesting relation between a parent and its children, we may partition the continuations set of every node into two subsets: αl, the continuations of the parent, and αls, the continuations of its children. We make the following restriction: the parent-child relation does not extend beyond two adjacent levels. Hence, αls contains the continuations of nodes at the lower adjacent level only; e.g. for sequential blocks, $\alpha ls = \{\}$. In what follows, we describe in detail the procedure for attributing continuations to nodes. That is also the procedure for computing the value of $\alpha\mathcal{L}$ for a given block.

Continuations may be attributed hierarchically, in a bottom-up fashion.

1. We make no difference between nodes denoting either single instructions or sequential blocks, and we will refer to them commonly as $\mathbf{lv_0}$ (read level-0) nodes. Such nodes do not introduce nesting, hence they have no children, i.e. $\alpha ls = \{\}$.
2. We then put in parallel $\mathbf{lv_0}$ nodes, exclusively, to form $\mathbf{lv1}$ nodes. Such nodes correspond to the nesting nodes mentioned earlier. The value of αls is given by the union of continuations αl of its constituents. e.g. $\alpha ls P_3 = \{\alpha l P_{31}, \alpha l P_{32}, \alpha l P_{33}\}$.
3. Again, putting exclusively $\mathbf{lv_1}$ nodes in parallel, or together with $\mathbf{lv_0}$ nodes, we obtain $\mathbf{lv_2}$ nodes. αls is the union of all the continuations of *adjacent* $\mathbf{lv_1}$ (and $\mathbf{lv_0}$) nodes, only. Hence the value of αls for a $\mathbf{lv_2}$ node does not contain the continuations of those $\mathbf{lv_0}$ nodes that are nested to $\mathbf{lv_1}$ nodes. e.g. $\alpha l P_{312x} \nsubseteq \alpha ls P_3$, although $\alpha l P_{312} \subseteq \alpha l P_{31} \subset \alpha ls P_3 \,\&\, \alpha ls P_{312} = \{..., \alpha l P_{312x}, ...\}$. This illustrates what we said earlier about αls: it contains only the continuations of the lower adjacent levels. We reiterate this construction procedure for higher-levelled nodes.

The value of $\alpha\mathcal{L}$ may be obtained by iteration on the level of a node considered as the root (of the graph), as follows:

$\mathbf{lv_0}$ root, no children: $\alpha l P \,\&\, \alpha ls P = \{\} \,\&\, \alpha\mathcal{L}P = \alpha l P$
$\mathbf{lv_1}$ root or parent, $\mathbf{lv_0}$ children only: $\alpha ls P = \bigcup_i \alpha l P_i \,\&\, \alpha\mathcal{L}P = \alpha l P \cup \alpha ls P$
$\mathbf{lv_2}$ root or parent, at least one $\mathbf{lv_1}$ child: $\alpha ls P = \bigcup_i \alpha l P_i \,\&\, \alpha\mathcal{L}P = \alpha l P \cup (\bigcup_i \alpha\mathcal{L}P_i)$
$\mathbf{lv_n}$ root or parent, at least one $\mathbf{lv_{n-1}}$ child: $\alpha ls P = \bigcup_i \alpha l P_i \,\&\, \alpha\mathcal{L}P = \alpha l P \cup (\bigcup_i \alpha\mathcal{L}P_i)$

Note. The introduction of a *nesting* step is what distinguishes the value of $\mathcal{L}$ from that of WH02' control variable ls [8]. Its effect is to delegate the instantiation of parallel (nested) nodes to the nesting node, which is a dummy. Thanks to that, control flows as in sequential programs, since the dummy node hides away the parallel structure of programs. It is also thanks to the nesting node that we solve the limitations of ls discussed earlier. Indeed, using WH02 steps, it is possible to jump to a step without care for its nesting level. The presence of the dummy step resolves this by imposing that control must enter into the dummy step first before it can then enter into the parallel steps.

In what follows we describe the semantics of $\mathcal{L}$ formally.

4   Continuations for Programs with Nested Parallelism

HH98 steps (Sect. 2) are programs that compute the control variable l. By analogy, we present programs that compute the control variable $\mathcal{L}$ instead. We follow the same methodology of Hoare and He [1, Chap. 6] that consists of starting with unstructured predicates (i.e. steps) and then adding more structure to obtain in turn target code programs, and then program blocks. In our case, after (re)defining steps, we shall restrict our programs to Reactive Processes and obtain, as a result, the theory of Reactive Process Blocks (Sect. 5) i.e. reactive processes that contain the control variable $\mathcal{L}$.

We now describe predicates whose alphabet include a set of continuations denoted by $\alpha\mathcal{L}$. $\alpha\mathcal{L}$ is partitioned into two subsets: αl, which contains the continuations at the current level of execution, and αls, which contains the continuations at the adjacent lower level of execution, w.r.t. nesting.

At first, each level of execution may be considered without regard for nesting. Then, every step is entered horizontally, and exits horizontally. In a graph, a level corresponds to a single horizontal line that links nodes arranged from left to right, according to their execution order. There is a node which has no horizontal predecessor, called the root of the level. Each node on a line is adjoined a continuation. We say that a node is entered horizontally if we can draw a line from the root leading to it viz. the value of $\mathcal{L}$ corresponds to the node's continuation.

In the case of nesting, in a graph, there is a vertical line linking the higher level, at the top, with its adjacent lower levels, all arranged as parallel horizontal lines. The root of the graph has neither vertical nor horizontal predecessors (i.e. there is no vertical/horizontal line leading to the graph-root); the root of a lower level has no horizontal predecessor and should have at least one vertical predecessor. A lower level (or child) node may be entered only if its parent has been entered first. That is, we can draw a vertical line from the parent node to the lower level line that contains the given child node, when traversing the graph of the step from its root to the given node. In other words, the value of $\mathcal{L}$ must hold both the parent and the child nodes continuations.

Definition 11. *Let P be a predicate describing a step. Let $\alpha\mathcal{L}P$ denote its set of continuations, and let $\mathcal{L}$ be the control variable for its execution. We may partition the set $\alpha\mathcal{L}P$ into two subsets αlP and αlsP such that:*

- *αlP denotes the set of all the continuations of P at a single level of execution.*
- *αlsP denotes the set of all the continuations of P at the adjacent lower level of execution.*

Control may enter into a step horizontally with regard to its own execution level, or vertically with regard to nesting. In either case, a step may be entered only when the value of $\mathcal{L}$ coincides with one of the step's entry points. Otherwise the step does nothing. Formally,

$$P = P \lhd \mathcal{L} \in \alpha\mathcal{L}P \rhd II$$

Some operators induce/embed a nesting relation (cf. below, e.g. parallel assembly) whilst others do not.

Definition 12 (Nesting relation). *Let P be a step, and $\mathbf{op}$ an operator on steps and which is closed.*
$\mathbf{op}$ *is said to* induce nesting *if, and only if, $\alpha l\,\mathbf{op}(P) \neq \alpha lP$ and $\alpha lP \subset \alpha ls\,\mathbf{op}(P)$: then, we say that $\mathbf{op}(P)$ is the* parent *of P, and is called a nesting step; or equivalently, we say that P is* nested *into $\mathbf{op}(P)$, and is called a nested step.*
Otherwise, i.e. if $\alpha l\,\mathbf{op}(P) = \alpha lP$, then $\mathbf{op}$ does not induce nesting.

The value of $\alpha\mathcal{L}P$ may only be given by recursion over the nesting level of P.

Definition 13 ($\mathbf{lv_k}$-steps, $\alpha\mathcal{L}$). *Let P be a step, then*

$$\alpha\mathcal{L}P \cong \alpha lP \cup \alpha lsP$$

where both αlP and αlsP are specified according to the level of the nested programs in the expression of P, as described subsequently.
We say that a program P is a $\mathbf{lv_0}$-step, denoted by $P = \mathbf{lv_0}(P)$, if, and only if, P has neither parent nor children, i.e. $\alpha lsP = \{\}$. Then

$$\alpha\mathcal{L}P \cong \alpha lP \cup \alpha lsP = \alpha lP$$

Let $\mathbf{op}$ be a binary operator that induces nesting. Then:

– *if P and Q are both $\mathbf{lv_0}$-steps, then we say that $\mathbf{op}(P, Q)$ is a $\mathbf{lv_1}$-step and*

$$\alpha l\,\mathbf{op}(P, Q) \cong \{\mathbf{nn}\} \qquad \alpha ls\,\mathbf{op}(P, Q) \cong \alpha\mathcal{L}P \cup \alpha\mathcal{L}Q = \alpha lP \cup \alpha lQ$$

– *if either P or Q is a $\mathbf{lv_1}$-step, or both are, then we say that $\mathbf{op}(P, Q)$ is a $\mathbf{lv_2}$-step and*

$$\alpha l\,\mathbf{op}(P, Q) \cong \{\mathbf{nn}\} \qquad \alpha ls\,\mathbf{op}(P, Q) \cong \alpha\mathcal{L}P \cup \alpha\mathcal{L}Q$$

– *if either P or Q is a $\mathbf{lv_k}$-step, or both are, then we say that $\mathbf{op}(P, Q)$ is a $\mathbf{lv_{k+1}}$-step and*

$$\alpha l\,\mathbf{op}(P, Q) \cong \{\mathbf{nn}\} \qquad \alpha ls\,\mathbf{op}(P, Q) \cong \alpha\mathcal{L}P \cup \alpha\mathcal{L}Q$$

where $\mathbf{op}(P, Q)$ is a nesting step and may have only one entry point, and only one exit point, both denoted by $\mathbf{nn}$ for convenience.

Consequence 1 *1.* $\mathbf{lv_0}$-*steps* do not *induce a nesting relation.*
2. $\mathbf{lv_0}$-*steps are* $\boxplus$-*closed. Hence, every operator that may be defined in terms of* $\boxplus$ *(such as* $\{\triangleleft b \triangleright, \square, \S\}$*) does not* induce *a nesting relation.*

The relation with HH98 steps is obvious:

Theorem 5. *HH98 steps are* $\mathbf{lv_0}$-*steps.*

Sequential Assembly (2). The sequential assembly is as defined by HH98. We simply redefine it here to account for the changes introduced.

$$P \boxplus Q \mathrel{\hat{=}} (P \triangleleft \mathcal{L} \in \alpha\mathcal{L}P \triangleright Q) \triangleleft \mathcal{L} \in (\alpha\mathcal{L}P \cup \alpha\mathcal{L}Q) \triangleright II$$
$$\alpha\mathcal{L}(P \boxplus Q) \mathrel{\hat{=}} \alpha\mathcal{L}P \cup \alpha\mathcal{L}Q$$
$$= \alpha lP \cup \alpha lQ$$

Parallel Assembly. Traditionally, control enters sequentially into a single step at any one time. However, when dealing with parallelism, control may enter sequentially into many steps at any one time. It is therefore possible for a step, upon exit, to indicate that many steps may be executed in parallel next (cf. WH02 [8]).

The selection of next parallel steps may be delegated to a dummy step, or *nesting step*, which is hence responsible of splitting control. In particular, thanks to the nesting step, we are able to 'guarantee by construction' that *none* of the component steps may be jumped into at random, and that *all* the component steps are *always* entered at the same time — it is necessary to enter the nesting step first.

We define below the parallel composition of steps, called *parallel assembly* and denoted by $//$. It states that the parallel assembly of two steps yields a third, nesting step. Such a step may have only one entry point, and only one exit point, both denoted by **nn**.

Definition 14. (Parallel assembly).

$$P//Q \mathrel{\hat{=}} (P \parallel Q) \triangleleft \{\mathbf{nn}\} \in \mathcal{L} \triangleright II$$
$$M(\mathcal{L}) \mathrel{\hat{=}} \mathcal{L}' = 1.\mathcal{L} \cup 2.\mathcal{L}$$
$$\alpha\mathcal{L}(P//Q) \mathrel{\hat{=}} \{\mathbf{nn}\} \cup \alpha\mathcal{L}P \cup \alpha\mathcal{L}Q$$

Instructions, Blocks, Program Blocks. In this section, we principally add more structure to the steps defined in the previous section.

First, we redefine the notion of single instruction.

Definition 15. (Single instruction(2)). *Let INST be a* $\mathbf{lv_0}$-*step, i.e.* $\alpha lsINST = \{\}$*, then*

$$m : INST \mathrel{\hat{=}} INST \triangleleft \mathcal{L} = \{m\} \triangleright II$$

is a single *instruction.*

We may distinguish two types of machine code blocks, according to the assembly operator used for their composition: (purely) sequential blocks (which we also call proper blocks) are the sequential assembly of single instructions (called machine code block in HH98 [1]); and parallel blocks (or nesting blocks) are the parallel assembly of single instructions.

Definition 16. (Proper-, nesting- block). *A proper block, say SeqB, is a program expressible as a sequential assembly of single instructions i.e.*

$$SeqB \mathrel{\widehat{=}} m_0 : INST_0 \boxdot m_1 : INST_1 \boxdot ... \boxdot m_n : INST_n$$
$$\alpha l(SeqB) \mathrel{\widehat{=}} \{m_i \mid 0 \leq i \leq n\}$$
$$\alpha ls(SeqB) \mathrel{\widehat{=}} \{\}$$

A nesting block, say ParB, is a program expressible as a parallel assembly of single instructions i.e.

$$ParB \mathrel{\widehat{=}} m_0 : INST_0 \mathbin{//} m_1 : INST_1 \mathbin{//} ... \mathbin{//} m_n : INST_n$$
$$\alpha l(ParB) \mathrel{\widehat{=}} \{\mathbf{nn}\}$$
$$\alpha ls(ParB) \mathrel{\widehat{=}} \{m_i \mid 0 \leq i \leq n\}$$

We expect any instruction to always pass control via a single exit point that may lead either to a proper instruction or to a nesting one. The definition of target code below reflects that expectation.

Definition 17. (Proper-, nesting- target code). *Let P be a step. Let S below denote the set of entry points of all the steps that will be executed in parallel next, and let F denote the corresponding set of exit points. If $\alpha lsP \neq \{\}$, then we say that any step of the form $\langle (s,S), P, (F,f) \rangle$ is in nesting target code, and defined by*

$$\langle (s,S), P, (F,f) \rangle \mathrel{\widehat{=}} (\mathcal{L} \in \{s\} \cup S)^{\top} \mathbin{\S} P \mathbin{\S} (\mathcal{L} \in F \cup \{f\})_{\perp}$$
$$= \mathbf{var}\mathcal{L} := \{s\} \cup S \mathbin{\S} P \mathbin{\S} (\mathcal{L} \in F \cup \{f\})_{\perp} \mathbin{\S} \mathbf{end}\,\mathcal{L}$$

However, if P is a $\mathbf{lv_0}$-step i.e. $\alpha lsP = \{\}$, then $S = \{\} = F$; we say that the step is in proper target code and we may write simply $\langle s, P, f \rangle$.

Notice above that the entry and exit points of the nesting step are independent of those of the steps supposed to execute in parallel. Upon entry, $\mathcal{L}$ is updated with the continuation s to ensure normal entry into the nesting step itself, and also with the set S so that the parallel steps may be entered conjointly afterwards. Upon exit, the value of $\mathcal{L}$ is first determined by a given merge function (cf. parallel assembly Definition 14) that ensures that $\mathcal{L}' \in F$ upon exiting the parallel assembly, and then $\mathcal{L}$ should be updated with the continuation f to provide normal exit out of the nesting step itself.

In what follows, we define the target code for the parallel composition operator $\|$ only.

The parallel composition of two steps simply yields a third, nesting step, which has its own distinct entry and exit points from those of the steps that are to be run in parallel. Each component step may start only when its continuation has been provided by the nesting step.

Definition 18. (Target code for parallel composition).

$$\langle(s_1, S_1), P, (F_1, f_1)\rangle \parallel \langle(s_2, S_2), Q, (F_2, f_2)\rangle \cong \exists(s, f) \bullet \langle(s, \{s_1, s_2\}), P//Q, (\{f_1, f_2\}, f)\rangle$$
$$\alpha l(P//Q) \cong \{s, f\}$$
$$\alpha ls(P//Q) \cong (\{s_1, f_1\} \cup S_1 \cup F_1) \cup (\{s_2, f_2\} \cup S_2 \cup F_2)$$

We expect the possibility of jumping into nested parallel steps. However, such jumps may not be left unguarded. The least requirement we can impose is that the continuation of the parent must figure in the definition of the jump statement together with the continuations of the children nodes to jump into.

Definition 19. (Vertical jump). $jump(f, F) \cong \mathcal{L} := \{f\} \cup F \lhd \mathcal{L} = \mathbf{n} \rhd II$

Placing a label to multiple steps at the same time for the purpose of running them in parallel may seem like an interesting feature at first, but it would only add pointless complications. It is sufficient for us to place labels in each program individually and then run the result (of each labelling procedure) in parallel.

In sum, in this section, we have defined the semantics of programs which may contain the control variable $\mathcal{L}$, thus extending the range of programs expressible using HH98 and WH02 to nested parallel programs. We have not discussed the case of Higher-order (HO) programs and this should be done, given that the theory of mobile processes for which we have built the continuations above relies on HO programming. We postpone such a discussion to Sect. 5.

5   Reactive Process Blocks

In this section we present the construction and semantics of Reactive Process Blocks (or RPB), based on the results obtained previously. RPB processes are meant to extend UTP-CSP processes with continuations. Since we are also interested in Higher-order programming, i.e. the possibility of calling a program within another program, we shall consider the extension of UTP-CSP with HO programming defined by Tang and Woodcock [6].

Alphabet. First, let us consider UTP-CSP processes as defined in [6]. The alphabet of a UTP-CSP process P is defined by

$$\alpha P \cong VarP \cup Obs \cup \mathcal{A}$$

where $Obs = \{\mathbf{o}, \mathbf{o}' \mid \mathbf{o} \in \{ok, tr, ref\}\}$ is the set of observational variables; $\mathcal{A}$ the set of events that P may perform (including communications), and $VarP$ the set of variables that P may use. We may extend such an alphabet with both $\alpha\mathcal{L}P$, the continuations of P, and $\mathcal{L}$, the control variable. This yields the following alphabet for P

$$\alpha P \cong VarP \cup \{\mathcal{L}\} \cup Obs \cup \mathcal{A} \cup \alpha\mathcal{L}P$$

Such an extension poses no difficulty at all, remembering that the alphabet of a predicate is simply a collection of symbols (otherwise meaningless on their own). We will refer to processes with such an alphabet as *reactive steps*.

Healthiness Conditions. UTP-CSP processes are characterised by a monotonic and idempotent healthiness condition $CSP = R \circ CSP1 \circ CSP2$.

The latter healthiness condition trivially holds under the extension of the alphabet proposed precedently. Nonetheless, that is not enough for characterising reactive steps. In order to achieve such a characterisation, it is necessary to regard the definition of steps given earlier as an additional healthiness condition that applies to UTP-CSP processes with $\{\mathcal{L}\}$ in their alphabet. We denote that healthiness condition by $RPB1$, i.e. $RPB1(P) = P \triangleleft \mathcal{L} \in \alpha\mathcal{L}P \triangleright II$.

The following law trivially holds:

$$RPB1 \circ CSP(P) = CSP \circ RPB1(P)$$

Both the control variable $\mathcal{L}$ and the observational variables ok and $wait$ allow reasoning about termination; in addition, $\mathcal{L}$ permits reasoning about control, while ok and $wait$ permit reasoning about intermediate stable states. We need to ensure that no contradiction arises from the definitions of each of these variables. Thus, we may define the following laws to ensure the consistency of the definitions of $\mathcal{L}$, ok and $wait$ variables.

Laws 1 (Consistency between $\mathcal{L}$, ok and $wait$). *The variables $wait$ and $\mathcal{L}$ must agree on the behaviour of a Step prior to its execution.*

A1 $P \wedge wait \Leftrightarrow P \wedge \neg (\mathcal{L} \in \alpha\mathcal{L}P)$

The variables ok and $\mathcal{L}$ must agree on the start of the execution.

A2 $P \wedge ok \Leftrightarrow P \wedge (\mathcal{L} \in \alpha\mathcal{L}P)$

The variables ok and $wait$, and $\mathcal{L}$ must agree on valid intermediate states.

A3 $P \wedge ok' \wedge wait' \Leftrightarrow P \wedge (\mathcal{L}' \in \alpha\mathcal{L}P)$

The variables ok and $wait$, and $\mathcal{L}$ must agree on the termination.

A4 $P \wedge ok' \wedge \neg wait' \Leftrightarrow P \wedge \neg (\mathcal{L}' \in \alpha\mathcal{L}P)$

Definition 20. $A \stackrel{\frown}{=} A1 \circ A2 \circ A3 \circ A4$

We may also define $RPB \stackrel{\frown}{=} A \circ RPB1 \circ CSP$.

We may now define reactive steps formally:

Definition 21 (Reactive steps). *Any predicate whose alphabet includes that for reactive processes, and, additionally, both $\alpha\mathcal{L}$, and $\mathcal{L}$, and that is RPB-healthy is called a* reactive step.

Basic Predicates and Operators.

We now give the semantics of some basic predicates and operators. Since we are building a target language for high-level UTP-CSP processes viz. that do not contain $\mathcal{L}$, we need to specify our basic instructions. The definition of target code earlier makes it possible of defining arbitrarily complex predicates even as single instructions. In what follows, we will consider a language with only two single instructions: assignment and action prefix.

The notation $m : INST$ may be considered as a predicate transformer, a function that takes a constant value m and a UTP-CSP process $INST$, and returns a reactive step with continuations $\{m\}$.

Assignment Instruction.

$$m : (x := e) \mathrel{\widehat{=}} (x := e)_{+\mathcal{L}} \lhd \mathcal{L} = \{m\} \rhd \mathit{II}_R$$
$$\alpha\mathcal{L}(m : (x := e)) \mathrel{\widehat{=}} \{m\}$$

Simple Action Prefix Instruction.

$$m : (a \to SKIP) \mathrel{\widehat{=}} (a \to \mathit{II})_{+\mathcal{L}} \lhd \mathcal{L} = \{m\} \rhd SKIP$$
$$(a \to SKIP) \mathrel{\widehat{=}} \boldsymbol{CSP1}(ok' \wedge do_A(a))$$
$$do_A(a) \mathrel{\widehat{=}} \Phi(a \notin ref' \lhd wait' \rhd tr' = tr \frown \langle a \rangle)$$
$$\Phi \mathrel{\widehat{=}} \boldsymbol{R} \circ and_B = and_B \circ \boldsymbol{R}$$
$$\alpha\mathcal{L}(m : (a \to SKIP)) \mathrel{\widehat{=}} \{m\}$$

where $and_B \mathrel{\widehat{=}} B \wedge X$, and $B \mathrel{\widehat{=}} (tr' = tr \wedge wait') \vee tr < tr'$, and X denotes any predicate of a given UTP theory.

We may then define, in an analogue way to HH98, basic (sequential) blocks, basic parallel blocks, and proper blocks (or reactive process blocks).

Assuming that every other operator is well-defined, we now turn to the case of higher-order (HO) programming. A HO program or *procedure* is one that may be assigned as the value of a HO process variable. $\{| P |\}$ denotes the procedure that, when executed, behaves like process P.

HO Variable Declaration. In UTP-CSP, the declaration of a HO variable h supposes that h may only contain as values procedures that have the same actions set $\mathcal{A}$. We may follow this idea for continuations too. We assume that any HO variable h may only receive for value procedures that have the same continuations. Thus, besides the latter assumption about continuations, there is no need for modifying the existing definition of variable declaration that was given for UTP-CSP processes in [6].

6   Conclusion

We have presented continuations for reactive processes, with an emphasis on the semantics for the parallel composition operator, and we have also defined continuations for HO programs. These results find an immediate application in the semantics for strong mobility for UTP-CSP which we aim to publish in the near future. The model presented in this paper does apply to all programs that may contain parallel operators, and not only to UTP-CSP. An interesting ongoing work is the study of the healthiness conditions *A1* to *A4*, in view of their eventual simplification.

Acknowledgments. We are grateful to the anonymous reviewers for their useful comments.

References

1. Hoare, C.A.R., He, J.: Unifying Theories of Programming. Prentice-Hall, Upper Saddle River (1998)
2. Hoare, C.A.R.: Communicating Sequential Processes. Prentice-Hall, Upper Saddle River (1985)
3. Roscoe, A.W.: The Theory and Practice of Concurrency. Prentice-Hall, Upper Saddle River (1998)
4. Cavalcanti, A., Woodcock, J.: A tutorial introduction to CSP in unifying theories of programming. In: Cavalcanti, A., Sampaio, A., Woodcock, J. (eds.) PSSE 2004. LNCS, vol. 3167, pp. 220–268. Springer, Heidelberg (2006). doi:10.1007/11889229_6
5. Tang, X., Woodcock, J.: Travelling processes. In: Kozen, D. (ed.) MPC 2004. LNCS, vol. 3125, pp. 381–399. Springer, Heidelberg (2004). doi:10.1007/978-3-540-27764-4_20
6. Tang, X., Woodcock, J.: Towards mobile processes in UTP. In: SEFM 2004, pp. 44–53. IEEE (2004)
7. Fuggetta, A., Picco, G.P., Vigna, G.: Understanding code mobility. In: TSE 1998, vol. 24, pp. 342–361. IEEE (1998)
8. Woodcock, J., Hughes, A.: Unifying theories of parallel programming. In: George, C., Miao, H. (eds.) ICFEM 2002. LNCS, vol. 2495, pp. 24–37. Springer, Heidelberg (2002). doi:10.1007/3-540-36103-0_5
9. Jahnig, N., Gothel, T., Glesner, S.: A denotational semantics for communicating unstructured code. In: FESCA 2015, EPTCS, vol. 178, pp. 9–21 (2015)
10. Reynolds, J.C.: The discoveries of continuations. LISP Symbolic Comput. **6**, 233–247 (1993)
11. Strachey, C., Wadsworth, C.P.: Continuations: a mathematical semantics for handling full jumps. Higher-Order Symbolic Comput. **13**, 135–152 (2000)
12. Danvy, O., Filinski, A.: Representing control: a study of the CPS transformation. Math. Struct. Comp. Sci. **2**, 361–391 (1992)
13. Felleisen, M., Friedman, D.P., Duba, B.F., Merrill, J.: Beyond continuations. Technical report, Indiana University Computer Science Department (1987)
14. Giorgi, J.F., LeMetayer, D.: Continuation-based parallel implementations of functional languages. In: LFP 1990, pp. 209–217. ACM (1990)
15. Moreau, L., Queinnec, C.: Partial continuations as the difference of continuations a duumvirate of control operators. In: Hermenegildo, M., Penjam, J. (eds.) PLILP 1994. LNCS, vol. 844, pp. 182–197. Springer, Heidelberg (1994). doi:10.1007/3-540-58402-1_14
16. Todoran, E., Papaspyrou, N.S.: Continuations for parallel logic programming. In: PPDP 2000, pp. 257–267. ACM (2000)

A Stepwise Approach to Linking Theories

Pedro Ribeiro$^{(\boxtimes)}$, Ana Cavalcanti, and Jim Woodcock

Department of Computer Science, University of York, York, UK
{pedro.ribeiro,ana.cavalcanti,jim.woodcock}@york.ac.uk

Abstract. Formal modelling of complex systems requires catering for
a variety of aspects. The Unifying Theories of Programming (UTP) distinguishes itself as a semantic framework that promotes unification of
results across different modelling paradigms via linking functions. The
naive composition of theories, however, may yield unexpected or undesirable semantic models. Here, we propose a stepwise approach to linking theories where we deal separately with the definition of the relation
between the variables in the different theories and the identification of
healthiness conditions. We explore this approach by deriving healthiness
conditions for *Circus Time* via calculation, based on the healthiness conditions of CSP and a small set of principles underlying the timed model.

Keywords: Theory engineering · *Circus* · CSP · UTP

1 Introduction

Systems exhibit several aspects of interest, including, for instance, state, behaviour, concurrency, object-orientation, time, and others. Several modelling paradigms capture one or a few of these aspects. The UTP of Hoare and He [1] is
distinctive as a relational semantic framework that supports unification of results
across different paradigms. Individual models can be studied in isolation using
different UTP theories, while their combinations can be studied by composing
theories. Of central importance to composition of theories are: a standard notion
of refinement across the theories, and the definition of pairs of monotonic linking
functions between them, usually Galois connections.

For example, in the UTP, functional total correctness is characterised by
the theory of designs, while reactive behaviour is captured using the theory of
reactive processes. Their combination yields a theory for the process algebra
Communicating Sequential Processes (CSP) [2]. Additions to that theory yield
theories in the *Circus* [3] family, where not only can state and behaviour be
captured together, but also time [4,5], object-orientation [6], and so on [7].

Combining paradigms is not trivial as their naive combination may produce
unexpected or undesirable semantic models. For example, it is often desirable
for the operators of the combined theory to preserve the semantics of the corresponding operators of the original theories, in the sense that, when they are

J.P. Bowen and H. Zhu (Eds.): UTP 2016, LNCS 10134, pp. 134–154, 2017.
DOI: 10.1007/978-3-319-52228-9_7

applied to predicates that correspond to those of the original theory, their behaviours are also in correspondence. To establish such a result, we need to identify Galois connections between the original and the combined theories.

We consider, for example, the theory of *Circus Time* [4], a discrete-time version of *Circus* that combines Z [8] and Timed CSP [9]. In *Circus Time*, data operations are instantaneous, and so every time property is explicitly specified: this is crucial to facilitate modelling and reasoning. It is not clear how to establish that the *Circus Time* theory preserves the semantics of the CSP operators, so that, when *Circus Time* operators are applied to (untimed) CSP processes, the resulting behaviour is consistent with that of the corresponding CSP operators.

Identifying a Galois connection that supports the proof that the operators in the *Circus Time* and CSP theories are consistent with each other is important, for example, to study external choice. The current definition [4] is not satisfactory: as pointed out in [10], external choice in *Circus Time* does not handle termination appropriately. We consider, for instance, $Wait\ d \ \Box \ Wait\ (d + m)$, a choice between terminating after d or after $d + m$ time units. Since, like in CSP, termination is not under the control of the environment, the choice should be resolved in favour of $Wait\ d$. However, this is not the case with the definition proposed in [4]. Finding an appropriate definition is challenging [11,12].

A Galois connection (L,R) is defined in [4]. L maps *Circus Time* processes to untimed *Circus* processes, while R is defined as the weakest inverse of L. For example, the application of L to $Wait\ d$ yields $Skip \ \sqcap \ Stop$, a process that may choose nondeterministically to terminate or deadlock. The results obtained for operators mapped through this linking function are not satisfactory. It is not clear how $Skip$ can be mapped into its *Circus Time* counterpart as a terminating process taking no time, at the same time that the timed counterpart of $Stop$ takes any amount of time. These desirable properties of the timed model make it less than obvious how to define an appropriate Galois connection.

In this paper, we present a general stepwise approach to linking theories that, by providing for a clear separation of concerns when linking theories, gives guidance as to how theories can be linked. We take inspiration from the calculational approach to data refinement based on auxiliary variables [13]. Accordingly, we use an intermediate super-theory with variables of both theories of interest.

In our approach, the link between the source and the super-theory adds the variables of the target theory. Another important component of a UTP theory are healthiness conditions, which identify the valid predicates over the theory variables. In our approach, healthiness conditions that the desired target theory must satisfy and coupling invariants relating variables of both theories are used to characterise the super-theory. The target theory is reached by removing the starting theory's variables. The opposite links can be constructed similarly.

We have applied our approach to *Circus Time* to construct a Galois connection that can justify its healthiness conditions and operators. In this example, we split the healthiness conditions in two categories: those that refer exclusively to concerns of the timed model are identified separately from those carried over from (untimed) CSP. The healthiness conditions of the original *Circus Time* theory are explained as combinations of these. We also justify the relationship between the observation variables of the two theories by considering separately the removal and introduction of variables, and the relationship between variables in the different theories. Our super-theory allows us to derive the healthiness conditions and operators of *Circus Time* as induced from the untimed model.

The remainder of this paper is organised as follows. In Sect. 2 we introduce the required UTP theories, including the theory of CSP and *Circus Time*. In Sect. 3 we discuss the stepwise linking approach. In Sect. 4 we use the proposed approach to build a super-theory of timed reactive processes, and ultimately derive a model for *Circus Time*. Finally, we conclude in Sect. 5 by summarizing our findings and discussing future work.

2   Preliminaries

UTP theories include relations defined by predicates P. They are characterised by three components: an alphabet, a set of healthiness conditions and a set of operators. The alphabet defines the free variables that can be used in the predicates. Also, the alphabet $\alpha(P)$ of a relation P is split into $in\alpha(P)$, which contains undashed variables corresponding to the initial observations, and $out\alpha(P)$ containing the dashed counterparts for after or final observations. The healthiness conditions are defined by monotonic idempotent functions; the theory contains only the healthy predicates: the fixed points of the healthiness conditions. The predicates can be defined using the operators of the theory.

Refinement is defined in all theories as universal reverse implication. In the UTP, total correctness is characterised through the theory of designs [1,14], whose healthiness conditions are named **H1** and **H2**. Every design P can be expressed in terms of pre and postcondition pairs, $(\neg P^f \vdash P^t)$, where $P^o = P[o/ok']$ and t and f correspond to *true* and *false*, respectively.

2.1   CSP

Programs characterised by continuous interactions with their environment are modelled in the UTP using the theory of reactive processes [1,15]. In addition to the variables, ok and ok' of the theory of designs, this theory includes the variables $wait$, tr, ref and their dashed counterparts, that record information about interactions with the environment.

This is a theory where observations of intermediate states of programs are recorded. The boolean variable $wait$ records whether the previous process is waiting for an interaction from the environment or, alternatively, has terminated. Similarly, $wait'$ ascertains this for the current process. The boolean variable ok indicates whether the previous process is in a stable state, while ok' records this information for the current process. If a process is not in a stable state, it is said to have diverged. A process starts executing only in states where ok and $\neg wait$ are *true*. Successful termination is characterised by ok' and $\neg wait'$ being *true*.

The actual interactions with the environment are represented using sequences of events, recorded by tr and tr'. The variable tr records the sequence of events that took place before the current process started, while tr' records the intermediate or final sequence of events that can be observed. Finally, ref and ref' record the set of events that may be refused by the process. Refusal sets allow the appropriate modelling of deadlock and nondeterminism [2].

The theory of reactive processes R is characterised by the functional composition ($\circ$) of three healthiness conditions [1,15] below, where function application binds stronger than function composition.

Definition 1 (Healthiness Conditions of Reactive Processes).

$$\mathbf{R1}(P) \mathrel{\widehat{=}} P \wedge tr \leq tr' \qquad\qquad \mathbf{R2}(P) \mathrel{\widehat{=}} P[\langle\rangle, (tr'-tr)/tr, tr']$$
$$\mathbf{R3}(P) \mathrel{\widehat{=}} \boldsymbol{I}_{rea} \lhd wait \rhd P \qquad\qquad \mathbf{R}(P) \mathrel{\widehat{=}} \mathbf{R3} \circ \mathbf{R1} \circ \mathbf{R2}(P)$$

$R1$ requires that in all circumstances the only change that can be observed in the final trace of events tr' is an extension of the initial sequence tr, while $R2$ requires that a process must not impose any restriction on the initial value of tr. Finally, $R3$ requires that if the previous process is waiting for an interaction with the environment, that is, $wait$ is $true$, then the process behaves as the identity of the theory $\boldsymbol{I}_{rea}$ [1,15].

The theory of CSP can be described by reactive processes that in addition satisfy the healthiness conditions $CSP1$ and $CSP2$ reproduced below [1,15].

Definition 2 (CSP).

$$\mathbf{CSP1}(P) \mathrel{\widehat{=}} P \vee \mathbf{R1}(\neg ok)$$
$$\mathbf{CSP2}(P) \mathrel{\widehat{=}} P \,;((ok \Rightarrow ok') \wedge tr' = tr \wedge ref' = ref \wedge wait' = wait)$$

The first healthiness condition $CSP1$ requires that if the previous process has diverged, that is, ok is $false$, then extension of the trace is the only guarantee. $CSP2$ is $H2$ restated with the extended alphabet of reactive processes.

A process that is R, $CSP1$ and $CSP2$-healthy can be described in terms of a design [1,15]. We reproduce this result below, where $P_w^o = P[o, w/ok', wait]$.

Theorem 1 (Reactive Design). *For every CSP process* $P, \mathbf{R}(\neg P_f^f \vdash P_f^t) = P$

This result is important as it allows CSP processes to be specified in terms of pre and postconditions, such as is the case for sequential programs, while the healthiness condition R enforces the required reactive behaviour.

2.2   Circus Time

Circus is a combination of Z, CSP and Dijkstra's language of guarded commands. Its semantics is also defined using reactive designs. The timed version *Circus Time* [4,5] provides facilities to explicitly model and reason about discrete time state-rich reactive systems. Observations are timed, so the trace of events

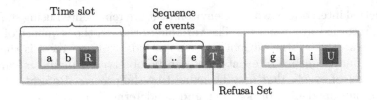

Fig. 1. A timed sequence.

and the set of refusals are recorded as pairs in a non-empty timed sequence tr_T, whose dashed counterpart is tr'_T, and where Σ is the set of all possible events. This is analogous to untimed CSP where tr and tr' are defined as sequences whose elements are drawn from Σ.

Definition 3. $tr_T, tr'_T : \mathrm{seq}_1(\mathrm{seq}\,\Sigma \times \mathbb{P}\,\Sigma)$

Here we use seq_1 following the Z notation [16] to denote a finite non-empty sequence. The variables ok, ok', $wait$ and $wait'$ retain the same meaning as in the untimed theory, and in that of CSP. For the purpose of our discussion, we adopt a model based on that of [4], but without considering state directly.

An illustration of a timed sequence consisting of three time slots is presented in Fig. 1. Each slot contains a pair, whose first component is a sequence of events, such as a followed by b, and whose second component is a refusal set (shaded in Fig. 1) such as R. This is useful to illustrate the intuition behind the healthiness conditions that we discuss in the sequel.

Healthiness Conditions. The first healthiness condition $\mathbf{R1_T}$ of the *Circus Time* theory ensures that the trace of events across time cannot be undone. It is the counterpart to $\mathbf{R1}$ and is defined as follows.

Definition 4. $\mathbf{R1_T}(P) \cong P \wedge \mathcal{E}(tr_T, tr'_T)$

It is a conjunctive healthiness condition [7] defined using the predicate $\mathcal{E}$.

Definition 5. $\mathcal{E}(s,t) \cong (front(s) < t) \wedge fst \circ last(s) \leq fst \circ head(t-front(s))$

Given two timed traces s and t, $\mathcal{E}$ requires the *front* (which for a given sequence yields all the elements except the last) of s to be a strict prefix of t, and in addition that the first component (as given by *fst*) of the *last* pair of s is a prefix of the first component of the *head* of the difference between t and *front*(s). If we consider s and t to be tr_T and tr'_T, respectively, then the strict prefixing $front(tr_T) < tr'_T$ requires that not only are the traces of previous time slots kept unchanged, but also the refusal sets. In addition, the difference $tr'_T - front(tr_T)$ yields the timed sequence corresponding to the current and future observations, and so the *head* corresponds to the first after observation in the current time slot. A pair of sequences satisfying $\mathbf{R1_T}$ is illustrated in Fig. 2. The functions *front*, *last*, *head*, *fst* and *snd* are those of Z [16] with expected meanings.

The counterpart to $\mathbf{R2}$ is $\mathbf{R2_T}$, which requires processes to be insensitive to events in the initial timed sequence tr_T.

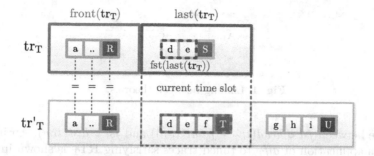

Fig. 2. Example of a pair of sequences tr_T and tr'_T satisfying **R1$_T$**.

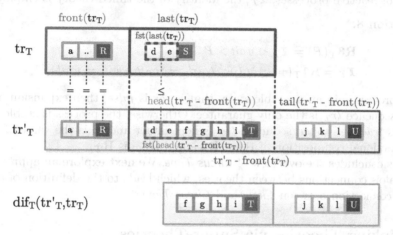

Fig. 3. Example application of dif_T.

Definition 6. R2$_\mathbf{T}$ $(P) \cong P[\langle(\langle\rangle, snd \circ last(tr_T))\rangle, dif_T(tr'_T, tr_T)/tr_T, tr'_T]$

It is defined by considering the substitution of tr_T by the timed sequence whose only element is a pair, where the trace is empty and the refusal set is the last observed in tr_T. The sequence tr'_T is substituted by the application of the function dif_T that captures the difference in events during the current time slot.

The function dif_T takes two timed traces tr'_T and tr_T, and yields a sequence whose first element is a pair containing the trace actually observed during that time slot, and the refusal set observed at the end of the time slot.

Definition 7.

$$dif_T(tr'_T, tr_T) \cong \left(\begin{array}{c} \langle \left(\begin{array}{c} fst \circ head(tr'_T - front(tr_T)) - fst \circ last(tr_T)), \\ snd \circ head(tr'_T - front(tr_T)) \end{array} \right) \rangle \\ \frown \\ tail(tr'_T - front(tr_T)) \end{array} \right)$$

The current sequence of time slots is obtained by the difference $tr'_T - front(tr_T)$. The actual events occurring during the first of those slots are obtained by the

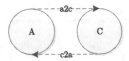

Fig. 4. Linking between theories.

difference between $fst \circ head(tr'_T - front(tr_T))$ and $fst \circ last(tr_T)$. An illustration of an application of dif_T to timed traces satisfying **R1$_T$** is shown in Fig. 3.

The counterpart to **R3** is **R3$_T$** below. Instead of $\boldsymbol{I}_{rea}$, the identity of the theory of reactive processes, $\boldsymbol{I}_T$, the identify of the timed theory is employed.

Definition 8.

$$\mathbf{R3_T}(P) \mathrel{\hat{=}} \boldsymbol{I}_T \lhd wait \rhd P$$
$$\boldsymbol{I}_T \mathrel{\hat{=}} \mathbf{R1_T}(\neg ok) \lor (ok' \land tr'_T = tr_T \land wait' = wait)$$

If the process is in an unstable state, that is, ok is *false*, then expansion of the timed sequence tr_T is the only guarantee. Otherwise, the process is stable, that is, ok is *true*, the timed sequence tr_T is kept intact and so is the value of *wait*. The functional composition of **R1$_T$**, **R2$_T$** and **R3$_T$** is **R$_T$**.

This concludes the overview of *Circus Time*. We next explore an approach to find Galois connections between theories, which leads to the definition of a new Galois connection between *Circus* and *Circus Time*.

3   Linking Theories via Super-Theories

The definition of linking functions between UTP theories with different alphabets involves introduction of variables of the target theory and removal of variables of the source theory (essentially a data refinement), while at the same time enforcing the healthiness conditions of the target theory. In other words, in addition to a data refinement, there is an application of the healthiness condition of the target theory. This is illustrated for two arbitrary theories A and C in Fig. 4, where a pair of linking functions $a2c$ and $c2a$ is shown.

When defining $a2c$ and $c2a$, a problem arises if the complete set of healthiness conditions of the target theory C is not known a priori. This is often the case when developing a new theory. An appealing approach is to calculate the healthiness conditions via application of $a2c$ to healthy predicates of A. If, however, finding a Galois connection, that is, defining $a2c$ and $c2a$ in the first place, is not immediately obvious, then this is not a solution.

For example, in the case of the link from *Circus* to *Circus Time* two choices arise naturally: every trace of events takes place in a single time slot, and so no time is actually added; or any amount of time can pass for any given trace. The latter violates **R1$_T$**, while the former does not capture an interesting correspondence between the models. The right approach lies between these two extremes.

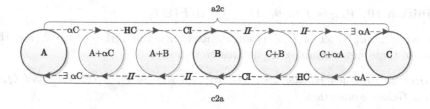

Fig. 5. Stepwise linking between theories.

We propose that, instead of exploring the links between the theories directly, we break down the linking functions into a series of functions that, when composed, achieve the same goal. We consider again the arbitrary theories depicted in Fig. 4, and suppose that we know only partially the set of healthiness conditions of the theory C, denoted by the function **HC**. To calculate those induced from theory A, we can proceed as depicted in Fig. 5.

The theories A and C are related through an intermediate super-theory B. The alphabet of B is the union of the alphabets of A and C: $\alpha B = \alpha A \cup \alpha C$. To relate the values of variables in αA and αC we introduce a coupling invariant **CI**, which is applied after **HC**, the known healthiness condition of the theory C that must be satisfied irrespective of those induced from A.

In what follows we define coupling invariants and characterise the properties required of **HC** to ensure that $a2c$ and $c2a$ form a Galois connection between the theories of interest. Finally, we present formal definitions for $a2c$ and $c2a$, and show that they form a Galois connection.

A coupling invariant is a monotonic and idempotent function **CI** defined by the general form below, where Q is a predicate relating variables.

Definition 9 (Coupling Invariant). $\mathbf{CI}(P) \mathrel{\widehat{=}} P \wedge Q$

If Q does not depend on P, then **CI** is a conjunctive healthiness condition [7]. A coupling invariant and the identity function I form a Galois connection as established by the following Lemma 1, following the result of Lemma 4.2.3 in [1].

Lemma 1. **CI** and I form a Galois connection in the domain of **CI**-healthy predicates.

Proof. $I \circ \mathbf{CI}(P) \sqsupseteq P$ {By definition of I and **CI** and predicate calculus}
and $\mathbf{CI} \circ I(Q) \sqsubseteq Q$ {By definition of I and predicate calculus, Q satisfies **CI**} □

We observe that in the proof of Lemma 1, we assume that I is applied to a **CI**-healthy predicate. This is because the Galois connection is established with the subset of interest of theory B that is **CI**-healthy.

Similarly, links related to the data refinement, in which one function introduces variables, and another function hides them, also form a Galois connection as established by the following Lemma 2. We use the operator $+C$, an alphabet extension with no particular value specified for variables in the set C.

Definition 10. $P_{+C} \cong P$, $with\ \alpha(P_{+C}) = \alpha(P) \cup C$

In words, the alphabet of P_{+C} is augmented with the variables in C, but the values of these new variables are not restricted.

Lemma 2. *Provided variables in αC are not free in P, $\exists \alpha C \bullet P$ and Q_{+C} form a Galois connection.*

Proof.

$$\exists \alpha C \bullet (P_{+C}) \qquad\qquad \{\text{Theory alphabet extension}\}$$
$$= \exists \alpha C \bullet (P) \qquad\qquad \{\text{Assumption: } c \text{ and } c' \text{ not free in } P\}$$
$$= P$$

$$(\exists \alpha C \bullet Q)_{+C} \qquad\qquad \{\text{Theory alphabet extension}\}$$
$$= (\exists \alpha C \bullet Q) \qquad\qquad \{\text{Predicate calculus}\}$$
$$\sqsubseteq Q$$

□

The remaining Galois connection to be established lies between the theory with variables of both A and B (depicted as $A + \alpha C$ in Fig. 5), and the theory whose predicates satisfy **HC** (depicted as $A + B$ in Fig. 5).

Lemma 3. **HC** *and I form a Galois connection in the domain of* **HC**-*healthy predicates, provided* **HC** *is a monotonic and idempotent function, and, for all P, either* **HC**$(P) \sqsupseteq P$ *(strengthening) or* **HC**$(P) \sqsubseteq P$ *(weakening), or both.*

Proof. **HC** $\circ\ I(Q) = Q$ $\{$Def. of I, and assumption: Q is **HC**-healthy$\}$
(Case: **HC** *is strengthening)*

$$I \circ \textbf{HC}(P) \qquad\qquad \{\text{Definition of } I\}$$
$$= \textbf{HC}(P) \qquad\qquad \{\text{Assumption: } \textbf{HC}(P) \sqsupseteq P\}$$
$$\sqsupseteq P$$

(Case: **HC** *is weakening)*

$$I \circ \textbf{HC}(P) \qquad\qquad \{\text{Definition of } I\}$$
$$= \textbf{HC}(P) \qquad\qquad \{\text{Assumption: } \textbf{HC}(P) \sqsubseteq P\}$$
$$\sqsubseteq P$$

□

When **HC** is applied to a predicate P that is **HC**-healthy, then **HC**$(P) = P$, and the proviso of Lemma 3 requiring strengthening or weakening is trivially satisfied. In the context of our approach, however, the proviso must also be satisfied when **HC** is applied to a predicate P that results from the application of

P_{+C}, that is, when the variables of set C are allowed to take arbitrary values by P. For example, we consider the case where **HC** is defined by a function like **R2**. This function is neither strengthening nor weakening when applied to unhealthy-predicates. We consider the following counter-example: $\mathbf{R2}(tr = \langle\rangle) = true$ and $\mathbf{R2}(tr \neq \langle\rangle) = false$. However, the application of $\mathbf{R2}(P)$ to a predicate P where tr and tr' take arbitrary values yields an equality.

As illustrated in Fig. 5 the linking function $a2c$ from A to C is the composition of several functions: a function that introduces the variables of C; the healthiness condition **HC**; the coupling invariant **CI**; followed by two applications of the identity function, and an existential quantification over all variables in A. We have a similar composition for $c2a$. Formally, we can describe $a2c$ and $c2a$ as follows: the identities do not need to be included in the composition.

Definition 11.

$$a2c(P) \ \widehat{=} \ \exists \alpha A \bullet \mathbf{CI} \circ \mathbf{HC}(P_{+C}) \qquad c2a(P) \ \widehat{=} \ \exists \alpha C \bullet \mathbf{CI} \circ \mathbf{HC}(P_{+A})$$

For variables that are simply aliases, the existential quantification at either end of the link is over the subset of those variables not present in the target theory. The relation established between variables could alternatively be defined using the data refinement approach of the UTP. However, to satisfy **HC** the invariants would need to be strengthened, and it is not clear how functions like **R2** could be justified purely by data refinement. Here we deal with these concerns piecewise.

The functions $a2c$ and $c2a$ form a Galois connection. This is our main result in this paper, established by the following Theorem 2.

Theorem 2. $a2c$ and $c2a$ form a Galois connection, provided **HC** is idempotent and monotonic, and **HC** is either strengthening or weakening, or both.

Proof. Follows from Lemmas 1 to 3 and Theorem 4.2.5 in [1] *(Galois connections compose).*

Our approach provides for a systematic way of studying the relationship between theories. As long as the known healthiness condition **HC** is weakening or strengthening, or both, then a Galois connection can be established. The coupling invariant can be tweaked as required to yield different Galois connections. Links between theories can be non-trivial due to the underlying differences in paradigm. The intermediate super-theory enables constructs from multiple theories to be considered together within the same alphabetized relation space, while still providing a Galois connection with the constituent theories.

This concludes our discussion on building super-theories. In the next section, we illustrate our approach by discussing how it can be used to build a model for *Circus Time* starting with the (untimed) CSP theory.

4   A Stepwise Approach Towards *Circus Time*

Here, we build a super-theory of timed reactive processes based on the CSP theory. Section 4.1 defines the alphabet and healthiness conditions of the super-theory, and coupling invariants that characterise the valid timed traces. The instance of **HC** in this example is the composition of the healthiness conditions we identify; similarly, the instance of **CI** is the composition of the coupling invariants. Defining **HC** and **CI** by composition of simpler functions gives a piecewise characterisation of properties of interest. This method is suggested by Theorem 2 and is an illustration the main feature of our stepwise approach to connecting theories. In Sect. 4.2 we calculate an explicit description of the linking function from (untimed) CSP to *Circus Time*, using Definition 11, and present the results obtained with our Galois connection.

4.1   Constructing the Super-Theory

The alphabet of the super-theory includes the union of alphabets of the theories of CSP and *Circus Time*, defined in Sect. 2; ok and ok' are common to both theories. Furthermore, we also add auxiliary variables tr_C and tr'_C to the super-theory to facilitate reasoning about traces in the current time slot.

Definition 12 (Alphabet).

$$tr, tr' : \text{seq}\, \Sigma \qquad\qquad tr_T, tr'_T : \text{seq}(\text{seq}\, \Sigma \times \mathbb{P}\, \Sigma)$$
$$wait, wait', ok, ok' : Boolean \qquad\qquad wait_T, wait'_T : Boolean$$
$$ref, ref' : \mathbb{P}\, \Sigma \qquad\qquad tr_C, tr'_C : \text{seq}\, \Sigma$$

In contrast with the treatment in [4], we require timed traces not to be empty by using a healthiness condition, defined in the sequel, rather than using the type system directly. This obviates the need to check intermediate calculations for type correctness with regards to this property.

Healthiness Conditions. Here, we identify minimal restrictions that are later used to justify the original healthiness conditions of *Circus Time*. With this approach, we consider issues related to time in isolation from those already captured by the healthiness condition of CSP.

TR0. The first condition of the super-theory requires that no sequence of events is empty: the length $\#tr_T$ of the initial trace tr_T is greater than zero.

Definition 13. TR0$(P) \mathrel{\widehat{=}} P \wedge \#tr_T > 0$

This makes operations on traces, such as *front*, well-defined. The corresponding restriction on tr'_T arises as a consequence of **TR0** and **TR1** defined next.

TR1. The second healthiness condition requires that time increases monotonically, that is, the length of the after timed trace tr'_T must be greater than or equal to the length of the current timed trace tr_T.

Definition 14. TR1$(P) \mathrel{\widehat{=}} P \wedge \#tr_T \leq \#tr'_T$

In the original *Circus Time* model [4], **TR0** and **TR1** are implicit.

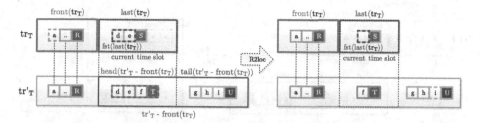

Fig. 6. Example of applying **R2loc$_T$**.

TR2. The third healthiness condition requires that previous observations across time cannot be changed and is defined as follows.

Definition 15. TR2$(P) \mathrel{\widehat{=}} P \wedge front(tr_T) \leq tr'_T$

In words, the *front* of the current timed sequence tr_T must be a prefix of tr'_T. In [4], this requirement is part of **R1$_T$**, but here it is studied in isolation.

An example of a relation that is **TR0**, **TR1** and **TR2**-healthy is depicted in Fig. 2. The healthiness conditions considered so far guarantee preservation of history before the current time slot, however, they are not sufficient to guarantee that **R1** is observed within the current time slot. Later in this section, we tackle this aspect by using coupling invariants related to tr_C and tr'_C.

TR3. The next healthiness condition defines for $wait_T$ part of what is established by **R3** for *wait*. It states that if the previous process is waiting in a stable state, then no explicit time is added and it continues waiting.

Definition 16. TR3$(P) \mathrel{\widehat{=}} P \wedge ((ok \wedge wait_T) \Rightarrow (\#tr'_T = \#tr_T \wedge wait'_T))$

This healthiness condition is essential to justify the definition of the timed identity $\mathbf{I}_T$. Further aspects of **R3**, including behaviour in the presence of divergence of the previous process are considered separately.

R2loc$_T$. The following healthiness condition captures part of **R2**, in that, if we ignore time and the events that happened in the previous time slot, then the counterpart to applying **R2** in the current time slot is **R2loc$_T$**.

Definition 17. R2loc$_T$ $(P) = P \begin{bmatrix} front(tr_T) \mathbin{\frown} \langle\langle\langle\rangle, snd \circ last(tr_T)\rangle\rangle / tr_T \\ front(tr_T) \mathbin{\frown} dif_T(tr'_T, tr_T) / tr'_T \end{bmatrix}$

A pictorial description of the application of **R2loc$_T$** is shown in Fig. 6. In the current time slot, the *front* of tr_T is maintained, while the last sequence of events is replaced by the empty sequence. Similarly, the subsequent observation of tr'_T is replaced with *front* of tr_T ($front(tr_T)$ is guaranteed to be a prefix of tr'_T when we consider relations that satisfy **TR0** and **TR1**) followed by the corresponding difference in events observed during the current time slots as given by dif_T.

For dif_T to be well-defined $fst(last(tr_T))$ must be a prefix of the sequence $fst(head(tr'_T - front(tr_T)))$. This is not an issue in the original *Circus Time* theory

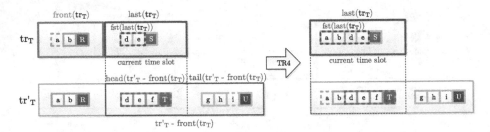

Fig. 7. Example of applying **TR4**.

as it includes **R1$_T$**, but the healthiness conditions above do not address this issue. One option is to consider this as a requirement for dif_T to be well-defined. Another option, which we choose to follow, is to enforce the counterpart to **R1** in the current time slot with the following healthiness condition.

Definition 18. $\mathbf{R1_C}(P) \cong tr_C \leq tr'_C$

This is a modelling decision: both options can justify **R1$_T$**. Later, a coupling invariant relates the values of tr_C and tr'_C with those of tr'_T and tr'_T.

TR4. The second requirement of **R2$_T$** is captured by the following healthiness condition **TR4** that requires processes not to depend on the time elapsed before them, irrespective of events that have happened. **R2loc$_T$** above captures insensitivity to events, whereas **TR4** captures insensitivity to time. A fixed point of **TR4** must allow the timed traces tr_T and tr'_T to be replaced with traces whose first time slots contain all events that have happened before, concatenated with any current events. In other words, the behaviour of a fixed point must be the same, even if no time had elapsed before.

Definition 19.

$$\mathbf{TR4}(P) \cong P \left[\begin{array}{l} \langle(Flat(tr_T), snd \circ last(tr_T))\rangle/tr_T \\ \left(\left\langle \left(\begin{array}{l} Flat(front(tr_T)) \frown head(tr'_T - front(tr_T))), \\ snd \circ head(tr'_T - front(tr_T)) \end{array} \right) \right\rangle \right) \\ \frown \\ tail(tr'_T - front(tr_T)) \end{array} \right/ tr'_T \right]$$

The sequence tr_T is replaced by a sequence with only one element: a pair whose first component is $Flat(tr_T)$, a projection on tr_T that yields the sequence of events in every first component of the pairs in tr_T, that is, all events that happened by the beginning of the current observation. Similarly, tr'_T is replaced by a sequence whose first pair has as first component the sequence of events observed up until the end of the current time slot. This includes the events in $front(tr_T)$ concatenated with those in the current time slot, given by $head(tr'_T - front(tr_T))$. An example of applying **TR4** is shown in Fig. 7.

The combination of **R2loc$_T$** and **TR4** corresponds to **R2$_T$** as established by the following Lemma 4. Proof of this and other results to follow that are not included in this paper are available in [17], with essential results having been checked using Isabelle/UTP [18].

Lemma 4. *Provided* $\#tr_T > 0$, $\mathbf{TR4} \circ \mathbf{R2loc_T}(P) = \mathbf{R2_T}(P)$.

This equality with $\mathbf{R2_T}$ holds only when $\mathbf{TR4}$ is applied after $\mathbf{R2loc_T}$. Although this may seem counter-intuitive, this requirement is a consequence of the order in which the substitutions of $\mathbf{TR4}$ and $\mathbf{R2loc_T}$ are applied.

TR. The healthiness condition corresponding to the functional composition of all the previous healthiness conditions is $\mathbf{TR}$.

Definition 20.

$$\mathbf{TR}(P) \cong \mathbf{TR0} \circ \mathbf{TR1} \circ \mathbf{TR2} \circ \mathbf{TR3} \circ \mathbf{TR4} \circ \mathbf{R2loc_T} \circ \mathbf{R1_C}(P)$$

This function is strengthening as established by the following Theorem 3.

Theorem 3. *Provided* tr_T *and* tr'_T *are not free in* P, $\mathbf{TR}(P) \sqsupseteq P$.

Proof.

$$
\begin{array}{lr}
\mathbf{TR}(P) & \{\text{Definition of } \mathbf{TR}\} \\
= \mathbf{TR0123} \circ \mathbf{TR4} \circ \mathbf{R2loc_T} \circ \mathbf{R1_C}(P) & \{\text{Lemma 4}\} \\
= \mathbf{TR0123} \circ \mathbf{R2_T} \circ \mathbf{R1_C}(P) & \{\text{Assumption: } tr_T \text{ and } tr'_T \text{ not free in } P\} \\
= \mathbf{TR0123} \circ \mathbf{R1_C}(P) & \{\text{Definition of } \mathbf{TR0} \text{ to } \mathbf{TR3}, \text{ predicate calculus}\} \\
\sqsupseteq \mathbf{R1_C}(P) & \{\text{Definition of } \mathbf{R1_C} \text{ and predicate calculus}\} \\
\sqsupseteq P &
\end{array}
$$

Following the approach outlined in Sect. 3, this result ensures that a linking function including $\mathbf{TR}$ as healthiness condition, yields a Galois connection.

This concludes the discussion of the healthiness conditions governing the timed aspects of the super-theory and *Circus Time*.

Coupling Invariants. In this section we define the coupling invariants that relate the value of variables in the super-theory.

CI0. The first coupling invariant relates the timed traces, tr_T and tr'_T, with their untimed counterparts, tr and tr'. The difference in traces in the untimed model $tr' - tr$ must be in agreement with the difference in events observed over all time units as given by the difference $Flat(tr'_T) - Flat(tr_T)$.

Definition 21.

$$
\mathbf{CI0}(P) \cong
$$
$$
P \wedge (tr'-tr) = Flat(tr'_T) - Flat(tr_T) \wedge Flat(tr_T) \leq Flat(tr'_T) \wedge tr \leq tr'
$$

For the differences to be well-defined we require $Flat(tr_T)$ to be a prefix of $Flat(tr'_T)$, and tr of tr'. While a direct equality could be used, rather than an equality between differences, it poses problems if **R2** were applied to **CI0** as it forbids insisting on a particular value for tr. Therefore, here we only consider the relationship between differences, an approach also followed in [19].

CI1. The second invariant requires refusals in the untimed ref variables and the timed traces variables tr_T to be in agreement.

Definition 22. $\mathbf{CI1}(P) \mathrel{\widehat{=}} P \wedge ref = snd \circ last(tr_T) \wedge ref' = snd \circ last(tr'_T)$

The value of ref must be the same as the refusal in the last time slot $last(tr_T)$ of tr_T, as given by the second component of $last(tr_T)$, whereas ref' must be the refusal in the last time slot $last(tr'_T)$, as given by the second component of $last(tr'_T)$, which may or may not be the same time slot as $last(tr_T)$.

CI2. The next invariant requires that termination without visible events in a stable state in the untimed model does not allow any time to pass.

Definition 23.

$$\mathbf{CI2}(P) \mathrel{\widehat{=}} P \wedge ((\neg wait' \wedge \neg P^f_f \wedge ok \wedge ok' \wedge tr' = tr) \Rightarrow \#tr'_T = \#tr_T)$$

That is, when $wait'$ is $false$, the precondition $\neg P^f_f$ of P is satisfied, and stability is preserved with ok and ok', and no event is observed $tr' = tr$, then no time must pass. Consequently, the CSP process $Skip$ in the context of the super-theory allows no time to pass. As previously indicated, this is required in $Circus\ Time$ to ensure that time passage is explicitly modelled. We note that data operations in $Circus\ Time$, like $Skip$, do not engage in events, and so, if not divergent, are instantaneous. So, time budgets and deadlines need to be explicitly defined.

CI3. The next invariant relates termination of interactions in both theories.

Definition 24. $\mathbf{CI3}(P) \mathrel{\widehat{=}} P \wedge wait_T = wait \wedge (\neg wait' \Rightarrow \neg wait'_T)$

It requires that termination, or not, of the previous process is the same in both models as $wait_T$ is equal to $wait$. On the other hand, termination of interactions in the untimed model, for the current process, implies termination in the timed model, but not vice-versa. If we were to admit $wait' = wait'_T$, then it would be impossible to define a process such as $Wait\ d$, since, when it terminates, **CI2** requires no time to pass, and thus d could never be greater than zero. On the negative side, if we consider the CSP process $Stop$ in the context of the super-theory, then it does not necessarily wait forever in the timed model. This is, however, unavoidable: if we were to admit $wait' \Rightarrow wait'_T$, then in the context of the super-theory $Stop$ would require non-termination appropriately, but $Skip$ would no longer require termination, and similarly $Wait\ d$ could still never terminate with d greater than zero due to **CI2**. We, therefore, need to provide a new definition of $Stop$ in the super-theory, which is not related to the CSP process $Stop$ by our Galois connection. It was the study of the super-theory, including both the $wait$ and $wait_T$ variables, that revealed the difficulties.

CI4. The final coupling invariant **CI4** relates the values of tr_C and tr'_C, and the values of tr_T and tr'_T, respectively.

Definition 25.

$$
\mathbf{CI4}(P) \mathrel{\widehat{=}} \begin{pmatrix} \textit{fst} \circ \textit{head}(tr'_T - \textit{front}(tr_T)) - \textit{fst} \circ \textit{last}(tr_T) = tr'_C - tr_C \land \\ P \land \\ tr_C \le tr'_C \land \textit{fst} \circ \textit{last}(tr_T) \le \textit{fst} \circ \textit{head}(tr'_T - \textit{front}(tr_T)) \end{pmatrix}
$$

The difference in traces between the variables tr'_C and tr_C, and the difference in events observed in the timed traces during the current time slot, as given by $\textit{fst} \circ \textit{head}(tr'_T - \textit{front}(tr_T))$ and $\textit{fst} \circ \textit{last}(tr_T)$, must be in agreement. Finally tr_C must be a prefix of tr'_C in order for the difference to be well-defined. Similarly, we also require the differences in the timed model to be prefixes. As discussed before, this aspect is part of $\mathbf{R1_T}$ in the original *Circus Time* theory.

CI. The complete relationship between timed and untimed variables is established by the coupling invariant **CI**, the composition of the previous invariants.

Definition 26. $\mathbf{CI}(P) = \mathbf{CI0} \circ \mathbf{CI1} \circ \mathbf{CI3} \circ \mathbf{CI2} \circ \mathbf{CI4}(P)$

We observe that **CI3** needs to be applied before **CI2** as the functions are not commutative; the others commute with each other.

Having defined both the healthiness condition **TR** and the coupling invariant **CI** of the super-theory, we now define the resulting Galois connection as described in Sect. 3. We have a pair of functions $csp2t$, mapping from untimed CSP to *Circus Time*, and $t2csp$ mapping in the opposite direction.

Definition 27.

$$
csp2t(P) \mathrel{\widehat{=}} \exists\, U\alpha \bullet \mathbf{CI} \circ \mathbf{TR}(P_{+T}) \quad t2csp(P) \mathrel{\widehat{=}} \exists\, T\alpha \bullet \mathbf{CI} \circ \mathbf{TR}(P_{+U})
$$

$$
\textit{where } T = \{tr_T, tr'_T, tr_C, tr'_C\}, \ U = \{tr, tr', \textit{ref}, \textit{ref}', \textit{wait}, \textit{wait}', tr_C, tr'_C\}
$$

That we have a Galois connection follows from Theorem 3 and Lemma 3.

This concludes the construction of the super-theory. In the following we explore the mapping of CSP operators into the super-theory and into *Circus Time*.

4.2   Using the Super-Theory

In this section we use the super-theory to relate CSP processes and their *Circus Time* counterparts. To that end, we first observe that the application of **TR** and **CI** to a reactive design yields a timed reactive process in the context of the super-theory of the form established by the following Theorem 4, where the function **S**, defined below, is used instead of **R**.

Definition 28. $\mathbf{S}(P) = \mathbf{R012_T} \circ \mathbf{CI0134} \circ \mathbf{R3_T} \circ \mathbf{R2}(P)$

The function **S** is the result of composing the healthiness conditions of the original *Circus Time* theory ($\mathbf{R0_T}$ to $\mathbf{R2_T}$, and $\mathbf{R3_T}$), together with our coupling invariants and **R2**. In the resulting design of Theorem 4, the conjunction in the postcondition is due to **CI2**: if the process terminates successfully in the untimed model, and without communicating any event, then time must not pass.

Theorem 4. *Provided ok' and $wait$ are not free in P,*

$$\mathbf{CI} \circ \mathbf{TR} \circ \mathbf{R}(P \vdash Q) = \mathbf{S}(P \vdash ((\neg wait' \wedge tr' = tr) \Rightarrow \#tr'_T = \#tr_T) \wedge Q)$$

We recall that all predicates of the CSP theory can be described as reactive designs, and so Theorem 4 describes all predicates of the super-theory. Similarly to CSP processes, they are the image of a design through a healthiness function. We observe that the proviso is standard for CSP processes, since their preconditions do not depend on the value of $wait$ as a result of **R3**.

Using Theorem 4, we can give a general characterisation of the result of applying $csp2t$ to a reactive design as established by the following Theorem 5, where $\phi \cong (Flat(tr'_T) = Flat(tr_T))$ and $f = false$ and $t = true$.

Theorem 5. *Provided tr_C and tr'_C are not free in P and Q, and ok' and $wait$ are not free in P,*

$$csp2t \circ \mathbf{R}(P \vdash Q) =$$
$$\mathbf{R_T} \begin{pmatrix} (\psi(P)[f/wait'] \vee wait'_T) \wedge \psi(P)[t/wait'] \\ \vdash \\ ((\phi \Rightarrow \#tr'_T = \#tr_T) \wedge \neg wait'_T \wedge \psi(Q)[f/wait']) \vee \psi(Q)[t/wait'] \end{pmatrix}$$

The proviso is satisfied by CSP processes as tr_C and tr'_C are not free in a reactive design. We obtain a timed reactive design with $\mathbf{R_T}$ applied. The design mentions the original pre and postconditions, P and Q, with ψ applied to them.

Definition 29. $\psi(P) \cong P \begin{bmatrix} \langle\rangle, Flat(tr'_T) - Flat(tr_T), wait_T/tr', tr', wait \\ snd \circ last(tr_T), snd \circ last(tr'_T)/ref, ref' \end{bmatrix}$

These substitutions are a consequence of the definition of the coupling invariants and the healthiness condition **R2** of the original reactive design.

In a CSP process $\mathbf{R}(P \vdash Q)$, we expect $wait'$ not to be constrained, or even free, in P. In this case, the precondition of $csp2t \circ \mathbf{R}(P \vdash Q)$ is simply $\psi(P)$. We do not have, however, a healthiness condition that ensures that $wait'$ is not free in P. So, the actual precondition of $csp2t \circ \mathbf{R}(P \vdash Q)$ requires that $wait'_T$ must hold if P requires $wait'$ to be true.

The postcondition considers two cases. The second case is simpler: $wait'$ is admitted to be *true* in Q, and so the postcondition is Q with the appropriate substitutions of ψ. The first case is when $wait'$ is admitted to be *false*: if no events are observed, that is, $Flat(tr_T) = Flat(tr'_T)$, then no time can pass, and termination also occurs in the timed model, with $wait'_T$ being *false*.

Having established the general results of mapping (untimed) CSP processes into the super-theory, and into *Circus Time*, in the remainder of this section we discuss the mapping of *Skip*, *Stop* and external choice.

Skip. The result of mapping *Skip* into the timed theory is established by the following Theorem 6.

Theorem 6. $csp2t(Skip) = \mathbf{R_T}(true \vdash \#tr'_T = \#tr_T \land \phi \land \neg wait'_T)$

The precondition is also *true*, while the postcondition requires termination in the timed model $\neg wait'_T$, that no events are observed, and that no time must pass. This is the original definition of *Skip* in *Circus Time* [4].

Stop. The result of mapping *Stop* through *csp2t* is established by Theorem 7.

Theorem 7. $csp2t(Stop) = \mathbf{R_T}(true \vdash Flat(tr'_T) = Flat(tr_T))$

Like in CSP the precondition is *true*, while the postcondition is rather different: it only states that no events are observed, but termination is not guaranteed. This is unlike the definition of timed $Stop_T$ [4] reproduced below.

Definition 30. $Stop_T \;\hat{=}\; \mathbf{R_T}(true \vdash Flat(tr'_T) = Flat(tr_T) \land wait'_T)$

The application of $t2csp$ to $Stop_T$, however, yields the *Stop* of CSP as required, since $wait'_T \Rightarrow wait'$ is enforced by **CI3**.

External Choice. Following from the result of Theorem 4, the next Theorem 8 establishes the induced definition of external choice in the super-theory.

Theorem 8. *Provided ok' and $wait$ are not free in P and Q,*

$$\mathbf{TR} \circ \mathbf{CI} \circ \mathbf{R}((P \vdash R) \,\square_{CSP}\, (Q \vdash S)) =$$

$$\mathbf{S}\left((P \land Q) \vdash \left(\begin{array}{l} ((R \land S) \vartriangleleft tr' = tr \land wait' \vartriangleright (R \lor S)) \\ \land \\ ((\neg wait' \land tr' = tr) \Rightarrow \#tr'_T = \#tr_T) \end{array} \right) \right)$$

The precondition is the conjunction of both preconditions just like in CSP, whereas the postcondition requires, in addition to that of CSP, immediate termination in the untimed model to become instantaneous. For example, in the case of the untimed process $Skip \,\square\, a \rightarrow Skip$, there is no agreement on waiting, so either *Skip* terminates instantaneously, or the prefixing on the event a terminates at any time, without any waiting period observed. So, we have unexpected behaviour in a timed setting: although *Skip* terminates immediately, it does not resolve the choice, and although $a \rightarrow Skip$ can take time, we cannot observe its stable waiting states. We note that, in (untimed) CSP, termination also does not resolve a choice, and the above is the definition in the super-theory. We consider next the result of mapping external choice through the super-theory into the timed model is established by the following Theorem 9.

Theorem 9. *Provided tr_C and tr'_C, and ok' and $wait$, are not free in P and Q,*

$$csp2t(\mathbf{R}(P \vdash S) \,\Box_{CSP}\, \mathbf{R}(Q \vdash R)) =$$

$$\mathbf{R_T} \left(\begin{array}{l} (\psi(P \wedge Q)[f/wait'] \vee wait'_T) \wedge \psi(P \wedge Q)[t/wait'] \\ \vdash \\ \left(\begin{array}{l} (\psi(R \wedge S)[t/wait'] \vartriangleleft \phi \vartriangleright \psi(R \vee S)[t/wait']) \\ \vee \\ ((\phi \Rightarrow \#tr'_T = \#tr_T) \wedge \psi(R \vee S)[f/wait'] \wedge \neg wait'_T) \end{array} \right) \end{array} \right)$$

This result closely follows that of Theorems 5 and 8. The precondition retains the conjunction of the original reactive design with appropriate substitutions.

In the postcondition there is a disjunction between, roughly, the usual conditional that characterises the choice, and an extra disjunct that stems from **CI**. It covers the possibility that one of the processes terminates, with $wait'$ being *false* in R or S, and termination also takes place in the timed theory, with $wait'_T$ being *false*, but it is instantaneous if no event is observed. The conditional considers the cases where R and S agree on waiting in the untimed model and, either no event is observed (ϕ) and R and S agree, or either process performs some visible event ($\neg\phi$). In any case, waiting in the untimed model does not lead to waiting in the timed model because of **CI3**. For example, the process *Skip* $\Box$ *Wait* 1 has only one possible behaviour: immediate and instantaneous termination. We note that *Skip* = *Wait* 0, and so *Skip* $\Box$ *Wait* 1 is a process of the form *Wait d* $\Box$ *Wait (d + m)* mentioned in Sect. 1.

We consider another example: *Wait* 1 $\Box$ *Wait* 2. In this case, the only possible agreement between the processes is to wait 1 time unit. Termination of either process with no visible events cannot be instantaneous and so the behaviour after 1 time unit is miraculous. Finally, we consider *Wait* 1 $\Box$ (*Wait* 2 ; $a \rightarrow$ *Skip*), where there is a choice between terminating after 1 time unit, or performing the event a after 2 time units. In this case, and following Theorem 9, the processes can only agree on waiting for 1 time unit. After 2 time units, the event a can still be observed, but between 1 and 2 time units the process is miraculous.

Ultimately the definition of external choice induced from (untimed) CSP does not satisfy the timed properties of interest, namely, that early termination of one of the processes leads to termination. The definition considered in [4] does not correspond to this induced definition either. The approach we propose allows the study of different timed models, and, consequently, different definitions of timed external choice, through Galois connections which preserve the properties of untimed CSP. These variations can be obtained by adjusting the coupling variants piecewise. Further work is necessary to explore other possibilities.

5   Conclusion

The composition of theories is crucial for the unification of results in the UTP. Galois connections are an essential tool for the theory engineer as part of studying multiple aspects and relating definitions amongst different models.

The approach we propose promotes separation of concerns: healthiness conditions are defined separately to the relation between variables of the theories. The coupling invariants can be adjusted to yield models satisfying different properties, and provided the healthiness conditions are strengthening or weakening, or both, then Galois connections can be established. Although, we have used this technique to study only *Circus* and *Circus Time*, we expect it to be of more general use because it is based on general ideas of data refinement. Confirmation of this generality, however, is still to be established.

We have applied our approach to find a Galois connection between CSP and *Circus Time* that can justify the definition of the healthiness conditions and operators of *Circus Time*. This is different to that proposed in [4]. Our construction relies on a set of principles underlying the timed model and the appropriate definition of coupling invariants. This approach provides a way to study the induced definitions of operators, such as *Skip*, *Stop* and external choice.

The definition obtained for timed external choice is not entirely satisfactory in light of desired properties. Different versions of this operator are considered in [11,12]. In pursuit of a suitable treatment of external choice, it remains for us to study the relationship between untimed CSP and those models through a super-theory construction that preserves the semantics of untimed CSP.

Acknowledgments. We would like to thank Simon Foster for his support regarding Isabelle/UTP. This work is funded by EPSRC grants EP/H017461/1 and EP/M025756/1.

References

1. Hoare, C.A.R., He, J.: Unifying Theories of Programming. Prentice Hall International Series in Computer Science. Prentice Hall, Upper Saddle River (1998)
2. Roscoe, A.W.: Understanding Concurrent Systems. Springer, London (2010)
3. Oliveira, M., Cavalcanti, A., Woodcock, J.: A UTP semantics for Circus. Formal Aspects Comput. **21**(1), 3–32 (2007)
4. Sherif, A., Cavalcanti, A.L.C., He, J., Sampaio, A.C.A.: A process algebraic framework for specification and validation of real-time systems. Formal Aspects Comput. **22**(2), 153–191 (2010)
5. Wei, K., Woodcock, J., Cavalcanti, A.: Circus Time with reactive designs. In: Wolff, B., Gaudel, M.-C., Feliachi, A. (eds.) UTP 2012. LNCS, vol. 7681, pp. 68–87. Springer, Berlin (2013). doi:10.1007/978-3-642-35705-3_3
6. Cavalcanti, A., Sampaio, A., Woodcock, J.: A Refinement Strategy for Circus. Formal Aspects Comput. **15**, 146–181 (2003)
7. Harwood, W., Cavalcanti, A., Woodcock, J.: A theory of pointers for the UTP. In: Fitzgerald, J.S., Haxthausen, A.E., Yenigun, H. (eds.) ICTAC 2008. LNCS, vol. 5160, pp. 141–155. Springer, Heidelberg (2008). doi:10.1007/978-3-540-85762-4_10
8. Woodcock, J., Davies, J.: Using Z: Specification, Refinement, and Proof. Prentice Hall, Upper Saddle River (1996)
9. Schneider, S.: Concurrent and Real-Time Systems: the CSP Approach. Worldwide Series in Computer Science. Wiley, New York (2000)

10. Wei, K., Woodcock, J., Cavalcanti, A.: New Circus Time. Technical report, University of York (2012). https://www.cs.york.ac.uk/circus/publications/techreports/reports/Circus%20Time.pdf
11. Butterfield, A., Gancarski, P., Woodcock, J.: State visibility and communication in unifying theories of programming. In: Third IEEE International Symposium on Theoretical Aspects of Software Engineering, TASE 2009, pp. 47–54, July 2009
12. Canham, S., Woodcock, J.: Three approaches to timed external choice in UTP. In: Naumann, D. (ed.) UTP 2014. LNCS, vol. 8963, pp. 1–20. Springer, Heidelberg (2015). doi:10.1007/978-3-319-14806-9_1
13. Morgan, C.: Programming from Specifications. Prentice Hall, Upper Saddle River (1994)
14. Woodcock, J., Cavalcanti, A.: A tutorial introduction to designs in unifying theories of programming. In: Boiten, E.A., Derrick, J., Smith, G. (eds.) IFM 2004. LNCS, vol. 2999, pp. 40–66. Springer, Berlin (2004). doi:10.1007/978-3-540-24756-2_4
15. Cavalcanti, A., Woodcock, J.: A tutorial introduction to CSP in *unifying theories of programming*. In: Cavalcanti, A., Sampaio, A., Woodcock, J. (eds.) PSSE 2004. LNCS, vol. 3167, pp. 220–268. Springer, Berlin (2006). doi:10.1007/11889229_6
16. Spivey, J.M.: The Z Notation: A Reference Manual. Prentice Hall, Upper Saddle River (1989)
17. Ribeiro, P.: Super-Theories. Technical report, University of York (2016). https://www-users.cs.york.ac.uk/pfr/reports/super-theories.pdf
18. Foster, S., Zeyda, F., Woodcock, J.: Isabelle/UTP: A Mechanised Theory Engineering Framework. In: Naumann, D. (ed.) UTP 2014. LNCS, vol. 8963, pp. 21–41. Springer, Heidelberg (2015). doi:10.1007/978-3-319-14806-9_2
19. Banks, M.J., Jacob, J.L.: On integrating confidentiality and functionality in a formal method. Formal Aspects Comput. **26**(5), 963–992 (2013)

An Axiomatic Value Model for Isabelle/UTP

Frank Zeyda[1], Simon Foster[2(✉)], and Leo Freitas[3]

[1] School of Computing, Teesside University, Middlesbrough TS1 3BA, UK
f.zeyda@tees.ac.uk
[2] Department of Computer Science, University of York, York YO10 5GH, UK
simon.foster@york.ac.uk
[3] School of Computing Science, Newcastle University, Newcastle NE1 7RU, UK
leo.freitas@ncl.ac.uk

Abstract. The Unifying Theories of Programming (UTP) is a mathematical framework to define, examine and link program semantics for a large variety of computational paradigms. Several mechanisations of the UTP in HOL theorem provers have been developed. All of them, however, succumb to a trade off in how they encode the value model of UTP theories. A deep and unified value model via a universal (data)type incurs restrictions on permissible value types and adds complexity; a value model directly instantiating HOL types for UTP values retains simplicity, but sacrifices expressiveness, since we lose the ability to compositionally reason about alphabets and theories. We here propose an alternative solution that axiomatises the value model and retains the advantages of both approaches. We carefully craft a definitional mechanism in the Isabelle/HOL prover that guarantees soundness.

1 Introduction

Much work has already been done in developing semantic models of particular programming languages and modelling notations. The Unifying Theories of Programming (UTP) [10] put forward an agenda of relating and combining such models in order to facilitate the development of sound foundations for highly-integrated languages that incorporate multiple paradigms, such as concurrency [16], object orientation [20], and time [21], to name a few only.

The importance of the UTP is to justify verification techniques that involve a heterogeneous set of notations, methods and tools. This is becoming an integral part of certification standards such as DO-178C in avionics [19], and motivated work in mechanising the UTP in theorem provers. Machine-checked proofs about the formalism(s) in use may thus become part of the certification evidence, in addition to verification proofs of actual systems and software components.

Several mechanisations of the UTP are currently available [3,6,7,17,25]. The majority of them uses HOL-based provers, namely ProofPower-Z [17,25] and Isabelle/HOL [6,7]. Only [3] develops a proof system and tool from scratch. The use of Isabelle/HOL in the aforementioned works is motivated by the high level

J.P. Bowen and H. Zhu (Eds.): UTP 2016, LNCS 10134, pp. 155–175, 2017.
DOI: 10.1007/978-3-319-52228-9_8

of adaptability and automation afforded by this prover. This is, for instance, due to its ability to interface with external tools such as powerful SMT solvers [1].

Although Isabelle/HOL appears to be an attractive choice for a proof tool, its type system forces us into a compromise when encoding the binding and predicate model of UTP theories. UTP theories are, in essence, characterised by subsets of predicates over some alphabet of variables. Predicates are typically encoded by sets of bindings, namely those that render the predicate true. Bindings associate alphabet variables with values. A fundamental part of any UTP reasoning framework is hence the representation of bindings and values.

Where the existing works on UTP mechanisation most notably differ is in how they encode the binding and value model of UTP theories. We here distinguish a deep and a shallow approach. In a deep approach as adopted by [14,17,25], a monomorphic value type with a fixed representation is introduced, typically as a datatype. This leads to a monomorphic binding model, and thereby, a monomorphic predicate model. It permits a high level of expressiveness by allowing us to define operators that inspect and modify the alphabets of predicates. A downside is that the value model must be *a priori* fixed and therefore cannot be extended. Moreover, certain constructions, such as arbitrary sets and functions, are difficult to support as they are not permissible in recursive datatype definitions.

In a shallow approach, as adopted by [5,6], the binding type is kept abstract by using a HOL type variable in place of it. This leads to a polymorphic (type-parametric) binding and predicate model. Therein, variables can only have an abstract representation, and we cannot prove properties about them until the binding model is (at least partially) instantiated — typically, using extensible record types to retain a degree of modularity. Doing so, however, forfeits the ability to compositionally reason about predicate alphabets. A crucial advantage of the shallow model is that UTP values can be drawn from *any* HOL type, and reasoning is much simplified since we are able to directly employ HOL theorems and tactics; the shallow model is moreover naturally extensible.

We here present an alternative and novel approach that uses an axiomatic value model. It combines the advantages of the deep and shallow approach, with no added complexity for the user. Our contribution here is not only relevant to mechanised proof support for the UTP, but indeed any kind of semantic language embedding in HOL. The choice of Isabelle/HOL is a pragmatic one: we benefit from an adaptable and open architecture, as well as powerful external proof tools that we can readily interface with. While dependently-typed logics and provers may tackle the issue we address in other ways, we nonetheless believe there is important scientific benefit in solving it in the context of HOL, too.

Our terminology of a deep and shallow approach ought not be confused with the terminology of a deep or shallow **embedding**. Whereas an embedding is classified as deep if it encodes the syntax of the embedded language, this paper is only concerned with the nature of semantic models. We remark that at the core, the UTP can in fact be viewed as a shallow embedding of program logic.

The structure of the paper is as follows. In Sect. 2, we review the UTP and Isabelle/HOL. Section 3 surveys the existing UTP mechanisations, comparing their encoding approaches for values and bindings in detail. Section 4 introduces our axiomatic value model in mathematical terms, and Sect. 5 describes its sound implementation in Isabelle/HOL. Lastly, in Sect. 6 we give an example of its use, and conclude and discuss future work in Sect. 7.

2 Preliminaries

In this section, we discuss preliminary material: the UTP in Sect. 2.1, and Isabelle/HOL in Sect. 2.2.

2.1 Unifying Theories of Programming

The Unifying Theories of Programming (UTP) [10] is a mathematical framework for describing and unifying the formal semantics of programming and modelling languages within the same descriptive environment of the alphabetised relational calculus. A UTP theory consists of an alphabet of variable names, a signature of language constructs, and a set of constraints (called healthiness conditions). Relations are encoded by alphabetised predicates: that is, predicates that contain additional information about the relation's alphabet.

Alphabets identify observational variables whose values are relevant to characterise system behaviour within a given paradigm. We use undecorated variables for initial, and dashed variables for intermediate or final observations. The alphabet of each theory contains variables relevant to the description of its programs, as well as auxiliary variables used to record aspects of the paradigm. For instance, the UTP theory of designs uses a boolean variable ok to record the program has started, and ok' to record that the program has terminated. The seminal book [10] on UTP is not precise on typing, but it is generally acknowledged that we operate in a typed language and logic setting, with common mathematical structures being available, such as sets, functions and sequences.

Through appropriate choice of variables and mathematical structures, it is possible to express the desired features of a programming notation in an elegant and concise way. The underlying UTP theory must select the appropriate and relevant subset of variables to represent intended behaviours. The signature of a theory is the language syntax, and the meaning of every program is given as a predicate restricted to the selected alphabet and signature.

Healthiness conditions formalise constraints on the semantic model: we only consider predicates that satisfy the healthiness conditions of a theory as valid models of computations within that theory. Importantly, healthiness conditions sometimes depend in their definition on the alphabet of the theory in which they reside. For instance, the theory of methods in [24] adds one constraint for each method variable m that is present in the theory's alphabet. This illustrates the nominal character of the UTP logic: variables are treated as first-class objects, with the αP operator yielding the alphabet of a predicate P as a set.

One can think of the UTP as a 'theory supermarket': whatever theoretical mechanisms are needed for a particular application, pick the appropriate UTP theories and link them to provide the laws and compositional refinement notion to verify specifications all the way down to code. The use of Galois connections is pervasive within UTP theories as a means to enable the description of formal links between a variety of paradigms, justifying the use of the same (formal) universe of discourse. In this utopian view of programming, the underlying mathematics are often challenging and profit from a mechanised reasoning framework, where the customer of the theory supermarket can be assured that the ingredients she picks soundly combine when preparing her theory.

Having said that, when it comes to making use of such theories in an industrial setting, or on examples beyond the blackboard, a suitable arrangement of technical details is required in order to use proof assistants. That is, before we can focus on any proof obligations born from modelling, we first need to shape and polish models to fit the needs of a mechanical theorem prover. The most fundamental problem tackled in this paper is therefore the description of an extensible and (expressively) rich value model. We claim this is as much part of UTP theory engineering as defining operators and healthiness conditions.

Our key objective here is to free the language designer from any restrictions that may be imposed by the embedding of the UTP logic in a HOL theorem prover; that is, without having to compromise on expressivity elsewhere.

2.2   Isabelle/HOL

Isabelle/HOL [13] is a popular theorem prover for Higher-Order Logic (HOL). It follows the design of LCF [9] in protecting the user from unsound deductions: theorems can only be generated through valid inferences that, ultimately, rely on the consistency of a small logic kernel of axiomatic rules only.

The Isabelle framework itself is agnostic to the logic being used. There exist, for instance, instantiations of it for First-Order Logic and Zermelo-Fraenkel set theory. Isabelle provides natural-deduction-style proof rules and an underlying proof engine to conveniently perform backward and forward inferences. In addition, several powerful external provers can be easily invoked from within Isabelle. A structured proof language called ISAR is also part of the system.

Types in Isabelle/HOL can be defined in various ways. The most basic type declaration is via a **typedecl** $('t_1, 't_2, \dots) T_{new}$, which introduces a new given type T_{new} without any constructor functions. The $'t_1$, $'t_2$, and so on, are possible parameters of the type. All we know about such types is that they are non-empty.

Type definitions are supported by way of:

$$\textbf{typedef } ('t_1, 't_2, \dots) \ T_{new} \ = \ S :: ('t_1, 't_2, \dots) \ T_{exists} \ \textsf{set}$$

where S is some (non-empty) subset of values of some existing type T_{exists} to which the newly-defined type is deemed to be isomorphic. We thus obtain a pair of abstraction and representation functions which are internally axiomatised to provide a bijection from S into the carrier set of T_{new}.

More sophisticated type definitions can be achieved with the **datatype** command for (co)inductive datatypes and **record** command to introduce extensible record types, although underneath the HOL system reformulates both in terms of plain **typedef**s. This definitional style of implementing high-level features guarantees that soundness is necessarily preserved.

Isabelle additionally supports type classes. They can be viewed as contractual specifications on types. A type may instantiate a particular type class C, and such can be formulated as a requirement 'a :: C on some type 'a. We note that the symbol '::' in HOL is used for both, typing and type-class membership.

3 UTP Embedding Approaches

In this section, we survey the existing mechanisations of the UTP and their approaches to encoding values, bindings and predicates. A complete list of current works is presented in Table 1. We note that there are three mechanisations that target ProofPower-Z, but they are very similar in how they encode the predicate and value model. All works except for $U \cdot (TP)^2$ are definitional, meaning that they extend HOL conservatively; this guarantees consistency of the embeddings. As $U \cdot (TP)^2$ uses its own logic, consistency must be argued by other means.

Table 1. Existing works that mechanise the UTP framework.

Name	Developers	Proof System
UTP in ProofPower-Z	Nuka [14], Oliviera [17], and Zeyda [25]	ProofPower-Z
Isabelle/*Circus*	Feliachi et al. [5,6]	Isabelle/HOL
Isabelle/UTP	Foster and Zeyda [7]	Isabelle/HOL
$U \cdot (TP)^2$ (Saoithín)	Butterfield [2,3]	Custom

All HOL-based embeddings create some type $\mathcal{P}$ for alphabetised predicates, either as a type synonym — in some cases with associated constraints, or HOL type definition. The model of $\mathcal{P}$ is typically the set of bindings $\mathbb{P}(\mathcal{B})$ over some binding type $\mathcal{B}$. In all works except Isabelle/*Circus*, $\mathcal{P}$ also includes explicit information about the predicate's alphabet. We note that Isabelle/*Circus* represents predicates as characteristic functions $\mathcal{B} \Rightarrow bool$, but this does not limit generality of our discussion, as being equivalent to a set-based encoding.

3.1 A Shallow Predicate Model

A shallow predicate model is adopted by Isabelle/*Circus* [5,6]. The binding notion is kept abstract, using a HOL type variable such as 's for it. UTP variables are likewise modelled abstractly, by way of pairs consisting of a getter and update function. The types of these functions are recaptured below.

$$get :: \text{'}s \Rightarrow \text{'}a \quad \text{and} \quad update :: \text{'}s \Rightarrow \text{'}a \Rightarrow \text{'}s$$

Above, $'a$ determines the HOL type of the variable. The *get* function extracts the value of the variable from a binding, and the *update* function modifies the binding to assign a new value to the variable. Variables hence do not have a symbolic identity that is, for instance, formalised by an encoding of names.

A key advantage of this approach is that UTP variables can range over arbitrary HOL types $'a$; a downside is that we cannot prove anything about them unless the binding type $'s$ is concretised, so that the *get* and *update* functions may be concretely defined. In Isabelle/*Circus*, instantiation of the binding type accompanies UTP theory development. It is done partially and incrementally, by way of extensible records. For instance, to encode the UTP theory of designs, we have to create a record type $(\!| ok :: bool, 'more |\!)$ to encode the variable *ok*. The type $'more$ here corresponds to the open extension of the record type and allows us to subsequently add further variables to that theory.

The use of extensible records retains a certain degree of modularity in defining generic connectives that apply to predicates with different alphabets. These connectives are typically encoded by operations on the binding sets. Unification of the binding types is therefore needed to apply these operators. As an example, we may unify the following binding types $(\!| ok :: bool, 'more |\!)$ and $(\!| ok :: bool, x :: nat |\!)$ by instantiating $'more$ with $(\!| x :: nat |\!)$. The first corresponds to the (extensible) design alphabet $\{ok :: bool, \dots\}$, and the second to the closed design alphabet $\{ok :: bool, x :: nat\}$ including a program variable x.

A ramification of this approach is that each time we introduce a variable, we effectively have to create a host-logic record type for it. It is therefore non-compositional in the treatment of alphabets. Variables, despite their abstract representation, are not first-class citizens in this treatment: we cannot create them on-the-fly or collect them in sets.

In a shallow model, the value universe $\mathcal{U}$ may potentially include any Isabelle/HOL type. The binding type $\mathcal{B}$ is equated with open and closed record types; this makes the predicate type $\mathcal{P}$ parametric in the extension type of (open) records. New record types are created through Isabelle's declarative mechanism, ensuring soundness. In this approach, complexity arises as record types have to be created as UTP theory development unfolds; complexity is, however, alleviated by a thin layer between object and host-logic value models.

3.2   A Deep Predicate Model

The ProofPower-Z works [14,17,25] use a deep predicate model by creating a fixed value universe $\mathcal{U}$ as an inductive datatype that supports the construction of various basic and composite values. Below, $\mathbb{F}(S)$ yields the finite subsets of S.

$$VALUE ::= Nat(\mathbb{N}) \mid Bool(\mathbb{B}) \mid Pair(VALUE \times VALUE) \mid Set(\mathbb{F}(VALUE)) \mid \dots$$

This approach leads to a monomorphic predicate type $\mathcal{P}$, because bindings $\mathcal{B}$ can be equated with the function space $VAR \Rightarrow VALUE$, where both the domain and range types are monomorphic. UTP variables (type VAR) are encoded symbolically as strings, with some added information for dashes and subscripts.

The work [25] adds to this a (monomorphic) model of types to formalise well-typed constructions. In that model, variables are encoded by name and type pairs.

In a deep predicate model, we are able to introspect and reason about the alphabets of predicates since variables are treated as first-class objects. This provides more expressivity to mechanise UTP theories, since functions can be formalised that manipulate predicates and their alphabets in any conceivable manner. We discuss an example where this is needed in Sect. 6.

A downside of the deep approach is that the value model is not extensible, since the *VALUE* type (universe) must be defined upfront. The use of datatypes imposes further restrictions. For instance, we cannot support general set-valued constructions as to avoid well-known inconsistencies [22], which is why the argument of *Set*(_) above must be a finite set. Recent advances in using categorical foundations for datatypes in Isabelle/HOL [23] have relaxed that restriction to furthermore permit infinite sets with bounded cardinalities, but this is still more restrictive than HOL sets in general.

The use of a deep model is often inevitable if we perform a deep embedding, since it enables us to formalise the mapping from syntax to semantics within the host logic. While a deep model offers more expressiveness at the level of predicates and UTP theories, it incurs restrictions with regards to what kind of values can be supported. Moreover, operators and theorems about (HOL) value types need to be 'lifted' into the unified *VALUE* type, resulting in a larger number of definitions and underlying proof infrastructure to burden the user.

3.3   A Hybrid Predicate Model

Isabelle/UTP [7] adopts a hybrid approach to alleviate some of the downsides of a deep predicate model while retaining its expressivity. Rather than using a polymorphic type $'s$ for bindings, it introduces an abstract type $'a$ for the values themselves. This type, unlike in Isabelle/*Circus*, does not need to be instantiated as the UTP theory hierarchy unfolds. Instead, we create type classes to inject particular desired HOL types into it. The type classes introduce the abstraction and representation function for the respective value. An example follows.

```
class INT_SORT =
  fixes MkInt :: "int ⇒ 'a::TYPED_VALUE"
  fixes DestInt :: "'a::TYPED_VALUE ⇒ int"
  assumes MkInt_inv : "DestInt(MkInt x) = x"
  assumes DestInt_inv : "y :ᵤ IntType ⟹ MkInt(DestInt y) = y"
```

The constant `IntType` and the operator $:_u$ are provided by the `TYPED_VALUE` type class, whose definition we omit for brevity. We can indeed think of the classes as type definitions that 'reuse' the target type to be defined. To prove consistency, we have to show that an aggregation of type classes (one for each value notion used by a UTP theory) can be instantiated. Logically, this corresponds to showing that the abstract value type has a model that satisfies the assumptions of all aggregated type classes. Yet in practice, such a proof has to be carried out for every UTP theory, based on what value notions are used by the theory.

With the above, we can formalise constraints on the value model of particular UTP theories through class constraints on $'a$. For instance, the theory of designs requires the presence of a value type to encode booleans for its auxiliary variables ok and ok', and this can be captured by a class constraint $'a ::$ BOOL_SORT on all definitional entities that play a part in the encoding of that UTP theory.

In this approach, the universe $\mathcal{U}$ need not be fixed upfront. We can inject new types into it as we go along. To prove consistency, which now becomes a 'proof obligation' to be discharged by the user, we are, however, still restricted to value notions that have a model within HOL. We note that the hybrid approach can be 'abused' as an axiomatic treatment, for instance, to support general sets and functions as UTP values but in doing so, we introduce the possibility of localised inconsistencies into the value model. This is not safe since the consistency issue then rests with the user rather than the mechanised framework.

In conclusion, it seems we cannot have our cake and eat it: none of the existing mechanised UTP systems gives us an unconstrained and provably-sound value model *and* an expressive (compositional) predicate model. In the remainder, we propose a new axiomatic approach that satisfies both desiderata.

4   An Axiomatic Value Model

We next describe our value model in general mathematical terms. Section 4.1 examines the HOL universe, and Sect. 4.2 our axiomatic UTP universe.

4.1   The HOL Universe

The standard set-theoretic semantics of HOL prescribes the von Neumann universe $V_{\omega+\omega} \setminus \{\varnothing\}$ (without the empty set) as a minimal model for its possible type constructions [18]. The von Neumann universe V_i is inductively defined for some index i by repeated application of the power-set for ordinal indices β, and generalised union for limit ordinals λ.

$$V_0 \mathrel{\hat{=}} \varnothing \qquad V_{\beta+1} \mathrel{\hat{=}} \mathbb{P}(V_\beta) \qquad V_\lambda \mathrel{\hat{=}} \bigcup_{\beta<\lambda} V_\beta$$

Each limit ordinal index corresponds to the union of all sets constructed up to that level. In HOL, every finite type is representable by some V_n (for $n \in \mathbb{N}_{>0}$), and every infinite type by some $V_{\omega+n}$. For example, nat and int correspond to V_ω, and real and nat set correspond to $V_{\omega+1}$. In Isabelle/HOL specifically, types can be constructed either by composition of existing parametric types, or by definition of new types through identification of a suitable non-empty subset of some existing type [11,12]. The built-in types of Isabelle/HOL are:

- the boolean type bool containing the elements True and False;

- the infinite type ind whose cardinality is that of the naturals;
- the parametric function type $\sigma \Rightarrow \tau$ for HOL types σ and τ.

From these three types, all standard HOL types can be produced, including the power type σ set ($\hat{=}$ $\sigma \Rightarrow$ bool), the product type $\sigma \times \tau$, and the sum type $\sigma + \tau$. The constructions are performed via the **typedef** command, though the σ set type is technically axiomatised in Isabelle/HOL. This, however, is merely for convenience — its definition as a function type is equally feasible. It shows though, in defence of our solution, that Isabelle/HOL itself does not shy away from axiomatisations where we can provide strong evidence for consistency.

We conclude that all types in Isabelle/HOL of higher cardinality than $|\mathbb{N}|$ must be constructed by a (finite) repeated application of the power-type constructor σ set, with their cardinality being bounded by $V_{\omega+n}$ for some $n \in \mathbb{N}$. Thus it is impossible to define a type as large as $V_{\omega+\omega}$ within HOL itself, when using only the standard mechanisms for type definition.

The above implies that it is not possible to define a universal type $\mathcal{U}$ in HOL into which all HOL types are injectable. The existence of such a type in HOL would moreover lead to inconsistency, since there would then have to exist an injection $\mathcal{U}$ set into $\mathcal{U}$ itself, which Cantor's theorem forbids. In introducing $\mathcal{U}$ axiomatically, namely for UTP value and type models, it is, in essence, the latter that we have to protect ourselves from.

There have been several attempts to formalise a larger universe in HOL than the standard definitional mechanisms allow. HOL-ST [8] is an experimental combination of HOL and set theory that axiomatises a universe consisting of ZFC set constructions. HOL-ST was later adapted to create Isabelle/HOLZF [15] which axiomatises the ZFC universe as a type ZF alongside other HOL types; the motivation of that work was to formalise the notion of *Partisan Games* [15] as they cannot be captured through permissible **datatype** constructions in HOL.

Our approach here has the same aim as HOL-ST in using an **axiomatization** to provide a type that is 'larger' than any type definable in HOL, but unlike HOL-ST we want to make it possible to directly inject existing HOL types in our new (axiomatic) type. For this, it is sufficient to declare a type UVal and postulate three axioms that provide injectivity and type reflection from HOL into UVal. The next section discusses the axiomatisation in general terms.

4.2   The UTP Universe

In this section, we give a semi-formal exposition of our axiomatic UTP universe, which will be formally mechanised in Sect. 5. We presuppose the existence of a class Type of HOL types, and also a universe HOL of HOL values. We recall that the latter cannot be defined in HOL as a set, and we therefore refer to it here as a (proper) class. For simplicity, we do not directly consider polymorphism and treat each type $\sigma \in$ Type as a fully-instantiated monomorphic type. Hence, no two types can possess a common element. Our objectives are:

- The creation of a universe type UVal into which the values of a suitable subset of permissible HOL types can be soundly injected;

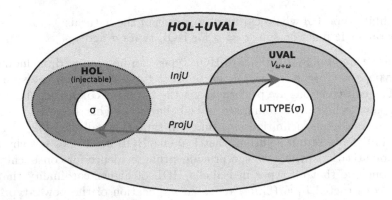

Fig. 1. Relation between the HOL and UVal universes.

– reflection of the HOL typing relation $v :: t$ into UVal, also allowing us to explicitly reason about typing within UVal.

Our universe will be implemented through monomorphic types. This enables us to form definitions and theorems that effectively quantify over HOL types. Each objective is characterised by an additional axiom that we will describe. These axioms are conceptual, and do not correspond precisely to the Isabelle axioms which cannot, for instance, have typing statements like $x :: \sigma$ as caveats or talk explicitly about the HOL universe of values. The axioms will therefore require some refinement before their implementation into Isabelle/HOL, which we describe in Sect. 5. We will also prove some necessary theorems implied by these axioms, which our implementation satisfies.

Our UTP universe is characterised by a declared Isabelle type UVal, together with a polymorphic injection function $InjU$: HOL $\Rightarrow$ UVal, a projection function $ProjU$: UVal $\Rightarrow$ HOL, and a type mapping $UTYPE$: Type $\Rightarrow$ UType. The application $UTYPE(\sigma)$ encodes a HOL type σ as a suitable value of a monomorphic type UType that represents HOL types. We also have a reflected typing relation $x :_u t$, for $x \in$ UVal and $t \in$ UType. We visualise the behaviour of these functions in Fig. 1. Every HOL type $\sigma \in$ Type can be injected into a corresponding subset of UVal, by application of $InjU$. Moreover, all values within UVal can be projected back to their corresponding HOL type.

We now formally specify the behaviour of these functions through three axioms that augment the axioms of HOL:

1. AxVALBIJ. For any $\sigma \in$ Type, $InjU$ is a bijection between the values of σ and those of $UTYPE(\sigma)$, with $ProjU$ being its inverse.
2. AxTYPEREFL. The reflected typing relation is sound and complete with respect to HOL typing, such that $InjU(x) :_u UTYPE(\sigma)$ if and only if $x :: \sigma$.
3. AxTYPENONEMPTY. For any $t \in$ UType, there exists a value $v \in$ UVal such that $v :_u t$.

Axiom AxVALBIJ indirectly ensures that the cardinality of any HOL type is less or equal than that of UVal, as stated by the following theorem.

Theorem 1. *For any* $\sigma \in \mathsf{Type}$, *the cardinality of* σ *is no greater than that of* UVal, *that is* $|\sigma| \leq |\mathsf{UVal}|$.

Proof. $InjU$, by AxVALBIJ, is an injection from σ to UVal. This is sufficient to demonstrate the required cardinality relationship. □

Furthermore, we can show that UVal has a strictly greater cardinality than any HOL type.

Theorem 2. *The cardinality of any HOL type* $\sigma \in \mathsf{Type}$ *is strictly less than the cardinality of* UVal, *that is* $|\sigma| < |\mathsf{UVal}|$.

Proof. We prove this by contradiction. Assume that $|\sigma| \geq |\mathsf{UVal}|$, then either $|\sigma| > |\mathsf{UVal}|$ or $|\sigma| = |\mathsf{UVal}|$.

- If $|\sigma| > |\mathsf{UVal}|$, we obtain a contradiction by Theorem 1.
- If $|\sigma| = |\mathsf{UVal}|$, from $\sigma \in \mathsf{Type}$ we also have that $\sigma\,\mathsf{set} \in \mathsf{Type}$. By Cantor's theorem we have that $|\sigma\,\mathsf{set}| > |\sigma|$, and hence $|\sigma\,\mathsf{set}| > |\mathsf{UVal}|$. Again, by Theorem 1 this leads to a contradiction. □

A corollary of Theorem 2 is that neither UVal nor any type with a cardinality equal to or greater than UVal can be a HOL type.

Corollary 1. $\forall t \bullet |\mathsf{UVal}| \leq |t| \Rightarrow t \notin \mathsf{Type}$

Proof. By Theorem 2 we have $|t| < |\mathsf{UVal}|$, and by transitivity of $<$ thus follows the contradiction $|\mathsf{UVal}| < |\mathsf{UVal}|$. □

It is therefore essential to ensure that UVal cannot be made an element of Type for our logic to remain consistent. We can also demonstrate a number of necessary consequences of the type reflection axiom AxTYPEREFL. Firstly, we require that each reflected type identify a unique HOL type.

Theorem 3. *The type mapping function* $UTYPE$ *is injective for* $\sigma, \tau \in \mathsf{Type}$. *That is,* $UTYPE(\sigma) = UTYPE(\tau)$ *implies that* $\sigma = \tau$ *for all* $\sigma, \tau \in \mathsf{Type}$.

Proof. Assume $UTYPE(\sigma) = UTYPE(\tau)$ for $\sigma, \tau \in \mathsf{Type}$. By non-emptiness of σ, there exists some value x with $x :: \sigma$. Thus $InjU(x) :_u UTYPE(\sigma)$ by axiom AxTYPEREFL, and $InjU(x) :_u UTYPE(\tau)$ since $UTYPE(\sigma) = UTYPE(\tau)$. Converse application of AxTYPEREFL finally yields $x :: \tau$. Because of disjointness of types in HOL, it follows that $\sigma = \tau$. □

Note that we cannot show from the axioms that all reflected types possess a witness. Namely, that for any $t \in \mathsf{UType}$, there exists a value $x \in \mathsf{UVal}$ such that $x :_u t$. To show this, a sufficient condition is that every element in UType is the image of some permissible HOL type $\sigma \in \mathsf{Type}$. In practice, this turns out to be too strong since, clearly, not all HOL types are permissible. The third axiom AxTYPENONEMPTY thus guarantees non-emptiness of all reflected types.

For those types that are not in the image of $UTYPE$, non-emptiness is all that we know about their values. For other types, which *are* in the image of $UTYPE$, the axiom does not add any new knowledge, since for those types we can already prove from the axioms AxVALBIJ and AxTYPEREFL that they are non-empty. Hence this additional axiom does not pose a risk to consistency.

5   Implementation in Isabelle/HOL

In this section, we describe our implementation in Isabelle/HOL of the axiomatic value model that was proposed in the previous section.

5.1   UTP Values and Types

UTP Types. Our goal is to associate UTP model types directly with (a subset of) the HOL types. HOL, in general, is not expressive enough to treat HOL types as values. However, the type-class mechanism is used in Isabelle/HOL to define an operator TYPEREP('a) that converts a HOL type 'a into a representation of that type as a HOL value. The representation is in terms of a datatype typerep, which is part of the standard HOL library and recaptured below.

datatype typerep = Typerep String.literal "typerep list"

It has a single constructor Typerep that takes both a string literal for the type's name, and a list of typerep objects corresponding to the arguments of a parametric type. The datatype encodes the structure of any monomorphic HOL type as a value, and is generally used as a limited facility to support reasoning about types in HOL. We effectively reuse it here to encode UTP model types, and for uniformity introduce a syntax abbreviation utype for it.

In order to apply the TYPEREP('a) operator to some type 'a, the type 'a must instantiate the type class typerep that defines how 'a is to be represented. That type class is typically instantiated automatically by Isabelle when new types are created with **typedef**. We may hence reasonably assume that all HOL types we like to use in UTP theories instantiate typerep.

We proceed by introducing a polymorphic typing operator. We note that an implicit default sort constraint was placed on 'a to be of class typerep.

definition p_type_rel :: "'a ⇒ utype ⇒ bool" (infix ":" 50) where
"x : t ⟷ TYPEREP('a) = t"

Above, x : t holds if the (HOL) value x is of UTP model type t. For instance, we can prove (1 :: nat) : TYPEREP(nat) but not 1 : TYPEREP(nat) since numbers in HOL are polymorphic objects. This means that the type of 1 corresponds to some type variable 'a of sort typerep. For such types, TYPEREP('a) cannot be simplified but we can still perform reasoning using unification. For this reason, our model in fact supports polymorphic types.

To facilitate proofs about typing, we provide a theorem attribute typing that collects all relevant theorems about typing, including the definitional theorem of p_type_rel. Simplification with added typing theorems typically discharges any kind of type conjecture, or otherwise reduces it to *false*. We implemented a hook into Isabelle/HOL's type definition packages that automatically collects the required theorems. This kind of proof engineering plays a crucial part in theory usability and proof automation, and is often overlooked in mechanisations.

We next examine the UTP value model. This is the core contribution of the novel mechanisation of the UTP in Isabelle/HOL that we developed.

UTP Values. In agreement with both Sect. 4.2 and the earlier ProofPower-Z works, we introduce a monomorphic type `uval` for our UTP value model. We thus are able to retain all of the expressiveness of a deep binding and predicate model as in the works [7,17,25]. However, rather than giving `uval` a concrete definition, for instance, by virtue of a **datatype**, we leave it uninterpreted.

typedecl uval

In languages like Z, the above corresponds to the definition of a given type. As explained in Sect. 2.2, such types are not equipped with an abstraction or representation function. All we know about them is that they are non-empty.

Construction, destruction and typing of values in `uval` are axiomatised by three polymorphic functions: `InjU`, `ProjU` and `utype_rel`. For the third, we introduce the infix notation v :_$_u$ t. The following **axiomatization** introduces these constants as well as their defining axioms. This formalises our earlier axioms in Sect. 4.2 and is all that is needed to reason about UTP model values.

> **axiomatization**
> — Universal abstraction, representation and model typing relation.
>   InjU :: "'a::injectable ⇒ uval" **and**
>   ProjU :: "uval ⇒ 'a::injectable" **and**
>   utype_rel :: "uval ⇒ utype ⇒ bool" (**infix** ":_$_u$" 50) **where**
> — Axioms that determine the semantics of the above functions.
>   InjU_inverse: "ProjU (InjU x) = x" **and**
>   ProjU_inverse: "y :_$_u$ TYPEREP('a) ⟹ InjU (ProjU y) = y" **and**
>   utype_rel_def: "(InjU x) :_$_u$ t ⟷ x : t" **and**
>   utypes_non_empty: "∃y. y :_$_u$ t"

The axioms have similarities with the standard axioms for type definitions [13]. First, we have a pair of injection theorems: `InjU_inverse` and `ProjU_inverse`. The first one is for the abstraction function (`InjU`), and the second one for the representation function (`ProjU`). An important difference to HOL type definitions is, however, that we do not merely inject the values of a single existing HOL type into the new type, but a universe of the values belonging to a collection of HOL types (HOL in Fig. 1). That universe is identified by the type class `injectable`, whose purpose is explained later on in Sect. 5.2. It usually includes values of infinitely many HOL types because of type parametricity.

Since we here inject the entire carrier (`UNIV`) of a HOL type 'a, contrary to **typedef**s there is no caveat present in the `InjU_inverse` injection theorem. Both injection theorems together implement the axiom AxVALBIJ in Sect. 4.2. The sort constraint 'a::`injectable` in the definition of the constants `InjU` and `ProjU` ensures that we cannot write any term `InjU` x where the argument x is not an injectable HOL type — Isabelle/HOL otherwise flags a type error. Likewise, the result of `ProjU` must always be chosen as to have an injectable type. The caveat of `ProjU_inverse` moreover ensures that the value we are projecting out of the UTP model and back into HOL has the correct type for the projection to be valid. Model typing x :_$_u$ t is formalised by lifting polymorphic typing into `uval`. Our third axiom `utype_rel_def` hence corresponds to AxTypeRefl and ensures completeness and soundness of the reflective typing relation.

The fourth axiom `utypes_non_empty` encodes AxTypeNonempty, capturing that all UTP model types are non-empty. If all `utype` elements corresponded to injectable HOL types, this would follow automatically. However, since there are some HOL types that are inherently not injectable, the axiom requires that even those types have at least one value, though we do not know anything else about such types. The need for the axiom is technical: we want to ensure that there is a well-typed 'total' binding whose variables must range over *any* HOL type.

The axiomatisation gives us the ability to control what HOL types we like to inject into the UTP value model. This is crucial as the injection of certain types can lead to inconsistencies. We next discuss this issue and explain how we ensure that unsoundness cannot emerge from inappropriate use of our axioms.

5.2   Controlling Injectability

The quintessential example that leads to inconsistency is injecting `uval` itself into the value model. Depending on the injection of other HOL types, in particular `'a set`, we are then able to derive a contradiction. Since `InjU` of (injectable!) type (`uval set`) $\Rightarrow$ `uval` cannot be injective due to Cantor's theorem, the axiom `InjU_inverse` above clearly is violated in that case.

We could naively have implemented a mechanism that prevents the user from instantiating `uval` as `injectable` but this is not enough: a clever user might circumvent that mechanism by defining a new HOL type (via a **typedef**) that is equipotent to `uval` or even larger, and then the same problem arises if that new type is made permissible for injection into `uval`.

To solve this problem in a universal and robust manner, we first mechanise a notion of type dependency. We recall a type definition generally has the form:

$$\textbf{typedef}\ (\text{'a, 'b}, \dots)\ \texttt{new\_type} = S :: (\text{'a, 'b}, \dots)\ T\ \texttt{set}$$

where the type term (`'a, 'b`, ...) T only involves currently existing HOL types and S is a non-empty subset of the values of (`'a, 'b`, ...) T. We observe that (`'a, 'b`, ...) `new_type` depends on the types occurring in T and the type variables `'a, 'b`, and so on. We formalise this dependency via a new type class `typedep`.

```
class typedep = typerep +
    fixes typedep :: "'a itself ⇒ typerep set"
```

This class extends Isabelle/HOL's existing class `typerep`. Any HOL type that instantiates it must additionally provide a function `typedep` that, given an element of `'a itself`, yields a set of type representations of HOL types that `'a` depends upon. The type constructor `'a itself` is primitive and conventionally used when a function is *polymorphically* parametrised by a HOL type. Polymorphism is crucial here since it determines resolution of `typedep` if applied to a particular HOL type. To simplify the application of `typedep`, we introduce a syntactic sugar that allows us to write TYPEDEP(T) for some HOL type T, instead of having to construct a corresponding value from 'a itself and then apply typedep to it. Examples are TYPEDEP(nat), TYPEDEP(nat set) and TYPEDEP('a set).

A subtle issue is how we ensure that the class typedep is instantiated correctly. Below we give an example of instantiating typedep for the function type.

```
instantiation "fun" :: (typedep, typedep) typedep
begin
definition typedep_fun :: "('a ⇒ 'b) itself ⇒ typerep set" where
"typedep_fun t = TYPEDEP('a) ∪ TYPEDEP('b)"
instance by (intro_classes)
end
```

We first observe that the definition of typedep for the function type 'a ⇒ 'b involves the recursive application of typedep (via the TYPEDEP(_) syntax) to the type parameters 'a and 'b, making precise that 'a ⇒ 'b depends on 'a and 'b. We secondly observe that a type representation of the function type does not itself occur in the right-hand side, namely there is no term such as ... ∪ {TYPEREP('a ⇒ 'b)} included. The reason for this is that we are only interested in dependency to *ground types*, namely those types that are not defined in terms of other types and thus form the roots of the dependency hierarchy. This also ensures efficient evaluation of TYPEDEP(_) as resulting terms may become large.

There are indeed only two genuine ground types in HOL: bool and ind. Also, any type declaration via a **typedecl** construct introduces a new ground type. Therefore, uval, in our formalisation, crucially becomes a ground type, too. Although HOL's set type ('a set) and function type ('a ⇒ 'b) are not introduced by a type definition, we do not consider them as ground types.

For a type definition, such as the one on page 14, we would need to perform the following instantiation:

```
instantiation new_type :: (typedep, typedep, ...) typedep
begin
definition typedep_new_type ::
   "('a, 'b, ...) new_type itself ⇒ typerep set" where
"typedep_new_type t = TYPEDEP(T)"
instance by (intro_classes)
end
```

We observe that the dependency of a new type ('a, 'b, ...) new_type is defined in terms of the dependency of its model type ('a, 'b, ...) T. While the instantiation is uniform and easy to perform, it would constitute a risk to rely on the user to perform it. Instead, we implemented a hook in Isabelle/HOL that executes such instantiations automatically and outside the control of the user for each new type defined via a type definition. Isabelle/HOL provides an interface that allows one to execute such hooks (see the Typedef.interpretation ML function within the HOL source code). It, fortunately, even does so retrospectively for existing types. This again means that the user — just like with typerep — does not have to be concerned with the instantiation of typedep and precludes any unsoundness potentially arising from wrongly instantiating that class. For convenience, we lastly make typedep the **default_sort** for free type variables.

We are now in a position to define the `injectable` class in a safe manner. This class, we endow with two assumptions that have to be discharged upon instantiation of any HOL type as `injectable`.

```
class injectable = typedep + order +
    assumes utype_is_not_uval : "TYPEREP('a) ≠ TYPEREP(uval)"
    assumes utype_not_dep_uval : "TYPEREP(uval) ⊈ TYPEDEP('a)"
```

The first assumption captures that the type we inject must not be the same as `uval`. The second uses the type-dependency mechanism by formalising that `uval` must not be in the set of types on which the type we inject depends. If both proof obligations can be discharged, we have established that injecting T into the UTP value model `uval` is safe and sound.

To facilitate the instantiation of HOL types as injectable, we provide an Isabelle command `inject_type` that discharges the above assumptions automatically. We note that this is for convenience and not for safety reasons — manual instantiation means that the proof obligations would still need to be discharged. Their proof is usually not difficult and can be done by rewriting and automatic reasoning. Again, to facilitate proofs, we introduce an attribute to record theorems that are relevant to reason about type dependency. They are automatically collected when new types are defined and the class `typedep` is instantiated.

By default, we inject a useful subset of existing HOL types into the UTP value model, including `unit`, `bool`, `nat`, `int`, `char`, `real`, `fun`, `set`, `list`, `prod`, `sum` and `option`. We can, however, inject any custom type definition or datatype in exactly the same manner, as illustrated in the next section. While our implementation requires, to a certain degree, low-level ML programming of the proof system, all of this is done outside the Isabelle/HOL kernel and code — we did not have to change the prover's source distribution in any way. We also implemented useful error reporting to the user when a type cannot be injected as failing the caveats of the `injectable` class. Lastly, we note that mutually-recursive datatypes are implicitly supported since Isabelle/HOL endows such types with a common model, so that the recursive type dependency disappears when the underlying (non-recursive) **typedef**s are constructed under-the-hood by Isabelle/HOL.

We claim that our implementation is LCF-sound: this means that incorrect use of our tool cannot result in inconsistency of the logic. We deconstruct the evidence for this through the following reasoning chain.

1. We consider the approach to be 'mathematically sound', as a consequence of restricting injectable types to those that do not depend on `uval` (Sect. 4);
2. In the mechanisation, we use a type class to restrict injection to permissible values only, which excludes constructs that attempt to inject invalid types *already at the level of HOL type analysis* (Sect. 5.1);
3. The injectability caveat is formalised and enforced by endowing the above type class with two assumptions (proof obligations) (Sect. 5.2);
4. The proof obligations rely on the correct instantiation of **typerep** and **typedep** classes, but both instantiations reside outside the control of the user.

Our tool is, thus, not only an Isabelle/UTP extension to enable richer UTP value models, but also a low-level Isabelle/HOL language extension. A final point to note is that `injectable` in our design also imports the type class `order`, since we assume that any UTP value model is equipped with an order. This opens up further possibilities to mechanise High-Order UTP, which adds support for higher-order programming to UTP. The reason for this is that HO UTP relies on order relations on values, namely to (re)define common UTP operators such as skip, assignment and variable blocks in this context (Chapter 9 of [10]).

6 Example: Mechanising a Theory of Object Orientation

As an example, we consider Santos' UTP theory of object orientation [20]. In what follows, we illustrate how the axiomatic value model enables us to easily encode that theory, using our tool. The Isabelle 2015 sources and a report are available from https://www.scm.tees.ac.uk/users/f.zeyda/utp2016/.

The UTP theory of object orientation is an extension of the UTP theory of designs, and, therefore, includes the auxiliary boolean variables ok and ok' to record termination. Besides, it also includes additional auxiliary variables to capture specific aspects of the object-oriented paradigm. These variables and their types explained below.

- cls of type $\mathbb{P}(CName)$ to record the names of classes used in the program;
- $atts$ of type $CName \nrightarrow (AName \nrightarrow Type)$ to record class attributes;
- sc of type $CName \nrightarrow CName$ to record the subclass hierarchy;
- an open set $\{\overline{m}_1, \overline{m}_2, \dots\}$ of procedure variables for method definitions;
- an open set $\{\overline{m}_1, \overline{m}_2, \dots\}$ of procedure variables for method calls.

Above, $CName$ is the set of all class names, $AName$ is the set of all attribute names, and $Type$ is defined as $CName \cup prim$ where the elements in $prim$ represent primitive types, like the integers or booleans. The functions $atts$ and sc are partial ($\nrightarrow$) since they only consider classes that are currently declared, namely those in cls. The function sc maps each class to its immediate superclass; the subclass relation is obtained via its reflexive and transitive closure: $C_{sub} \preceq C_{super} =_{def} (C_{sub}, C_{super}) \in sc^*$. There also exists a special class **Object** $\in CName$ that does not have a superclass.

The above description, which was taken from the literature, indeed gives us a very clear idea of how to design the value encoding for that theory. In doing so, however, we do not want to be constrained by a mechanised framework. The axiomatic value model lets us work at the level of HOL, using its definitional features as needed. Below we introduce the necessary types.

```
datatype cname = Object | Class "string"
datatype aname = Attr "string"
datatype prim = int | bool
datatype atype = PType "prim" | CType "cname"
```

Above, `cname` encodes $CName$, `aname` encodes $AName$, `prim` encodes $prim$, and `atype` encodes $Type$. The next step is to inject these types into the universal value type `uval`. As explained in the previous section, this is easily done with the following set of commands.

```
inject_type cname
inject_type aname
inject_type prim
inject_type atype
```

Behind the scene, the implementation of the **inject_type** command discharges the proof obligations that establish that the injections are sound. Here, this is the case since `uval` does not occur in the above **datatype** definitions.

It is worth noting that in order to support injection of datatypes into `uval`, we did not have to interface in any way with Isabelle's datatype package. This is because, ultimately, the definitional implementation of datatypes implies that everything boils down to plain type definitions, and our tool can readily handle those. For the same reason, **record** types are also supported out-of-the-box, as well as any other custom types that are definitional, which is the norm.

Healthiness Conditions. The theory has seven healthiness conditions. They are characterised by invariants that constrain the permissible values of *cls*, *atts* and *sc*, as well as the procedure variables for methods. Table 2 summarises the first six constraints, which are related to *cls*, *atts* and *sc*. Intuitively, the invariant **OO1** requires **Object** always to be a valid class of the program. **OO2** and **OO3** determine the shape of the subclass relation: it has to be a tree with **Object** at its root. Attributes have to be defined for all classes (**OO4**), they have to be unique (**OO5**), and their types, if they are not primitive, must refer to declared classes (**OO6**). A further healthiness condition (**OO7**) not in Table 2 is inherited from the UTP theory of methods in [24]. Its shape is given below, where the function **SIH**(_) is part of the UTP theory of invariants [4] and performs the conversion of invariants into design predicates over before and after states.

$$\mathbf{OO7}(P) = \mathbf{SIH}(\forall\, \overline{m}\,\overline{\overline{m}} \mid \{\overline{m}, \overline{\overline{m}}\} \subseteq \alpha P \bullet [\forall\, args \bullet \overline{m}(args) \Leftrightarrow \overline{\overline{m}}(args)]_0)(P)$$

Table 2. Healthiness conditions for the theory of object orientation.

Name	Invariant	Description
OO1	**Object** $\in$ *cls*	**Object** is always a class of the program
OO2	dom *sc* = *cls* \ **Object**	Every class except **Object** has a superclass
OO3	$\forall\, C$: dom *sc* $\bullet$ $(C, Object) \in sc^+$	**Object** is at the top of the class hierarchy
OO4	dom *atts* = *cls*	Attributes are defined for all classes
OO5	$\forall\, C_1, C_2$: dom *atts* $\mid C_1 \neq C_2 \bullet$ dom$(atts(C_1)) \cap$ dom$(atts(C_2)) = \varnothing$	Attribute names are unique across classes
OO6	ran($\bigcup$ ran *atts*) $\subseteq$ *prim* $\cup$ *cls*	Attributes have primitive or class types

This healthiness condition establishes a correspondence between procedure variables that are used for definition (double overbar) and call (single overbar) of methods. The purpose of **OO7**(P) is beyond the technical scope of this paper; we, however, observe that the quantifier above ranges over variables $\overline{m}$ and $\overline{\overline{m}}$ within the alphabet of predicate P. Encoding this condition may not be possible in a shallow model that does not allow us to quantify over alphabets.

We lastly present an example that illustrates how we encode the healthiness conditions. While a deep approach is non-negotiable in this case, the axiomatic value model enables us to express everything in terms of HOL concepts. This is done by 'lifting' HOL predicates into deeply-encoded UTP predicates. The lifting is performed by a simple rewrite engine that we implemented as part of the tool. With it, we may, for example, encode **OO5** as follows.

```
definition OO5 :: "upred" where
"OO5 = (∀ C1 ∈ dom atts .
         ∀ C2 ∈ dom atts . C1 ≠ C2 |
         dom (atts·C1) ∩ dom (atts·C2) = {})ₚ"
```

The tool that performs the lifting is invoked via the $(\_)_p$ construct. Inside the brackets, we may write plain HOL. The beauty of this is that we do not have to be concerned with redefining any of the HOL operators that are used, such as $\in$, $\cap$, dom, and so on, for our value model, and neither recast laws and tactics for proof support. Our approach enables the development of a generic rewrite tool that circumvents all of this so that the user is able to work exclusively in HOL; the underlying details of the deep encoding are by and large concealed.

There are some useful aspects of the implementation that did not discuss. For instance, we also provide a mechanism for parsing and rewriting HOL variables into UTP variables, in a way that we can take advantage of type-checking and unification. Our system is flexible: we can always escape the parser to combine unprocessed HOL with lifted predicate terms.

7   Conclusion

We have presented a novel approach to axiomatically encode value models of language embeddings. While we applied our work to the problem of mechanising the UTP framework, it remains applicable to *any* deep language embedding. The problem we addressed is to relax common restrictions on deep value models in HOL to support, for instance, general sets and functions. Our key contribution is the design of a solution and tool in Isabelle/HOL that is definitionally sound.

Beyond this, we put forward an approach to UTP theory engineering that enables and advocates working at the level of HOL rather than the formalised concepts and idioms of a particular mechanised framework. We claim that this is the crux in attracting academics to use a mechanised framework or theorem prover for the UTP, as we cannot expect users to acquire detailed knowledge of a mechanised framework or the nitty-gritty of a proof system. We hope that this work will set the future direction for UTP proof support, but accept that there is a price to pay in the currency of axioms for having our cake and eating it!

Future work will extend our mechanisation to be competitive with the currently available systems Isabelle/*Circus* [6] and Isabelle/UTP [7] in terms of the number of laws and mechanised theories. This work is mostly clerical and should not take a lot of time and effort. A second future work will isolate those parts that are independent of the UTP and only concerned with the value model, and publish this separately for the Isabelle/HOL community as a stand-alone tool.

Acknowledgement. We would like to thank the anonymous reviewers for their helpful suggestions and conscientious reading of the paper.

References

1. Blanchette, J.C., Böhme, S., Paulson, L.C.: Extending sledgehammer with SMT solvers. In: Bjørner, N., Sofronie-Stokkermans, V. (eds.) CADE 2011. LNCS (LNAI), vol. 6803, pp. 116–130. Springer, Heidelberg (2011). doi:10.1007/978-3-642-22438-6_11
2. Butterfield, A.: Saoithín: a theorem prover for UTP. In: Qin, S. (ed.) UTP 2010. LNCS, vol. 6445, pp. 137–156. Springer, Heidelberg (2010). doi:10.1007/978-3-642-16690-7_6
3. Butterfield, A.: The logic of $U \cdot (TP)^2$. In: Wolff, B., Gaudel, M.-C., Feliachi, A. (eds.) UTP 2012. LNCS, vol. 7681, pp. 124–143. Springer, Berlin (2013). doi:10.1007/978-3-642-35705-3_6
4. Cavalcanti, A., Wellings, A., Woodcock, J.: The safety-critical java memory model formalised. Formal Aspects Comput, **25**(1), 37–57 (2013)
5. Feliachi, A., Gaudel, M.-C., Wolff, B.: Unifying theories in Isabelle/HOL. In: Qin, S. (ed.) UTP 2010. LNCS, vol. 6445, pp. 188–206. Springer, Heidelberg (2010). doi:10.1007/978-3-642-16690-7_9
6. Feliachi, A., Gaudel, M.-C., Wolff, B.: Isabelle/*Circus* a process specification and verification environment. In: Joshi, R., Müller, P., Podelski, A. (eds.) VSTTE 2012. LNCS, vol. 7152, pp. 243–260. Springer, Berlin (2012). doi:10.1007/978-3-642-27705-4_20
7. Foster, S., Zeyda, F., Woodcock, J.: Isabelle/UTP: a mechanised theory engineering framework. In: Naumann, D. (ed.) UTP 2014. LNCS, vol. 8963, pp. 21–41. Springer, Heidelberg (2015). doi:10.1007/978-3-319-14806-9_2
8. Gordon, M.: Set theory, higher order logic or both? In: Goos, G., Hartmanis, J., Leeuwen, J., Wright, J., Grundy, J., Harrison, J. (eds.) TPHOLs 1996. LNCS, vol. 1125, pp. 191–201. Springer, Heidelberg (1996). doi:10.1007/BFb0105405
9. Gordon, M.J., Milner, A.J., Wadsworth, C.P.: Edinburgh LCF: A Mechanised Logic of Computation. LNCS, vol. 78. Springer, Heidelberg (1979)
10. Hoare, T., Jifeng, H.: Unifying Theories of Programming. Prentice Hall Series in Computer Science. Prentice Hall, Upper Saddle River (1998). http://www.unifyingtheories.org/
11. Iancu, M., Rabe, F.: Formalising foundations of mathematics. Math. Struct. Comput. Sci. **21**(Special Issue 04), 883–911 (2011)
12. Kunčar, O., Popescu, A.: A consistent foundation for Isabelle/HOL. In: Urban, C., Zhang, X. (eds.) ITP 2015. LNCS, vol. 9236, pp. 234–252. Springer, Heidelberg (2015). doi:10.1007/978-3-319-22102-1_16

13. Nipkow, T., Wenzel, M., Paulson, L.C. (eds.): Isabelle/HOL: A Proof Assistant for Higher-Order Logic. LNCS, vol. 2283. Springer, Berlin (2002). 3540433767
14. Nuka, G., Woodcock, J.: Mechanising a unifying theory. In: Dunne, S., Stoddart, B. (eds.) UTP 2006. LNCS, vol. 4010, pp. 217–235. Springer, Heidelberg (2006). doi:10.1007/11768173_13
15. Obua, S.: Partizan games in Isabelle/HOLZF. In: Barkaoui, K., Cavalcanti, A., Cerone, A. (eds.) ICTAC 2006. LNCS, vol. 4281, pp. 272–286. Springer, Heidelberg (2006). doi:10.1007/11921240_19
16. Oliveira, M., Cavalcanti, A., Woodcock, J.: A UTP semantics for Circus. Formal Aspects Comput. 21(1), 3–32 (2007)
17. Oliveira, M., Cavalcanti, A., Woodcock, J.: Unifying theories in ProofPower-Z. Formal Aspects Comput. 25(1), 133–158 (2013)
18. Pitts, A.: Part III: The HOL Logic. In: Gordon, M.J.C., Melham, T.F. (eds) Introduction to HOL: A Theorem-Proving Environment for Higher-Order Logic, pp. 191–232. Cambridge University Press, March 1993
19. RTCA, Inc.: Formal Methods Supplement to DO-178C and DO-278A. Technical report DO-333, RTCA, Washington, DC 20036, USA, December 2011
20. Santos, T., Cavalcanti, A., Sampaio, A.: Object-orientation in the UTP. In: Dunne, S., Stoddart, B. (eds.) UTP 2006. LNCS, vol. 4010, pp. 18–37. Springer, Heidelberg (2006). doi:10.1007/11768173_2
21. Sherif, A., Cavalcanti, A., Jifeng, H., Sampaio, A.: A process algebraic framework for specification and validation of real-time systems. Formal Aspects Comput. 22(2), 153–191 (2010)
22. Spivey, M.: The consistency theorem for free type definitions in Z. Formal Aspects Comput. 8(3), 369–375 (2015)
23. Traytel, D., Popescu, A., Blanchette, J.C.: Foundational, compositional (Co)datatypes for higher-order logic: category theory applied to theorem proving. In: Proceedings of LICS 2012, pp. 596–605. IEEE, June 2012
24. Zeyda, F., Cavalcanti, A.: Higher-order UTP for a theory of methods. In: Wolff, B., Gaudel, M.-C., Feliachi, A. (eds.) UTP 2012. LNCS, vol. 7681, pp. 204–223. Springer, Heidelberg (2013). doi:10.1007/978-3-642-35705-3_10
25. Zeyda, F., Cavalcanti, A.: Mechanical reasoning about families of UTP theories. Sci. Comput. Program. 77(4), 444–479 (2012)

UTP Semantics for rTiMo

Wanling Xie$^{(\boxtimes)}$ and Shuangqing Xiang

Shanghai Key Laboratory of Trustworthy Computing,
School of Computer Science and Software Engineering,
East China Normal University, Shanghai, China
mmrs_113_213@163.com

Abstract. rTiMo is a real-time version of TiMo (Timed Mobility),
which is a process algebra for mobile distributed systems. In this paper,
we investigate the denotational semantics for rTiMo. A trace variable tr
is introduced to record the communications among processes as well as
the location where the communication action takes place. Based on the
formalized model, we study a set of algebraic laws, especially the laws
about the migration and communication with real-time constraints. In
order to facilitate the algebraic reasoning about the parallel expansion
laws, we enrich rTiMo with a form of *guarded choice*. This enables us
to convert every parallel construct to a guarded choice.

1 Introduction

With the development of cloud computing, mobile applications play an important role in modern distributed systems. Analyzing and verifying the ever
increasing complexity of mobile applications effectively is of great significance.

In recent years, some work has been done to explore the formal modeling
and analysis of mobile distributed systems [1–8]. Lakos has used a Petri Net
formalism, called Mobile Petri Nets [1], to model and simulate Mobile IP [3].
Ma et al. [2] have proposed a new formal method called Extended Elementary
Object System (EEOS), and they also have presented a model for a generic secure
mobile-agent system based on EEOS, which supports strong mobility and secure
mobility of a mobile agent. Braghin et al. [4] have introduced a framework for
the modeling and verification of mobile programs, which supports exhaustive
analysis of security policies. The time-related aspects of process migration and
interaction have been studied in [5–8].

Ciobanu et al. [5] have first introduced a process algebra called TiMo (Timed
Mobility) for mobile systems, where it is possible to add timers to the basic
actions in addition to process mobility and interaction. Their model of time is
based on local clocks. Aman et al. [6] have extended the TiMo family [9–11] by
introducing a real-time version named rTiMo in which a global clock is used.
The rTiMo processes can move between different locations of a mobile distributed
system and communicate locally with other processes. Real-time constrains are
used to control migration and communication. In [6], they also have investigated
the operational semantics of rTiMo. However, we can see that their work does
not cover the denotational semantics and algebraic semantics of rTiMo.

© Springer International Publishing AG 2017
J.P. Bowen and H. Zhu (Eds.): UTP 2016, LNCS 10134, pp. 176–196, 2017.
DOI: 10.1007/978-3-319-52228-9_9

Hoare and He advocate three different styles of mathematical representations, including operational semantics, denotational semantics and algebraic semantics [12,13] in their Unifying Theories of Programming (UTP) [14]. Denotational semantics provides mathematical meanings to programs. Algebraic semantics fits well with symbolic calculation of parameters and structures of an optimal design. The algebraic approach has been successfully applied in provably-correct compilation [15–17].

This paper considers the denotational semantics for rTiMo, which can provide the precise understanding of the rTiMo formalism and deduce interesting properties of programs. In our semantic model, we introduce a variable tr to record the communications among processes. Based on the formalized denotational semantics, we investigate a set of algebraic laws, which not only comprises algebraic laws similar to traditional algebraic laws of programming, but also contains algebraic laws about migration and communication with time constraints. In order to facilitate algebraic reasoning about parallel expansion laws, we enrich rTiMo with a guarded choice construct which is classified into three types: communication guarded choice, delay guarded choice and hybrid guarded choice. From a set of parallel expansion laws that we have explored, we are able to show that every parallel construct can be converted to a guarded choice.

The remainder of this paper is organized as follows. Section 2 introduces the syntax of rTiMo and the concept of guarded choice which is used to study the parallel expansion laws. We investigate the semantic model of rTiMo and healthiness conditions which a program should satisfy in Sect. 2. Section 3 explores the denotational semantics of rTiMo using the UTP approach. Section 4 presents a set of algebraic laws, including the basic algebraic laws and the parallel expansion laws which enable us to convert a parallel construct to a guarded choice. Section 5 concludes the paper.

2   The Semantic Model

In this section, we first introduce the syntax of rTiMo in Sect. 2.1. The denotational semantic model for rTiMo is presented in Sect. 2.2.

2.1   The Syntax of rTiMo

rTiMo is a real-time version of TiMo [5], which is a process algebra for mobile distributed systems. rTiMo processes can move between different locations in a distributed environment and communicate locally with other processes, which means that processes from different locations cannot communicate with each other. The syntax of rTiMo is given in Table 1 as it has been introduced in [6]. We agree on the following assumptions:

- Loc is a set of locations, l is a location or a location variable.
- $Chan$ is a set of communication channels, a is a communication channel and hence $a \in Chan$.

- u is a tuple of variables and v is a tuple of expressions built from values, variables and permissible operations.
- t is a timeout (deadline) of an action and $t \in \mathbb{R}$.

In rTiMo, process migration and communication are controlled by using real-time constraints. Timeouts are specified by a superscript $^{\triangle t}$.

1. $a^{\triangle t}!\langle v \rangle$ *then* P *else* Q indicates that an output process can send message v for a period of t time units via channel a. When the message v is sent successfully within t time units, the next process is P. If the communication does not happen before the timeout t, the communication attempt is aborted and the next process is Q.
2. $a^{\triangle t}?(u)$ *then* P *else* Q stands for an input process whose waiting time interval is t time units. When the process receives a message via channel a within t time units, the control passes to process P. If the communication does not take place before the deadline t, the waiting process gives up and it switches to the alternative process Q. The input process binds the variable u within P (but not within Q).
3. $go^{\triangle t}l$ *then* P denotes a migration process that moves to location l precisely after t time units.
4. 0 denotes the process that terminates without taking any time.
5. $P \mid Q$ stands for parallel composition.
6. $l[[P]]$ specifies a process P running at location l.
7. $L \mid L \mid N$ indicates that a network can be a located process or can be built from its components $L \mid N$.

Table 1. rTiMo syntax

Processes	$P, Q ::= a^{\triangle t}!\langle v \rangle$ *then* P *else* Q $\mid$	(output)
	$a^{\triangle t}?(u)$ *then* P *else* Q $\mid$	(input)
	$go^{\triangle t}l$ *then* P $\mid$	(move)
	0 $\mid$	(termination)
	$P \mid Q$	(parallel)
Located processes	$L ::= l[[P]]$	
Networks	$N ::= L \mid L \mid N$	

In order to support our algebraic expansion laws, we enrich rTiMo with a new concept, called guarded choice, which is classified into three types:

1. $[\![_{i \in I}\{g_i \to N_i\}$ is communication guarded choice where g_i is a communication guard. The guard is instantaneous which means that it happens without any time delay. The guard can be expressed as $a!\langle v \rangle@l$, $a?(u)@l$ or $a.\{v/u\}@l$,

where $a!\langle v\rangle@l$ $(a?(u)@l)$ indicates that the output (input) action happens at location l and uses the channel a, $a.\{v/u\}@l$ denotes that the communication over channel a takes place at location l and the variable u is replaced by the message v.

2. $\#t \rightarrow N$ is delay guarded choice, where $\#t$ means delaying t time units.
3. The third guarded choice is hybrid guarded choice, which has the following form, where the notation $N_1 \oplus N_2 \oplus N_3$ denotes N_1 has higher priority than N_2 and N_2 has higher priority than N_3:

$$\|_{i \in I}\{g_i \rightarrow N_i\}$$
$$\oplus \ \exists t' \in (0...t) \bullet (\#t' \rightarrow (\|_{i \in I}\{g_i \rightarrow N_i'\}))$$
$$\oplus \ \#t \rightarrow N'$$

2.2   The Semantic Model

In this section, the denotational semantic model for rTiMo is investigated. Our approach is based on the relational calculus [14]. We introduce a pair of variables st and st' into our semantic model in order to denote the execution state of a program. st represents the initial execution state of a program before its activation and st' stands for the final execution state of the program during the current observation. A program may have two execution states:

1. *completed state* : A program has reached the *completed state* when it terminates successfully. "$st = completed$" indicates that the previous program has terminated successfully and control passes to the current program. "$st' = completed$" indicates that the current program has terminated successfully and control passes to the next program.
2. *wait state* : A program may wait for communicating with another program via a specific channel or moving from one location to another after the given time units. "$st = wait$" indicates that the predecessor of the current program is in a waiting state. Thus, the current program cannot be activated. "$st' = wait$" indicates that the current program itself is in a waiting state. Thus, the next program cannot be activated.

We describe the behavior of a process in terms of a trace of snapshots which record the sequence of the communication actions that the process is able to engage in. In our semantic model, we introduce a variable tr to denote that trace. The behavior of a communication action is specified by a snapshot which can be expressed as a triple (t, κ, l) where:

- t indicates the time when the communication action terminates.
- κ denotes the message transmitted via a specific channel at the termination of a communication action. And the form of κ is $a.v$, where a indicates the communication channel and v is the message transmitted. We define $\mathbf{Chan}(\kappa)$ to obtain the communication channel and $\mathbf{Mess}(\kappa)$ to obtain the message, i.e., if $\kappa = a.v$, then $\mathbf{Chan}(a.v) = a$ and $\mathbf{Mess}(a.v) = v$.

– l records the location at which the communication action takes place.

The observations of an rTiMo program can be described by a tuple:

$$(time, time', st, st', tr, tr')$$

where,

– $time$ and $time'$ respectively denote the start point and the end point of the time interval over which the observation is recorded.
– st represents the initial execution state of the program before its activation and st' stands for its final execution state during the current observation.
– tr represents the initial trace of a program over the interval which is passed by its predecessor. tr' stands for the final trace of a program over the interval. $tr' - tr$ denotes the sequence of snapshots contributed by the program itself during the interval.

Example 2.1.
$$N_1 = l_1[[go^{\triangle 3}l_2 \text{ then } a^{\triangle 2}!\langle v_1 \rangle \text{ then } b^{\triangle 3}?(u_2) \text{ else } 0]],$$
$$N_2 = l_2[[a^{\triangle 6}?(u_1) \text{ then } b^{\triangle 2}!\langle v_2 \rangle \text{ else } 0]].$$

Above, we use the following shorthand notations:

$$b^{\triangle 3}?(u_2) \text{ stands for } b^{\triangle 3}?(u_2) \text{ then } 0 \text{ else } 0$$
$$b^{\triangle 2}!\langle v_2 \rangle \text{ stands for } b^{\triangle 2}!\langle v_2 \rangle \text{ then } 0 \text{ else } 0$$

Consider the trace of $N_3 = N_1 \mid N_2$. Assume the activation time of N_3 is at 0.

According to the syntax of rTiMo, the migration process moves to location l_2 from location l_1 after 3 time units. Thus, the communication action happens at time 3.

One possible trace of N_1 is given as below:

$$\langle (3, a.v_1, l_2), (3, b.\{m/u_2\}, l_2) \rangle$$

where $m \in \textbf{Type}(b)$ and $\textbf{Type}(b)$ stands for the type of the messages which can be transformed along channel b.

A possible trace of N_2 is shown next:

$$\langle (3, a.\{m/u_1\}, l_2), (3, b.v_2, l_2) \rangle$$

where $m \in \textbf{Type}(a)$ and $\textbf{Type}(a)$ denotes the type of the messages that channel a can communicate.

Hence, the one trace of N_3 is as follows:

$$\langle (3, a.\{v_1/u_1\}, l_2), (3, b.\{v_2/u_2\}, l_2) \rangle \qquad \square$$

Next we consider the healthiness conditions rTiMo programs should satisfy. In our semantics model, the variable tr is used to record the execution trace of a program, so this variable cannot be shortened. A formula P satisfies the healthiness condition $(H1)$.

$(H1)$ $P = P \wedge Inv(tr)$,

where $Inv(tr) =_{df} tr \preceq tr'$, which states that tr is a prefix of tr'.

As we have mentioned earlier on, a program may wait for communicating with another program via a specific channel or moving from one location to another after a given time delay. For the migration process $home[[go^{\triangle 5} shop \ then \ P]]$ which indicates that process P moves to location $shop$ from location $home$ after 5 time units: if process P is asked to start in a waiting state of $go^{\triangle 5} shop$, then P keeps itself unchanged; i.e., it satisfies the following healthiness condition.

$(H2)$ $P = \Pi \lhd st = wait \rhd P$,

where $\Pi =_{df} (st' = st) \wedge (time' = time) \wedge (tr' = tr)$

and $P \lhd b \rhd Q =_{df} (b \wedge P) \vee (\neg b \wedge Q)$

The variable $time$ is used to record the progress of a program, thus, P should satisfy the following healthiness condition.

$(H3)$ $P = P \wedge (time \leq time')$

The definition of H function can be given as follows:

$$H(X) =_{df} \Pi \lhd st = wait \rhd (X \wedge Inv(tr) \wedge time \leq time')$$

From the definition of H function, we know that $H(X)$ satisfies the healthiness conditions $(H1)$, $(H2)$ and $(H3)$. The H function is used to define the denotational semantics for the rTiMo model.

3 Denotational Semantics

In this section, we present the denotational semantics for rTiMo. We use $\textbf{beh}(l[[P]])$ to describe the behavior of a process running at location l after it is activated.

3.1 Basic Commands

We first investigate the behavior of a migration process $l[[go^{\triangle t} l' \ then \ P]]$, it indicates that process P moves to location l' after t time units.

$\mathbf{beh}(l[[go^{\triangle t}l' \ then \ P]]) =_{df}$

$$H\left(\left(\begin{array}{c} (st' = wait \ \wedge \ time' - time < t) \\ \vee \\ (st' = completed \ \wedge \ time' = time + t) \end{array}\right) \wedge \ tr' = tr\right) ; \mathbf{beh}(l'[[P]])$$

For t time units, the migration process is in a waiting state and its trace is unchanged. After t time units, the migration action terminates successfully and the trace also remains unchanged. We record the terminal time of the migration action using $time' = time + t$ which is also the activation time of the next action. After the completion of the migration action, the subsequent behavior of the program is the behavior of process P which runs at location l'.

The input process $l[[a^{\triangle t}?(u) \ then \ P \ else \ Q]]$ indicates that if the program successfully receives an input via channel a within t time units, then process P gets the control. On the other hand, if the communication does not happen before the deadline t, the waiting process gives up and it switches to the alternative process Q. The notation $tr_1 \hat{} tr_2$ is used to denote the concatenation of the two traces tr_1 and tr_2.

$\mathbf{beh}(l[[a^{\triangle t}?(u) \ then \ P \ else \ Q]]) =_{df}$

$$\left(\begin{array}{c} \left(\exists m \in \mathbf{Type}(a) \bullet \left| H \begin{array}{c} (st' = wait \ \wedge \ tr' = tr \ \wedge \\ 0 < time' - time < t) \ \vee \\ (st' = completed \ \wedge \\ append(a?(u)@l) \ \wedge \\ 0 \leq time' - time < t) \end{array} \right. ; \mathbf{beh}(l[[\{m/u\}P]])\right) \\ \vee \\ H\left(st' = completed \ \wedge \ tr' = tr \ \wedge \ time' = time + t\right) ; \mathbf{beh}(l[[Q]]) \end{array}\right)$$

where

$append(a?(u)@l) =_{df}$
$\quad tr' = tr\hat{}\langle(time', a.m, l)\rangle \ \wedge \ \neg(\forall t' \in (time', \infty) \bullet tr' = tr\hat{}\langle(t', a.m, l)\rangle)$

Here, $\mathbf{Type}(a)$ represents the type of the messages that channel a can communicate. There are two alternative behavior branches to describe the execution of the input process.

- **Case 1**: within t time units, the input action either waits for receiving a message via a specific channel, or communicates with the corresponding output action successfully. If the input action waits for receiving a message, the execution state is *wait* and the trace is unchanged. If the input action happens successfully, the execution state is *completed* and the snapshot $(time', a.m, l)$

contributed by the input action is attached to the end of the program trace. The predicate $\neg(\forall t' \in (time', \infty) \bullet tr' = tr^\wedge \langle (t', a.m, l) \rangle)$ is used to ensure that the input action takes place as soon as it is enabled. The subsequent behavior of the program is determined by process P from location l. The notation $\{m/u\}P$ denotes P in which all free occurrences of a variable u are replaced by m.

- **Case 2**: the input action does not take place before the deadline t, the execution state is *completed* and the trace remains unchanged. In this case, the subsequent behavior of the program is the behavior of the alternative process Q from location l.

The output process $l[[a^{\triangle t}!\langle v \rangle \ then \ P \ else \ Q]]$ means that if the program sends the message v along channel a within t time units successfully, the control passes into process P. On the other hand, if the communication does not happen before the timeout t, the communication gives up and the control passes into process Q.

$$\mathbf{beh}(l[[a^{\triangle t}!\langle v \rangle \ then \ P \ else \ Q]]) =_{df}$$

$$
\begin{pmatrix}
H \begin{pmatrix} (st' = wait \ \wedge \ tr' = tr \ \wedge \ 0 < time' - time < t) \ \vee \\ (st' = completed \ \wedge \ append(a!\langle v \rangle @l) \ \wedge \\ 0 \le time' - time < t) \end{pmatrix} ; \mathbf{beh}(l[[P]]) \\
\vee \\
H \left(st' = completed \ \wedge \ tr' = tr \ \wedge \ time' = time + t \right) ; \mathbf{beh}(l[[Q]])
\end{pmatrix}
$$

where

$$append(a!\langle v \rangle @l) =_{df}$$
$$tr' = tr^\wedge \langle (time', a.v, l) \rangle \ \wedge \ \neg(\forall t' \in (time', \infty) \bullet tr' = tr^\wedge \langle (t', a.v, l) \rangle)$$

3.2 Guarded Choice

As mentioned earlier, the guarded choice has three types: communication guarded choice, delay guarded choice and hybrid guarded choice. Now we give the denotational semantics for these three types of guarded choice.

Communication Guarded Choice. We first consider the communication guarded choice, which is composed of a set of communication guarded components. There are three types of the communication guard: $a!\langle v \rangle @l$, $a?(u)@l$ and $a.\{v/u\}@l$, which all have been described earlier.

$$\mathbf{beh}(\|_{i \in I}\{g_i \to N_i\}) =_{df} \bigvee_{i \in I} \mathbf{beh}(g_i \to N_i), \ where$$

if $g = a!\langle v\rangle@l$, then

$\mathbf{beh}(g \to N) =_{df}$

$H\left(st' = completed \;\wedge\; append(a!\langle v\rangle@l) \;\wedge\; time' = time\right) ; \mathbf{beh}(N)$

if $g = a?(u)@l$, then

$\mathbf{beh}(g \to N) =_{df}$

$$\left(\exists m \in \mathbf{Type}(a) \bullet \left(H\left(\begin{array}{c} st' = completed \;\wedge \\ append(a?(u)@l) \;\wedge \\ time' = time \end{array}\right) ; \mathbf{beh}(\{m/u\}N)\right)\right)$$

if $g = a.\{v/u\}@l$, then

$\mathbf{beh}(g \to N) =_{df}$

$H\left(st' = completed \;\wedge\; append(a.\{v/u\}@l) \;\wedge\; time' = time\right) ; \mathbf{beh}(\{v/u\}N)$

where

$append(a.\{v/u\}@l) =_{df}$
$\quad tr' = tr^\frown\langle(time', a.v, l)\rangle \;\wedge\; \neg(\forall t' \in (time', \infty) \bullet tr' = tr^\frown\langle(t', a.v, l)\rangle)$

Delay Guarded Choice. For the delay guarded choice, it consists of only one time delay component.

$\mathbf{beh}(\#t \to N) =_{df}$

$$H\left(\left(\begin{array}{c} (st' = wait \;\wedge\; time' - time < t) \\ \vee \\ (st' = completed \;\wedge\; time' = time + t) \end{array}\right) \wedge \; tr' = tr\right) ; \mathbf{beh}(N)$$

Hybrid Guarded Choice. The hybrid guarded choice has the following form:
$$N = \|_{i\in I}\{g_i \to N_i\}$$
$$\oplus \exists t' \in (0...t) \bullet (\#t' \to (\|_{i\in I}\{g_i \to N_i'\}))$$
$$\oplus \#t \to N'$$
where, $\|_{i\in I}\{g_i \to N_i\}$ is communication guarded choice and $\#t \to N'$ is delay guarded choice. $\#t' \to (\|_{i\in I}\{g_i \to N_i'\})$ consists of a delay guard followed by a communication guarded choice where $t' \in (0...t)$.

$$\mathbf{beh}(N) =_{df}$$

$$
\begin{pmatrix}
\bigvee_{i \in I} \mathbf{beh}(g_i \rightarrow N_i) \\
\vee \\
\bigvee_{1 \leq i \leq n} \left(H \left(\begin{array}{c} (st' = wait \,\wedge\, tr' = tr \,\wedge\, \\ 0 < time' - time < t) \,\vee\, \\ (st' = completed \,\wedge\, append(g_i) \,\wedge\, \\ 0 < time' - time < t) \\ \vee \end{array} \right) ; \mathbf{beh}(N_i') \right) \\
H \left(st' = completed \,\wedge\, tr' = tr \,\wedge\, time' = time + t \right) ; \mathbf{beh}(N')
\end{pmatrix}
$$

3.3 Parallel Composition

In this section, we explore the behavior of a network which is composed of a set of located processes running in parallel. Let P and Q be the processes. The parallel composition $l[[P]] \mid l'[[Q]]$ performs process P from location l and process Q from location l' running in parallel, where l and l' can be the same or different locations. Its behavior is the composition of the behaviors of the two parallel components by merging their traces together. The composition is described by the following definition.

$$\mathbf{beh}(l[[P]] \mid l'[[Q]]) = \mathbf{beh}(l[[P]]) \mid \mathbf{beh}(l'[[Q]])$$

where,

$$l[[P_1]] \mid l'[[P_2]] =_{df}$$

$$
\begin{pmatrix}
\exists\ st_1, st_1', st_2, st_2', tr_1, tr_1', tr_2, tr_2', time_1, time_1', time_2, time_2' \bullet \\
tr_1 = tr_2 = tr \,\wedge\, st_1 = st_2 = st \,\wedge\, time_1 = time_2 = time \,\wedge\, \\
P_1[st_1, st_1', tr_1, tr_1', time_1, time_1'/st, st', tr, tr', time, time'] \,\wedge\, \\
P_2[st_2, st_2', tr_2, tr_2', time_2, time_2'/st, st', tr, tr', time, time'] \,\wedge\, \\
Merge
\end{pmatrix}
$$

The first three predicates in the definition $l[[P_1]] \mid l'[[P_2]]$ describe the two independent behaviors of process P_1 from location l and P_2 from location l' running in parallel. The last predicate $Merge$ mainly does the merge of the contributed traces of the two behavioral branches for recording the communications, which is defined as below.

$$
Merge =_{df} \begin{pmatrix}
(st_1' = completed \,\wedge\, st_2' = completed) \Rightarrow st' = completed \,\wedge\, \\
(st_1' = wait \,\vee\, st_2' = wait) \Rightarrow st' = wait \,\wedge\, \\
\exists s \in (tr_1' - tr) \mid (tr_2' - tr) \bullet tr' = tr \,\widehat{}\, s \,\wedge\, \\
time' = \mathbf{max}\{time_1', time_2'\}
\end{pmatrix}
$$

The final execution state of the behavior of the parallel composition is determined by the two parallel components together. The contributed traces of the two behaviors for recording the communication can be merged. And the terminal time of the parallel composition is the maximum between the two terminal times of the parallel components.

We introduce some notations. The notation $\mathbf{head}(s)$ is used to denote the first snapshot of the trace s and $\mathbf{tail}(s)$ is used to denote the result of removing the first snapshot in the trace s. We use the projections to select the components of a snapshot:

$$\pi_1((t,\kappa,l)) =_{df} t \qquad \pi_2((t,\kappa,l)) =_{df} \kappa \qquad \pi_3((t,\kappa,l)) =_{df} l$$

The merging of the contributed traces of the two behaviors for recording the communication can be defined as follows.

$$\epsilon \mid \epsilon =_{df} \{\epsilon\}$$

$$s \mid \epsilon =_{df} \{s\}$$

$$\epsilon \mid t =_{df} \{t\}$$

$$s \mid t =_{df} \left\{ \left(\left(\left(\begin{array}{c} \left(\begin{array}{c} \langle (t_1, \kappa_1, l_1) \rangle \widehat{\ }(\mathbf{tail}(s) \mid \mathbf{tail}(t)) \\ \vartriangleleft t_1 = t_2 \vartriangleright \\ \{\epsilon\} \end{array} \right) \\ \vartriangleleft \mathbf{Chan}(\kappa_1) = \mathbf{Chan}(\kappa_2) \vartriangleright \\ \left(\begin{array}{c} (\mathbf{head}(s)\widehat{\ }(\mathbf{tail}(s) \mid t) \cup \mathbf{head}(t)\widehat{\ }(s \mid \mathbf{tail}(t))) \\ \vartriangleleft t_1 = t_2 \vartriangleright \\ \left(\begin{array}{c} \mathbf{head}(s)\widehat{\ }(\mathbf{tail}(s) \mid t) \\ \vartriangleleft t_1 < t_2 \vartriangleright \\ \mathbf{head}(t)\widehat{\ }(s \mid \mathbf{tail}(t)) \end{array} \right) \end{array} \right) \end{array} \right) \\ \vartriangleleft l_1 = l_2 \vartriangleright \\ \left(\begin{array}{c} (\mathbf{head}(s)\widehat{\ }(\mathbf{tail}(s) \mid t) \cup \mathbf{head}(t)\widehat{\ }(s \mid \mathbf{tail}(t))) \\ \vartriangleleft t_1 = t_2 \vartriangleright \\ \left(\begin{array}{c} \mathbf{head}(s)\widehat{\ }(\mathbf{tail}(s) \mid t) \\ \vartriangleleft t_1 < t_2 \vartriangleright \\ \mathbf{head}(t)\widehat{\ }(s \mid \mathbf{tail}(t)) \end{array} \right) \end{array} \right) \end{array} \right) \right) \right\}$$

where,

$$t_1 = \pi_1(\mathbf{head}(s)), \quad \kappa_1 = \pi_2(\mathbf{head}(s)), \quad l_1 = \pi_3(\mathbf{head}(s)),$$

$$t_2 = \pi_1(\mathbf{head}(t)), \quad \kappa_2 = \pi_2(\mathbf{head}(t)), \quad l_2 = \pi_3(\mathbf{head}(t)).$$

The result of merging two empty traces is still empty. For the two traces which are required to be merged, if one of them is empty and the other is non-empty, the result of trace merging follows the nonempty one. If both traces are nonempty, the result of trace merging is obtained according to the fourth trace-merging definition.

Example 3.1. Consider the network $N_1 \mid N_2$ in Example 2.1, where

$$N_1 = l_1[[go^{\triangle 3}l_2 \ then \ a^{\triangle 2}!\langle v_1 \rangle \ then \ b^{\triangle 3}?(u_2) \ else \ 0]],$$
$$N_2 = l_2[[a^{\triangle 6}?(u_1) \ then \ b^{\triangle 2}!\langle v_2 \rangle \ else \ 0]].$$

And we have the following shorthand notations:

$$b^{\triangle 3}?(u_2) \ stands \ for \ b^{\triangle 3}?(u_2) \ then \ 0 \ else \ 0$$
$$b^{\triangle 2}!\langle v_2 \rangle \ stands \ for \ b^{\triangle 2}!\langle v_2 \rangle \ then \ 0 \ else \ 0$$

Assume that the activated time of N_1 and N_2 is at 0. As mentioned earlier, the trace of N_1 is below:

$$s = \langle (3, a.v_1, l_2), (3, b.\{m/u_2\}, l_2) \rangle$$

And the trace of N_2 is below:

$$t = \langle (3, a.\{m/u_1\}, l_2), (3, b.v_2, l_2) \rangle$$

By using the trace merging rules, we can obtain

$$s \mid t \ = \ \langle (3, a.\{v_1/u_1\}, l_2) \rangle {^\frown}(s' \mid t')$$
$$and \quad s' \mid t' \ = \ \langle (3, b.\{v_2/u_2\}, l_2) \rangle {^\frown}(s'' \mid t'')$$
$$and \quad s'' \mid t'' = \langle \rangle$$

where

$$s' \ = \ \langle (3, b.\{m/u_2\}, l_2) \rangle, \ t' = \langle (3, b.v_2, l_2) \rangle$$
$$s'' = \langle \rangle, \ t'' = \langle \rangle$$

Finally, we obtain the trace of the network by merging s and t below:

$$\langle (3, a.\{v_1/u_1\}, l_2), (3, b.\{v_2/u_2\}, l_2) \rangle \qquad \square$$

4   Algebraic Properties

Our work towards the formalization of rTiMo aims to deduce its interesting properties, which are usually expressed using algebraic laws and Eq. [14]. In this section, we explore a set of algebraic laws for rTiMo including basic algebraic laws and a set of parallel expansion laws.

4.1   Basic Algebraic Laws

If a migration action has a timer which equals to 0, then process P migrates from location l to l' without any time delay.

(move-1) $l[[go^{\triangle 0}l' \ then \ P]] = l'[[P]]$

A communication action has a timer which equals to 0, the process $a^{\triangle 0} *$ *then P else Q* continues as the alternative process Q. Here, $* \in \{!\langle v\rangle, ?(u)\}$.

(output-1) $l[[a^{\triangle 0}!\langle v\rangle \ then \ P \ else \ Q]] = l[[Q]]$

(input-1) $l[[a^{\triangle 0}?(u) \ then \ P \ else \ Q]] = l[[Q]]$

For the located migration process $l[[go^{\triangle t}l' \ then \ P]]$, it first delays t time units, then process P moves to location l'.

(move-2) $l[[go^{\triangle t}l' \ then \ P]] = \#t \to l'[[P]]$ where $t > 0$.

For the output process, if the output action happens at the start of the program, the subsequent process is P. On the other hand, the output process needs to wait for the specific input action trigged. If the waiting time t' ranges in $(0...t)$, the subsequent process is still P. The subsequent process is Q when the output process delays t time units, which means that the communication gives up and the control passes into the alternative process Q.

$$
\begin{aligned}
\textbf{(output-2)} \ & l[[a^{\triangle t}!\langle v\rangle \ then \ P \ else \ Q]] \\
= \ & a!\langle v\rangle @l \to l[[P]] \\
& \oplus \exists t' \in (0...t) \bullet (\#t' \to (a!\langle v\rangle @l \to l[[P]])) \\
& \oplus \#t \to l[[Q]], \text{ where } t > 0.
\end{aligned}
$$

Proof

RHS

$= \{$Def of Hybrid Guarded Choice$\}$

$$\begin{pmatrix} H(st' = completed \ \wedge \ append(a!\langle v\rangle @l) \ \wedge \ time' = time); \mathbf{beh}(l[[P]]) \\ \vee \\ H\begin{pmatrix} (st' = wait \ \wedge \ tr' = tr \ \wedge \ 0 < time' - time < t) \ \vee \\ (st' = completed \ \wedge \ append(a!\langle v\rangle @l) \ \wedge \\ 0 < time' - time < t) \end{pmatrix} ; \mathbf{beh}(l[[P]]) \\ \vee \\ H\left(st' = completed \ \wedge \ tr' = tr \ \wedge \ time' = time + t\right); \mathbf{beh}(l[[Q]]) \end{pmatrix}$$

$= \{(H(X1); Y) \bigvee (H(X2); Y) = H(X1 \vee X2); Y\}$

$$\begin{pmatrix} H\begin{pmatrix} (st' = completed \wedge append(a!\langle v\rangle @l) \wedge time' = time) \ \vee \\ (st' = wait \ \wedge \ tr' = tr \ \wedge \ 0 < time' - time < t) \ \vee \\ (st' = completed \ \wedge \ append(a!\langle v\rangle @l) \ \wedge \\ 0 < time' - time < t) \end{pmatrix} ; \mathbf{beh}(l[[P]]) \\ \vee \\ H\left(st' = completed \ \wedge \ tr' = tr \ \wedge \ time' = time + t\right); \mathbf{beh}(l[[Q]]) \end{pmatrix}$$

$= \{$Logical Equivalence$\}$

$$\begin{pmatrix} H\begin{pmatrix} (st' = wait \ \wedge \ tr' = tr \ \wedge \ 0 < time' - time < t) \ \vee \\ (st' = completed \ \wedge \ append(a!\langle v\rangle @l) \ \wedge \\ (time' = time \ \vee \ 0 < time' - time < t)) \end{pmatrix} ; \mathbf{beh}(l[[P]]) \\ \vee \\ H\left(st' = completed \ \wedge \ tr' = tr \ \wedge \ time' = time + t\right); \mathbf{beh}(l[[Q]]) \end{pmatrix}$$

$= \{(time' = time \ \vee \ 0 < time' - time < t) = 0 \le time' - time < t\}$

$$\begin{pmatrix} H\begin{pmatrix} (st' = wait \ \wedge \ tr' = tr \ \wedge \ 0 < time' - time < t) \ \vee \\ (st' = completed \ \wedge \ append(a!\langle v\rangle @l) \ \wedge \\ 0 \le time' - time < t) \end{pmatrix} ; \mathbf{beh}(l[[P]]) \\ \vee \\ H\left(st' = completed \ \wedge \ tr' = tr \ \wedge \ time' = time + t\right); \mathbf{beh}(l[[Q]]) \end{pmatrix}$$

$= \{$Def of Output Process$\}$

LHS

(input-2) $l[[a^{\triangle t}?(u) \ then \ P \ else \ Q]]$

$$= \ a?(u)@l \to l[[P]]$$

$$\oplus \exists t' \in (0...t) \bullet (\#t' \to (a?(u)@l \to l[[P]]))$$

$$\oplus \#t \to l[[Q]], \ where \ t > 0.$$

The input process has the similar description with the output process.

4.2   Algebraic Laws for Parallel Composition

Process 0 is the identity of parallel composition.

(para-1) $P \mid 0 = P = 0 \mid P$

The parallel composition $\mid$ is symmetric and associative.

(para-2) $P \mid Q = Q \mid P$

(para-3) $P \mid (Q \mid R) = (P \mid Q) \mid R$

(para-4) Let $N_1 = l[[a^{\triangle t}!\langle v \rangle \ then \ P \ else \ Q]]$

$$N_2 = l[[a^{\triangle t'}?(u) \ then \ P' \ else \ Q']]$$

$$N_3 = N_1 \mid N_2, \ where \ t > 0 \ and \ t' > 0.$$

Then, $N_3 = a.\{v/u\}@l \to (l[[P]] \mid l[[\{v/u\}P']])$

In the law **(para-4)**, an output process, from location l, succeeds in sending the message v over channel a to an input process from location l without any time delay. Both processes continue to execute at location l, the first one as P, the second one as $\{v/u\}P'$.

(para-5) Let $N_1 = l[[go^{\triangle t_1}l_1 \ then \ P_1]]$

$$N_2 = l[[go^{\triangle t_2}l_2 \ then \ P_2]]$$

$$N_3 = N_1 \mid N_2, \ where \ t_1 > 0 \ and \ t_2 > 0.$$

Then, we have the following two cases:

$$t_1 < t_2: N_3 = \#t_1 \to (l_1[[P_1]] \mid \#(t_2 - t_1) \to l_2[[P_2]])$$

$$t_1 = t_2: N_3 = \#t_1 \to (l_1[[P_1]] \mid l_2[[P_2]])$$

Law **(para-5)** is about the one for the parallel composition of two migration processes. N_3 delays t_1 time units first (we assume t_1 is the smaller delay), process P_1 then moves to location l_1 and the second process still needs to wait $t_2 - t_1$ time units. For the case $t_1 = t_2$, P_2 moves to location l_2 after delaying t_1 time units.

$$(\textbf{para-6}) \text{ Let } N_1 = l[[a^{\triangle t_1}!\langle v \rangle \text{ then } P \text{ else } Q]]$$

$$N_2 = l[[go^{\triangle t_2} l' \text{ then } P']]$$

$$N_3 = N_1 \mid N_2, \text{ where } t_1 > 0 \text{ and } t_2 > 0.$$

Then we have three cases for N_3:

$t_1 < t_2$: $N_3 = a!\langle v \rangle @l \rightarrow (l[[P]] \mid N_2)$

$\quad \oplus \exists t' \in (0...t_1) \bullet (\#t' \rightarrow (a!\langle v \rangle @l \rightarrow l[[P]] \mid \#(t_2 - t') \rightarrow l'[[P']]))$

$\quad \oplus \#t_1 \rightarrow (l[[Q]] \mid \#(t_2 - t_1) \rightarrow l'[[P']])$

$t_1 = t_2$: $N_3 = a!\langle v \rangle @l \rightarrow (l[[P]] \mid N_2)$

$\quad \oplus \exists t' \in (0...t_1) \bullet (\#t' \rightarrow (a!\langle v \rangle @l \rightarrow l[[P]] \mid \#(t_2 - t') \rightarrow l'[[P']]))$

$\quad \oplus \#t_1 \rightarrow (l[[Q]] \mid l'[[P']])$

$t_1 > t_2$: $N_3 = a!\langle v \rangle @l \rightarrow (l[[P]] \mid N_2)$

$\quad \oplus \exists t' \in (0...t_2) \bullet (\#t' \rightarrow (a!\langle v \rangle @l \rightarrow l[[P]] \mid \#(t_2 - t') \rightarrow l'[[P']]))$

$\quad \oplus \#t_2 \rightarrow (l[[a^{\triangle t_1 - t_2}!\langle v \rangle \text{ then } P \text{ else } Q]] \mid l'[[P']]).$

For the parallel composition of an output process and a migration process indicated in law (**para-6**), we have to consider the three cases: $t_1 < t_2$, $t_1 = t_2$ and $t_1 > t_2$. In the case $t_1 < t_2$, i.e., if the output action occurs at the start of the program, the output process evolves as process P from location l and the migration process keeps itself unchanged. On the other hand, the output action enters a waiting state, if the waiting time t' ranges in $(0...t_1)$, N_3 delays t' time units first, the output action happens and the output process continues as P from location l, the migration process should still wait $t_2 - t'$ time units. If the output action does not take place before the timeout t_1, N_3 delays t_1 time units, the output process continues as the alternative process Q from location l and the migration process still needs to wait $t_2 - t_1$ time units.

$$(\textbf{para-7}) \text{ Let } N_1 = l[[a^{\triangle t_1}!\langle v \rangle \text{ then } P_1 \text{ else } Q_1]]$$

$$N_2 = l[[b^{\triangle t_2}?(u) \text{ then } P_2 \text{ else } Q_2]]$$

$$N_3 = N_1 \mid N_2, \text{ where } 0 < t_1 < t_2.$$

Then, $N_3 = a!\langle v\rangle@l \to (l[[P_1]] \mid N_2)\lbrack b?(u)@l \to (N_1 \mid l[[P_2]])$

$\qquad \oplus \exists t' \in (0...t_1) \bullet (\#t' \to ($

$\qquad\qquad a!\langle v\rangle@l \to (l[[P_1]] \mid l[[b^{\triangle t_2 - t'}?(u) \ then \ P_2 \ else \ Q_2]])$

$\qquad\qquad \lbrack b?(u)@l \to (l[[a^{\triangle t_1 - t'}!\langle v\rangle \ then \ P_1 \ else \ Q_1]] \mid l[[P_2]])))$

$\qquad \oplus \#t_1 \to (l[[Q_1]] \mid l[[b^{\triangle t_2 - t_1}?(u) \ then \ P_2 \ else \ Q_2]])$

In law **(para-7)**, the output process and the input process do not share the same communication channel, which means that there is no message communication between them. The law **(para-7)** describes the following three cases:

- **Case 1**: At the start point of the program, at least one of output action over channel a ($a!\langle v\rangle@l$) and input action over channel b ($b?(u)@l$) occurs, the first action of N_3 is either $a!\langle v\rangle@l$ or $b?(u)@l$. When $a!\langle v\rangle@l$ is the first action of N_3, the output process continues to be process P_1 from location l and the input process remains unchanged. If the first action of N_3 is $b?(u)@l$, the output process keeps itself unchanged and the input process continues as process P_2 from location l.
- **Case 2**: N_3 enters the waiting state, if the waiting time t', which denotes the time $a!\langle v\rangle@l$ or $b?(u)@l$ happens, ranges in $(0...t_1)$, N_3 delays t' time units first and the next action is either $a!\langle v\rangle@l$ or $b?(u)@l$.
- **Case 3**: If neither $a!\langle v\rangle@l$ nor $b?(u)@l$ takes place before the timeout t_1, then N_3 delays t_1 time units first, the output process continues as process Q from location l and the timer for the input process is $\triangle^{t_2-t_1}$.

(para-8-1) Let $N = \lbrack\!\lbrack_{i\in I}\{g_i \to N_i\}$ and $M = \lbrack\!\lbrack_{j\in J}\{h_j \to M_j\}$.

Assume that there is no message communication between N and M.

Then, $N \mid M = \lbrack\!\lbrack_{i\in I}\{g_i \to (N_i \mid M)\}\lbrack\!\lbrack\!\lbrack_{j\in J}\{h_j \to (N \mid M_j)\}$

Law **(para-8-1)** reflects the parallel composition of two communication guarded choices, in which two communication components do not share the same communication channels, which means there is no message communication between them. The case that two parallel communication components can communicate with each other is illustrated in law **(para-8-2)**.

(para-8-2) Let $N1 = \lbrack\!\lbrack_{i\in I}\{g_i \to N1_i\}$ and $M1 = \lbrack\!\lbrack_{j\in J}\{h_j \to M1_j\}$,

$\qquad N = N1\lbrack\!\lbrack\!\lbrack_{k\in K}\{a_k!\langle v_k\rangle@l_k \to N2_k\}$,

$\qquad M = M1\lbrack\!\lbrack\!\lbrack_{k\in K}\{a_k?(u_k)@l_k \to M2_k\}$.

Assume that there are no communications between $N1$ and $M1$.

Then, $N \mid M = \|_{i \in I}\{g_i \rightarrow (N1_i \mid M)\}$

$$\|_{j \in J}\{h_j \rightarrow (N \mid M1_j)\}$$

$$\|_{k \in K}\{a_k.\{v_k/u_k\}@l_k \rightarrow (N2_k \mid M2_k)\}$$

(para-9) $\|_{i \in I}\{g_i \rightarrow N_i\} \mid \#t \rightarrow N = \|_{i \in I}\{g_i \rightarrow (N_i \mid \#t \rightarrow N)\}$

Law **(para-9)** indicates the parallel composition of communication guarded choice and delay guarded choice, the communication guard g_i is executed first, the subsequent network evolves as $(N_i \mid \#t \rightarrow N)$.

Law **(para-10)** stands for the parallel composition of communication guarded choice and hybrid guarded choice.

(para-10) Let $N = \|_{i \in I}\{g_i \rightarrow N_i\}$,

$$M = \|_{j \in J}\{h_j \rightarrow M_j\}$$

$$\oplus \exists t' \in (0...t) \bullet (\#t' \rightarrow (\|_{j \in J}\{h_j \rightarrow M'_j\}))$$

$$\oplus \#t \rightarrow M'.$$

Then, $N \mid M = \|_{i \in I}\{g_i \rightarrow (N_i \mid M)\}\|\|_{j \in J}\{h_j \rightarrow (N \mid M_j)\}\|N'$

where $N' = \|_{i \in I}\{g_i \rightarrow N_i\} \mid \|_{j \in J}\{h_j \rightarrow M_j\}$, whose result is able to be obtained by applying the laws **(para-8-1)** and **(para-8-2)**.

(para-11-1) $\#t_1 \rightarrow N_1 \mid \#(t_1 + t_2) \rightarrow N_2 = \#t_1 \rightarrow (N_1 \mid \#t_2 \rightarrow N_2)$

(para-11-2) $\#t_1 \rightarrow N_1 \mid \#t_1 \rightarrow N_2 = \#t_1 \rightarrow (N_1 \mid N_2)$

Laws **(para-11-1)** and **(para-11-2)** represent the parallel composition of two delay guarded choices.

Law **(para-12)** stands for the parallel composition of delay guarded choice and hybrid guarded choice.

(para-12) Let $N = \|_{i \in I}\{g_i \rightarrow N_i\}$

$$\oplus \exists t' \in (0...t_1) \bullet (\#t' \rightarrow (\|_{i \in I}\{g_i \rightarrow N'_i\}))$$

$$\oplus \#t_1 \rightarrow N',$$

$$M = \#t_2 \rightarrow M'.$$

Then, $N \mid M$ has three cases:

$$t_1 < t_2: N \mid M = \|_{i \in I}\{g_i \rightarrow (N_i \mid M)\}$$
$$\oplus \exists t' \in (0...t_1) \bullet (\#t' \rightarrow (\|_{i \in I}\{g_i \rightarrow N_i'\} \mid \#(t_2 - t') \rightarrow M'))$$
$$\oplus \#t_1 \rightarrow (N' \mid \#(t_2 - t_1) \rightarrow M')$$

$$t_1 = t_2: N \mid M = \|_{i \in I}\{g_i \rightarrow (N_i \mid M)\}$$
$$\oplus \exists t' \in (0...t_1) \bullet (\#t' \rightarrow (\|_{i \in I}\{g_i \rightarrow N_i'\} \mid \#(t_2 - t') \rightarrow M'))$$
$$\oplus \#t_1 \rightarrow (N' \mid M')$$

$$t_1 > t_2: N \mid M = \|_{i \in I}\{g_i \rightarrow (N_i \mid M)\}$$
$$\oplus \exists t' \in (0...t_2) \bullet (\#t' \rightarrow (\|_{i \in I}\{g_i \rightarrow N_i'\} \mid \#(t_2 - t') \rightarrow M'))$$
$$\oplus \#t_2 \rightarrow (N1 \mid M')$$

where,

$$N1 = \|_{i \in I}\{g_i \rightarrow N_i\}$$
$$\oplus \exists t' \in (0...t_1 - t_2) \bullet (\#t' \rightarrow (\|_{i \in I}\{g_i \rightarrow N_i'\}))$$
$$\oplus \#(t_1 - t_2) \rightarrow N'$$

Law **(para-13)** stands for the parallel composition of hybrid guarded choice and hybrid guarded choice.

(para-13) Let $N = \|_{i \in I}\{g_i \rightarrow N_i\}$
$$\oplus \exists t' \in (0...t_1) \bullet (\#t' \rightarrow (\|_{i \in I}\{g_i \rightarrow N_i'\}))$$
$$\oplus \#t_1 \rightarrow N',$$
$$M = \|_{j \in J}\{h_j \rightarrow M_j\}$$
$$\oplus \exists t' \in (0...t_2) \bullet (\#t' \rightarrow (\|_{j \in J}\{h_j \rightarrow M_j'\}))$$
$$\oplus \#t_2 \rightarrow M', \text{ where } t_1 < t_2.$$

Then, $N \mid M = \|_{i \in I}\{g_i \rightarrow (N_i \mid M)\}\|\|_{j \in J}\{h_j \rightarrow (N \mid M_j)\}\|R$

$$\oplus \exists t' \in (0...t_1) \bullet \left(\#t' \rightarrow \left(\begin{array}{l} \|_{i \in I}\{g_i \rightarrow (N_i' \mid M1)\} \\ \|\|_{j \in J}\{h_j \rightarrow (N1 \mid M_j')\}\|R1 \end{array} \right) \right)$$

$$\oplus \#t_1 \rightarrow (N' \mid M2)$$

where,

$$R = \|_{i \in I}\{g_i \to N_i\} \mid \|_{j \in J}\{h_j \to M_j\},$$

$$R1 = \|_{i \in I}\{g_i \to N_i'\} \mid \|_{j \in J}\{h_j \to M_j'\},$$

$$N1 = \|_{i \in I}\{g_i \to N_i\}$$

$$\oplus \exists t'' \in (0...t_1 - t') \bullet (\#t'' \to (\|_{i \in I}\{g_i \to N_i'\}))$$

$$\oplus \#(t_1 - t') \to N',$$

$$M1 = \|_{j \in J}\{h_j \to M_j\}$$

$$\oplus \exists t'' \in (0...t_2 - t') \bullet (\#t'' \to (\|_{j \in J}\{h_j \to M_j'\}))$$

$$\oplus \#(t_2 - t') \to M',$$

$$M2 = \|_{j \in J}\{h_j \to M_j\}$$

$$\oplus \exists t'' \in (0...t_2 - t_1) \bullet (\#t'' \to (\|_{j \in J}\{h_j \to M_j'\}))$$

$$\oplus \#(t_2 - t_1) \to M'$$

The results of R and $R1$ can be achieved according to the laws (para-8-1) and (para-8-2).

5 Conclusion

rTiMo is a real-time version of TiMo, which is a process algebra for mobile distributed systems. In this paper, we have studied the denotational semantics for rTiMo via the concept of UTP [14]. In addition, a set of algebraic laws have been investigated, especially the algebraic laws which can stand for the time-related features of rTiMo. In order to deal with the parallel expansion laws, we have introduced the concept of guarded choice. From a set of parallel expansion laws, we can see every parallel construct can be converted to a guarded choice.

For the future, we want to continue our work on rTiMo. We plan to explore the linking theories [18–20] between the three semantics of rTiMo. And a proof system based on Hoare Logic [21] is also planned to be investigated.

Acknowledgments. This work was partly supported by the Danish National Research Foundation and the National Natural Science Foundation of China (Grant No. 61361136002) for the Danish-Chinese Center for Cyber Physical Systems. It was also supported by National Natural Science Foundation of China (Grant No. 61321064) and Shanghai Collaborative Innovation Center of Trustworthy Software for Internet of Things (No. ZF1213).

References

1. Lakos, C.A.: A Petri net view of mobility. In: Wang, F. (ed.) FORTE 2005. LNCS, vol. 3731, pp. 174–188. Springer, Heidelberg (2005). doi:10.1007/11562436_14
2. Ma, L., Tsai, J.J.P.: Formal modeling and analysis of a secure mobile-agent system. IEEE Trans. Syst. Man Cybern. Part A **38**(1), 180–196 (2008)

3. Lakos, C.: Modelling mobile IP with mobile petri nets. In: Jensen, K., Billington, J., Koutny, M. (eds.) ToPNoC III. LNCS, vol. 5800, pp. 127–158. Springer, Heidelberg (2009). doi:10.1007/978-3-642-04856-2_6

4. Braghin, C., Sharygina, N., Barone-Adesi, K.: A model checking-based approach for security policy verification of mobile systems. Formal Asp. Comput. 23(5), 627–648 (2011)

5. Ciobanu, G., Koutny, M.: Timed mobility in process algebra and Petri nets. J. Log. Algebr. Program. 80(7), 377–391 (2011)

6. Aman, B., Ciobanu, G.: Real-time migration properties of rTiMo verified in UPPAAL. In: Hierons, R.M., Merayo, M.G., Bravetti, M. (eds.) SEFM 2013. LNCS, vol. 8137, pp. 31–45. Springer, Heidelberg (2013). doi:10.1007/978-3-642-40561-7_3

7. Ciobanu, G., Koutny, M., Steggles, L.J.: Strategy based semantics for mobility with time and access permissions. Formal Asp. Comput. 27(3), 525–549 (2015)

8. Aman, B., Ciobanu, G.: Verification of bounded real-time distributed systems with mobility. In: Proceedings of the 9th Workshop on Verification and Evaluation of Computer and Communication Systems, VECoS 2015, Bucharest, Romania, September 10–11, pp. 109–120 (2015)

9. Ciobanu, G., Koutny, M.: Timed migration and interaction with access permissions. In: Butler, M., Schulte, W. (eds.) FM 2011. LNCS, vol. 6664, pp. 293–307. Springer, Heidelberg (2011). doi:10.1007/978-3-642-21437-0_23

10. Ciobanu, G., Juravle, C.: Flexible software architecture and language for mobile agents. Concurrency Comput.: Pract. Experience 24(6), 559–571 (2012)

11. Ciobanu, G., Koutny, M.: Pertimo: a model of spatial migration with safe access permissions. Comput. J. 58(5), 1041–1060 (2015)

12. Plotkin, G.D.: A structural approach to operational semantics. J. Log. Algebr. Program. 60–61, 17–139 (2004)

13. Hoare, C.A.R., Hayes, I.J., He, J., Morgan, C., Roscoe, A.W., Sanders, J.W., Sørensen, I.H., Spivey, J.M., Sufrin, B.: Laws of programming. Commun. ACM 30(8), 672–686 (1987)

14. Hoare, C.A.R., He, J.: Unifying Theories of Programming. International Series in Computer Science. Prentice Hall, Upper Saddle River (1998)

15. He, J.: Provably Correct Systems: Modelling of Communication Languages and Design of Optimized Compilers. International Series in Software Engineering. The McGraw-Hill, New York City (1994)

16. Hoare, C.A.R., He, J., Sampaio, A.: Normal form approach to compiler design. Acta Inf. 30(8), 701–739 (1993)

17. Duran, A., Cavalcanti, A., Sampaio, A.: An algebraic approach to the design of compilers for object-oriented languages. Formal Asp. Comput. 22(5), 489–535 (2010)

18. Zhu, H., He, J., Qin, S., Brooke, P.J.: Denotational semantics and its algebraic derivation for an event-driven system-level language. Formal Asp. Comput. 27(1), 133–166 (2015)

19. Zhu, H., Yang, F., He, J., Bowen, J.P., Sanders, J.W., Qin, S.: Linking operational semantics and algebraic semantics for a probabilistic timed shared-variable language. J. Log. Algebr. Program. 81(1), 2–25 (2012)

20. Zhu, H., He, J., Li, J., Bowen, J.P.: Algebraic approach to linking the semantics of web services. ISSE 7(3), 209–224 (2011)

21. Apt, K.R., de Boer, F.S., Olderog, E.: Verification of Sequential and Concurrent Programs. Texts in Computer Science. Springer, Heidelberg (2009)

UTPCalc — A Calculator for UTP Predicates

Andrew Butterfield[⊠]

Trinity College Dublin, Dublin, Ireland
andrew.butterfield@cs.tcd.ie

Abstract. We present the development of the UTP-Calculator: a tool, written in Haskell, that supports rapid prototyping of new theories in the Unifying Theories of Programming paradigm, by supporting an easy way to very quickly perform test calculations. The emphasis during the calculator development was keeping it simple but effective, and relying on the user to have the expertise to check its output. It is not intended to supplant existing theorem prover or language transformation technology. The tool is designed for someone who is both very familiar with UTP theory construction, and familiar enough with Haskell to be able to write pattern-matching code. In this paper we describe how this tool can be used to assist in theory development, by describing the key components of the calculator and how various aspects of such a theory might be encoded. We finish with a discussion of our experience in using the tool.

1 Introduction

1.1 Motivation

The development of a Unifying Theory of Programming (UTP) can involve a number of false starts, as alphabet variables are chosen and semantics and healthiness conditions are defined. Typically, some calculations done to check that everything works end up revealing problems with the theory. So an iteration occurs by revising the basic definitions, and attempting the calculations again.

We have recently started to explore using UTP to describe shared-variable concurrency, by adapting the work of the UTP semantics for Unifying Theories of Parallel Programming (UTPP) [20]. We have reworked it to use a system for generating unique labels, in order to give a slight improvement to the compositionality of the semantics. This we call a Unifying Theory of Concurrent Programming (UTCP) [6].

We illustrate the calculator here with, as a running example, the definition of the UTP semantics of an atomic action. We assume basic atomic actions A, B which modify the shared global state (program variables), represented by observation variables s, s'. The concurrent flow of control is managed by using

A. Butterfield—This work was supported, in part, by Science Foundation Ireland grant 10/CE/I1855 to Lero - the Irish Software Engineering Research Centre (www.lero.ie).

© Springer International Publishing AG 2017
J.P. Bowen and H. Zhu (Eds.): UTP 2016, LNCS 10134, pp. 197–216, 2017.
DOI: 10.1007/978-3-319-52228-9_10

labels associated with language constructs, which are added to and removed from a global label-set as execution proceeds. We represent this label-set using observations ls, ls'. Our main change to the original UTPP theory is to provide a mechanism to create unique labels, to be associated with both the beginning and end of each language construct. This results in three static observables: a generator g; and two labels in and out. So our UTCP theory is based on a non-homogeneous relation with alphabet s, s', ls, ls', g, in, and out. See [6] for details.

Our running example is the need to calculate the outcome of sequentially composing (;;) two basic atomic actions (A, B), that are lifted $(\mathbf{A}(\_))$ to the full alphabet by adding control-flow, and are then run in order to see their dynamic behaviour:

$$run(\mathbf{A}(A) \;;; \mathbf{A}(B))$$

We hope that the final result would be

$$(A \; ; B) \wedge ls' = \{\ell_{g:}\}$$

We have the standard UTP sequential composition of A and B defined on s, s', and an assertion that the termination label $\ell_{g:}$ is the sole member of the final label-set.

The theory with its somewhat unusual arrangement of observation variables did *not* emerge as an immediate and obvious solution, but as a result of many trial calculations. These trial calculations exposed two problems: one was the difficulty in reading very long complex set-based expressions in order to assess their correctness. The second was the sheer length and drudgery of these calculations, often involving many repetitions of very similar steps.

To be specific, the calculator described in this paper is intended to be used for *calculation*, and not *theorem proving*. In particular, it is designed to help solve the problem just described above. Both the starting predicate and the final result have free variables and are not theorems. That means counter-example generators like Nitpick or Alloy are not helpful.

If we consider the reasoning processes used in the development and deployment of a theory, we can see a spectrum ranging from informal, through to fully mechanised: hand calculation; simulation; proof assistant; and automated theorem provers. The level of detail, complexity, and rigour rises as we proceed along the spectrum. The calculator described here is designed to assist with the exploratory hand-calculation phase early on, by making it easier to calculate, and to manually check the outcomes. It is not intended to provide the soundness guarantees that are quite rightly expected from the tools further along the spectrum.

1.2   Structure of This Paper

In Sect. 2 we discuss related work to justify our decision to develop the calculator. The key design decisions and tool architecture is then described in Sect. 3. Three key components of the system are then discussed: Dictionaries (Sect. 4);

Expressions (Sect. 5); and Predicates (Sect. 6). In Sect. 7 we describe how to encode laws and then conclude (Sect. 8).

2 Related Work

There are lots of tools for assisting with the kinds of calculations we are trying to perform, ranging from calculators [3], through rewrite/transformation systems (CIP-S [1], Stratego [16], ASF+DSF [15]Maude [7] HATS [19]) to full-blown theorem provers (Isabelle/HOL [12], CoQ [2], PVS [14]) including those that support equational reasoning (Isabelle/ISAR [18]).

Most of the above have a considerable body of work behind them, both in terms of theory and tool development, and provide very comprehensive coverage of their problem domain, be it rewriting, program transformation or theorem proving. However many are tied to specific languages, or have limited ability to allow the user to customise the target language. In particular, it is not clear in any of them, how to achieve the ability to do rapid calculation with a high degree of ease in proof-reading its output.

Within the UTP community, there has been considerable work using Proof-Power-Z, such as the deep embedding into Z of an imperative language whose semantics were given using UTP [13] and re-working the mechanisation of UTP in order to better support the hierarchical nature of UTP theory building [21]. There is also work on embedding UTP into Isabelle/HOL [9]. This contains a considerable amount of infrastructure to support UTP's alphabetised predicates in a general way, with UTP forming a third sub-syntax in addition to Isabelle/HOL's inner and outer syntaxes. It continues to undergo continuous improvement [8].

Like all high-quality state-of-the-art tools, CoQ, Isabelle/HOL, ProofPower-Z and PVS all have in common that they work best when used in the manner for which they were designed—in none of these cases does this manner match the way we wish to work in UTP, as described in the introduction, without at least a steep learning curve.

We briefly considered using the $U \cdot (TP)^2$ theorem prover [4,5], which does support both equational reasoning, plus a mode in which calculations can be from a starting predicate, as we require. However, it would have required a lot of setup effort, in particular to build the support theories about sets and labels and generators. Also, it is currently not in an ideal state, due to difficulties installing the relevant third-party software libraries on more recent versions of Haskell.

However, as part of other ongoing work, we had developed a parser and some initial analysis tools in Haskell [11], and this software contained abstract syntax and support for general predicates. It became really obvious that this could be quickly adapted, to mechanise the checking calculations, that were being performed during each attempt. In particular, the key inspiration was the observation, that the pattern of each calculation was very uniform and similar. So a decision was taken to construct the calculator described in this paper. It also has the advantage that it runs on standard Haskell, and hence it is much easier to future-proof.

3   Design and Architecture

3.1   Key Design Decisions

Taking into account the repetitive nature of the calculations, and the need for shorthand notations we very rapidly converged on four initial design decisions:

1. All calculation objects are written directly in Haskell, to avoid having to implement a parser.
2. The expression and predicate datatype declarations would be very simple, with only equality being singled out.
3. Provide a good way to pretty-print long predicates that made it easy to see their overall structure.
4. Rely on a dictionary based system to make it easy to customise how specific constructs were to be handled.

From our experience with the $U \cdot (TP)^2$ theorem-prover we also decided the following regarding the calculation steps that would be supported:

– We would not support full propositional calculus or theories of numbers or sets. Instead we would support the use of hard-coded relevant laws, typically derived from a handwritten proof.
– We would avoid, at all costs, any use of quantifiers or binding constructs.
– The calculator user interface would be very simple, supporting a few high level commands such as "simplify" or "reduce". In particular, no facility would be provided for the user to identify the relevant sub-part of the current goal to which any operation should be applied. Instead the tool would use a systematic sweep through the predicate to find the first applicable calculation step of the requested kind, and apply that. Our subsequent experience with the calculator indicates that this was a good choice.

3.2   The Calculator REPL

The way the calculator is designed to be used is that a function implementing a calculator Read-Execute-Print-Loop (REPL) is given a dictionary and starting predicate as inputs. Calculator commands include an ability to undo previous steps ('u'), request help ('?'), and to signal an exit from the calculator ('x'). However, of most interest are the five calculation commands. The first is a global simplify command ('s'), that scans the entire predicate from the bottom-up looking for simplifiers for each composite and applying them. Simplifiers are captured as **eval** or **prsimp** components in dictionary entries.

The other four commands work by searching top-down, left-to-right for the first sub-component for which the relevant dictionary calculator function returns a changed result. Here is where we have a reduced degree of control, which simplifies the REPL dramatically, but has turned out to be effective in practice.

Here is a sample run obtained when calculating the effect of $run(\mathbf{A}(A)$;; $\mathbf{A}(B))$, from the introduction. For convenience we predefined the predicate $\mathbf{A}(A)$;; $\mathbf{A}(B)$ in Haskell as

```
athenb = pseq [patm (PVar"A"),patm (PVar "B")]
```

Here PVar is a constructor of the predicate datatype Pred (See Sect. 6), while pseq and patm are convenient functions we wrote to build instances of ;; and A(_) respectively. We invoked the calculator as follows, where dictUTCP is the dictionary for this theory:

```
calcREPL dictUTCP (run athenb)
```

We then proceeded to interact (the prompt " ?,d,r,l,s,c,u,x :-" shows the available commands):

```
 1 run(A(A) ;; A(B))
 2 ?,d,r,l,s,c,u,x :- d
 3 ="defn. of run.3"
 4    (A(A) ;; A(B))[g::,lg,lg,lg:/g,in,ls,out]
 5 ; ~ls(lg:) * (A(A) ;; A(B))[g::,lg,lg:/g,in,out]
 6 ?,d,r,l,s,c,u,x :- d
 7 = "defn. of ;;"
 8    (A(A)[g:1,lg/g,out] \/
 9    A(B)[g:2,lg/g,in])[g::,lg,lg,lg:/g,in,ls,out]
10 ; ~ls(lg:) * (A(A) ;; A(B))[g::,lg,lg:/g,in,out]
11 ?,d,r,l,s,c,u,x :- s
12 = "simplify"
13    A(A)[g:::1,lg,lg,lg::/g,in,ls,out] \/
14    A(B)[g:::2,lg::,lg,lg:/g,in,ls,out]
15 ; ~ls(lg:) * (A(A) ;; A(B))[g::,lg,lg:/g,in,out]
16 .... 10 more steps
17 A /\ ls' = {lg::} ; B /\ ls' = {lg:}
18 ?,d,r,l,s,c,u,x :- r
19 = "ls'-cleanup"
20 (A ; B) /\ ls' = {lg:}
```

Lines 2, 6, 11, and 18 show the user entering a single key command at the prompt. Lines 3, 7, and 19 show a short string identifying the relevant definition or law. Lines 1, 4–5, 8–10, 17 and 20 show various stages of the calculation.

3.3 Pretty-Printing

For the calculator output, it is very important that it be readable, as many of the predicates get very large, particularly at intermediate points of the calculation. For this reason, a lot of effort was put into the development of both good pretty-printing, and ways to highlight old and new parts of predicates as changes are made. The key principle was to ensure that whenever a predicate had to split over multiple lines, that the breaks are always around the top-most operator or composition symbol, with sub-components indented in, both after and *before*. An example of such pretty-printing in action is shown in Fig. 1 The top-level

```
   D(out)
\/ (       ~ls(out)
        /\ (D(lg) \/ A(in,lg,a,in,lg,lg) \/ D(out) \/ A(lg,out,b,lg,out,out))
      ; W(D(lg) \/ A(in,lg,a,in,lg,lg) \/ D(out) \/ A(lg,out,b,lg,out,out)))
```

Fig. 1. Pretty-printer output

structure of this is $D(out) \vee ((\neg ls(out) \wedge \ldots); W(\ldots))$ where the precedence ordering from tightest to loosest is $\wedge, ;, \vee$.

The pretty printing support can be found in `PrettyPrint.lhs`, which was written from scratch, but inspired by writings of Hughes [10] and Wadler [17] on the subject. In addition to the layout management aspects of pretty-printing there is also a need for a support for shorthand notations. We illustrate this in Sect. 5.

Display Convention. In the rest of this paper, code that is part of the underlying calculator infrastructure is shown as a simple verbatim display, thus:

```
underlying UTPCalc code
```

while code supplied by the user to set it up for a particular theory under investigation is shown enclosed in horizontal lines:

```
user-supplied theory customisation code
```
---

4   Dictionaries

The approach taken is to provide a dictionary that maps names to entries that supply extra information. The names can be those of expression or predicate composites, or correspond to variables, and a few other features of note. All of the main calculator functions are driven by this dictionary, and the correct definition of dictionary entries is the primary way for users to set up calculations. The dictionary datatype (`Dict s`), parameterised with a generic type `s`, is critical to the functioning of the calculator.

```
type Dict s = M.Map String (Entry s)
-- M is the renamed import of Data.Map
```

It is the basic way in which the user of the calculator describes the alphabet, definitions and laws associated with their theory.

The dictionary uses the Haskell `String` datatype for keys, and contains four different kinds of entries: alphabets, expressions, predicates and laws.

```
data Entry s = AlfEntry .. | ExprEntry .. | PredEntry .. | LawEntry ..
```

For simplicity, there is only one namespace involved, and some names are reserved for special purposes. These are listed in Fig. 2. There are ten names that describe different (overlapping) parts of the theory alphabet (Fig. 2). While it is possible to define these individually, this can be quite error-prone, so a function is provided to construct all these entries from three basic pieces of information: program variable names ('script', Scr); auxiliary variable names ('model',Mdl), e.g. variables like *ls* that don't represent variable values, but instead some other observable program property of interest); and static parameter variable names (Stc).

```
stdAlfDictGen :: [String] -> [String] -> [String] -> Dict s
```

All lists contain undashed names, with dashes added when required by the function. So, the alphabet entries for the UTCP theory are defined as follows:

```
dictAlpha = stdAlfDictGen ["s"] ["ls"] ["g","in","out"]
```

All of these entries will be of kind AlfEntry, i.e., just lists of the relevant variables.

```
AlfEntry { avars   :: [String]}
```

There are two important utility functions, one that builds dictionaries from lists of string/entry pairs, and another that merges two dictionaries, resolving conflicts by merging entries if possible, otherwise favouring the second dictionary:

```
makeDict :: [(String, Entry s)] -> Dict s
dictMrg :: Dict s -> Dict s -> Dict s
```

5   Expressions

In Fig. 3 we show the Haskell declarations of the datatypes used to represent expressions and substitution. Both types are parameterised on a generic state type s, which allows us to be able to reason independently of any particular notion of state. We provide booleans (B), integers (Z), values of the generic state type (St), and named function application (App). We also have substitution (Sub), which pairs an expression with a substitution (Substn), which is a list of variable/expression pairs. The deriving clause for Expr enables the Haskell default notions of equality, ordering and display for the type.

5.1   Set Expressions

We shall explore the use of the Expr datatype by indicating how the notions of sets and some basic operators could be defined with the calculator. We shall represent sets as instances of App with the name "set", and the subset relation as an App with name "subset", so the set $\{1, 2\}$ and predicate $S \subseteq T$ would be represented by App"set" [Z 1,Z 2], and App "subset" [Var "S",Var "T"] respectively. In practice, we would define constructor functions to build these:

```
data Expr s
  = St s | B Bool | Z Int | Var String
  | App String [Expr s] | Sub (Expr s) (Substn s) | Undef
  deriving (Eq, Ord, Show)
type Substn s = [(String,Expr s)]
```

Fig. 3. Expression and substitution datatypes (`CalcTypes.lhs`)

```
set es = App "set" es
subset s1 s2 = App "subset" [s1,s2]
```

There is a standard interface for defining expression simplifiers: define a function with the following type:

```
Dict s -> [Expr s] -> (String, Expr s)
```

The first argument, of type `Dict`, is the dictionary currently in use. The second argument is the list of sub-expressions of the `App` construct for which the simplifier is intended. The result is a pair consisting of a string and an expression. If the simplification succeeds, then the string is non-empty and gives some indication for the user of what was simplified. In this case the expression component is the simplified result. If the simplification has no effect, then the string is empty, and the expression returned is not defined.

The following code defines a simplifier for "subset", which expects it to have precisely two set components:

```
evalSubset d [App"set" s1,App "set" s2] = dosubset d s1 s2
evalSubset _ _ = none -- predefined shorthand for ("",Undef)
```

The two underscores in the second line are pattern matching wildcards, so this catches all other possibilities. It makes use of the following helper, which gets the two lists of expressions associated with each set:

```
dosubset d es1 es2 -- is es1 a subset of es2 ?
  | null (es1 \\ es2)  = ( "subset", B True )
  | all (isGround d) ((es1 \\ es2) ++ es2)
                       = ( "subset", B False )
  | otherwise          = none
```

If the result of removing es2 from es1 is null it then returns true. If not, then if all elements remaining are "ground", i.e., contain no variables, it returns false. Otherwise, we cannot infer anything, so return none.

5.2   Rendering Expressions

The UTCP theory definitions and calculations involve a lot of reasoning about sets, leading to quite complicated expressions. To avoid complex set expressions that are hard to parse visually, a number of simplifying notations are desirable, so that a singleton set $\{x\}$ is rendered as x and the very common idiom $S \subseteq ls$ is rendered as $ls(S)$, so that for example, $ls(in)$ is short for $\{in\} \subseteq ls$. This shrinks the expressions to a much more readable form, mainly by reducing the number of infix operators and set brackets.

When rendering expressions, if an `App` construct is found, then its name is looked up in the dictionary. If an `ExprEntry` is not found, then the default rendering is used, in which `App "f" [e1,e2,..,en]` is converted into `f(e1,e2,..,en)`. Otherwise, a function of type `Dict s - > [Expr s] - > String`, in that entry, is used to render the construct.

As far as expressions are concerned, they become strings, and so are viewed as atomic by the predicate pretty-printer (see Sect. 6). So, we could show singleton sets without enclosing braces by defining:

```
showSet d [elm] = edshow d elm      -- drop {,} from singleton
showSet d elms = "{" ++ dlshow d "," elms ++ "}"
```

Here `edshow` (expression-dict-show) displays its `elm` argument, while `dlshow` (dictionary-list-show) displays the expressions in `elms` separated by the `","` string. Similar tricks are used to code a very compact rendering of a mechanism that involves unique label generator expressions that involve very deep nesting, such as:

$$\pi_2(new(\pi_1(new(\pi_2(split(\pi_1(new(g))))))))$$

This can be displayed as `lg:2:`, using a very compact shorthand described in [6] which we do not explain here.

5.3   Expression Equality

In contrast to the way that the subset predicate is captured as an expression above, the notion of expression equality is hardwired in, as part of the predicate abstract syntax (see Sect. 6). The simplifier will look at the two expression arguments of that construct, and if they are both instances of `App` with the same name, will do a dictionary lookup, to see if there is an entry, from which an equality checking function can be obtained (`isEqual` component). This has the following signature:

```
Dict s -> [Expr s] -> [Expr s] -> Maybe Bool
```

The `Maybe` type constructor is standard Haskell, defined as

```
data Maybe t = Nothing | Just t
```

It converts a type `t` into one which is now "optional", or equivalently has a undefined value added.

The equality testing function takes a dictionary and the two expression lists from the two `App` instances and either returns `Nothing`, if it cannot establish the truth or falsity of the equality, or `Just` the appropriate result. Suitable code for `"set"` is the following

```
eqSet d es1 es2
= let ns1 = nub (sort es1)
      ns2 = nub (sort es2)
  in if all (isGround d) (ns1++ns2)
     then Just (ns1==ns2) else Nothing
```

The standard function nub removes duplicates, which we do after we sort. If both lists are ground we just do an equality comparison and return Just it. Otherwise, we return Nothing.

5.4 The Expression Entry

The dictionary entry for expressions has the following form:

```
ExprEntry
    { ecansub :: [String]
    , eprint :: Dict s -> [Expr s] -> String
    , eval :: Dict s -> [Expr s] -> (String, Expr s)
    , isEqual :: Dict s -> [Expr s] -> [Expr s] -> Maybe Bool}
```

One big win in using a functional language like Haskell, in which functions are first class data values, is that we can easily define datatypes that contain function-valued components. We make full use of this in three of the entry kinds, for expressions, predicates and laws.

The eprint, eval and isEqual components correspond to the various examples we have seen above. The ecansub component indicates those variables occurring in the App expression list for which it is safe to replace in substitutions.

To understand the need for ecansub, consider the following shorthand definition for an expression:

$$D(L) \mathrel{\widehat{=}} L \subseteq ls$$

in a context where we know that L is a set expression defined only over variables g, in and out. The variable ls is not free in the lhs, but does occur in the rhs. A substitution of the form $[E/ls]$ say, would leave the lhs unchanged, but alter the rhs to $L \subseteq E$. For this reason the entry for D would need to disallow substitution for ls. The ecansub entry lists the variables for which substitution is safe with the expression as-is. With the definition above, the value of this entry should be ["g","in","out"]. If we want to state that any substitution is safe, then we use the "wildcard" form: ["*"]. We choose to list the substitutable variables rather than those that are non-substitutable, because the former is always easy to determine, whereas the latter can be very open ended.

Given all of the above, we can define dictionary entries for set and subset as

```
setUTCPDict = makeDict
  [ ("set",(ExprEntry ["*"] showSet evalSet eqSet))
  , ("subset",(ExprEntry ["*"] showSubSet evalSubSet noEq)) ]
```

Here noEq is an equality test function that always returns Nothing.

```
data Pred s = T | F | PVar String | Equal (Expr s) (Expr s) | Atm (Expr s)
            | Comp String [Pred s] | PSub (Pred s) (Substn s)
```

Fig. 4. Predicate datatype (`CalcTypes.lhs`)

6   Predicates

In Fig. 4 we show the Haskell declarations of the datatypes to represent predicates. Similar to expressions we have basic values such as true (`T`) and false (`F`), with predicate-valued variables (`PVar`), and composite predicates (`Comp`) which are the predicate equivalent of `App` (see Sect. 5). We also have two ways to turn expressions into predicates. One (`Atm`) lifts an expression, which should be boolean-valued into an (atomic) predicate, while the other is an explicit representation (`Equal`) for expression equality. We can also substitute over predicates (`PSub`).

In many ways, we define our predicates of interest in much the same was as done for expressions. Basic logic features such as negation, conjunction, etc., are not built in, but have to be implemented using `Comp`. A collection of these are pre-defined as part of the calculator, in the Haskell module `StdPredicates`.

There are a few ways in which the treatment of predicates differ from expressions:

- The simplifier and some of the infrastructure for handling laws treats `PVar` in a special way. It is possible to associate an `AlfEntry` in the dictionary with a `PVar`, so defining its alphabet. This can be useful when reasoning about atomic state-change actions which only depend on s and s'. Such entries will be looked up when certain side-conditions are being checked.
- We distinguish between having a definition/expansion associated with a `Comp`, and having a way to simplify one.
- Rendering predicates involves the pretty printer so the interface is more complex. We explain this below.

6.1   Coding Atomic Semantics

Formally, using our shorthand notations, we define atomic behaviour as in UTCP as:

$$\mathbf{A}(A) \mathrel{\widehat{=}} ls(in) \wedge A \wedge ls' = ls \ominus (in, out)$$

where A and $\mathbf{A}(\_)$ are as in the introduction, and $S \ominus (T, V)$ is notation from [20] that stands for $(S \setminus T) \cup V$.

Coding a Definition. We want to define a composite, called "A" (representing $\mathbf{A}$). We define a function that takes a single predicate argument and applies $\mathbf{A}$ to it

```
patm pr = Comp "A" [pr] -- we assume pr has only s, s' free
```

We can now code up its definition, which takes a dictionary, and a list of its sub-components and returns a string/predicate pair, interpreted in the same manner as the string/expression pair returned by the expression simplifier.

One way to code this is as follows. First define our variables and expressions, because these get used in a variety of places.

```
ls = Var "ls" ; ls' = Var "ls'"
inp = Var "in" -- 'in' is a Haskell keyword
out = Var "out"
lsinout = App "sswap" [ls,inp,out]
```

Here, "sswap" is our name for $\ominus$, and note that Haskell identifiers can contain the prime (') character. We then define our atomic predicates ($ls(in)$ and $ls' = ls \ominus (in, out)$)

```
lsin = Atm (App "subset" [inp,ls])
ls'eqlsinout = Equal ls' lsinout
```

Finally we can define $\mathbf{A}(a)$ as their conjunction, where `mkAnd` is a smart constructor for `Comp "And"`, defined in `StdPredicates.lhs`.

```
defnAtomic d [a] = Just ("A",mkAnd [lsin,a,ls'eqlsinout],True)
```

Coding for Pretty Printing. For rendering `Comp` predicates, we are going to generate an instance of the pretty-printer type `PP`, using a dictionary and list of sub-predicates, with two additional arguments: one of type `SubCompPrint` which is a function to render sub-components, and one of type `Int` which gives a precedence level. The type signature is

```
SubCompPrint s -> Dict s -> Int -> [Pred s] -> PP
```

The function type is

```
type SubCompPrint s  =  Int -> Int -> Pred s -> PP
```

It takes two integer arguments to begin. The first is the precedence level to be used to render the sub-component, while the second should denote the position of the sub-component in the sub-component list, counting from 1. The third argument is the sub-predicate to be printed. To render our atomic construct we can define the pretty-printer as follows:

```
ppPAtm sCP d p [pr]
        = pplist [ ppa "A" , ppbracket "(" (sCP 0 1 pr) ")"]
```

The functions `pplist`, `ppa` and `ppbracket` build instances of `PP` that respectively represent lists of PP, atomic strings, and an occurrence of PP surrounded by the designated brackets. Note that the `SubCompPrint` argument (`sCP`) is applied to `pr`, with the precedence set to zero as it is bracketed, and the sub-component number set to one as `pr` is the first (and only) sub-component. We will show how the pretty-printing for sequential composition (;;) in UTCP is defined, to illustrate the support for infix notation.

```
ppPSeq sCP d   p [pr1,pr2]
= paren p precPSeq
    ( ppopen   (pad ";;") [ sCP precPSeq 1 pr1
                          , sCP precPSeq 2 pr2 ] )
```

Here pad puts spaces around its argument, and so its use here is equivalent to ppa " ;; ", while ppopen uses its first argument as a separator between all the elements of its second list argument. The paren function takes two precedence values, and a PP value, and puts parentheses around it if the first precedence number is greater than the second. The variable precPSeq is the precedence level of sequential composition, here defined to be tighter than disjunction, but looser than conjunction, as defined in module StdPrecedences. Note, once more, the use of sCP, and how the 2nd integer argument corresponds to the position of the sub-predicate involved.

The Predicate Entry

The dictionary entry for predicates has the following form:

```
PredEntry
  { pcansub :: [String]
  , pprint  ::
  SubCompPrint s -> Dict s -> Int -> [Pred s] -> PP
  , alfa :: [String], pdefn  :: Rewrite s, prsimp ::
  Rewrite s}
type Rewrite s   =   Dict s -> [Pred s] -> RWResult s
type RWResult s  =   Maybe ( String, Pred s, Bool )
```

Fields pcansub and prsimp are the predicate analogues of ecansub and eval in the expression entry. Here pprint plays the same role as eprint, but is oriented towards pretty printing. The alfa component allows a specific alphabet to be associated with a composite —if empty then the dictionary alphabet entries apply.

The pdefn component, of the same type as prsimp, is used when the user invokes the Definition Expansion command from the REPL. The calculator searches top-down, left-right for the first Comp whose pdefn function returns a changed outcome.

A RWResult can be Nothing, in which case this definition expansion or simplifier was unable to make any changes. If it was able to change its target then it returns Just(reason,newPred,isTopLevel). The string reason is used to display the justification for the calculation step to the user. The isTopLevel flag is a hint to the change-highlighting facilities of the pretty-printer infrastructure.

The dictionary entry for our atomic semantics is then:

```
patmEntry=("A",PredEntry [] ppPAtm [] defnAtomic (pNoChg "A"))
```

The function pNoChg creates a simplifier that returns Nothing.

7 Laws

In addition to the global simplifier and definition expansion facility, we have three broad classes of laws that can be invoked from the REPL: Reduce; Conditional Reduce; and Loop Unroll.

The way the latter three laws are applied is somewhat different to the behaviour of either the simplifier or definition expansion. Instead the reserved dictionary key "laws" is used to lookup a special dictionary entry

```
LawEntry { reduce  :: [RWFun s]
         , creduce :: [CRWFun s], unroll ::
[String -> RWFun s] }
```

7.1 Reduce

The reduce component of the LawEntry is a list of RWFun, which are defined as follows:

```
type RWFun s = Dict s -> Pred s -> Pred s -> RWResult s
```

The first predicate argument is used to supply an invariant assertion for those reduction rules that require one. It is a recent new feature of the calculator, not required for this UTCP theory, and its use is beyond the scope of this paper.

When asked to do a reduce, the calculator then does a top-down, left-to-right search, where at each point it tries all the laws in its reduce list, in order, with the current composite being passed in as the second predicate argument. It terminates at the point of first success (a non-Nothing outcome). A reduce law is an equation of the form $P = Q$, where we search for instances of P and replace them with the corresponding instance of Q. The idea is that we pattern-match on predicate syntax with the second predicate argument, to see if a law is applicable (we have its lefthand side), and if so, we then build an appropriate instance of the righthand-side. The plan is that we gather all these pattern/outcome pairs in one function definition, which will try them in order. This is in direct correspondence with Haskell pattern-matching. So for UTCP we have a function called reduceUTCP, structured as follows:

```
reduceUTCP d inv (...1st law pattern...) = 1st-outcome
reduceUTCP d inv (...2nd law pattern...) = 2nd-outcome
...
reduceUTCP _ _ _ = Nothing  -- catch-all at end, no change
```

A simple example of such a pattern is the following encoding of $II; P = P$:

```
reduceUTCP d inv (Comp "Seq" [(Comp "Skip" []), pr])
   =  Just ( ";-1unit", pr, True )
```

The pattern matches a composite called "Seq", with a argument list containing two predicates. The first predicate pattern matches a "Skip" composite with no further sub-arguments. The second argument pattern matches an arbitrary predicate (P in the law above). The righthand side constructs a `RWResult` return value, with the string being a justification note that says a reduction-step using a law called ";-lunit" was applied, and noting that the top-level composite (the "Seq") was modified.

7.2   Conditional Reduce

A `CRWResult` is a `RWResult` that has been adapted, so that instead of returning one result if successful, it returns a list of possible results, each paired with a side-condition predicate.

```
type CRWResult s  =  Maybe ( String, [( Pred s, Pred s, Bool)] )
type CRWFun s     =  Dict s -> Pred s -> CRWResult s
```

A conditional reduce law is an equation as per reduce, but with conditional outcomes, e.g. $P = Q_1 \triangleleft C \triangleright Q_2$. Matching an instance of P will return a list of two pairs, the first being (C, Q_1), the second $(\neg C, Q_2)$. No attempt is made to evaluate C, but instead the REPL asks the user to choose. This is a key design decision for the calculator. A general purpose predicate evaluator requires implementing lots of theories about numbers, sets, lists, and whatever else might be present. Given the scope and purpose of this calculator it is much more effective to let the user choose.

For an example, here is one pattern of the conditional reduce function for UTCP. Given x a list of unique variables, and e a list of the same length of expressions, with $x \subseteq \{s, ls\}$ we have:

$$c[e/x] \implies (c * P)[e/x] = P[e/x]; c * P$$
$$\neg c[e/x] \implies (c * P)[e/x] = II[e/x]$$

```
creduceUTCP d (PSub w@(Comp"Iter" [c,p]) sub)
 | isCondition c && beforeSub d sub
 = Just( "loop-substn", [ctrue,cfalse] )
 where
   csub = PSub c sub
   ctrue  = (          csub, mkSeq (PSub p sub) w, diff )
   cfalse = ( mkNot csub, PSub mkSkip sub,          diff )
```

Here `mkSeq`, `mkNot` and `mkSkip` build sequential composition, negations and standard UTP skip (II) respectively. Both `isCondition` and `beforeSub` ensure that their arguments contain no dashed variables.

7.3   Loop Unroll

Iteration is typically defined in UTP as the least fixed point w.r.t. the refinement ordering that also involves sequential composition, which itself is defined using existential quantification, and II.

$$c * P \cong \mu L \bullet (P; L) \lhd c \rhd II$$
$$P; Q \cong \exists s_m, ls_m \bullet P[s_m, ls_m/s', ls'] \wedge Q[s_m, ls_m/s, ls]$$
$$II \cong s' = s \wedge ls' = ls$$

We do not want to explicitly handle quantifiers, or fixed-points. Instead we prefer to use the loop unrolling law, as this is much more useful for the kinds of calculations we encounter.

$$c * P = (P; c * P) \lhd c \rhd II$$

Even more useful are ones that split the conditional and unroll a number of times (; binds tighter than $\vee$ but looser than $\wedge$):

$$c * P = \neg c \wedge II \vee c \wedge P; c * P$$
$$= \neg c \wedge II \vee c \wedge P; c \wedge II \vee c \wedge P; c * P$$
$$= \ldots$$

The loop unroll functions are like those for reduce but have an extra string argument: `unroll ::  [String -> RWFun s]`. When the user enters a command of the form `"lsss"`, the loop unroll facility is activated, and the string `"sss"` is passed as the first argument to the functions above. It is up to the user to decide how to interpret these strings—but the most useful is to treat them as specifying the number of unrollings to do. We won't give an example here of the use of unrolling.

7.4 Bringing It All Together

We make these two reduction functions "known" to the calculator by adding them into a dictionary.

```
lawsUTCPDict
 = makeDict [("laws", LawEntry [reduceUTCP] [creduceUTCP] [])]
```

We then can take a number of partial dictionaries and use various dictionary functions, defined in `CalcPredicates`, to merge them together.

```
dictUTCP = foldl1 dictMrg [ alfUTCPDict , ..., lawsUTCPDict]
```

The main method of working with dictionaries is to construct small ones focussed on some specific area of interest. These can then be combined in different ways to provide a number of complete dictionaries that can vary in the order in which things are tried.

8 Conclusions

We have presented a description of a calculator written in Haskell, that allows the encoding of an UTP theory under development, in order to be able to rapidly perform test calculations. This helps to check that predictions of the theory match expectations. The tool was not designed to be a complete and sound theory development system, but instead to act as a rapid-prototype tool to help smoke out problems with a developing theory. This approach relies on the developer to be checking and scrutinising everything.

8.1   Costs vs. Benefits

As far as the development of the UTCP theory is concerned, the costs of developing and customising the calculator have been well compensated for by the benefits we encountered. This also applies to ongoing work to develop a fully compositional UTP theory of shared-state concurrency that does not require *run*. We note a few observations based on our experience using the calculator.

The "first-come, first-served" approach used by the calculator is surprisingly effective. We support a system of equational reasoning where reductions and definitions replace predicates with ones that are equal. In effect this means that the order in which most of these steps take place is immaterial. Some care needs to be taken when several rules apply to one construct, but this can be managed by re-arranging the order in which various patterns and their side-conditions can be checked.

The main idea in using the calculator is to find a suitable collection of patterns, in the right order, to be most effective in performing calculations. The best way to determine this is to start with none, run the calculator and when it stalls (no change is happening for any command), see what law would help make progress, and encode it. This leads to an unexpected side-effect of this calculator, in that we learnt what laws we needed, rather than what we thought we would need.

Effective use of the calculator results in an inexorable push towards algebras. By this we do not mean the Kleene algebras, or similar, that might characterise the language being formalised. Rather we mean that the most effective use of the calculator results when we define predicate functions that encapsulate some simple behaviour, and demonstrate, by proofs done without the calculator, some laws they obey, particularly with respect to sequential composition. In fact, one of the 'algebras' under development for the fully compositional theory, is so effective, that many of the test calculations can actually be done manually. However some, most notably involving parallel composition, still require the calculator in order to be feasible.

8.2   Correctness

An issue that can be raised, given the customisation and lack of soundness guarantees, is how well has the calculator been tested? The answer is basically that the process of using it ensures that the whole system is comprehensively tested. This is because calculations fail repeatedly. Such failures lead to a post-mortem to identify the reason. Early in the calculator development, the reason would be traced to a bug in the calculator infrastructure. The next phase has failures that can be attributed to bugs in the encoding of laws in Haskell, or poor ordering in the dictionary. What makes the above tolerable is that the time taken to identify and fix each code problem is relatively short, often a matter of five to ten minutes. The final phase is where calculation failures arise because of errors in the proposed theory—this is the real payback, as this is the intended purpose of the tool. The outcome of all of this iterative development is a high degree of confidence in the end result. In the author's experience, the cost of all the above failures is considerably outweighed by the cost of trying to do the check calculations manually.

There are no guarantees of soundness. But working on any theory by hand faces exactly the same issues — a proof or calculation by hand always raises the issue of the correctness of a law, or the validity of a "proof-step" that is really a number of simpler steps all rolled into one. In either case, by hand or by calculator, the theory developer has a responsibility to carefully check every line. This is one reason why so much effort was put into pretty-printing and marking. The calculator's real benefit, and *main design purpose*, is the ease with which it can produce a calculation and transcript.

In effect, this UTP Calculator is a tool that assists with the validation of UTP semantic definitions, and is designed for use by someone with expertise in UTP theory building, and a good working knowledge of Haskell.

8.3   Future Work

We plan a formal release of this calculator as a Haskell package. A key part of this would be comprehensive user documentation of the key parts of the calculator API, the standard built-in dictionaries, as well as a complete worked example of a theory encoding. There are many enhancements that are also being considered, that include better transcript rendering options (e.g. LaTeX) or ways to customise the REPL (e.g. always do a simplify step after any other REPL command). Also of interest would be finding a way of connecting the calculator to either the $U \cdot (TP)^2$ theorem-prover [4] or the Isabelle/UTP encoding [9] in order to be able to validate the dictionary entries. All the code described here is available online at https://bitbucket.org/andrewbutterfield/utp-calculator.git as Literate Haskell Script files (.lhs) in the src sub-directory.

References

1. Bauer, F.L., Ehler, H., Horsch, A., Möller, B., Partsch, H., Paukner, O., Pepper, P.: The Munich Project CIP, Volume II: The Program Transformation System CIP-S. LNCS, vol. 292. Springer, Heidelberg (1987). doi:10.1007/3-540-18779-0
2. Bertot, Y., Castéran, P.P.: Interactive Theorem Proving and Program Development: Coq'Art: The Calculus of Inductive Constructions. Texts in Theoretical Computer Science. Springer, Heidelberg (2004)
3. Bird, R.: Thinking Functionally with Haskell. Cambridge University Press, Cambridge (2014)

4. Butterfield, A.: Saoithín: a theorem prover for UTP. In: Proceedings of Unifying Theories of Programming - Third International Symposium, UTP 2010, Shanghai, China, 15–16 November 2010, pp. 137–156 (2010). http://dx.doi.org/10.1007/978-3-642-16690-7_6

5. Butterfield, A.: The logic of $U \cdot (TP)^2$. In: Unifying Theories of Programming, 4th International Symposium, UTP 2012, Paris, France, 27–28 August 2012, Revised Selected Papers, pp. 124–143 (2012). http://dx.doi.org/10.1007/978-3-642-35705-3_6

6. Butterfield, A., Mjeda, A., Noll, J.: UTP semantics for shared-state, concurrent, context-sensitive process models. In: Bonsangue, M., Deng, Y. (eds.) TASE 2016 10th International Symposium on Theoretical Aspects of Software Engineering, pp. 93–100, IEEE, July 2016

7. Clavel, M., Durán, F., Eker, S., Lincoln, P., Martí-Oliet, N., Meseguer, J., Talcott, C.: The Maude 2.0 system. In: Nieuwenhuis, R. (ed.) RTA 2003. LNCS, vol. 2706, pp. 76–87. Springer, Heidelberg (2003). doi:10.1007/3-540-44881-0_7

8. Foster, S., Woodcock, J.: Mechanised theory engineering in isabelle. In: Irlbeck, M., Peled, D.A., Pretschner, A. (eds.) Dependable Software Systems Engineering, NATO Science for Peace and Security Series, D: Information and Communication Security, vol. 40, pp. 246–287. IOS Press (2015). http://dx.doi.org/10.3233/978-1-61499-495-4-246

9. Foster, S., Zeyda, F., Woodcock, J.: Isabelle/UTP: a mechanised theory engineering framework. In: Naumann, D. (ed.) UTP 2014. LNCS, vol. 8963, pp. 21–41. Springer, Heidelberg (2015). doi:10.1007/978-3-319-14806-9_2

10. Hughes, J.: The design of a pretty-printing library. In: Jeuring, J., Meijer, E. (eds.) AFP 1995. LNCS, vol. 925, pp. 53–96. Springer, Heidelberg (1995). doi:10.1007/3-540-59451-5_3. http://www.cs.chalmers.se/~rjmh/Papers/pretty.ps

11. Marlow, S. (ed.): Haskell 2010 Language Report. Haskell Community (2010). https://www.haskell.org/definition/haskell2010.pdf

12. Nipkow, T., Paulson, L.C., Wenzel, M.: Isabelle/HOL – A Proof Assistant for Higher-Order Logic. LNCS, vol. 2283. Springer, Heidelberg (2002). http://link.springer.de/link/service/series/0558/tocs/t2283.htm

13. Nuka, G., Woodcock, J.: Mechanising a unifying theory. In: Dunne, S., Stoddart, B. (eds.) UTP 2006. LNCS, vol. 4010, pp. 217–235. Springer, Heidelberg (2006). doi:10.1007/11768173_13

14. Shankar, N.: PVS: combining specification, proof checking, and model checking. In: Srivas, M., Camilleri, A. (eds.) FMCAD 1996. LNCS, vol. 1166, pp. 257–264. Springer, Heidelberg (1996). doi:10.1007/BFb0031813

15. Van Den Brand, M.G.J., Heering, J., Klint, P., Olivier, P.A.: Compiling language definitions: the ASF+SDF compiler. ACM Trans. Program. Lang. Syst. **24**(4), 334–368 (2002)

16. Visser, E.: Stratego: a language for program transformation based on rewriting strategies system description of stratego 0.5. In: Middeldorp, A. (ed.) RTA 2001. LNCS, vol. 2051, pp. 357–361. Springer, Heidelberg (2001). doi:10.1007/3-540-45127-7_27

17. Wadler, P.: A prettier printer. In: Gibbons, J., de Moor, O. (eds.) The Fun of Programming (Cornerstones of Computing), Chap. 11, pp. 223–244, Palgrave - Macmillan, March 2003

18. Wenzel, M.: The Isabelle/Isar reference manual, June 2010. http://www.cl.cam.ac.uk/research/hvg/Isabelle/dist/Isabelle/doc/isar-ref.pdf

19. Winter, V., Beranek, J.: Program transformation using HATS 1.84. In: Lämmel, R., Saraiva, J., Visser, J. (eds.) GTTSE 2005. LNCS, vol. 4143, pp. 378–396. Springer, Heidelberg (2006). doi:10.1007/11877028_15
20. Woodcock, J., Hughes, A.: Unifying theories of parallel programming. In: George, C., Miao, H. (eds.) ICFEM 2002. LNCS, vol. 2495, pp. 24–37. Springer, Heidelberg (2002). doi:10.1007/3-540-36103-0_5
21. Zeyda, F., Cavalcanti, A.: Mechanical reasoning about families of UTP theories. Electr. Notes Theor. Comput. Sci. **240**, 239–257 (2009). http://dx.doi.org/10.1016/j.entcs.2009.05.055

Author Index

Printed in the United States
By Bookmasters